C0-AOC-299

BATTLESHIPS

BATTLESHIPS

PETER HORE

LORENZ BOOKS

This book is dedicated to my children: Eleanor, Geoffrey, Tamsin and Isabel – that they may remember 'sic transit gloria mundi'.

This edition is published by Lorenz Books

Lorenz Books is an imprint of Anness Publishing Ltd
Hermes House, 88–89 Blackfriars Road, London SE1 8HA
tel. 020 7401 2077; fax 020 7633 9499
www.lorenzbooks.com; info@anness.com

© Anness Publishing Ltd 2005

UK agent: The Manning Partnership Ltd,
6 The Old Dairy, Melcombe Road, Bath BA2 3LR;
tel. 01225 478444; fax 01225 478440;
sales@manning-partnership.co.uk

UK distributor: Grantham Book Services Ltd,
Isaac Newton Way, Alma Park Industrial Estate,
Grantham, Lincs NG31 9SD;
tel. 01476 541080; fax 01476 541061; orders@gbs.tbs-ltd.co.uk

North American agent/distributor: National Book Network,
4501 Forbes Boulevard, Suite 200, Lanham, MD 20706;
tel. 301 459 3366; fax 301 429 5746; www.nbnbooks.com

Australian agent/distributor: Pan Macmillan Australia,
Level 18, St Martins Tower, 31 Market St, Sydney, NSW 2000;
tel. 1300 135 113; fax 1300 135 103;
customer.service@macmillan.com.au

New Zealand agent/distributor: David Bateman Ltd,
30 Tarndale Grove, Off Bush Road, Albany, Auckland;
tel. (09) 415 7664; fax (09) 415 8892

All rights reserved. No part of this publication may be reproduced, stored in a retrieval system, or transmitted in any way or by any means, electronic, mechanical, photocopying, recording or otherwise, without the prior written permission of the copyright holder.

A CIP catalogue record for this book
is available from the British Library.

Publisher: Joanna Lorenz
Editorial Director: Judith Simons
Project Editors: Sarah Uttridge and Molly Perham
Copy Editor: Tim Ellerby
Designer: Ian Sandom
Jacket Designer: Mike Reynolds
Production Controller: Pedro Nelson

10 9 8 7 6 5 4 3 2 1

PAGE 1: **USS *Alabama***
PAGES 2–3: **USS *North Carolina***

Contents

6 Introduction

The History of Battleships
10 The Russian War
11 Swedish influences in the United States Navy
12 *Captain* and the end of sail
14 The Battle of Lissa
16 The Battle of Tsushima
18 The Great White Fleet
20 Cuniberti, Scott and Sims
22 *Goeben* and battleships in the Black Sea
24 Jacky Fisher
26 The Anglo-German naval race
28 The Battle of the Falklands
30 New bottles for old wine
32 North Sea actions 1914–15
34 The Battle of Jutland
36 The scuttling at Scapa Flow
38 The naval treaties
40 The Indian Ocean
42 Cunningham and the battleship war in the Mediterranean
44 Nemesis at Pearl Harbor
46 Hunt for the *Bismarck*
48 Battleship versus battleship in the Pacific
50 Battleship war in the Pacific
52 The German navy in World War II
54 Convoy PQ17 and the Battles of the Barents Sea and the North Cape
56 Where are they now?

Pre-Dreadnoughts
60 *Gloire*
62 *Warrior*
64 The first *Monitor*
66 *Virginia*
67 Broadside ironclads
68 The monitors
70 The rams
71 Barbettes
72 Turret ships
74 Coast defence ships
75 Royal Sovereign class
76 *Hood/Renown*

77 *Centurion* and *Barfleur*
78 Majestic class
79 Canopus class
80 Formidable class
81 London class
82 Duncan class
83 King Edward VII class
84 Swiftsure class
85 Lord Nelson class
86 *Maine/Texas*
87 Indiana class
88 *Iowa*
89 Kearsarge class
90 Illinois class
91 Maine class
92 Virginia class
93 Connecticut class
94 Vermont class
95 Mississippi class
96 Fuji and Shikishima class
97 *Mikasa* and *Asahi*
98 Brandenburg class
99 Kaiser class/Wittelsbach class
100 Braunschweig class
101 Deutschland class
102 *Brennus* turret ship/
Charles Martel class
103 Charlemagne class
104 Iéna class
105 République class/Liberté class
106 Danton class
108 Italia class
109 Ruggiero di Lauria class
110 Re Umberto class
111 Ammiraglio di Saint Bon class
112 Regina Margherita class
113 Regina Elena class
114 *Sissoi Veliki*
115 Admiral Ushakov class
116 Petropavlovsk class
117 *Rostislav*
118 Peresviet class
119 *Potemkin*
120 *Retvisan* and *Tsessarevitch*
121 Borodino class
122 Evstafi class/
Imperator Pavel class
123 Habsburg class/
Erzherzog Karl class

World War I
126 *Dreadnought*
128 Bellerophon class
129 St Vincent class
130 *Invincible*, *Indomitable*
and *Inflexible*
132 *Neptune*, *Colossus*
and *Hercules*
133 Indefatigable class
134 *Australia*
135 *New Zealand*
136 Orion Class
137 Lion Class
138 *Queen Mary* and *Tiger*
139 King George V class
140 Iron Duke class
142 Queen Elizabeth class
144 Royal Sovereign class
145 *Erin*
146 *Agincourt*
148 *Canada*
149 Renown class
150 *Courageous*, *Glorious*
and *Furious*
152 South Carolina class
153 Delaware class/
Florida class
154 Wyoming class/
New York class
155 Nevada class
156 Pennsylvania class/
New Mexico class
157 Kashima class/
Satsuma class
158 Tsukuba class/Ibuki class
159 Fuso class
160 Kongo class
162 Ise class
163 Nassau class
164 Helgoland class
165 Kaiser class/König class
166 Bayern class
167 *Von der Tann*
168 *Moltke* and *Goeben*
169 *Seydlitz*/Derfflinger class
170 Courbet class
172 Bretagne class
173 Normandie class
174 *Dante Alighieri*
175 Conte di Cavour class
176 Caio Duilio class
177 Gangut class

178 Imperatritsa Mariya class
179 *Imperator Nikolai 1/*
Borodino class
180 Radetzky class
181 Tegetthoff class
182 Sverige class
183 *De Zeven Provincien*
184 España class
185 *Kilkis* and *Lemnos*
186 *Yavuz Sultan Selim*
187 Rivadavia class
188 Minas Gerais class
189 Almirante Latorre class

World War II
192 *Hood*
194 *Queen Elizabeth* –
modernized
196 Royal Sovereign class
198 *Nelson* and *Rodney*
200 King George V class
202 Lion class and *Vanguard*
204 Colorado class
208 North Carolina class
210 South Dakota class
214 Iowa class and *Iowa*
216 *New Jersey*
218 *Missouri*
220 *Wisconsin*
222 *Kentucky* and
Illinois/Alaska class
223 Montana class
224 *Nagato* and *Mutsu*
226 *Kaga* and *Tosa*
228 Yamato class
232 *Deutschland* (*Lützow*) and
Admiral Scheer
234 *Admiral Graf Spee*
236 *Scharnhorst* and *Gneisenau*
238 *Bismarck*
240 *Tirpitz*
242 *Dunkerque* and *Strasbourg*
243 Richelieu class
244 Conte di Cavour class (1933)
245 Caio Duilio class (1937)
246 Vittorio Veneto class
248 Sovyetskiy Soyuz class

250 Glossary
251 Key to flags
252 Acknowledgements
254 Index

Introduction

A basic style of sailing ship, capable of taking its place in the line of battle, or a "line-of-battle ship", from which the term battleship is derived, had dominated warfare at sea from the 16th to the 19th century. Then, just as the British navy delivered the victory of sea power in 1815 at the Battle of Trafalgar, new technology became available, which would revolutionize battleship design.

This revolution encompassed the use of steam engines at sea, breech-loading guns, the rotating turret, armour and above all the increase in size of ships. At one stage a British prime minister complained that ship design was a changing fashion like ladies' hats. There were developmental dead ends as well. The paddle ship with its exposed wheels was useless as a vehicle of war; the paddlewheels and boxes were too vulnerable to damage and restricted the size of broadside armament that could be mounted. However the paddle ship was useful for towing sailing ships into action.

Other lines of development took unexpected turns. The monitor was designed for coastal defence and for war in the estuaries and rivers, and was highly successful in the American Civil War. However when given a little more sea-keeping capability, the monitors became a powerful weapon of offence, mounting some of the largest guns, which were taken from their "big sister" battleships. In two world wars monitors were used in operations from the Arctic to Africa, and indeed at the end of their lives the shore-bombardment role of some battleships could be compared to that of an over-large

TOP: **USS _Merrimac_ engages USS _Monitor_.** ABOVE: **HMS _Warrior_ was so strongly built that she has survived until today. She has been beautifully restored and can be seen in Portsmouth, England.**

monitor. In this sense the monitor stands in line with the development of the cruise and ballistic missiles launched from submarines.

The battleship itself, broadly defined here as a capital ship mounting guns of 255mm/10in calibre or more, took on many different shapes for the first 20 years of its life as a distinct species. Designers faced difficult choices, weight being a primary driver in the decisions which had to be made. Many early designs had large, heavy barbettes which meant a low freeboard and loss of sea-keeping – the alternative was a high-sided ship with a consequent loss of stability. This period was marked by some exceedingly odd and ugly ships.

By the end of the 19th century the design of the battleship had more or less settled on a ship of about 10,160 tonnes/ 10,000 tons carrying two twin barbettes or turrets, one forward

and one aft, sometimes with side-by-side funnels, and a speed of 18 knots was considered fast. Then, a British admiral, Jacky Fisher, changed everything with his concept of a battleship which would "dread nought". It was not his idea alone. The Italian naval engineer Vittorio Cuniberti's proposals for an all-big-gun ship were widely published and there were simultaneous developments in the same direction in several other countries, as well. However, it was Fisher's energy, enthusiasm and drive which brought the first ship, HMS *Dreadnought* into being, and halted warship-building worldwide while friends and rivals considered what had been achieved. Although the design was not perfect, the ship was revolutionary in nearly every respect and thereafter battleships had to be classified by reference to this one ship: battleships had become pre-Dreadnoughts, Dreadnoughts or super-Dreadnoughts.

Once the 20,320 tonnes/20,000 tons and 20 knots barrier had been broken, there was only one direction in which development could go and, within 10 years, subsequent generations of Dreadnoughts had reached 30,480 tonnes/ 30,000 tons and 30 knots. Eventually the largest ships of this type exceeded 60,960 tonnes/60,000 tons. Secondary armament was re-introduced to deal with torpedo boats and later for anti-aircraft use. Triple and even quadruple turrets were fitted along with ramps and then catapults for aircraft, and oil replaced coal. Reciprocating engines were replaced by steam turbines and in some cases by diesel engines.

TOP: **Battleships were still fought in the line of battle which maximized the number of guns that could be brought to bear on a target. The smoke from burning coal advertised their position.** ABOVE: **Big-gun ships still needed to be protected against smaller craft.** ABOVE LEFT: **Each shell was the size of a man.**

There were only two large-scale fleet actions involving this type: the Battle of Tsushima in 1905 between pre-Dreadnoughts and the Battle of Jutland in 1918 between Dreadnoughts. There were also actions in World War II, but battleships were soon relegated to auxiliary roles such as forming an anti-aircraft screen to defend aircraft carriers and for shore bombardment. By the end of World War II the type was obsolete, although in the US Navy (USN) the battleship lingered on, seeing action in the Vietnam War and the 1990–1 Gulf War.

This book looks first at the fascinating history of the battleship, from the first broadside ironclads of the mid-19th century through the development of the Dreadnoughts and on to the last battleships built during World War II. It also chronicles the main battles and naval operations mounted by the world's foremost naval powers, notably Britain, the United States, Germany, France, Italy and Japan. The country-by-country chronological directories that follow describe the most famous of these ships in three sections: Pre-Dreadnoughts, battleships of World War I and battleships of World War II. This then is the story, told through the lives of individual ships, of the development, deployment and demise of one type of ship which dominated naval strategy for 150 years.

The History of Battleships

The term battleship derives from "line-of-battle ship", meaning a ship strong enough to fight in the line of battle – but there was confusion of nomenclature. *Warrior,* laid down in 1859, was certainly the strongest ship of her time yet she was never officially a battleship, only a frigate (because of her single gun deck), though later she was rated an armoured cruiser. The French called all the new battleships that developed in the later 19th century and 20th century *cuirassé*, and the Spanish called them *acorazado*, but these terms concentrated on the protective nature of armour. When the Germans came to build their navy they were more precise, using the terms *linienschiff, panzerschiff, schlachtschiff* and *schlachtkreuzer* to indicate different waypoints in the development of the battleship. The British navy began to re-introduce the term battleship around 1880 to mean a recognizable type of ship that was heavily armed and armoured. As technology advanced with the advent of steam, with propellers, breech-loading guns, turret mountings, turbines, armour plating, gun propellant and explosive power, so the modern battleship evolved.

LEFT: **A view taken onboard a USA battleship of the New Mexico class during the capture of Saipan in 1944. A sister ship follows next astern and the USS *Pennsylvania* completes the line ahead.**

LEFT: **The Crimean War was in fact a campaign and part of a larger war, more accurately known as the Russian War 1854–6, which raged on a global scale, and depended heavily upon sea power as this crowded anchorage in the Crimea shows.** BELOW: **For an attack upon Kinburn, the French navy devised some armoured box-like ships, just visible through the smoke, with which they could approach the low-lying Russian fortifications. These craft, which were little more than rafts, are generally considered the genesis of the modern battleship.**

The Russian War

By the time of the Russian War of 1854–6, all the ingredients for a revolution in battleship design and construction were in place. Steam propulsion had been successfully applied at sea to a large number of paddle ships and shortly thereafter many wooden walls had been converted to screw-steam propulsion. British shipyards were proficient in building iron hulls, armour was beginning to be applied to warships and guns were increasing in killing-power.

The actual impetus for the development of the battleship grew out of the campaign in the Black Sea, which is sometimes erroneously known as the Crimean War. The combined British and French fleets, which arrived in the Black Sea in March 1854, were massively superior to any force that the Russians could put to sea. The problem faced by the allies was therefore how to take the war to their opponents.

In November 1853 a Russian fleet had destroyed a squadron of Turkish frigates using shell fire. Louis Napoleon III, who considered himself an artillery expert, proposed a shellproof battery for dealing with the threat and for attacking the coast.

Technology was just about to produce 100mm/4in armour plate and this was tested independently in Britain and France to construct a number of batteries, with their armour fitted together with tongue-and-groove joints and bolted to the hull. The resulting vessels were scarcely manoeuvrable under their own steam power and were unwieldy under sail, which meant that they had to be towed for most of their passage.

In 1855 three French batteries saw action at Kinburn in the Crimea, where, in flattery to the Emperor, they were credited with destroying Russian shore positions. A more realistic assessment is that the low-lying Russian earthworks were flattened by mortar and bomb fire and blasted at close range by the accompanying battleships. Nevertheless, Kinburn saw the first use of armoured steam warships in battle.

The British took this basic idea a step further and built an immense fleet of gunboats and mortar vessels with which to attack St Petersburg – the news alone was sufficient to bring the Tsar to the negotiating table. On St George's Day 1856, the Royal Navy organized a review of their fleet to remind the Russians and the rest of the world of its power. The war was no sooner over than France began to think up ways of designing a ship that could challenge the Royal Navy, resulting in Dupuy de Lôme designing the first seagoing ironclad, *Gloire*.

Swedish influences in the United States Navy

The lessons of the Russian War and developments in warship design were noted in the USA where three Swedes, Ericsson, Fox and Dahlgren, strongly influenced the early United States Navy (USN).

John Ericsson had been an engineer in the Swedish Army when he moved to Britain in 1826 to sell his ideas, not all of them successful, for steam engines, screw propellers, large guns and even engines driven by hot air instead of steam. Ericsson was recruited to work in the USA and, with Robert Stockton, designed the heavily armed screw-driven USS *Princeton*. However, after an explosion in one of *Princeton*'s guns, for which Ericsson's design was blamed, he took up a career in civil engineering until the outbreak of the American Civil War. Ericsson designed and built a revolutionary armoured ship, *Monitor*, carrying her guns in a rotating turret, which like many of his designs was novel but not entirely successful. Active until his death at age 83, Ericsson continued to produce ideas for submarines, self-propelled torpedoes and heavy ordnance.

John Dahlgren was the son of the Swedish consul in Philadelphia, who after some years in the USN started work in the Washington Navy Yard, helping to found the USN's ordnance department. He designed the Dahlgren gun, a smoothbore cannon made in a variety of sizes, which became the standard weapon of the Union navy during the American Civil War. In 1863 he commanded the South Atlantic Blockading Squadron and saw his guns in action at Charleston.

Gustavus Vasa Fox retired after nearly 20 years in the USN. In the American Civil War, after volunteering to command an expedition to relieve the garrison at Fort Sumter, Fox was appointed chief clerk of the Department of the Navy and then Assistant Secretary of the Navy, where his honesty and efficiency were much needed. Fox effectively became the chief of naval operations. He kept in touch personally with senior officers and planned many of the navy's campaigns against the Confederacy. Fox was also a keen advocate of new technology including Ericsson's *Monitor*.

In mid-1866 Fox crossed the Atlantic in the monitor *Miantonomoh*, demonstrating the sea-worthiness of a low-freeboard, armoured turret ship. Fox visited northern Europe, including Russia, and the officers of his squadron used the opportunity to collect naval intelligence. However, Fox soon resigned from office to enter business. The USN went into a decline that lasted for the next few decades and the early promise of an oceanic navy went unfulfilled.

BELOW: **The USN continued to build low-freeboard monitors and to make trans-Atlantic crossings until the 20th century: here a US monitor passes a high-sided broadside French ship, herself a survivor from an earlier age.**
RIGHT: **One of the first acts of the newly pacified USA was to send a naval mission to Europe led by the Secretary of the Navy Gustavus Fox, in the un-seaworthy-looking monitor** *Miantonomoh*.

Captain and the end of sail

Captain Cowper Phipps Coles was first inspired to design turntable mountings for heavy guns following the use of ordnance mounted on rafts during the Crimean War.

Coles was well aware of the disadvantage of a broadside battery in a steamship being that only half the armament could be brought to bear, and then only on one side or other of the ship's heading, thus restricting ships to fight broadside-on as they had always done under sail. He advocated turrets for warships and had invented a working mounting so that the guns could be brought to bear at more or less any bearing. Furthermore it was recognized that the weight of Coles's mountings required them to be mounted on the centreline of warships, unlike swivel guns which had long been mounted along the sides.

Even before the clash between *Monitor* and *Merrimac*, the British Admiralty had tried Coles's revolving turrets in *Trusty* in 1861, and in 1862 had ordered a coast defence ship *Prince Albert* and converted *Royal Sovereign*, a 120-gun three-decker, for coastal defence, each with no less than four turrets. The success of these ships and news from the USA led to the design of *Monarch*, the first ocean-going turret ship, armed with four 305mm/12in guns in two turrets. Inefficient engines with high coal consumption meant that ships like *Monarch* still required sails for long passages. However, the forest of masts and rigging which a sailing ship needed was incompatible with centreline turrets which required clear arcs of fire to be effective. Coles proposed the use of tripod masts to help solve this problem.

Coles was critical of the design of *Monarch*: she was a high-freeboard ship and he was convinced that a low-freeboard design, such as that of *Monitor*, would give additional protection. After he had won the backing of Parliament, the public and *The Times* newspaper, the Admiralty reluctantly ordered a ship from Lairds at Birkenhead to be built to Coles's specification.

Whilst *Captain* was being built between 1867 and 1870 there was insufficient attention to weight control and consequentially she was 813 tonnes/800 tons heavier than planned. Edward Reed, the Admiralty's Chief Constructor, was already concerned about the stability of Coles's design which would have a freeboard of just 2.44m/8ft; however the additional weight reduced this to just 2m/6ft 6in. The metacentric height was very small so that she rolled slowly; at 14 degrees of heel her gunwales were in the water, and at 21 degrees she was unsafe.

Captain was the first ship of her size to have twin screws, another of Coles's ideas, but she was also given a large sail plan of some 3,715sq m/40,000sq ft.

Two revolving centre-line turrets, with twin 305mm/12in, 25.5-tonne/25-ton, muzzle-loading rifled guns firing 270kg/600lb shells, were mounted on the main deck. The stern, midships and forecastles were linked by a flying deck, and restricted the angles of fire or "A" arcs of the guns. The three strongly built masts with tripod supports instead of traditional standing rigging were fitted. On trials *Captain* appeared to confound her critics; she manoeuvred well under

LEFT: **Despite *Captain*'s high sides and continuous upper deck, the men in white uniforms show how low in the ship the guns were mounted. It is evident from the photograph that *Captain* was a low freeboard barbette ship with a dangerously heavy top hamper, which would eventually prove fatal.**
ABOVE: **A close-up of one of *Captain*'s massive turrets shows that the deck above is only a flying bridge. This arrangement kept the rigging clear of the arcs of fire.**

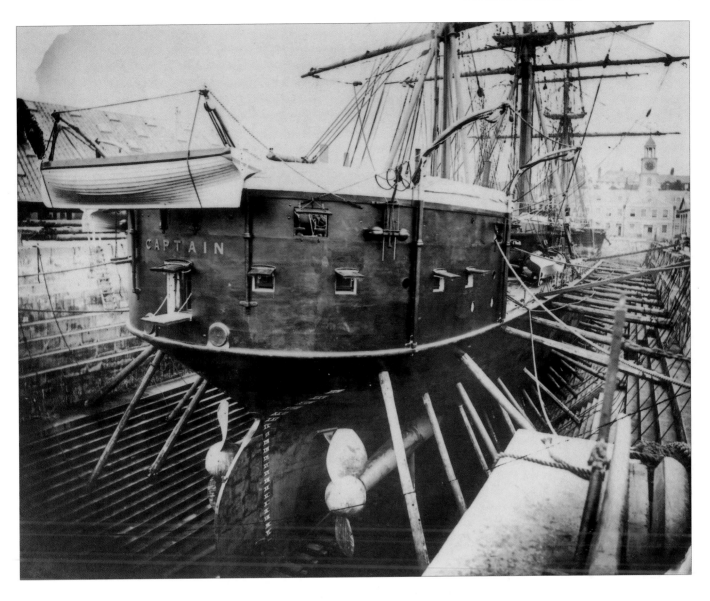

power and was a steady gun platform. However, the results of heeling experiments, in the summer of 1870, were not made known to the Admiralty or to the ship before she sailed to join the Channel Squadron. In her was Coles, as an observer, and among the midshipmen was the son of Sir Hugh Childers, First Lord of the Admiralty, who had backed Coles against the advice of his own Board of Admiralty.

West of Cape Finisterre Admiral Sir Alexander Milne, Commander-in-Chief of the Mediterranean fleet, had witnessed gunnery practice onboard *Captain*, and as the wind freshened he returned to his flagship, *Lord Warden*. Shortly after midnight on September 7, a strong gust of wind blew out many sails throughout the fleet. *Captain,* however, was knocked over and capsized, sinking quickly, with the loss of 481 of her 499 crew. Ironically, had she been a less strongly built ship the masts might have broken away and saved her.

In the inquiry which followed, blame was shared between the Admiralty, Coles himself and the builder. However, following the disaster no more broadside or central battery ships were laid down, and shortly afterwards the Royal Navy began to reduce the rig of its capital ships, the loss of *Captain* marking the beginning of the end of sail in the Royal Navy.

ABOVE: **A view of *Captain* under construction when her designers and builders lost control of her weight. The photograph shows just how little freeboard she had.** BELOW: **_Captain_'s first voyage was a success and, although this fanciful picture shows her in a storm, with water spilled across her decks, she caused no concern for her stability. She was so strongly built that instead of her sails blowing out or her masts going overboard, the freshening wind caused her to capsize.**

The Battle of Lissa

The Battle of Lissa in the Adriatic in 1866 was the first fleet engagement involving ironclad ships. Even a tactical victory for the Austrians could not save the war for them, but when the gunnery of the day proved ineffective against armour, other navies drew the wrong lessons and ramming was given a bogus tactical status for the rest of the century.

Italy was allied with Prussia, which was fighting Austria for dominance of the German states in the Austro-Prussian or Seven Weeks War. After Prussia had defeated Austria on land, Italy, wanting to gain Italian-speaking provinces from Austria, attempted to use its navy to make territorial gains, and bombarded the island of Lissa or Vis in the eastern Adriatic. The Italian fleet commanded by Admiral Carlo Persano including the broadside ironclads, *Regina Maria, Pia San Martino, Castelfidardo, Ancona, Re d'Italia, Re di Portogallo, Principe di Carignano, Terribile,* and *Formidabile,* the turret ram *Affondatore,* and the coast defence ships *Palestro* and *Varese,* then commenced an assault on the island of Lissa.

The Austrian Admiral Wilhelm von Tegetthoff guarded the Adriatic cities of Pola and Trieste until he became convinced that the island of Lissa was the Italians' main effort and he immediately set sail for the island. His fleet consisted of the 90-gun ship of the line *Kaiser,* and the broadside ironclads *Erzherzog Ferdinand Max, Habsburg, Kaiser Max, Prinz Eugen, Juan de Austria, Drache* and *Salamander.*

As Persano prepared to land on July 20, after two days of bombardment, Tegetthoff appeared out of the fog from the north-west, his fleet formed into a wedge with the elderly

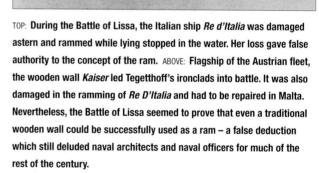

TOP: **During the Battle of Lissa, the Italian ship *Re d'Italia* was damaged astern and rammed while lying stopped in the water. Her loss gave false authority to the concept of the ram.** ABOVE: **Flagship of the Austrian fleet, the wooden wall *Kaiser* led Tegetthoff's ironclads into battle. It was also damaged in the ramming of *Re D'Italia* and had to be repaired in Malta. Nevertheless, the Battle of Lissa seemed to prove that even a traditional wooden wall could be successfully used as a ram – a false deduction which still deluded naval architects and naval officers for much of the rest of the century.**

Kaiser in the centre of an arrowhead formation of seven ironclads, followed by a second wedge of wooden warships and a convoy of troops.

Though some of Persano's ironclads were absent, he was still numerically superior but his forces were divided and unprepared. Furthermore, he was caught in the middle of landing troops and with boats in the water. Persano divided his strength by distributing his ironclads into mixed squadrons, with older wooden and sailing ships, and decided, apparently at a late moment, to command his fleet from the *Affondatore.* Forming a hurried line of battle, he is alleged to have said disparagingly of the Austrians, "Here come the fishermen".

Battle commenced at 10.30, when Tegetthoff, still in wedge formation, increased speed and broke the Italian line, rather like Nelson at Trafalgar, ordering his ironclads to turn to port and to sink the enemy centre with their rams. The leading Austrian ironclads then turned to port to attack the Italian centre. In the fierce close-quarters mêlée which ensued, wreathed in smoke from the guns and funnels, Tegetthoff was able to concentrate his seven ironclads against four Italian ironclads. There were several attempts at ramming in which Ferdinand Max and Palestro succeeded in ramming each other, and Persano in Affondatore twice missed hitting Kaiser. Then, when Re d'Italia's stern was damaged and she lay stopped in the water, Tegetthoff rammed her at about 11 knots and she sank in a few minutes. Even Kaiser somehow managed to damage her bows and had to be sent to the Royal Navy base at Malta for repairs.

Following two hours of manoeuvring, shortly after noon, the Austrian ships were north of Lissa and the Italians to the west; Lissa had been saved. Gunfire continued until mid-afternoon, and at about 14.30 Palestro exploded following a fire which had been started during the morning's action. The Italians, now short of coal, retired to Ancona.

The deciding factor in this battle was that the Austrians were better led and better trained, overcoming the Italians' superiority in numbers and quality of ships; however, this was to be overlooked by commentators at the time. Despite the fury of the fight, few ships suffered significant damage and most attempts at ramming had been unsuccessful. However the Battle of Lissa influenced ship design for the rest of the century, leading to some ships being specifically designed for ramming, even after improvements in gunnery and the development of the torpedo made such tactics suicidal.

The ram has enjoyed a modern reincarnation as the streamlined bulbous bow of merchant ships and in "chin sonars" for frigates, but there is no evidence that it aided ship performance in the 19th century, although architects may have unconsciously discovered how to streamline their designs.

ABOVE: The Italian coast defence ship *Palestro* and the German battleship *Erzherzog Ferdinand Max* rammed each other during the course of the Battle of Lissa in 1866. BELOW: Austria's toehold on the Adriatic included the ancient city-port of Venice and this made her a sea power: the Austrian admiral Wilhelm von Tegetthoff fought in the North Sea as well as at the Battle of Lissa. The Austro-Hungarian navy had global aspirations which included deployments beyond the Mediterranean to the West Indies during the Spanish American War and to China. BOTTOM: Late in the deployment and immediately before the battle the Italian Admiral Carlo Persano transferred his flag to *Affondatore* and lost control of his fleet.

The Battle of Tsushima

The imperial rivalry between Russia and Japan over control of Manchuria and Korea brought about one of the most decisive battles of naval history. Japan had defeated China in a war in 1894–5, but had been denied her conquests, particularly of Port Arthur on the Liaotung Peninsula, by the international community. In 1896 Russia made a treaty with China which included the right to extend the Trans-Siberian railway across Manchuria to the Russian port of Vladivostok, and two years later gained a lease over Port Arthur. Japan rapidly expanded its army, whilst the railway, which was completed in 1904, enabled Russia to begin a slow build-up of its forces in the Far East. However, when Russia reneged on an agreement to withdraw troops from Manchuria, Japan launched a surprise attack and bombarded Port Arthur and the Russian ships there. The Japanese army overran Korea and the Russian army fell back; Port Arthur was besieged and surrendered on January 2, 1905.

Meanwhile the Russian Baltic Fleet, renamed the Second Pacific Squadron, was despatched from Europe under the command of Admiral Rozhdestvenski. This might have been a fine demonstration of the use of sea power, but the logistic difficulties facing Rozhdestvenski were enormous. Britain, allied with Japan, would not sell coal or grant harbour facilities to the Russians. France, however, granted access to its colonial ports and Germany chartered-out a fleet of 60 colliers of the Hamburg-Amerika Line. Nevertheless, the Russian ships were not designed for a 29,000km/18,000-mile voyage nor for tropical conditions, and Russian morale, as well as equipment, seem to have broken down. A Third Pacific Squadron, composed of weak and elderly ships, transited the Suez Canal to join Rozhdestvenski at Madagascar, where he was delayed while fresh contracts were being drawn up for the supply of

TOP: **The Battle of the Yalu River on August 10, 1904, preceding the Battle of Tsushima. Here the Japanese ships in traditional line-ahead fire the opening shots of the engagement.** ABOVE: **The Japanese fleet under manoeuvre. Every calibre of weapon was fitted in the pre-Dreadnoughts, including machine-guns for anti-torpedo boat defence. These pictures show once more how coal-burning gave away the position of pre-Dreadnought and Dreadnought era battleships. Coal also limited the endurance, measured in speed and range, of coal-powered steamships.**

coal. Kamranh Bay in French Indo-China was the last port before the motley Russian fleet crossed the South China Sea; British-owned Singapore and Hong Kong were, of course, denied to Rozhdestvenski.

There were two routes from Kamranh to Vladivostok. East about the Japanese home islands would require Rozhdestvenski to coal at sea while exposed and open to Japanese attack. The direct route lay west of Japan and led via Tsushima Strait into the Sea of Japan. Steaming slowly to conserve fuel and keep his fleet together, he entered the strait on the night of May 26/27, where the Japanese fleet, commanded by Admiral Togo, was waiting.

Togo was one of several Japanese officers who had been trained by the Royal Navy and he had studied in England from 1871–8. As captain of the cruiser *Naniwa* he had sunk a Chinese troopship en route for Korea, thus precipitating the Sino-Japanese war. His Nelson-like order before the Battle of Tsushima was "The fate of the Empire rests upon this one battle; let every man do his utmost."

Togo's cruisers spotted the Russians heading north-east and reported this by radio. By mid-morning Rozhdestvenski was being followed by two Japanese divisions and Togo while the main battle fleet was approaching from the north. Rozhdestvenski attempted to form a line of battle as ships appeared from the mist and vanished again, but missed signals and poor seamanship threw his ships into confusion.

When the mist cleared in the early afternoon, Togo's concentrated, disciplined and faster fleet was north-east of Rozhdestvenski and on an opposite course. Using his speed, Togo crossed the Russian fleet, which was now in two columns, led his fleet in a 180-degree turn and steadied on a parallel course on the Russians' port side. Later he again crossed the Russians' line of advance, though by now they were in disarray.

The Russians fought bravely but the battle was soon decided. Rozhdestvenski's flagship was one of four Russian battleships destroyed by the concentrated fire of Togo's ships, and with the loss of any kind of central command the battle

TOP: **The Russian *Osliabia*, a Peresviet class battleship, sunk at the Battle of Tsushima in May 1905. Togo's victory over Rozhdestvenski's fleet gave Japan victory in the war.** ABOVE LEFT: **The Russian battleship *Tsessarevitch* photographed in Port Arthur in 1904 where she was blockaded. Her funnels show damage received during the Battle of the Yalu River. The Russians fought bravely in all their engagements, but they were overwhelmed by numbers or by superior logistics.** ABOVE: **A Japanese print showing the destruction of the Russian flagship. Victory marked the ascendancy of the Imperial Japanese Navy and Togo was hailed as the new Nelson.**

became a mêlée and then a massacre. Of the Russian fleet of 45 ships, only two destroyers and the light cruiser *Almaz* reached Vladivostok, and six others reached neutral ports. The rest were sunk, beached, or surrendered.

The battle gave victory to the Japanese in the war, and the annihilation of the Russian fleet altered the balance of power in Europe. Royal Navy officers witnessed the battle from Japanese ships and noted the effectiveness of heavy guns at long range.

The Great White Fleet

The voyage of the Great White Fleet in 1907–9, despatched round the world by the American President Theodore Roosevelt, marked the coming of age of the United States Navy (USN) following a period of revival. The voyage also marked the beginning of the "American" century, presaging the leading role which the USN would take in the 20th century. However despite newspaper acclaim and public pride in the USA, the fleet was obsolescent and to naval planners the voyage revealed strategic weaknesses.

Roosevelt was a navalist who been influenced by and then in turn influenced the American naval strategist Alfred Mahan. As a young man Roosevelt had written *The Naval War of 1812*, which praised the performance of the USN in that war somewhat uncritically, and he had also contributed to Laird Clowes's seven-volume history of the Royal Navy. When Roosevelt became president of the USA, after a period of naval expansion which he himself had helped to stimulate, Japan was beginning to be seen as more of a threat than Britain.

In the summer of 1907 Roosevelt approved a proposal that the American battle fleet should make a demonstration by deploying from the Atlantic to the Pacific coast of the USA. The USN had been considering sending a fleet on a deployment into the Pacific for some time, though quite when Roosevelt agreed that this should become a circumnavigation is not clear. Roosevelt probably only came gradually upon the idea that such a move would act as a deterrent to the Japanese, impress the American taxpayer, and garner support for more battleships. The long deployment round South America and through the Magellan Straits would also help show the need for the Panama Canal.

ABOVE: **American battleships at Port Said, Egypt. The voyage of the Great White Fleet relied upon a fleet of hired British colliers and upon British-controlled facilities like the Suez Canal.** BELOW: *Connecticut* **leads battleships of the US Atlantic Fleet in 1907. The paint scheme was responsible for the name "white fleet", the supply of coal restricted its operations and smoke gave away its position.**

ABOVE: **Life onboard – a scene which must have been familiar throughout all fleets over many years; peeling vegetables. By the age of steam, however, scurvy was almost unknown.** ABOVE RIGHT: **Rear Admiral C. M. Thomas, USN, onboard *Minnesota*, 1907. The admiral's use of a handheld signal book is another scene which would have been familiar in the age of sail.** RIGHT: **Fourth of July festivities onboard the battleship *Connecticut* in 1908 during the Great White Fleet's historic circumnavigation.**

The battleships were accompanied by several auxiliary ships and on the first part of their voyage by a flotilla of early destroyers. The 14-month-long voyage by 14,000 sailors covered some 22,500km/43,000 miles and made 20 landfalls on six continents. They were led initially by Rear Admiral "Fighting Bob" Evans who had made his career in the Spanish-American War.

Significantly the fleet's first visit was to the British island of Trinidad in the West Indies for coal, and then, on the first leg of its voyage, to Rio de Janeiro, Chile, Peru, Mexico, and on to San Francisco, where *Alabama* and *Maine* were replaced by *Nebraska* and *Wisconsin*. The fleet then visited Hawaii, Auckland, Sydney and Melbourne. The celebrations when the Great White Fleet arrived in Australia in 1908 were only surpassed by those which had been held for the federation of Australia. Over 80,000 people stood on South Head to watch the fleet enter Sydney Harbour and crowds, parties, speeches and parades greeted the Americans. This did not stop American officers using the opportunity to draw up plans to invade or capture these ports in the event of war with the British Empire.

The fleet then steamed on to Yokohama, Manila, Colombo and Suez, where it arrived on January 3, 1909. The voyage had become something of a race to be home before Roosevelt's successor was sworn in as the new president, and not even an earthquake in Sicily could delay the fleet very much; they were back in Hampton Roads, Virginia, on February 22, 1909.

The voyage of the Great White Fleet may have served its purpose politically, but before they had even set out, every ship had been rendered obsolescent by the launch of the British all-big-gun battleship *Dreadnought*. Just as significantly, the fleet had found there were few American bases to support it and instead the ships had had to rely upon another fleet, of some 50 chartered colliers. Good Welsh or Appalachian coal was unobtainable and the colliers often turned up late with very inferior coal. Worse, the colliers were nearly all British. The lesson was clear; impressive as the Great White Fleet was, the USN would have to – and did – develop its own logistical train.

Within only a few months of returning to the USA the battleships of the Great White Fleet were painted grey and their pole masts were replaced by lattice masts.

The 18 new battleships of the Great White Fleet

Alabama	Kearsarge	Missouri	Vermont
Connecticut	Kentucky	Nebraska	Virginia
Georgia	Louisiana	New Jersey	Wisconsin
Illinois	Maine	Ohio	
Kansas	Minnesota	Rhode Island	

Cuniberti, Scott and Sims

In addition to Fisher, three men stand out as having strongly influenced the development of the big gun and the design of the *Dreadnought*. The Italian naval architect and engineer Vittorio Cuniberti was descended from a successive line of innovative Italian naval architects such as Brin and Micheli. At the beginning of the 20th century Cuniberti had drawn up plans for a ship with a single calibre of big guns, but the project was regarded as too ambitious for the Italian navy, and in 1902 he was given permission to publish an article in *Jane's Fighting Ships*, then a newly established publication. The article was entitled: "An Ideal Battleship for the British Fleet" and his ideas were for "a moderate-sized, very swift vessel with the greatest possible unified armament". An article that was published three years earlier in German in the *Marine Rundschau*, "Ein neuer Schlachtschifftypus" had attracted little attention, but by 1904 navies around the world were about to analyse the Battle of Tsushima and its implications for warship design.

At this time guns were laid by eye, so the direction officer needed to see the fall of shot in order to estimate the range adjustment. Cuniberti and others appreciated that as guns of all calibre improved and could be fired to the limits of visual observation it was increasingly difficult to distinguish the fall of

ABOVE: **Cuniberti's ideas were taken up in several countries, where some smaller navies did not slavishly copy Fisher's Dreadnought but designed all-big-gun ships from first principles, like the small but purposeful and elegant *España*, seen here.**

one shot and thus make the appropriate corrections. Cuniberti actually lampooned the American practice of fitting up to four different calibres, writing, "Looking to America, one realizes that chaos reigns in the designing department of the United States Navy, and hardly a month seems to pass without a new type being brought out, more and more loaded with guns." Whether Cuniberti's ideas actually influenced any British decision or the ideas arose spontaneously and simultaneously in different navies is not known but Fisher was the first to implement them.

Meanwhile in the Royal Navy, Percy Scott was improving the accuracy of gun laying. Scott is best known for his efforts during the Boer War in 1899 when as captain of the cruiser *Terrible* he designed makeshift gun carriages for the ship's guns so they could be taken up-country by a naval brigade to help the army at the siege of Ladysmith. He was training commander at the gunnery school, HMS *Excellent*, in

Portsmouth, 1890–3, a member of the Ordnance Committee, 1893–6, captain of HMS *Excellent* in 1904, and Inspector of Target Practice in 1908, and in 1916 he was called from retirement to create the Anti-Aircraft Corps for the defence of London against air attack. Scott was a prolific inventor who devised a loading tray to teach faster loading, a "dotter" designed to help his gun layers record accurate bearings, and introduced director firing from a centralized position in the ship. The gunnery technology of the day was capable of firing a shell ten miles, and Scott helped the Royal Navy to hit targets at these ranges more accurately. After the war he argued that the advent of submarines and aeroplanes meant that the day of the battleship, which his inventions had helped to perfect, was over.

William Sims, a Canadian by birth, joined the USN and between regular appointments was a naval attaché in Europe. Sims reported on new ship designs and improvements in gunnery and wrote directly to President Theodore Roosevelt criticizing the efficiency of the USN. He supported Roosevelt in arguing for the USN adopting an all-big-gun Dreadnought fleet against others, including the now elderly Mahan who advocated a mixed calibre and a "balanced fleet". Roosevelt made Sims his protégé and he went on to introduce the continuous aim method developed by Scott to the USN. He commanded the battleships *Minnesota*, 1909–11 and *Nevada*, 1916–17. Sims was briefly president of the US Naval War College but in March 1917 he was made the USN's representative in London. When the USA entered World War I he took command of all American destroyers operating from British bases, helping to establish convoys to overcome the strangulating effect of German U-boats. Like Scott he became an apostate regarding battleships and in retirement was an advocate of naval aviation. Despite the contributions these men made, the modern battleship is indelibly linked with Fisher and his *Dreadnought*.

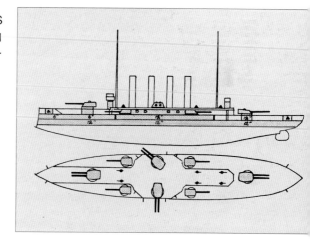

TOP LEFT: **Percy Scott taught the Royal Navy to shoot and he was a prolific inventor. He later argued against the retention of the battleship because it was rendered obsolescent by new weapons.**
TOP RIGHT: **As a junior officer William Sims supported Theodore Roosevelt by advocating an ocean-going fleet.** ABOVE: **A line drawing of Cuniberti's proposed all-big-gun battleship: even Cuniberti retained some smaller guns, essential for anti-torpedo defence. His proposals, however, did not go as far as having the guns on the centreline so that they could all be brought to bear on one target.**

21

Goeben and battleships in the Black Sea

The bombardments by the German Admiral Wilhelm Souchon of the French ports in North Africa at Bône and Philippeville on August 3, 1914, were the first shots of the war at sea in World War I. His subsequent escape through the Mediterranean was a disgrace to the all-powerful Royal Navy and the arrival of his modern battlecruiser at Constantinople later that month brought Turkey into the war on the side of the Central Powers. Souchon's bombardment of Odessa on October 29 opened the war between Turkey and Russia, but, when he met a squadron of Russian pre-Dreadnoughts in the Black Sea, Souchon failed to use his speed and firepower to destroy his foe.

At the outbreak of war Souchon commanded the only German ships in the Mediterranean, the modern battlecruiser *Goeben* and the light cruiser *Breslau*. His orders were to cooperate with the Austro-Hungarian and Italian fleets and interdict the passage of French troops across the Mediterranean. When Austria declared war against Serbia on July 28, *Goeben* and *Breslau* were at Pola and by August 1, when Germany declared war on Russia, Souchon's ships had moved to Brindisi, where, fearing internment after Italy had declared its neutrality, he sailed west in the direction where the Royal Navy thought he might make for the Atlantic. Though Britain had yet to join the war, the battlecruisers *Indomitable*

ABOVE: **The German *Goeben*, having altered the balance of power in the Dardanelles and Black Sea, hoisted the Turkish flag and was briefly captured at Novorossiysk before being handed back to the Turks in November 1918.**

and *Indefatigable* looked for Souchon, and met him on August 4 returning eastwards. Both sides were at action stations but their guns were trained fore and aft, and as the British turned to follow, Souchon increased speed and gradually lost sight of the British battlecruisers.

Souchon coaled at Messina, feinted towards the Adriatic and headed for the Dardanelles: he was found again by the Royal Navy which acted timidly and he escaped to Constantinople. Meanwhile on August 2, two Turkish battleships completing in British yards, *Resadiye* and *Sultan Osman I* (formerly the Brazilian *Rio de Janeiro*), were confiscated by the Royal Navy and commissioned as *Erin* and *Agincourt*.

On August 16 Germany announced the sale of Souchon's squadron to Turkey as *Sultan Yavuz Selim* and *Middilli*, Souchon became commander-in-chief of the Turkish battlefleet and his German crew continued to man their ships.

On November 18, 1914, *Goeben* intercepted the Russian battlefleet consisting of the pre-Dreadnoughts *Estavii*, *Ioann Zlatoust* (both 1903), the 1905 *Pantelimon*, the 1895 *Rostislav*,

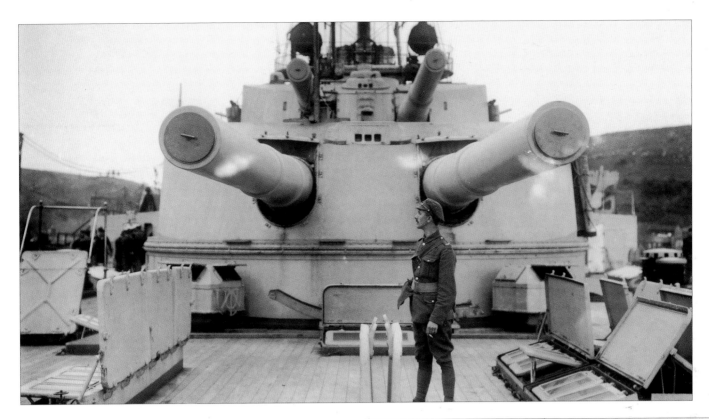

and the 1891 turret ship *Tri Sviatitelia* returning from bombarding Turkish positions. Souchon was eager for a fight and expected to find the Russians easy prey, but he was unpleasantly surprised by the weight and accuracy of the Russian fire.

Poor visibility eliminated *Goeben*'s guns' range advantage, and the Russians, who had learned some lessons from their defeat at Tsushima, were practised as a centralized firing unit. This meant that the centre ship in a three-ship group would pass ranges and bearings to coordinate the fire of the other ships. The older *Rostislav* and *Tri Sviatitelia* were not part of the firing unit and were free to fire on *Breslau*.

In the quarter hour's engagement which ensued, at ranges of 5–8km/3–5 miles, *Breslau* took shelter on *Goeben*'s disengaged side from the hail of fire and *Goeben* was hit 14 times, mainly by *Evstafii*. *Evstafii* was hit four times before *Goeben* veered off into the mist and did not attempt to renew the engagement.

Thereafter there was stalemate in the Black Sea, and *Goeben* did not challenge the Russian pre-Dreadnought Black Sea Fleet. While the Russians operated as a squadron they were relatively free to bombard Turkish ports and positions until even *Goeben* was affected by coal shortages.

After many other actions, *Goeben* and *Breslau* sortied from the Dardanelles to raid Salonika on January 20, 1918, where they sank the British 355mm/14in gun monitor *Raglan* and the smaller 235mm/9.2in gun *M28*. *Breslau* was mined and sunk and *Goeben* was beached after hitting three mines herself. She was repaired in time for the surrender of the mutinous Black Sea Fleet on May 2, 1918.

Rebuilt in 1927–30, and again in 1938 and 1941, she was renamed *Yavuz Selim*. The ex-*Goeben* was offered back to

TOP: **A close-up of *Goeben* after turrets while under military guard. Presumably no officer is watching this man smoke.** ABOVE: ***Goeben*, the ever-elusive German battleship, at last in British hands. From her escape from the Royal Navy in the Mediterranean in 1914 until the Armistice in 1918, *Goeben*, whether she was German or Turkish, had a major impact on the strategic balance in the Black Sea and altered great power politics.**

Germany in 1963 but the offer was refused and so after a period as a museum ship she was scrapped in 1976. Souchon's own career ended in ignominy when in late October 1918 he was removed from his command at Kiel by mutineers.

Jacky Fisher

Jacky Fisher, or Admiral of the Fleet Lord Fisher of Kilverstone, was the father of the Dreadnought revolution, a revolution which changed naval warfare and the balance of power between nations. Fisher linked the old sailing navy with the new, having been nominated by the last of Nelson's captains. As a young officer he served in the Crimea and in China at the battle of Fatshan Creek. Specializing in gunnery, he served on *Warrior* when she was new, and was responsible for a number of innovations including the introduction of electrical firing circuits in the guns of *Ocean* in 1869, and helped to found the Royal Navy's experimental school in HMS *Vernon*. Later he commanded the battleship *Inflexible* at the bombardment of Alexandria in 1882 and took command of the Naval Brigades when they landed.

As Director of Naval Ordnance Fisher introduced a range of modern weapons to the Royal Navy and as an admiral he was responsible, as Third Sea Lord, for delivering the ships ordered under the Naval Defence Act of 1889. Whilst serving as Commander-in-Chief, Mediterranean, he concentrated on firing at long ranges, taught the fleet to manoeuvre in tight formations at maximum speed, and studied the tactics that this implied. Then as Second Sea Lord he reformed the officer and rating structure and training which he implemented whilst Commander-in-Chief, Portsmouth.

From the 1880s onwards Fisher increasingly turned to politics to promote the Royal Navy and his ideas, using his friendship with the journalist W T Stead. He also made influential friends in royal circles and amongst politicians, particularly Winston Churchill.

Fisher brought this powerful suite of technical, strategic and political skills, together with his forceful character, to the office of First Sea Lord in 1904. He advocated the use of submarines and ensured that at the outbreak of World War I the Royal Navy had one of the largest fleets of submarines. Whilst in the Mediterranean he had conceived the idea of the large armoured cruiser, which became the battlecruiser, and though he could not solve the problem of ships having to fight in line-of-battle, he proposed the creation of mixed "fleet units". In response to the danger posed by the rise of the German fleet, Fisher concentrated the Royal Navy in home waters, and needing the manpower for new, larger warships, he controversially paid off many older ships on overseas stations as they were too weak and too slow. Above all, however, Fisher pressed for speed and hitting power in warships.

LEFT: **A famous picture of Fisher's protégé, John Jellicoe, mounting a ladder onboard the battleship *Iron Duke*. Jellicoe was a man consumed by self-doubt, despite the impression of dynamism given by this picture.** BELOW: **An unusual picture of Fisher relaxing with visitors onboard the battleship *Renown*.**

The concept of the all-big-gun battleship was not new. The Italian designer Vittorio Cuniberti had written about it and been published in Germany and Britain, and similar ideas were being developed in the USA. Fisher's critics said that by building the all-big-gun battleship he made every other battleship obsolete including all the Royal Navy's, but it seems that it was an idea whose hour had come, and for once the Royal Navy was first. *Dreadnought* was Fisher's brainchild and it was his fanatic drive and energy which made the development time so short: within months he had decided upon the 305mm/12in gun armament and opted for every innovation available, Professor Barr's 2.74m/9ft optical rangefinder accurate to 6,400m/7,000yd, steam turbines rather than reciprocating engines, and enhanced underwater protection. By robbing the Lord Nelson class of their guns Fisher was able to claim that he had built *Dreadnought* in twelve months and she was officially completed on Trafalgar Day 1906. However, Fisher also made personal enemies, and was forced to retire in 1910, continuing to give advice from retirement in France. He became mentor to Winston Churchill when he was First Lord of the Admiralty, and it was under his tutelage that Churchill persuaded the British government to take a stake in the Anglo-Iranian Oil Company (which grew into British Petroleum) in order to ensure oil supplies for the Royal Navy. Then, after Prince Battenberg was forced to resign as First Sea Lord in 1914 on grounds of his German background Fisher was recalled. As First Sea Lord he was responsible for sending battlecruisers to the South Atlantic in response to the German victory at Coronel, but subsequently fell out with Churchill over his interference in operational matters during the Dardanelles campaign, and resigned.

Fisher was also responsible for advancing the career of John Jellicoe. Jellicoe was not an inspirational leader like Fisher and failed to make best use of his ships when Fisher's mighty fleet of Dreadnoughts was tested at the Battle of Jutland in 1916.

ABOVE: **Jacky Fisher, as he was universally known, seized upon good ideas and turned them into his own but he also had the energy and force of character to make them happen.** BELOW: **Fisher had many ideas, including the concept of a fleet unit and the battlecruiser, and he was an advocate of the submarine. But his greatest brainchild, for which he is best known, was *Dreadnought*, a new type of warship that made all preceding battleships obsolescent, and from which the type took its name.**

The Anglo-German naval race

In the early 20th century the Royal Navy was at the height of its power, was superior by a ratio of two to one to any other navy, and had been at peace for the best part of 100 years – there had been no general war since 1815. The French navy had not really been a threat for many years, and the Russian navy had suffered a crushing defeat at Tsushima in 1905 by the Japanese navy which was under British tutelage. However, the German navy was beginning to grow and establish overseas bases, and the United States Navy (USN) had shown its potential by the cruise of the Great White Fleet in 1907–9.

Royal Navy relations with the USN were cordial and Sims, for example, had been one of the first foreign visitors to inspect *Dreadnought*. On a personal level many British and German officers knew and liked each other, but relations with the German state deteriorated. Kaiser Wilhelm II and naval chief Admiral von Tirpitz wanted a modern navy for personal and prestigious reasons as much as for securing an overseas empire, and they wanted a large navy even if this meant challenging the Royal Navy. The Kaiser's brother, Prince Henry of Prussia, who was also an honorary Admiral in the Royal

ABOVE: **As well as Dreadnought-type battleships, the German navy also employed airships to carry out reconnaissance for the High Seas Fleet.** BELOW LEFT: **Grand Admiral Alfred von Tirpitz who encouraged the German Kaiser to challenge the Royal Navy by building up a "Riskflotte", which helped bring about World War I.**

Navy, made the German navy a respectable profession for ambitious young Germans, while the Kaiser ordered the works of the American naval strategist, Captain Mahan, to be translated and placed in the wardrooms of all his ships. Wilhelm II had absorbed the lesson from his reading of Mahan that a large navy and great power status were synonymous. Perhaps also his cousins on the British throne with their command of the Royal Navy gave him an inferiority complex. The Kaiser was ably assisted by Tirpitz, who had joined the Prussian navy in 1865 and then the navy of the new German Empire when it formed in 1871. Tirpitz, who had commanded the East Asiatic Squadron in 1896–7 when a treaty was concluded with China, returned to Berlin to commence his challenge to the Royal Navy by building up the German navy.

Up until the 1890s the German navy had been a coastal defence force. However, harnessing German industrial power, new German Navy Laws in 1898, 1900, 1908 and 1912 envisaged a balanced fleet which by 1920 would include 38 battleships. Tirpitz's concept was of a *riskflotte* or risk fleet: he reasoned that Britain would not go to war with Germany if Germany possessed a significant fleet, because, although the Royal Navy would win any campaign at sea, it would be so weakened that the two-power standard would be broken and Britain exposed to defeat at sea by France, Russia or even the USA.

RIGHT: **This photograph dated November 28, 1918, shows the German fleet at Scapa Flow after the British Grand Fleet had escorted it into internment.** BELOW: **King Edward VII of Great Britain and his nephew Kaiser Wilhelm II of Germany – it was partly Wilhelm's jealousy of his uncle which drove him to build up the German navy. Books have been written about the extent to which Anglo-German rivalry was a personal affair between the British and German royal families, and a political inevitability of German reunifications in the late 19th century.** BELOW RIGHT: **The German navy at Kiel before World War I, making its challenge to the Royal Navy.** BOTTOM: **This photograph is entitled "the last [large calibre] firing of the German fleet" and shows the effect of firing a broadside – and the resulting smoke. The extent of the German challenge to Britannia's rule of the waves was taken seriously by the Royal Navy.**

The result was somewhat different. Britain became concerned that German naval expansion would provoke French and Russian shipbuilding, and therefore concluded a treaty with Japan. The treaty allowed the Royal Navy to maintain only token forces in the East, and other steps were taken to reduce British imperial commitments: Jacky Fisher brought many ships home from their overseas stations, and paid off older warships to man the new. The larger countries of the British Empire were urged to help create an empire navy by establishing their own navies, like the Royal Australian Navy. Then in 1904 Britain unexpectedly joined in an *entente cordiale* with her long-time enemy, France, and, after the annihilation of the Russian navy at the Battle of Tsushima, Britain and Germany were left to face each other across the North Sea. The launch of *Dreadnought* in 1905 temporarily halted battleship building in Germany, while the German navy designed new ships, but once the naval arms race started afresh it became one of the catalysts of World War I. As war loomed, the French navy was persuaded to concentrate its forces in the Mediterranean, while the Royal Navy took on the defence of the North Sea and northern France.

Despite the efforts of Wilhelm II and Tirpitz, the German battleship building programme never came near to matching the Royal Navy and the challenge tailed off with the approach of war as the German army diverted resources from Wilhelm's navy. In the same period 1907–16, USA completed 14 battleships, Japan and France seven each, Italy and Austro-Hungary five each, Brazil and the Argentine two.

The Battle of the Falklands

The Battle of the Falklands in 1914 was regarded as a triumphant vindication of Jacky Fisher's much-criticized concept of the battlecruiser, a name given by the British Admiralty in 1911 to a new class of heavily armed cruisers.

The outbreak of World War I found Admiral von Spee, commanding the German East Asiatic Squadron, cut off in the western Pacific, with half the world and the Royal Navy between him and home. Without supplies of coal Spee's chances of reaching Germany were slim, and he headed for the west coast of South America, detaching one cruiser to make a diversion into the Indian Ocean. The British divided their forces, and a mixed squadron of elderly ships under Admiral Cradock entered the eastern Pacific. The German squadron contained two large vessels, *Scharnhorst* and *Gneisenau*, which were crack gunnery ships. When Cradock clashed with Spee's squadron off Coronel, the Germans were able to hold him at long range, and the British cruisers *Good Hope* and *Monmouth* were sunk on November 1, 1914.

This blow to British prestige unleashed all the latent energy and resource of the oldest and most powerful of the navies. All available cruisers were ordered to concentrate in the River Plate, and from Britain, two of the latest and fastest battle

ABOVE: **The battlecruiser** *Invincible* **was flagship of the British squadron at the Battle of the Falklands in December 1914. Admiral Sturdee's rapid deployment to the South Atlantic, ordered pre-emptorily when more work was still needed in the dockyards at Devonport, was timely and he beat the German admiral to the Falklands by only a few hours.**

cruisers, *Inflexible* and *Invincible*, were detached from the Grand Fleet and hurried south under the command of Admiral Sturdee – both battlecruisers still had some dockyard mateys working onboard. Sturdee's order gave him an almost free hand, and, as Commander-in-Chief South Atlantic and Pacific, the largest geographical command ever entrusted to a single admiral. The British force concentrated at the Abrolhos Islands and then steamed on southwards with the ships formed in a scouting line at 19km/12-mile intervals.

Sturdee's ships arrived at the Falklands on December 7, 1914, and as the British coaled their ships, the Germans arrived the following morning. As Spee turned away, his ships belching black smoke, Sturdee ordered his ships to sea and the chase began with the Germans already hull down on the Southern horizon. Spee ordered his light ships to make for South American ports whilst the *Scharnhorst* and *Gneisenau*

prepared to take on the British battlecruisers, who, each flying three ensigns, caught up and commenced firing shortly after 13.00. The Germans were in line abreast chased by the British in quarter line. The fall of shot threw up mountains of water, the peaks rising to over 90m/300ft above the water, but there were few hits at long range.

As *Scharnhorst* and *Gneisenau* turned to port, their firing was "beautiful to watch", with perfect ripple salvos all along their sides. A brown coloured puff with a centre of flames masked each gun as it fired, straddling the British ships, and causing splinter damage. In *Inflexible*, one officer noted, "We could hear the shells coming with a curious shrill whine which gradually got deeper and then pop, pop as they burst in the water". In the German ships the long-range plunging fire of 305mm/12in shells was devastating: one German survivor reported that he could feel his whole ship shake and the decks rippled like a caterpillar. At about 14.00 Spee altered course and drew out of range, but by 15.00 the British had closed the range again, and a fierce exchange began. At 15.40 Spee turned 180 degrees away, and Sturdee turned his ships together to port. Then at 16.20 the *Scharnhorst* suddenly turned over and sank.

TOP: **When Spee's German squadron was spotted approaching the Falklands, the British cruiser *Kent* was at anchor and so the first ship to get under way.**
ABOVE LEFT: ***Invincible* making an immense amount of smoke in order to work to her full speed of 22 knots, and flying a battle ensign (probably taken from the cruiser *Carnarvon*).** ABOVE; **The German battleships *Scharnhorst* (seen here when new in 1910) and *Gneisenau* formed the core of Admiral von Spee's squadron, whose route home was barred by the Royal Navy.**

An hour later, after both British battlecruisers had concentrated their fire on *Gneisenau*, she too stopped, gradually turned over and sank. Over 2,000 men were killed in the blazing wrecks or drowned in the freezing waters. Only the German cruiser *Dresden* escaped from the Battle of the Falklands and she was to be hunted down later. Within months of the outbreak of war the German navy's attempts at commerce raiding using surface ships had been brought to an end.

The British battlecruisers had proved they could protect trade and pursue a fleeing enemy, but whether they could also provide a heavy scouting force to the main fleet or close support to the battlefleet would be proved at the Battle of Jutland in 1916.

New bottles for old wine

Even before their heyday at the Battle of Jutland in 1916, the construction of battleships was beginning to falter. In World War I Britain and Italy both had the same operational requirement to manoeuvre on the flanks of their armies and to bombard the enemy with heavy guns. Full-sized battleships, whether obsolete or not, were unsuitable to operate in shallow waters and so specialized ships were built. Although none of these ships bore any resemblance to the low-freeboard monitors of the previous century, the name "monitor" was applied to the resulting single-turret ships.

On the rivers and coasts of the northern Adriatic, the Italian navy converted barges captured from the Austrians into gun platforms, creating a class of monitor that was largely un-armoured. The largest of these were the *Alfredo Cappellini* and *Faa di Bruno,* which used the guns from the battleships *Francesco Morosini* and *Cristoforo Colombo*. The *Monte Santo* and *Monte Sabotino* had guns from the Caracciolo class of battleships, which had been cancelled in 1916.

In Britain, 355mm/14in guns intended for Greece were purchased from their American maker and fitted to the new monitors, which, presumably under Churchill's influence, were

given the names *Admiral Farragut, General Grant, Robert E. Lee* and *Stonewall Jackson*. However, following protests from the USA their names were changed to *Abercrombie, Havelock, Raglan* and *Roberts*.

During 1914 and 1915 the Majestic class of 1890s vintage pre-Dreadnoughts were laid up to provide their 305mm/12in guns for the Lord Clive class of monitors, this time all named after British generals. Three of these, *Lord Clive, Prince Eugene* and *General Wolfe,* were later fitted with a single 455mm/18in gun in a fixed mounting.

ABOVE RIGHT: **In the line of evolution of the battleship,** *Glatton* **(1871) represents an obscure type designed both for coastal defence and bombardment of the enemy coastal targets.** BELOW: **The Royal Navy took the concept of the coast attack ship and built a large number of monitors during World War I. One of the last of these was** *Terror,* **sunk in the Mediterranean in 1941.**

Strangely, the next two monitors were named after French generals, *Marshal Ney* and *Marshal Soult*. They were built with 305mm/12in turret guns taken from the battleship *Ramillies,* thus delaying her completion until 1917. Many smaller monitors were also built, including two coastal defence battleships bought from the Norwegians while under construction, *Gorgon* (ex *Nidaros*) and *Glatton* (ex *Bjorgvin*). Last, largest and most successful to be built were two 380mm/15in gun monitors, *Erebus* and *Terror*. *Erebus* survived torpedoing in 1917, but was sunk by a German dive-bomber off North Africa in 1941.

Characteristic of the new British monitors was their seaworthiness and they saw action in the Dardanelles, in the Adriatic and on the Belgian coast. At the end of the war some were sent to the White Sea and the Baltic to fight the Bolsheviks. Many of the new monitors also carried a single aeroplane for spotting the fall of shot, until they were replaced by shore-based aircraft of the newly formed Royal Naval Air Service. In World War I the Royal Navy led the world in naval aviation and two ships, the battlecruiser *Furious* and the battleship *Eagle* (formerly the Chilean *Almirante Cochrane*) were converted to aircraft carriers. *Furious*, designed as a light battlecruiser with two single 455mm/18in guns, underwent two conversions. In the first conversion she was given a flying-off deck by covering over her forecastle. The aircraft were then recovered from the water by crane after flying off.

In September 1917 she was taken in hand again, her remaining big gun removed and she was given a full length flightdeck. In June 1918 *Furious*'s Camel fighters drove off enemy aircraft and in July they successfully attacked Zeppelin sheds at Tondern in what must rate as the first carrier-borne aircraft strike. *Furious* also served in World War II.

In 1918 the partly completed *Almirante Cochrane* was also purchased for conversion to a through-deck aircraft carrier, although she was not completed until the 1920s. Amongst several other cancelled aircraft carrier projects, the first modern purpose-built aircraft carrier in the world was *Hermes,* laid down in 1918 and completed in 1924.

TOP: **While Germany concentrated on lighter-than-air machines, such as the Zeppelin, the Royal Navy developed the use of fixed-wing aircraft. At first each battleship and cruiser was fitted with one or two aircraft, but soon it was realized that a dedicated ship was needed. As the battleship approached its zenith, the Royal Navy began to build dedicated aircraft carriers. The light battlecruiser *Furious*, with her two single 455mm/18in guns, was converted in two stages.** ABOVE MIDDLE: **The after turret was removed to make a hybrid ship but this was unsuccessful.** ABOVE: **In 1917 she was fully converted before being completely rebuilt between the wars.**

In the USN a class of fast, heavy battlecruisers intended as a counter to the Japanese Kongo class and the British Hoods was cancelled. The two hulls were then taken in hand and built into aircraft carriers, the *Lexington* (CV2) and *Saratoga* (CV3). Likewise steel assembled for *Ranger* was used to build the USN's first purpose-built carrier. However the story of these ships belongs to another book. Aircraft carriers would replace battleships as the capital ships of the future.

North Sea actions 1914–15

The Battle of Heligoland Bight was the first major surface action at sea in World War I when, in late August 1914, Commodore Tyrwhitt, based at Harwich, conducted a sweep into the Heligoland Bight with cruisers and destroyers, while Beatty's First Battle Cruiser Squadron provided cover. On the morning of August 28 Tyrwhitt sank some torpedo boats but was soon outnumbered by the rapid reaction of German cruisers, and as Tyrwhitt fell back on the British battlecruisers, *New Zealand* and *Invincible* were damaged and the cruiser *Arethusa* had to be towed home. The German light cruisers *Mainz* and *Köln* were sunk and three other German cruisers were damaged, further enhancing Beatty and Tyrwhitt's reputations as fighting admirals.

Thereafter, the German tactics were to make raids into the North Sea with the hope of drawing individual British ships and formations into U-boat traps where the Royal Navy's numerical superiority could be whittled away until the German High Seas Fleet could meet the British Grand Fleet on more or less equal terms.

On December 16, 1914, the High Seas Fleet Scouting Group, as the German battlecruisers were known, bombarded the English east coast towns of Hartlepool, Whitby and Scarborough. Several hundred civilians were killed or wounded, though not without a coastal battery damaging some of the German ships including the armoured cruiser *Blücher*. Intelligence had given the Royal Navy warning of the raid and six battleships, four battlecruisers and several

TOP: **The German battle fleet during firing practice and manoeuvring for the photographer.** ABOVE: **The Dreadnought revolution coincided with the centenary of the Battle of Trafalgar in 1805, and the names of the new battleships reflect the Nelson age. This is the British battleship *Temeraire* painted by A. B. Cull.**

cruisers, under Admiral Warrender, were deployed. However, the German admiral, Hipper, and his battlecruisers *Seydlitz*, *Moltke, Von der Tann*, and *Derfflinger,* plus cruisers and destroyers, was covered by the High Seas Fleet under its Commander-in-Chief, Ingenohl.

Warrender saw Ingenohl's ships and closed, mistaking the High Seas Fleet for the smaller raiding force, while Ingenohl mistook the British force for Jellicoe's Grand Fleet of Battle. Ingenohl acted cautiously, ordering Hipper to proceed with his bombardment without apparently telling him of the British ships, while withdrawing the High Seas Fleet towards its bases. Warrender chased Ingenohl until he realized that the east coast ports to the north of his position were under attack, when he turned towards Hipper.

Meanwhile, eight pre-Dreadnoughts were sailed from Rosyth and the Grand Fleet from Scapa Flow, all three movements threatening to encircle Hipper: however, inept communications by the British allowed him to escape.

When the Germans attempted to repeat their successful raid on the east coast ports in January 1915 the British were pre-warned, again by intelligence, and better prepared. As a result Hipper's three battlecruisers were intercepted by Beatty's five battlecruisers at the Battle of Dogger Bank on January 24, the first direct clash between such ships.

Consequently the armoured cruiser *Blücher* was sunk and Hipper's flagship, the battlecruiser *Seydlitz*, was damaged, while on the British side Beatty's own flagship, *Lion*, was also badly damaged. Nevertheless Beatty transferred to *New Zealand* and continued his pursuit of the Germans until the threat of mines and U-boats caused him to break off the attack. Dogger Bank was a moral victory for the Royal Navy but not a decisive battle, although it made the German navy ever more cautious in its excursions into the North Sea.

One of the more memorable images of the war at sea is that of *Blücher* capsizing with her sides covered with men. *Blücher* was last in the German battle line formation, where she was repeatedly hit. At a range of 18,000m/20,000yds, a shell from *Princess Royal* penetrated her forward ammunition handling spaces causing a catastrophic fire. Beatty might have been able to do more damage to the other German ships but his fleet concentrated their fire on *Blücher* and allowed the other German vessels to escape, although *Seydlitz* was badly damaged and on fire. Like other German ships *Blücher* proved difficult to sink: a torpedo provided the *coup de grâce*.

TOP LEFT: **The Indefatigable class of battlecruisers, one of which was *Australia*, bore the brunt of the North Sea actions. Often by the time squadrons of the Grand Fleet could deploy from Scapa Flow, the Germans had returned to harbour.** TOP RIGHT: **Returning from the bombardment of English east coast towns in January 1915, the armoured cruiser *Blücher* was caught by British forces and sank.** ABOVE: ***Derfflinger* was one of the three battlecruisers under the command of the German admiral Hipper.**

The Battle of Jutland followed much the same theme, with a threatened raid intending to draw out the British fleet which would then be destroyed piecemeal. After Jutland the High Seas Fleet rarely left the Heligoland Bight, and there were few opportunities for the British Grand Fleet to come to grips with its enemy, while Beatty kept the Grand Fleet ready at Scapa Flow.

The Battle of Jutland

Jutland was the greatest battleship engagement of all time. On the outbreak of World War I most Royal Navy officers expected a decisive battle, *der Tag* (the day), between the battleships of the Grand Fleet, commanded by Admiral Jellicoe, and the German High Seas Fleet, commanded by Admiral von Pohl. However, German strategy was defensive, and on sweeps into the North Sea, the Germans avoided contact with the larger Grand Fleet. On the other hand, Beatty, in command of the British battlecruisers, adopted an aggressive strategy and at the Battles of the Heligoland Bight in December 1914 and of Dogger Bank in January 1915 the Germans were lucky to escape without serious losses.

However, when Admiral von Scheer replaced Pohl in command of the High Seas Fleet in January 1916, he prepared a strategy of attrition to counter the Royal Navy's distant blockade. He hoped to defeat the British by making hit-and-run raids on North Sea coastal towns that would bring the ships into battle piecemeal where they would be destroyed by minefields, submarines and local concentrations of superior numbers of German surface warships.

In May 1916 Scheer sent his battlecruisers out, under Admiral Hipper, hoping to draw Beatty's battlecruisers on to the High Seas Fleet. However, when British naval intelligence became aware of these plans, the Grand Fleet sailed from Scapa Flow as well as the battlecruisers from Rosyth.

TOP: **Close-up of the German battlecruiser *Seydlitz* on fire during the Battle of Jutland. Despite her after-turrets being burned out she reached Germany and was repaired.** ABOVE: **The British battleship *Warspite* flying three battle ensigns at about 18.00 during the "run to the north" on May 31, 1916. The German fleet is to the south-east.**

At 15.20 on May 31, 1916, the cruiser *Galatea* made the time-honoured signal "Enemy in sight" and Beatty turned his battlecruisers to the south-east to engage, opening fire at extreme range. As Beatty closed the range, *Indefatigable* and *Queen Mary* were hit and blew up and he uttered his infamous remark that there was "something wrong with our bloody ships today". Later it was thought that the British practice of achieving rapid fire by storing ready-use ammunition in exposed positions might have been the cause of losing these fine ships.

Beatty also lost contact with the supporting Fifth (Fast) Battle Squadron, and, after he had sighted the German High Seas Fleet, at 16.46 he turned towards Jellicoe, thus ending the first phase of the battle known as the run to the south.

At 17.33 Jellicoe and Beatty sighted each other's forces. Warned of the presence of the High Seas Fleet, Jellicoe now deployed the Grand Fleet into line of battle and crossed the head of the German line, but as he did so a third battlecruiser, *Invincible*, was hit and also blew up. At 18.33 Scheer ordered a simultaneous 16-point (180-degree) turn: to Jellicoe it seemed that the Germans had vanished in the haze. Twenty minutes later Scheer ordered another turn and again the head of his line came under fire, then at 19.18 he ordered a final 16-point turn.

Meanwhile Jellicoe, fearing a torpedo attack and unwilling to risk a night action, had made two alterations of course away from the Germans. Jellicoe was much criticized for this: had he taken greater risks at this stage of the battle, there is every possibility that he would have inflicted heavy casualties on the Germans.

As night fell the battlecruisers engaged each other, but during the night Scheer set course for Horns Reef while Jellicoe steered for the Ems River. There were plenty of skirmishes, but no one informed Jellicoe that Scheer was crossing behind him and by morning the seas were empty.

Jutland was a material and tactical victory for Scheer and the High Seas Fleet, and the Germans scored a propaganda victory too by the way they reported the battle first. However, it was a strategic victory for the Grand Fleet. While the Germans inflicted losses on the numerically superior Grand Fleet in the ratio of three to one, they had failed to break the British blockade or to wrest control of the North Sea from the Royal Navy.

On the other hand, the Royal Navy had failed to achieve the expected new Trafalgar, and the Navy and its public were bitterly disappointed. The German navy did not come out again until a mutiny and the armistice in 1918. Churchill summed affairs up when he said that Jellicoe was the only person who could have lost the war in an afternoon. The controversy about whether he could have done more continues to the present.

RIGHT: **John Jellicoe was Commander-in-Chief of the British Grand Fleet at the Battle of Jutland, the only man, Churchill said, who could have lost World War I in an afternoon.** FAR RIGHT: **Admiral Scheer commanded the German High Seas Fleet in 1916. His ships sank more than the British and his superior tactical handling of the fleet outwitted Jellicoe.** BELOW: **A German picture of the destruction of the British battlecruiser *Queen Mary* during the Battle of Jutland or Skagerrakschlacht at 16.26 on May 31, 1916. Beatty, when he saw his ships blowing up, asked if there was something wrong with the British ships.**

BRITISH LOSSES	GERMAN LOSSES
Battlecruisers	**Battlecruisers**
Indefatigable	None
Queen Mary	**Pre-Dreadnoughts**
Invincible	*Pommern*
Pre-Dreadnoughts	**Armoured Cruisers**
None	None
Armoured Cruisers	**Light Cruisers**
Black Prince	*Elbing*
Defence	*Frauenlob*
Warrior	*Rostock*
Light Cruisers	*Wiesbaden*
None	**Destroyers**
Destroyers	*S35*
Ardent	*V4*
Fortune	*V27*
Nestor	*V29*
Nomad	*V48*
Shark	**Crew Killed**
Sparrowhawk	2551
Tipperary	
Turbulent	
Crew Killed	
6097	

The scuttling at Scapa Flow

According to the terms of the armistice which brought about a temporary halt to the hostilities of World War I in continental Europe, Germany was obliged to have all her U-boats and about 70 surface warships interned, whose fate would then be decided by the treaty negotiations at Versailles.

When the German fleet steamed for the Firth of Forth they were met at sea by Beatty's Grand Fleet which had formed two parallel columns, comprising nearly 400 warships including 13 squadrons of battleships, battlecruisers and cruisers and the USN Sixth Battle Squadron. The Allied ships were at action stations even though their guns were trained fore and aft.

The German fleet arrived at the Firth of Forth on the morning of November 21. Beatty had no intention of treating this as merely an internment of the German navy, but was determined by stage management to make this an abject surrender, equivalent to major defeat in battle. The German navy was in an incipient state of mutiny, which Beatty dealt with by telling the plenipotentiaries of the Sailors' and Workers' Soviet of the North Sea command to "go to hell", and ordered that "the German flag will be hauled down at sunset and will not be hoisted again without permission".

Over the next few days the German ships were moved in groups to Scapa Flow, where they were all assembled by November 27. By mid-December 1918 the 20,000 crew members who had sailed the ships to Scapa Flow were reduced to maintenance crews of less than 5,000 officers and men, and in June 1919 these were further reduced to skeleton crews of less than 2,000.

TOP: *Seydlitz* leads the German battlecruisers into Scapa Flow on November 21, 1918. ABOVE: A close-up of the *Seydlitz* such as the British had not seen during the war. For four years the British Grand Fleet and the German High Seas Fleet had occupied each others' thoughts and actions. When they finally met, the British fleet was ready for action, though guns were trained fore and aft.

The armistice was extended several times while the treaty negotiations continued, in which, as far as the Royal Navy was concerned, the British were just as anxious to destroy the naval power of Germany as they were to prevent an increase in naval power of any other nation by the acquisition of the German ships. Finally it was agreed that all the interned ships should be surrendered and under the terms of the Treaty of Versailles Germany would only be allowed to keep six of her oldest pre-Dreadnought battleships of the Deutschland or Braunschweig classes, six light cruisers, 12 destroyers and no submarines.

LEFT: German battleship *Kaiser* taken from the air on November 21, 1918. BELOW LEFT: David Beatty, Jellicoe's successor as the Commander-in-Chief of the British Grand Fleet, caught open-mouthed as he watches the German High Seas Fleet entering an internment which he was determined to turn into surrender. BELOW: The wreck of the proud *Seydlitz* after she had been scuttled on June 21, 1919. The salvage of the German fleet took many years: the ships were raised and towed, mostly keel-up, to Scotland where they were broken up in the inter-war years. Some of the work was contracted out, so that by the 1930s there were German tugs, flying the Nazi's Swastika flag, engaged in towing the hulks between Scapa Flow and the Firth of Forth.

However, rather than allow the Royal Navy to seize his ships, Reuter, the German admiral at Scapa Flow, was making preparations to scuttle them. After he had read the details of the Treaty of Versailles in *The Times* newspaper, his only source of reliable intelligence, Reuter sent the cryptic message "Paragraph eleven. Confirm" on June 21, 1919, which was his order to scuttle the fleet. Although the British First Battle Cruiser Squadron immediately returned from exercises it was too late to prevent the German action.

Over 406,420 tonnes/400,000 tons of warships were sunk, including ten battleships (*Kaiser, Prinzregent Luitpold, Kaiserin, König Albert, Friedrich der Grosse, König, Grosser Kurfüst, Kronprinz Wilhelm, Markgraf,* and *Bayern*), and five battle-cruisers (*Seydlitz, Moltke, Von der Tann, Derfflinger* and *Hindenburg*), and also five cruisers and 31 other ships. Twenty-four other ships, including the battleship *Baden*, were beached by the British to prevent them from sinking. Officially the British were outraged and attempted to blame the government in Berlin for ordering the scuttling, but in private senior officers of

the Royal Navy were relieved that the German navy, once the second most powerful in the world, had been reduced to a minor status, and that the problem of what to do with the interned ships had been resolved. Perversely Admiral Scheer, the last commander-in-chief of the High Seas Fleet, took pride that the honour of the German navy had somehow been saved.

The remnants of the old Imperial German Navy became the Reichsmarine in April 1919 under the Weimar Republic and were given the task of defending the German Baltic coast against attacks by the Bolsheviks who were consolidating their grip on the Russian state. Salvage operations on the sunken ships at Scapa Flow lasted over the next two decades. It was an ignominious end to Germany's imperial and naval ambitions.

The naval treaties

There were a number of international treaties that attempted to limit naval armaments, including the size and number of battleships. At the end of World War I the most modern units of the German High Seas Fleet had been interned at Scapa Flow, where they were scuttled in 1919, and Britannia, or rather the Royal Navy, once more ruled the waves. However, Japan, which had been following a British naval tradition and an ally since the Anglo-Japanese Treaty of 1902, and the USA, which had sent a squadron of battleships to join the Grand Fleet at Scapa Flow, represented new challenges.

The 1916 US Naval Program had called for ten battleships and six battlecruisers, which would give the United States Navy (USN) a fleet of modern battleships. In contrast, all the Royal Navy's battleships, except *Hood,* which was still incomplete, were pre-war. The Japanese also had a battleship-building programme, as did France and Italy. Then in November 1921, US President Harding convened a naval disarmament conference in Washington.

To the surprise of the British, the USA offered to scrap much of the 1916 and later programmes, and proposed a ten-year holiday on new construction. Specifically, the USA proposed that a ratio should be agreed for the number of ships which should be scrapped, and that the number of battleships retained by each nation should be used to calculate the numbers of other warships each nation could keep. Battleships would only be replaced when they were 20 years old and then they could not exceed 35,560 tonnes/35,000 tons standard displacement (the displacement of a ship fully equipped for sea except for fuel).

TOP: **USN warships being scrapped at Philadelphia in the 1920s. On the right is the battleship *Maine* (down by the bows) and centre (with her cage masts still in place) is the battleship *Wisconsin*. The Washington Naval Treaty caused the world's fleets to be culled.** ABOVE: **The first of a series of interwar naval conferences was staged in Washington in this specially converted theatre, where the delegates knew that they had the opportunity to make history.**

After weeks of negotiation, a formula was agreed of British to American to Japanese battleships in the ratio of 5:5:3, and to limit battleship guns to 405m/16in. A separate Four Power Treaty, which included France, attempted to neutralize the Western Pacific and ended the period of Anglo-Japanese cooperation. France and Italy were given smaller ratios, but France obtained parity in submarine numbers with Britain and the USA. The tonnage and gun size of cruisers was also limited, but not the number, Britain insisting that she needed large numbers of cruisers for the protection of Empire trade. The size of aircraft carriers was set at a maximum of 27,500 tonnes/27,000 tons, and the total tonnage was agreed for Britain and the USA as 35,560 tonnes/35,000 tons each, Japan 82,300 tonnes/81,000 tons, and France and Italy as 61,000 tonnes/60,000 tons each.

The Washington Naval Treaty of 1922, which seemed to have curtailed Anglo-American rivalry while making it impossible for Japan to challenge the USA in the Pacific, was to be effective for 15 years. Several issues remained unresolved but a subsequent naval arms limitation conference at Geneva in 1927 was not successful and France and Italy refused to attend. The British wanted to revise the Washington Treaty to allow 30,500-tonne/30,000-ton battleships with 340mm/13.5in guns. Britain and the USA disagreed about the number of cruisers that should be allowed – the USA wanted parity at 254,000–305,000 tonnes/250,000–300,000 tons for all cruisers. However, the Royal Navy thought it needed over 406,500 tonnes/400,000 tons for the defence of the Empire, and Japan wanted a limit on heavy, 205mm/8in-gun cruisers. The British hoped to set a new limit on the tonnage of submarines. However, the conference formally broke up without agreement though desultory talks continued, while the USA endeavoured to build cruisers to match those of the Royal Navy.

The controversy about cruisers continued at the London Conference of 1930. The Royal Navy conceded a limit of 25,400 tonnes/25,000 tons standard displacement and 305mm/12in guns, and the life was extended to 26 years. This was not accepted, but the numbers of battleships were reduced to a ratio of 15:15:9. A second London Conference was convened in 1935 at which Britain and the USA refused to grant parity to Japan, as this would have given her local superiority in the Far East. Japan then gave notice that she would withdraw from the original Washington Treaty, and Italy followed suit. The main benefit of this conference was the agreement signed by Britain, France and the USA that provided for notice to be given of intended construction. Italy, Germany, Poland and the Soviet Union later assented to this.

TOP: **The Japanese delegation, which came to Washington in 1921, included Count Shidehara (second left) and Admiral Kato. They were disappointed not to achieve parity with Britain and the USA.** ABOVE: **The guns of scrapped warships photographed lying in Philadelphia Navy Yard in 1923.**

Battleship numbers in 1939

COUNTRY	IN SERVICE	UNDER CONSTRUCTION
Britain	15	5
France	7	4
Germany	5	4
Italy	4	4
Japan	10	4
USA	15	8
Total	56	29

In 1935, Britain also agreed to an Anglo-German Naval Agreement that allowed Germany 35 per cent of the British tonnage in all classes of warships.

The Indian Ocean

The World War II battleship campaign in the Indian Ocean is one of the least known and studied, but nevertheless features many key aspects of battleship warfare. Two German surface raiders visited the Indian Ocean: the pocket battleship *Graf Spee* in October 1939, where she claimed a small tanker of 717 tonnes/706 tons south-west of Madagascar and then escaped back into the South Atlantic before Anglo-French hunting groups could find her, and the pocket battleship *Admiral Scheer*, which reached as far as the Seychelles in spring 1941 and was lucky to evade the hunting British cruisers. The purpose of these raids was to cause British and allied warships to disperse and to make them introduce the convoy system, which the Germans regarded as inefficient. However these raids were so short-lived that they had little effect on the actual distribution and deployment of Allied warships.

Until 1942, however, the Indian Ocean remained a relatively safe theatre of operations for the Royal Navy. Admiral Sir James Somerville, who had successfully commanded the battleships and aircraft carriers of Force H based at Gibraltar, had been sent to command a new Eastern Fleet based in Ceylon (Sri Lanka). Somerville formed his fleet in two groups, a fast division consisting of the battleship *Warspite* and two carriers, *Indomitable* and *Formidable*, and a slow division composed of the four battleships *Resolution*, *Ramillies*, *Royal Sovereign* and *Revenge*, and the carrier *Hermes*. Both

ABOVE: *Warspite* formed part of the fast division of Admiral Somerville's Eastern Fleet as he manoeuvred to avoid succumbing to superior Japanese naval power. BELOW: The slow division of Somerville's fleet comprised four elderly battleships, including *Ramillies*, which would have been no match for Nagumo's carriers. Thousands of men were engaged, and put at risk, in this strategic deployment.

Colombo and Trincomalee were poorly defended and Somerville made a secret base at Addu Atoll in the Maldives.

In early April the Japanese navy struck into the Indian Ocean. A force of carriers and cruisers entered the Bay of Bengal and sank 23 ships of 113,800 tonnes/112,000 tons, while Japanese submarines attacked shipping on the west coast of India. Meanwhile a strong carrier group (the same ships as had attacked Pearl Harbor) escorted by four fast battleships reached for Ceylon. However, the Japanese admiral Nagumo lost the element of surprise when his force was sighted on April 4 south of Ceylon, and Somerville was able to clear his ships from their ports.

Between April 5 and 9 Japanese air attacks were frustrated, and only a British destroyer and an armed merchant cruiser were caught in harbour, and two heavy cruisers were discovered at sea and sunk. Somerville's aggressive spirit led him to attempt a counter-attack, and the elderly carrier *Hermes* and two of her escorts were sunk when returning to Colombo. The Japanese then left the Indian Ocean, and Somerville, uncertain of where his enemy was, retired, sending his slow group to East Africa and his fast group to Bombay. The Japanese had thus secured their perimeter and reached the high tide of their expansion for little cost in either material or ships.

The British were now concerned about further Japanese raids into the Indian Ocean and about the neutrality of Madagascar, held by the Vichy French. A large force including two carriers and the battleship *Ramillies* was assembled at Durban for Operation Ironclad, the occupation of Diego Suarez, a natural harbour at the northern end of Madagascar. There on May 30 the Japanese counter-attacked using midget submarines and *Ramillies* was severely damaged, needing to be towed back to Durban for temporary repairs.

Thereafter Somerville's Eastern Fleet was reduced to reinforce other theatres, and throughout August he carried out diversionary raids using the carrier *Illustrious* and the battleships *Warspite* and *Valiant*. From September to November 1942 the remainder of the island of Madagascar was occupied and the Indian Ocean was relatively quiet for the next year, during which Axis submarines scored some successes.

In January 1944 the British Eastern Fleet was strengthened by the arrival of *Queen Elizabeth, Valiant, Renown* and several

ABOVE: **The Japanese admiral Nagumo, who had planned and led the air strike on Pearl Harbor, hoped to catch the British in Trincomalee, but Somerville was warned and escaped to a secret anchorage.**

carriers. This was in preparation for a series of strikes against Japanese-held positions on Sumatra beginning on April 19, by which time the Eastern Fleet included the Free French battleship *Richelieu*. Thereafter the war in the Indian Ocean was increasingly prosecuted using carrier-based aircraft, and in August *Valiant* was badly damaged and never again fully repaired after the dry dock she was in collapsed.

In November 1944 the British Eastern Fleet was split into the British East Indies Fleet including the battleships *Queen Elizabeth* and *Renown*, and the British Pacific Fleet based in Australia including the battleships *Howe* and *King George V*. Aircraft carriers, however, predominated in both fleets as the battle moved out of the Indian Ocean. After World War II the Indian Ocean once more became a naval power vacuum, until the growth of the Indian navy in the late 20th century.

RIGHT: **Later in the war the British Eastern Fleet was strengthened by the deployment of fast battleships like *Valiant* and several aircraft carriers. The distances involved were huge and Trincomalee became an important staging post and centre for training for the fleet both in its attack on the Japanese-held East Indies, and in its deployment to the east of Australia, where the British Pacific Fleet would be based.**

LEFT: The 380mm/15in guns of the battleship *Valiant* firing a broadside; astern of her are *Barham* and *Warspite*. These three ships, based at Alexandria in Egypt, formed the backbone of Cunningham's fleet.
ABOVE: "ABC" or Admiral Sir Andrew Cunningham, Commander-in-Chief of the British Mediterranean Fleet, was the greatest British Admiral since Nelson.
BELOW: The battleship *Renown* and the aircraft carrier *Ark Royal* belonged to Force H, which held the western end of the Mediterranean and could be deployed into the Atlantic.

Cunningham and the battleship war in the Mediterranean

The actions between the British and Italian fleets in the Mediterranean in 1940–3 were some of the last involving battleship against battleship, with characteristics reminiscent of the North Sea battles of World War I and a foretaste of the carrier battles in the Pacific. The driving spirit of the British Mediterranean Fleet was "ABC" Cunningham, who in June 1939 became Commander-in-Chief, Mediterranean Fleet, and is widely regarded as the greatest admiral since Nelson.

After the fall of France, the Royal Navy's first objective was the neutralization of the French fleet. When the French turned down all British suggestions to neutralize their fleet at Mers-el-Kebir, Admiral Somerville, commanding Force H, reluctantly fired upon his former allies. The battleship *Bretagne* blew up, *Provence* and *Dunkerque* were badly damaged, but *Strasbourg* escaped to Toulon. *Dunkerque* was torpedoed a few days later by *Ark Royal*'s aircraft. At Alexandria Cunningham persuaded the French Admiral Godfrey to agree to demilitarize his flagship, *Lorraine*.

In July 1940 Cunningham sailed from Alexandria with *Warspite*, *Malaya* and *Royal Sovereign*, and the aircraft carrier *Eagle* to cover convoys in the central Mediterranean. Intelligence told Cunningham that two Italian battleships, *Giulio Cesare* and *Conte di Cavour*, were escorting a convoy to North Africa, and Cunningham changed course to cut them off. *Warspite* hit *Giulio Cesare* at extreme range and as the Italians retreated Cunningham pursued them to within sight of

Calabria, scoring a moral victory which would set the tone for the rest of this war. Off Cape Spartivento on November 27, Force H, led by Somerville in *Renown*, exchanged long-range shots with *Vittorio Veneto* and *Guilio Cesare*, but, handicapped by the slower *Ramillies*, Somerville could not close with his quarry. A few weeks later, on February 9, 1941, Somerville took *Renown*, *Malaya* and the aircraft carrier *Ark Royal* into the Gulf of Genoa to bombard and mine Genoa, Leghorn and La Spezia. This time it was the Italian fleet which was too late to catch the British.

LEFT: **Aerial reconnaisance after the Fleet Air Arm attack on** *Taranto* **showed one Italian Cavour class battleship badly damaged, one beached with a heavy list to starboard and the other with her stern submerged and leaking oil.** ABOVE: **The Italian battleship** *Caio Duilio* **photographed on the morning after the attack, with the whole of her starboard side submerged.** BELOW: **The sad end for one of** *Illustrious*'s **Swordfish, recovered from the harbour after the attack on** *Taranto*. **Despite their frailty, the Swordfish could survive considerable damage.**

When Cunningham planned Operation Judgement in November 1941 – a complex passage of ships through the Mediterranean and an attack on the Italians in Taranto harbour – the Italians outnumbered Cunningham in every class of ship except carriers. *Malaya, Ramillies, Valiant* and *Warspite* formed the covering force, while torpedo-bombers from the carrier *Illustrious* sank or badly damaged *Vittorio Veneto, Caio Duilio* and *Conte di Cavour*. Japanese naval officers studied the results as they prepared for an attack on the US fleet at Pearl Harbor.

At the Battle of Cape Matapan in March 1941, the Italians sent the battleship *Vittorio Veneto* to interrupt British convoys south of Greece, and, again warned by intelligence, Cunningham sailed his ships. British cruisers retired eastwards towards Cunningham's battleships, hoping to draw the Italians into a trap, while the Italian Admiral Iachino hoped to catch them between his heavy cruisers and the *Vittorio Veneto*. However, aircraft from the carrier *Formidable* attacked the Italian battleship, and, without his own air cover, Iachino realized he must retreat westwards. *Vittorio Veneto* was hit once by torpedo, and the heavy cruiser *Pola* was stopped, also by a torpedo.

Iachino ordered ships to protect *Pola*, but shortly after ten o'clock that night, radar in the British battleships revealed their position. Immediately, *Barham, Valiant* and *Warspite* opened fire at close range sinking two Italian heavy cruisers, and in the night fighting which followed two Italian destroyers and *Pola* were sunk.

However, the end of the battleship age was marked in the Mediterranean by the dramatic sinking of the elderly *Barham*, which on November 25, 1941, with the battleships *Queen Elizabeth* and *Valiant* formed part of Force K hunting for Italian

convoys off North Africa. She was hit by three torpedoes from the German submarine *U-331*, quickly capsized and blew up with large loss of life.

Battleships played a supporting role in the Allied landings in North Africa and Sicily and in Italy. In November 1942 three US battleships covered the landings at Casablanca, whilst in the Mediterranean Force H covered the landings in Algeria. At Salerno in September 1943 the heavy guns of *Warspite* and *Valiant*, turned on targets ashore, played a major role in stopping a German counter-attack.

The surrender of the Italian fleet released the Royal Navy's capital ships for duties elsewhere and the war at sea in the Mediterranean was then mostly conducted by light ships. Nevertheless, during Operation Dragoon, the last major landings in the Mediterranean, in southern France, there were five battleships, one British, three American and a Frenchman, fighting for the liberty of France.

LEFT: **Pearl Harbor, December 7, 1941: a Japanese aerial picture that shows "battleship row" already under attack. A British officer who visited earlier and saw the Americans' lack of preparedness had noted "you can't miss".** ABOVE: **Admiral Isoroku Yamamoto, architect of the pre-emptive attack on Pearl Harbor, who realized that the only hope of defeating the USA was to wipe out its fleet. He might have succeeded but intelligence did not tell him that the USN carriers were not present.**

Nemesis at Pearl Harbor

When the British battleship *Warspite* visited Pearl Harbor in August 1941 one of her officers, a veteran of the Fleet Air Arm in the Mediterranean, saw battleship row and remarked, "Blimey, you can't miss!" The Imperial Japanese Navy (IJN) had followed events in the Mediterranean, particularly the attack on Taranto in which a handful of unsophisticated biplanes had crippled the Italian battle fleet.

The Washington Naval Treaty was aimed at preventing a naval arms race and forbade the building of naval bases closer to Japan than Singapore (UK) and the Philippines (USA). However, the Anglo-Japanese treaties were not renewed, and after the conquest of Manchuria in 1937, Japan invaded China. The USA aided China and imposed sanctions on Japan, eventually cutting off the supply of oil and raw materials. By 1940, Japan had aligned herself with Nazi Germany and was developing plans to occupy South-east Asia and seize the resources she needed. The Japanese army and navy were well versed in amphibious warfare and naval aviation, but the threat to Japanese plans was the US Navy (USN) fleet based at Pearl Harbor, Hawaii. Earlier in the century, the IJN had launched a pre-emptive strike on Port Arthur, and now Admiral Yamamoto devised a plan to annihilate the USN with a surprise attack.

The key element of Yamamoto's plan was the surprise use of aircraft carriers and naval aircraft on a scale never seen before. Training began in the spring of 1941, and the plan was approved in October. The carrier force commanded by Vice Admiral Chuichi Nagumo consisted of six heavy aircraft carriers and their escorts, and a submarine force was deployed to sink any American warships that escaped from Pearl Harbor. Nagumo's fleet assembled in a remote anchorage in the Kurile Islands and crossed the northern Pacific unobserved. By dawn on Sunday December 7, 1941, the Nagumo fleet was some 320km/200 miles north of Hawaii.

At 06.00, the first wave of 181 planes composed of torpedo bombers, dive-bombers and fighters attacked the USN's Pacific Fleet at its anchorage and achieved complete surprise. There were more than 90 ships at anchor in Pearl Harbor, including eight battleships, seven in a row off Ford Island, and the *Pennsylvania* in dry dock close by. Within minutes of the first attack, all had been bombed and torpedoed. *West Virginia* sank quickly; *Oklahoma* turned turtle; a fire in *Arizona* ignited the forward magazine and she blew up; *California, Maryland, Tennessee, Pennsylvania,* and *Nevada* were also damaged.

Half an hour later, a second wave of 170 Japanese planes made a concentrated attack on *Nevada*, which despite damage got underway. However, *Nevada* had to be beached to keep the channel clear. The Japanese attack on Pearl Harbor ended shortly before 10.00 am, by which time 21 USN ships were sunk or damaged including, in addition to the battleships, three cruisers, four destroyers, a seaplane tender, the former battleship *Utah* (converted to a target), a repair ship, a minelayer, a tug and a floating dock. The Japanese had also

ABOVE: *Nevada* was the only USN battleship to get underway during the attack and is seen here moving away from other burning ships. Her ensign is still in the harbour position. RIGHT: The battleships *West Virginia* and *Tennessee* still upright but burning fiercely after the attack was over. Both ships were later repaired and fought in the Pacific theatre. BELOW RIGHT: *Arizona* was not to be so lucky. After a raging fire reached her forward magazine, she blew up. The US President called it "a day of infamy", and the effect of the attack was to shock and mobilize the American people and especially the USN. It was inevitable that the USA with its superior industrial might would eventually prevail over Japan.

struck at the airfields of Hawaii, where over 188 US aircraft were destroyed and 159 damaged, mostly on the ground.

Japanese losses were less than 10 per cent of the attacking aircraft, yet the attack on Pearl Harbor was not as successful as it might have been. By chance, there were no USN aircraft carriers in harbour. The carriers *Enterprise* and *Lexington* were at sea delivering aircraft reinforcements to other American Pacific bases and *Saratoga*, which might also have been present, was in refit on the West Coast. Damage to the harbour installations was slight, and these were quickly brought back into full use, and all but three ships sunk or damaged at Pearl Harbor were salvaged. Of the battleships, *Arizona* was too badly damaged to be raised, *Oklahoma* was raised but considered too old to be worth repair, and *Utah* was already considered obsolete.

President Roosevelt called the attack on Pearl Harbor "a day of infamy", while the blow to American prestige and anger at the sudden and unexpected strike precipitated the USA into World War II, with the USA declaring war on Germany as well as Japan.

Hunt for the *Bismarck*

TOP LEFT: **This stern view of the German battleship *Bismarck* gives some idea of the strength and size of the German monster. Nevertheless, though she sank the British *Hood*, her career was measured in months.** ABOVE: **Battle at sea between battleships took place at long range and often all either side saw of the enemy was distant smoke on the horizon.**

Following the success of Operation Berlin in which the battleships *Scharnhorst* and *Gneisenau* had sunk 22 allied merchant ships during a two-month raid into the Atlantic, a new operation was planned. Operation Rheinübung would use Germany's newest and most powerful battleship, *Bismarck*. Originally, it was intended that *Scharnhorst* and *Gneisenau* would sail from Brest too, but neither was operational after being bombed. Consideration was also given to delaying the operation until *Tirpitz* was worked up, but the German leadership could not wait and the heavy cruiser *Prinz Eugen* was selected as *Bismarck*'s consort. The supporting force consisted of two supply ships, five tankers and two scouting ships despatched secretly into the Atlantic.

However, both warships were seen heading north off the Swedish coast and Fleet Air Arm reconnaissance confirmed that they had sailed from Bergen. *Bismarck* and the cruiser *Prinz Eugen* were next detected in the Denmark Strait late on May 23, by the watching British heavy cruisers *Suffolk* and *Norfolk*, who shadowed until the morning of May 24, 1940, when the battlecruiser *Hood* and the new battleship *Prince of Wales* came into action.

At 05.32, *Hood* opened fire on *Prinz Eugen* at 21km/13 miles range, and both German ships replied, firing at *Hood*. A fire started on *Hood*'s upper deck and at about 06.00 the *Bismarck*'s fifth salvo hit and *Hood* blew up. The German fire now shifted to *Prince of Wales*, hitting several times and killing or wounding everyone on the bridge except the captain. However, *Bismarck* had been hit with two or three 355mm/14in shells before breaking off the action.

Although *Bismarck* was losing fuel and shipping water, the German admiral, Lütjens, decided to continue his North Atlantic sortie. With one boiler room out of action and speed reduced to 28 knots, he first feinted north while ordering *Prinz Eugen* to proceed independently, and then resumed a course towards western France.

Around midnight Fleet Air Arm Swordfish torpedo bombers from the carrier *Victorious* found *Bismarck*, launched their torpedoes and hit her amidships on the armoured belt, with no apparent effect. Then during the night, *Bismarck* shook off *Norfolk* and *Suffolk*, which had been keeping contact by radar. Lütjens now had a chance to escape but, assuming that he was still being shadowed by radar, he thought that nothing would be lost by a long signal to Germany that gave away his position.

After 30 hours without a sighting, a Catalina flying-boat of the RAF, flown by a USN officer, Ensign Smith, spotted *Bismarck* on May 26. He held contact under fire while radioing *Bismarck*'s position and the cruiser *Sheffield* was able to resume shadowing.

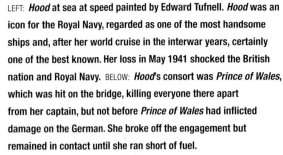

LEFT: *Hood* at sea at speed painted by Edward Tufnell. *Hood* was an icon for the Royal Navy, regarded as one of the most handsome ships and, after her world cruise in the interwar years, certainly one of the best known. Her loss in May 1941 shocked the British nation and Royal Navy. BELOW: *Hood*'s consort was *Prince of Wales*, which was hit on the bridge, killing everyone there apart from her captain, but not before *Prince of Wales* had inflicted damage on the German. She broke off the engagement but remained in contact until she ran short of fuel.

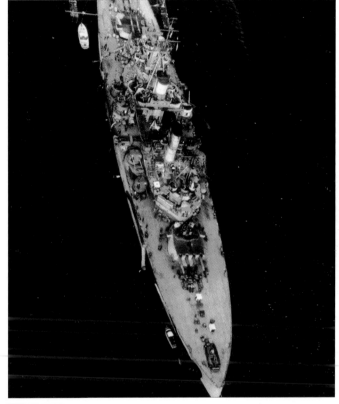

ABOVE: In the final stage of the battle, *Rodney* closed to a few thousand metres/yards to pulverize *Bismarck* at the modern equivalent of point blank range while the battleship *King George V* stood off and hit *Bismarck* with plunging fire.

Meanwhile the Royal Navy was gathering in the Atlantic. On May 22, Admiral Tovey with the capital ships *King George V* and *Repulse* and the carrier *Victorious* had steamed west and south from Scapa Flow. *Rodney* and *Ramillies* had left their convoys and were steaming south-west and Captain Vian with the Fourth Destroyer Flotilla had left a troop convoy to sail east. *Bismarck*, although more than 600 miles from France, might yet reach safety before the Royal Navy could catch up.

However, Force H, consisting of the battlecruiser *Renown* and carrier *Ark Royal* were approaching from Gibraltar. A torpedo strike by Swordfish biplanes on the afternoon of May 26 found the shadowing *Sheffield* in error. As darkness fell, a second strike found its target but cloud offered little protection against *Bismarck*'s radar laid guns, and as the Swordfish converged from different bearings, *Bismarck* used her heavy

guns to raise walls of water against the frail aircraft. Many aircraft were damaged but none were lost and two torpedoes hit their target, jamming the rudders and dooming *Bismarck*. As engineers tried to free her steering, *Bismarck* steered north towards the British, while Captain Vian and his destroyers, including the Polish *Piorun*, made a series of torpedo attacks.

At 08.45 on May 27, Tovey's heavy ships caught up and opened fire. At first, *Bismarck*'s reply was accurate but she quickly became a wreck as *Rodney*'s 405mm/16in guns found the enemy range. *Rodney* closed to 3,650m/4,000 yards to fire at point blank range while *King George V*'s fire from 12,800m/ 14,000 yards plunged down on *Bismarck*, and, within 30 minutes, coordinated resistance had ceased. The fire-control positions were out of action, communications to the engine rooms and compartments below the armoured deck had been lost, and fires raged. A myth would grow up that *Bismarck*'s crew scuttled her, but between 10.15 and 10.35, the cruiser *Dorsetshire* torpedoed *Bismarck* from port and starboard, finally causing *Bismarck* to heel over and sink in five minutes. Only 115 men survived from a crew of more than 2,000.

Battleship versus battleship in the Pacific

LEFT: **The modern *Washington* photographed off New York in August 1942. Her encounter with the elderly Japanese *Kirishima* in November was the last battleship-to-battleship engagement.** BELOW: ***Kirishima,* built as a battlecruiser, had been modernized with new guns and new armour in the interwar years and the Japanese navy rated her as a battleship. She is seen here in Sukumo Bay, 1937. The cut-away forecastle discloses her World War I origins and the upright funnels suggest a British provenance to her design.**

The last great battle involving battleships would not be until the Battle of Leyte Gulf in October 1944, but by then battleships were ancillary to aircraft carriers and naval aircraft. However, the last battle in which battleship fought battleship in the Pacific was during the epic months-long struggle between the Japanese and the Americans over Guadalcanal in the Solomon Islands. The Japanese hoped to turn the Solomons into a base to cut off Australia, and in 1942 started to build airfields along the chain of islands. In turn, the Americans wanted to use Guadalcanal as their base of operations against the Japanese further north.

The first Battle of Savo took place on 12/13 November as the Japanese tried to reinforce their troops on the island and to bombard Henderson airfield: the Japanese force was centred on the battleships *Hiei* and *Kirishima*. The ensuing battle by night and in heavy rain was disorganized and both sides suffered as their formations passed through each other. The American cruisers and destroyers suffered more but the Japanese battleship *Hiei* sank next day.

Two nights later, on November 14/15, the Japanese *Kirishima*, the heavy cruisers *Atago* and *Takao*, the light cruisers *Nagara* and *Sendai*, and nine destroyers tried to bombard Henderson Field again.

Although *Kirishima* was constructed as a battlecruiser and completed in 1915, she had twice been modernized, in 1927–30 and 1935–6: her armour was improved, she was lengthened and had modern machinery installed. Armed with eight 355mm/14in guns, the Japanese rated her as a battleship.

She had received light damage during a night action off Guadalcanal on November 12/13, when she met the Americans again. Her opponents this time were the two new battleships *Washington* and *South Dakota*, both completed within the last few months and armed with nine 405mm/16in guns, and their escort of four destroyers.

The Americans were in line ahead, in the order: four destroyers, *Washington* and *South Dakota* as they made a sweep north between Russell and Guadalcanal, then east and south-east, passing north of Savo. At about midnight contacts were seen on radar to the east, and *Sendai* and a destroyer immediately came under heavy fire. A few minutes later *Nagara* and the Japanese destroyers engaged the American destroyers, sinking three and damaging the fourth.

However, *South Dakota* had been illuminated and came under particularly heavy gun and torpedo attack. None of the 30 torpedoes hit her but she was hit several times by shellfire and lost electrical supply to her radar. According to the American admiral's official report, "What appeared to be the South Dakota was seen at about 01.21 at a considerable distance to the south-eastward between this ship and Guadalcanal on a southerly course".

Meanwhile *Washington*, which had not been engaged by the Japanese, succeeded in closing the range. From 00.16 to 00.19 *Washington* fired 42 405mm//16in rounds and her gunnery was highly effective. Fire opened at 17,000m/ 18,500yd range and hits were obtained by the third salvo.

She opened fire again between 01.00 and 01.07 after the target had been tracked by radar. The range was 7,700m/8,400yd and a hit was probably obtained on the first salvo and certainly on the second. *Kirishima* was hit nine times and burst into flames. Her return fire ceased and she was seen on radar to perform a 500-degree turn and draw off to the north-east.

The last major Japanese naval thrust at Guadalcanal had been turned back. *Washington* had done what she had been designed for and defeated one of her kind. In fact, *Washington* was the only American battleship to defeat another battleship. All the other battleship duels between the USN and the Imperial Japanese Navy involved ship- or land-based aircraft.

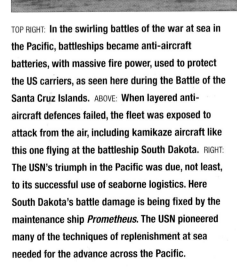

TOP RIGHT: In the swirling battles of the war at sea in the Pacific, battleships became anti-aircraft batteries, with massive fire power, used to protect the US carriers, as seen here during the Battle of the Santa Cruz Islands. ABOVE: When layered anti-aircraft defences failed, the fleet was exposed to attack from the air, including kamikaze aircraft like this one flying at the battleship South Dakota. RIGHT: The USN's triumph in the Pacific was due, not least, to its successful use of seaborne logistics. Here South Dakota's battle damage is being fixed by the maintenance ship *Prometheus*. The USN pioneered many of the techniques of replenishment at sea needed for the advance across the Pacific.

Battleship war in the Pacific

During World War II, the conflict in the east was primarily a naval war. After the Japanese attack on Pearl Harbor and the sinking of *Repulse* and *Prince of Wales* on December 10, 1941, the Japanese enjoyed an unbroken series of victories. Their aim was to occupy the American bases at Guam and Wake, capture the Philippines, seize Burma, Malaya, Singapore, and the Dutch East Indies, and then to fortify a ring of islands in the south and the central Pacific. The plan seemed to be successful and by early 1942 the Japanese had conquered an empire.

However, Japanese expansion reached its high-water mark in March 1942. The US Navy (USN) had been studying its strategy for a war in the Pacific for many years. The result was Plan Orange, which envisaged a campaign stretching across the Pacific Ocean and culminating in a decisive battle with the Imperial Japanese Navy (IJN). Accordingly, Admiral Nimitz began his counter-attack and in May 1942 the Japanese advance was stopped at the Battle of the Coral Sea. A month later, the Japanese suffered a major defeat at the Battle of Midway in the central Pacific. In August 1942, US Marines landed on Guadalcanal, beginning a month-long battle for possession. USN carrier-borne aircraft had supported the landings, but when the carriers withdrew the Japanese were able to counter-attack, and at the Battle of Savo Island, the Japanese navy sank four heavy cruisers, including the Australian *Canberra*, and one destroyer. Neither side could establish clear naval nor air superiority and the success of the campaign swung in the balance: Guadalcanal became a battle of attrition and in such a campaign the Americans were bound eventually to win.

The USN's strategy required resources and it required the development of the tactics and techniques of amphibious warfare and naval air power. Battleships were to play an

ABOVE: **Three ships from the South Dakota class were present at the Battle of Leyte Gulf: *South Dakota*, *Massachusetts* and *Alabama*. Here one of them fires a broadside from her main batteries.** LEFT: **Admiral Chester W Nimitz, the USN Commander-in-Chief Pacific during World War II, who led the US naval offensive, first from the Solomon Islands in 1942 to the north and west, and then, in 1944, to the coasts of the Japanese islands.**

ancillary role, bombarding enemy positions ashore and providing anti-aircraft defence for the fleet: as the war developed, USN battleships were massively rearmed with light guns. In November 1943, American industrial might was able to provide Nimitz with the strength he needed for an island-hopping campaign, and when US Marines met stubborn resistance and learned costly lessons, Nimitz opted to avoid strongly held islands and strike at the enemy's weakest points.

In 1944 and 1945 these hops developed into leaps as two amphibious offensives developed, American General MacArthur advancing via New Guinea into the Philippines and Nimitz reaching 3,200km/2,000 miles across the ocean from the Gilbert Islands to Okinawa. It was clear that while the Americans could replace their resources, the Japanese could not. At the Battle of the Philippine Sea in what USN pilots called "the great Marianas turkey shoot", Japanese naval air power was destroyed.

In October 1944, the Japanese navy planned to use their last carriers, including two hybrid conversions from battleships, *Ise* and *Hyuga*, to decoy American forces away from the beachheads of Leyte Gulf to enable their battleships to bombard them and to destroy the shipping offshore. The plan almost succeeded, with two battleship forces planned to converge on the invasion beaches. A southern force consisted of the battleships *Fuso* and *Yamashiro*, while a central force contained the five battleships *Yamato*, *Musashi*, *Nagato*, *Kongo* and *Haruna*. Opposing them were the six USN battleships *Iowa*, *New Jersey*, *Massachusetts*, *South Dakota*,

Washington, and *Alabama:* however, the USN fleet also contained 32 aircraft carriers and over 1,700 aircraft with experienced pilots, whereas the Japanese could only muster three carriers and fewer than 200 planes. The battle raged over several hundred miles of sea and although the Japanese reached the invasion beaches, they did not press home their attack. At the end of the Battle of Leyte Gulf, the Imperial Japanese Navy had effectively ceased to exist.

Japanese resistance did not end with the destruction of their fleet and in April 1945 off Okinawa, the Japanese launched large-scale suicide raids resulting in 26 Allied warships being sunk and many more damaged. A date had been set for the invasion of Japan when atomic bombs were dropped on Hiroshima and Nagasaki on August 6 and 9, 1945, and in Tokyo Bay on September 2, 1945, the battleship *Missouri* provided a theatrical background for the signing of the Japanese surrender. Also present were the American battleships *Colorado, Mississippi, Idaho, New Mexico, Iowa, South Dakota* and *West Virginia*, and the British battleships *King George V* and *Duke of York*.

The USA emerged from the war with global commitments and the largest navy the world had ever seen, but the age of the battleship was almost over.

ABOVE LEFT: **Many lonely beaches became battlegrounds, such as this beach in Leyte Gulf where Japanese shipping was bombed and strafed from the air by the advancing Allies' naval aircraft.** LEFT: **By 1945 nowhere was safe for Japanese battleships, not even their own home port of Kure, seen here under high level attack by the USAF.** ABOVE: **As Japanese air power waned, the Japanese resorted to kamikaze or suicide attacks, in which young inexperienced pilots tried to crash their aircraft into Allied ships. The damage caused – seen here in the Australian cruiser *Australia* – could be severe.**

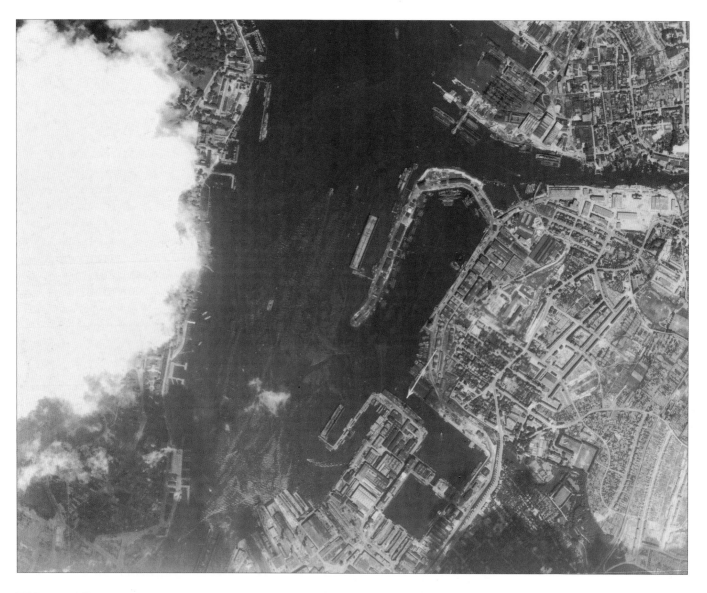

The German navy in World War II

In 1933–6 the revived German navy completed building the pocket battleships *Deutschland, Admiral Scheer* and *Admiral Graf Spee*. In 1935 the Anglo-German Naval Agreement was concluded, which allowed the Germans to build up to 35 per cent of the British warship tonnage. The Germans also drew up a secret "Plan Z" which by 1945 would give their navy six battleships, four pocket battleships and four battlecruisers in addition to the four battleships and three pocket battleships already in existence. However the outbreak of hostilities was to intervene well before this plan could be fulfilled.

In August 1939 two German pocket battleships, their supply ships and a force of U-boats were deployed into the Atlantic. On September 30, *Admiral Graf Spee* sank her first ship, and seven British and French hunting groups including three battleships were formed to hunt her down. After a brief sortie in November into the Indian Ocean, *Admiral Graf Spee* returned to the South Atlantic. On December 13 she met Force G, consisting of one heavy and two light cruisers, and was driven into Montevideo and scuttled.

ABOVE: **Through the cloud, aerial reconnaissance of Kiel, the German navy's base at the eastern or Baltic end of the Kiel canal, shows *Scharnhorst* alongside and vulnerable to attack.**

Meanwhile her sister ship *Deutschland* sank two ships in the North Atlantic and was ordered home where Hitler, fearing a loss of prestige should she be damaged or sunk under the name of the fatherland, had her renamed *Lützow*.

In early October *Gneisenau* sortied off Norway in a repeat of World War I tactics, to draw British ships within range of German U-boats and aircraft. *Hood, Nelson, Repulse, Rodney* and *Royal Oak* all sailed but did not make contact.

On November 23 *Scharnhorst* and *Gneisenau*, while attempting a breakout into the Atlantic, sank the armed merchant cruiser *Rawalpindi* but returned to Germany to avoid the searching British ships.

During the Norway Campaign in spring 1940 the battlecruisers *Scharnhorst* and *Gneisenau* covered the northern landings, and were briefly engaged by the British *Renown*, with

LEFT: *Scharnhorst* and *Gneisenau* were blockaded in western France for many months, but in February 1942 made a daring dash up the English Channel. Their escape was a tactical defeat for the Royal Navy but a strategic blunder for the Germans.

mutual, slight damage. The Germans escaped in a snowstorm and there were to be no other battleship-to-battleship engagements. However *Scharnhorst* was hit by a torpedo from the destroyer *Acasta* and again on June 13 by aircraft from *Ark Royal*. On June 20 *Gneisenau* was torpedoed by the submarine *Clyde*, blowing a huge hole in her bows. As a result both ships were out of action until the end of the year.

Between October 1940 and March 1941 *Admiral Scheer* raided in the Atlantic and Indian Oceans, sinking 16 ships of 100,650 tonnes/99,059 tons, including the armed merchant cruiser *Jervis Bay* and five ships of convoy HX84. The disruption to convoys across the Atlantic had a very serious effect on Britain, and diverted battleships to convoy protection. On February 8, 1941, *Scharnhorst* and *Gneisenau* found convoy HX106 escorted by *Ramillies* but declined to attack and *Ramillies* was too slow to catch them up. In March *Scharnhorst* and *Gneisenau* were sighted by aircraft from *Malaya* escorting convoy SL67 but again they escaped, finally taking refuge in Brest having sunk 22 merchant ships.

The hunt for the *Bismarck* is told separately, but her loss marked the end of independent raiding by German surface warships in the Atlantic, and when in June *Lützow* attempted a breakout she was torpedoed and forced to return to Germany.

The ships at Brest suffered repeated bomber attacks, and on February 11–13, 1942, they made a daring escape. The Channel Dash of *Scharnhorst, Gneisenau* and the cruiser *Prinz Eugen* was an embarrassment and a tactical defeat, but also a strategic gain for the Royal Navy. The Brest Squadron ceased to be a threat to convoys, the heavy ships were damaged by mines and two weeks later *Gneisenau* was so badly bombed at Kiel that she never went to sea again.

TOP RIGHT: **At the end of the Norway Campaign in the spring of 1940, during the invasion and counter-invasion of Norway by Germany and by Britain and her allies, the British carrier *Glorious* was caught and sunk by the German navy on June 8. Here the German warship *Scharnhorst* fires on the carrier.** RIGHT: **The German warships *Scharnhorst*, *Gneisenau* and *Hipper* at anchor in a Norwegain fjord in 1940.**

Thereafter the concentration of German ships in Norwegian waters dominated Royal Navy strategy in the north. The convoys had to be given strong escorts, including ships such as the battleships *Duke of York, Renown* and *King George V*, together with aircraft carriers.

Between March 6 and 9, 1942, *Tirpitz* was hunted by the British Home Fleet but when she was located, aircraft from the carrier *Victorious* failed to press home the attack. However *Tirpitz* never put to sea again. The story of convoy PQ17 and the Battles of the Barents Sea and of North Cape in 1942 and 1943 is also told separately.

Tirpitz was finally destroyed by RAF action in November 1944. In March 1945 *Gneisenau* was sunk as a block ship at Gdynia, in April *Admiral Scheer* was bombed and capsized, and shortly before Germany surrendered on 8 May, *Lützow*, the last of the German battleships, was scuttled.

Convoy PQ17 and the Battles of the Barents Sea and the North Cape

Hitler became obsessed with the idea that the British would invade Norway, and he wanted his heavy ships stationed there, where they were also a threat to the Arctic convoys which the Allies were pushing through to Russia. By July 1942 the threatening German ships consisted of *Tirpitz*, *Lützow*, *Admiral Scheer* and others. So when convoy PQ17 of 36 ships left Iceland on June 27 the escort consisted of American and British cruisers and destroyers, and the covering force contained the British *Duke of York* and carrier *Victorious*, and the USN battleship *Washington*. When on July 3 a false appreciation of intelligence led the Admiralty in London to withdraw the escort and concentrate the fleet against a reported movement by *Tirpitz*, there was a massacre of the convoy by U-boats and aircraft. Only 11 ships eventually reached Archangel over the next few days and weeks. In fact *Tirpitz*'s sortie was half-hearted, but the threat was sufficient to denude the convoy of its escort and halt Arctic convoys for the next three months.

In December 1942 convoy JW51B of 14 ships sailed from Scotland for Russia escorted by destroyers under the command of Captain Rupert Sherbrooke in *Onslow*, and covered by the cruisers *Jamaica* and *Sheffield*. Opposing the convoy were *Tirpitz* and *Lützow*, the cruisers *Admiral Hipper*, *Köln* and *Nürnberg*, and several destroyers. This long series of quickly changing and confused actions became known as the Battle of the Barents Sea.

As the convoy passed south of Bear Island in the darkness and snow, *Lützow*, *Hipper* and six destroyers put to sea to intercept it, and, on the morning of New Year's Eve, *Hipper* and three destroyers attacked the convoy from the north, driving it towards Lützow in the south. *Hipper* first fired on the destroyer *Obdurate*, but her approach to the convoy was thwarted by the destroyers *Onslow*, *Orwell* and *Obedient*, although Sherbrooke (who was subsequently awarded the VC) was badly wounded.

TOP: **Throughout World War II the German navy used the Norwegian fjords to try and outflank the Royal Navy and as bases for sorties into the Atlantic, or to attack Russian conveys. Here *Admiral Hipper*, *Admiral Scheer* and escorts leave for an operation.** ABOVE: **Threat of German capital ships to the Russian convoy caused the allies much anxiety, and in July 1942, after convoy PQ17 had been ordered to scatter, the route was abandoned until the days grew shorter.**

TOP LEFT: **A World War I picture of Admiral Franz von Hipper, who led the German battlecruisers at the Battle of Jutland in 1916.** ABOVE: **The Germans tried to hide their ships using camouflage and smokescreens when attacked.** LEFT: **The heavy cruiser *Hipper*, shown here at anchor in a Norwegian fjord, was part of the forces that threatened allied convoys.** BELOW: **Admiral Sir Bruce Fraser, photographed in January 1944 on the quarterdeck of *Duke of York* with his band of brothers, after the last-ever action between capital ships in home waters.**

Hipper sank a minesweeper and damaged the destroyer *Achates*, but when the British cruisers announced their arrival with accurate radar-laid gunfire *Hipper* was damaged and an escorting destroyer, *Friedrich Eckoldt*, was sunk. *Hipper* still tried to get into the convoy but the destroyers skilfully used smoke and the threat of torpedoes to keep her out.

Meanwhile *Lützow* approached from the south but was timidly managed and driven off by the remaining British destroyers: by noon of a very short midwinter's day both German ships were withdrawing, chased by their smaller opponents. The convoy reached Kola without loss whilst *Hipper* never saw action again, and *Lützow*'s intended breakout into the Atlantic was thwarted. When Hitler learned that the heavy German units had been driven off by light cruisers and destroyers, he raged, calling the heavy ships a waste of resources and ordering them to be paid off. The order was rescinded but Grand Admiral Raeder resigned.

Nearly one year later, on December 20, 1943, convoy JW55B consisting of 19 ships sailed for Russia covered by *Duke of York* and the cruiser *Jamaica*, while the return convoy RA55A sailed from Kola on December 23 protected by the cruisers *Belfast*, *Norfolk* and *Sheffield*. On Christmas Day *Scharnhorst* and five destroyers sailed to intercept. As convoy JW55B passed south of Bear Island in stormy weather, *Scharnhorst*'s approach was detected on radar and she was fired on and hit by the cruiser *Norfolk*. As *Scharnhorst* tried to

work to the north round the convoy, she was again engaged by the British cruisers and hit, although *Norfolk* was in turn badly damaged by 280mm/11in shells.

Scharnhorst then turned south away from the convoy but she was shadowed on radar, and her position reported to *Duke of York*, who was in an ideal position to the south-west to cut off her retreat. In a coordinated attack the cruisers fired starshells and attacked from one side of *Scharnhorst* while *Duke of York*, with the cruiser *Jamaica* close astern to confuse German radar, attacked from the other. The British battleship's 355mm/14in guns soon found their range and *Scharnhorst* was quickly silenced and finished off by some 10 or 11 torpedoes, sinking with huge loss of life.

The Battle of the North Cape was the last battleship-on-battleship action that took place between the Royal Navy and the German navy.

Where are they now?

Plenty of examples of battleships from all three phases of their development are still in existence today. Of the first phase, from what might be called the dead-end lines of development, a number of examples can be seen. The *Huascar*, a turret ship built in 1865 for the Peruvian navy, survives in Talcahuano, Chile. The 1868 French-built *Schorpioen* of the Netherlands navy, one of four ships of her class, can be seen at the Royal Netherlands Navy Museum at Den Helder. *Cerberus*, an 1870s British monitor, is a wreck off the coast of southern Australia, and the contemporary turret ram *Buffel* is in Rotterdam, the Netherlands. Two other monitors also survive – the coastal monitor *Solve*, with her fixed gun, is at Gothenburg, Sweden, and *M33,* a small bombardment monitor which saw much service in World War I, is at Portsmouth, England.

Warrior, the first broadside ironclad, is the only surviving example of the 45 iron hulls built by the Royal Navy between 1861 and 1877. She was obsolete within a decade of being built and placed in reserve. After her masts and guns were stripped she became a depot ship in Portsmouth, attached to the experimental and torpedo training school, to supply steam and electricity. She was sold in 1924 and became an oil fuel hulk at Pembroke Dock, Wales. Over the next 50 years some 5,000 ships refuelled alongside her. In 1979 *Warrior* was sold to a trust that had the vision of restoring her, which they did at Grays Shipyard in Hartlepool, and she is now on display as a museum ship in Portsmouth, England.

Mikasa, the 1902 pre-Dreadnought flagship of the Japanese navy at the Battle of Tsushima, is embedded in concrete in Yokosuka, Japan.

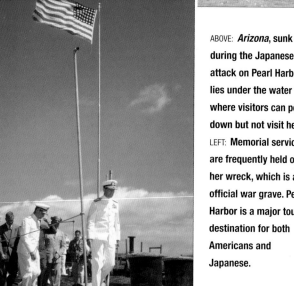

ABOVE: *Arizona*, sunk during the Japanese attack on Pearl Harbor, lies under the water where visitors can peer down but not visit her.
LEFT: Memorial services are frequently held over her wreck, which is an official war grave. Pearl Harbor is a major tourist destination for both Americans and Japanese.

The World War I USN battleship *Texas* is preserved at Houston, Texas, although she is displayed in the blue camouflage colour scheme and state of modernization which she was given in World War II. Other preserved USN battleships from World War II include *North Carolina* at Wilmington, *Massachusetts* at Fall River, *Alabama* at Mobile, *Iowa* at Suisun Bay, *New Jersey* at Camden, *Missouri* at Pearl Harbor, and *Wisconsin* at Norfolk.

The 1889 British pre-Dreadnought *Hood* lies upside down outside the breakwater at Portland, England, where she was sunk as a block ship in 1914. The wreck of the 1893 USS *Massachusetts* is an underwater archaeological preserve off Pensacola, Florida.

The short-lived 1911 British battleship *Audacious* lies where she settled in 1914 off Northern Ireland, and is not much visited.

From the epic battle in the North Sea in 1916, the 1908 German battleship *Thuringen* was used by the French navy as a target after World War I and large parts of her wreck can be seen from the shore at Plouhinec, France. *Ostfriesland*, also a veteran of Jutland, was ceded to the USA and expended as a target. Her wreck now lies 97km/60 miles off the Virginia Capes in deep water. *Lützow*, damaged and scuttled during the battle, lies 177km/110 miles from the Danish coast in 44m/144ft of water. One of her turrets lies besides the wreck, the other underneath the upturned hull, and 305mm/12in ammunition is scattered across the seabed. The remains of *Indefatigable*, the first capital ship to be sunk at Jutland, lie in the same general area, as does *Invincible,* broken in half by the explosion that ripped through her. *Queen Mary* was the second ship to blow up at Jutland, and her wreck was located in the 1990s, in a shattered condition.

Arizona and *Utah* in Pearl Harbor and *Royal Oak* at Scapa Flow are designated war graves, as are most of the other wrecks listed here.

The Japanese *Nagato*, laid down in 1917, was sunk at Bikini Atoll and lies upside down on the bottom of the lagoon at a depth of 55m/180ft in clear warm water, where she is reckoned to be the best battleship dive in the world.

The German pocket battleship *Graf Spee* was scuttled off Montevideo, Uruguay, where parts have been salvaged and there are proposals to lift the remains. *Repulse* and *Prince of Wales* were sunk by Japanese aircraft off the coast of Malaya, and both wrecks are regularly visited by the Royal Navy, who "fly" the White Ensign from their upturned hulls.

Finally, the mighty German battleship *Tirpitz* was broken up in the 1950s in the Norwegian fjord where she was eventually sunk, but large parts of the ship still litter the seabed.

ABOVE LEFT: **A piece of armour plate from the wreck of the Japanese *Yamato*.** ABOVE: **Two of her shells. The cars in the background give some idea of their size. The massive scale of the armour and armament were no proof against bombs and torpedoes from naval aircraft.** BELOW: **Attempts were being made to lift *Utah*, and she was still leaking oil as late as 1944. Eventually the decision was made to leave her as a war grave.**

Pre-Dreadnoughts

The pre-Dreadnought battleships were a bewildering variety of vessels. Once the propeller had been married to steam propulsion, the choice for naval architects was between broadside and turreted guns. The first turrets were fitted on to small ships. Because of their weight, they could not be mounted in larger ships until steam engines became more reliable and the top hamper represented by masts and sails could be done away with. As armour temporarily outstripped the effectiveness of guns, the ram was thought to be the weapon of choice at sea and survived a remarkably long time until the torpedo and long range guns became available. Once all the elements of the modern battleship were present, the final problem to solve was that of hitting the target at long range. Before the use of radar, the only way of spotting the fall of shot was by eye and for accurate range-finding a single large calibre with all the guns slaved to a single fire control was necessary. Only when all these design problems had been resolved and the technology developed could the modern Dreadnought battleship come into being.

LEFT: *Implacable* sweeping majestically out of Malta, whose harbours were the proud base of the Royal Navy for more than a century and a half.

Gloire

In the Russian War 1854–6 Britain and France had formed an unlikely alliance against Russia, and during the war both navies had constructed armoured floating batteries, and used these to effect in the Black Sea against shore targets. Once the war was over France continued to develop the concept of an ironclad ship, primarily as a means of opposing her ancient enemy, Britain, and between 1858 and 1861 ordered no less than 16 broadside ironclads.

The first three, designed by Dupuy de Lôme, were Gloire and Invincible, laid down at Toulon in 1858, and, a few months later, Normandie at Cherbourg.

They were wooden-hulled and clad in wrought-iron armour. The hulls were 0.6m/2ft thick and covered by an armoured belt over 100mm/4in thick which extended from stem to stern and to 1.83m/6ft below the waterline, and there was a thinner layer of plating under the wooden upper deck. In the style of the screw ships that Gloire would replace, she was pierced for 38 guns on the main deck, although she never seems to have carried so many, an arrangement carried over from the days of sail. The armament differed throughout the class and with time. In Gloire, the original guns themselves were 160mm/6.4in rifled muzzle-loaders, although in an age when the technology of

ABOVE: **Despite having been recent allies in the Russian War, the French began building new ships in the late 1850s which would challenge the Royal Navy. The first of these was** *Gloire*, **a wooden-hulled ironclad ship incorporating the lessons which had been learned about the effect of modern guns. The use of wood limited the length of the hull.**

guns was also evolving rapidly, these were successively replaced by breech-loaders of different sizes. There were also four Paixhans shell guns on the upper deck.

Originally barquentine-rigged, the sail area was doubled to 2,500sq m/27,000sq ft when these ships were converted to ship-rig, but they were no more successful, despite French insistence upon building four of the class. Normandie and Invincible were built of poor timber that soon rotted and both were hulked up in 1871–2. Nevertheless, Normandie was the first armoured ship to cross the Atlantic, when she was sent to Mexico in 1862–3 in furtherance of Napoleon III's ambitions to found an empire there, but she returned with a centuries-old problem, an outbreak of yellow fever. Gloire lasted until 1879.

Ships of the Gloire class rolled badly and were not otherwise successful ships, nevertheless to France must go the honour of building the first armoured battleship.

When intelligence reached Britain of these new ships, there was an immediate response in the building of *Warrior*, a ship in every respect superior to *Gloire*. *Warrior* was not only larger by nearly 4,065 tonnes/4,000 tons, but faster and more heavily armed. Symbolically, the second of these ships was named *Black Prince*. It is surprising, therefore, that France, having introduced the first innovation, continued with her programme to build ships that were so much weaker than the British vessels.

Innovation nevertheless continued, and on the same day that *Gloire* was ordered, so was the iron-hulled *Couronne*. Though launched and completed after the *Warrior*, due to alteration to her plans during building, *Couronne* was another first for France: the world's first iron-hulled armoured battleship. Though similar in appearance to *Gloire*, her armour was unusual, consisting of a sandwich of teak, an iron lattice-work and more teak clad in iron plating. The upper deck armour was thicker, but did not cover the engine room spaces. There was no compartmentation, and in her last manifestation she was armed with eight 240mm/9.4in and four 190mm/7.6in guns on the main gundeck and two 120mm/4.7in and 12 1-pounder guns on the upper deck.

The French programme seemed unstoppable, and included two two-decker ironclads, also designed by Dupuy de Lôme and the only ships of their type ever built, *Magenta* and *Solferino*. They were also the first ships to have a spur ram, which projected 19.5m/64ft and was covered by a 14,225kg/14 ton steel cone, though their wide turning circle rendered them tactically unsuitable for ramming. The armament varied throughout their careers, and eventually the lower gundeck was removed. In another novelty, they carried two howitzers on the upper deck, capable of raining fire on an enemy ship.

Seemingly content with the *Gloire* design, a class of ten ships were all laid down in 1861, and all were wooden-hulled except the last, *Heroine*. Although the design had started a

TOP: **The British response to *Gloire* was immediate. *Warrior* was an iron-built, armoured ship, twice as big, twice as fast and twice as powerful as the French *Gloire* and her sisters.** ABOVE: **With the launch of *Warrior*, and *Black Prince* – a name surely chosen to send a message to the French – Britain and the Royal Navy announced their intention to maintain supremacy at sea.**

revolution and precipitated a naval arms race with Britain, many of these were still afloat in the 1890s when developments in gunnery made them obsolete, so strongly built were the hulls.

Gloire class

Class: *Gloire, Invincible, Normandie.* Launched 1859–61
Dimensions: Length (at waterline) – 77.9m/255ft 6in
Beam – 17m/55ft 9in
Draught – 8.5m/27ft 10in
Displacement: 5,720 tonnes/5,630 tons
Armament: Main – 36 x 160mm/6.4in RML guns
Machinery: 1-shaft HRCR, 8 oval boilers, 1,864kW/2,500ihp
Performance: 13 knots
Complement: 570 men

Warrior

By the mid-1850s, and the end of the Russian War, Britain was the world's foremost industrial nation and the Royal Navy had an overwhelming superiority in three-decker screw ships. It was policy to observe other nations' innovations and then use Britain's industrial and shipbuilding might to maintain the Royal Navy's supremacy. News from France of *Gloire* called this policy into action and in 1859 two ships were ordered, *Warrior* and *Black Prince*, designed by chief constructor Isaac Watts and engineer John Scott Russell. Unlike *Gloire* they were constructed of iron frames (in which the Victorian engineers excelled), which allowed a longer and stronger ship.

They were initially classed as frigates, because of their single main gundeck, and when completed they were the world's most powerful warships. Their strength lay not only in a broadside, on build, of ten 110-pounder, 26 68-pounder and four 70-pounder guns, but a complement of over 700 seamen and marines with field guns, muskets and cutlasses for warfare ashore.

Their high length-to-beam ratio (6.5:1) and fine lines forward and aft made them fast ships, though at slow speed they were not very handy. Ship-rigged, *Warrior* had a lifting screw and logged 13 knots under sail, while *Black Prince*, with a fixed screw, managed only 11 knots, but under combined sail and steam both ships could reach 17 knots. With taller funnels for increased draught to the boilers *Warrior* exceeded 14 knots under steam alone. The armour belt over the midships sections was 64.9m/213ft long and 6.7m/22ft deep and consisted of iron plates 4.6m/15ft by 0.9m/3ft and weighing 4,060kg/4 tons each which slotted together by tongue and groove. Other novel features included steam-driven capstans and watertight, armoured bulkheads fore and aft, and double bottoms that were compartmented. They were quite simply the biggest, the fastest and best armed and armoured ships in the world.

However, the British Admiralty was more concerned about the increased costs than the threat from France, so while continuing to build older-style wooden ships, the follow-on ships, *Defence* and *Resistance*, were smaller by about one third (6,100 tonnes/6,000 tons rather than 9,140 tonnes/9,000 tons). Then, when the French announced a programme to construct 30 seagoing ironclads, work on wooden line-of-battle ships halted. Instead two more ships of the Defence class, *Hector* and *Valiant,* were laid down, as were four *Warrior*-sized ships, the four-masted *Achilles*, and the magnificent five-

BELOW: *Warrior* was so strongly built that she has survived until today and can now be seen as a beautifully restored museum ship in Portsmouth, where, with her towering masts, she is one of the first and most memorable sights to greet the visitor to the several naval museums there.

LEFT: **An interior view of the preserved and restored** *Warrior*. **Modern armour and heavy guns were not all – on the bulkhead behind the gun is a rack of small arms, intended for use when** *Warrior* **landed her sailors and marines for power projection ashore.** BELOW: *Warrior* **shortly after she arrived at Hartlepool for restoration by the Warrior Preservation Trust.** BOTTOM: *Warrior* **in dry dock sometime in the 1870s. Her figurehead has been beautifully restored.**

masted 10,770 tonne/10,600 ton *Minotaur, Agincourt* and *Northumberland*. Also five (originally eight) 90-gun two-deckers, *Prince Consort, Caledonia, Ocean, Royal Oak* and *Royal Alfred*, were converted on the slips to wooden broadside ironclads and some purpose-built wooden broadside ironclads, including *Lord Clyde* and *Lord Warden*, were built to use up existing timber stocks. All of these ships were larger, faster and better armed than the Provence class, to a degree that ought to have deterred the French. By 1867, the Royal Navy had completed 19 broadside battery ships, easily outbuilding the French whose challenge collapsed for want of finance, industrial capacity and adequate designs.

The only area in which the British ironclads were possibly inferior was that they were armed with muzzle-loading guns. When *Warrior* was completed in 1861, Armstrong rifled breech-loaders were widely fitted throughout the fleet, but a series of accidents from flaws in the steel barrels and in the breech mechanisms caused these to be abandoned. For the next few years, the British Navy reverted to using a muzzle-loading rifled gun until by the 1880s the technology was sufficiently advanced, in other navies, for a reliable breech-loading gun to replace smooth bore guns.

These ships spanned an age of change. *Achilles* as completed in 1864 was the only British warship with four masts and had the largest sail area of any British warship. *Lord Warden* (1867) at 7,968 tonnes/7,842 tons was the heaviest wooden ship ever built and *Minotaur* the first ship to carry a searchlight. The *Hector* as a tender at the Royal Navy's

experimental school, Vernon, was the first ship to be fitted with wireless, in 1900. Many of these ships also had exceptionally long lives: *Minotaur* and *Black Prince* were broken up in 1923, *Achilles* in 1925, *Northumberland* in 1927, *Defence* in 1935, *Valiant* in 1957, and *Agincourt* not until 1960. *Warrior* is still afloat and has been fully restored as a museum ship. She was restored internally and externally at Hartlepool before being towed to her present berth in Portsmouth.

Warrior

Class: *Warrior, Black Prince.*
Launched 1860–1
Dimensions: Length (at waterline) –
115.9m/380ft 2in
Beam – 18m/58ft 4in
Draught – 7.9m/26ft
Displacement: 9,284 tonnes/9,137 tons
Armament: Main – 4 x 205mm/8in MLR guns
Secondary – 28 x 180mm/7in MLR
and 4 x 20pdr BL guns
Machinery: 1-shaft, Penn HSET, 10 rectangular
boilers, 3,928kW/5,267ihp
Performance: 14 knots
Complement: 707 men

The first *Monitor*

*M*onitor was only one of 17 proposals considered by the Federal government of the USA in 1861, of which three were selected for construction: the conventional broadside-ironclad *New Ironsides*, the armoured ship *Galena*, and the wholly unconventional *Monitor,* which was designed by John Ericsson. Ericsson's ship was an armoured wooden raft, with a lower hull 38m/126ft long and 10.3m/34ft wide, overhung, turtle-fashion, by a platform 52.5m/172ft long and 12.5m/41ft wide: the overhang protected the sides, propeller and screw from ramming.

The USN had asked for a speed of 8 knots, but *Monitor*'s best speed was only 6 knots. Worse, the freeboard was only 35.5cm/14in, though the largely submerged hull, often awash, was less susceptible to rolling. The hatches, however, could only be opened in the calmest of weather and the hawse pipe in the hull was very near the waterline. The forced-air ventilators were 1.37m/4ft 6in high and the two square funnels were 1.83m/6ft high: even with forced ventilation temperatures inside *Monitor* were intolerable.

Ericsson's original sketch called for 150mm/6in armour on the side and 50mm/2in on the deck, made up of individual 25.4mm/1in plates bolted or riveted together. This, it was

TOP: *Merrimac* **was rated by the USN as an auxiliary screw frigate when her burned hulk was captured alongside by the Confederate forces, who rebuilt her as an ironclad.** ABOVE: **John Ericsson, who was one of a group of Swedes who strongly influenced the USN in the mid-19th century. Ericsson was a prolific inventor who designed the first monitor.**

calculated, would have sunk the *Monitor* and the side armour was reduced to 50mm/2in except around the turret where it was 200–230mm/8–9in. A pilothouse on the foredeck was built of 230mm/9in iron blocks.

So, Ericsson's heavily armoured, shallow-draft iron hull with its low profile had good protection against cannon shot and the unusual construction protected the vital parts from damage by

LEFT: **The launch of the first monitor. The name was chosen because, according to Gustavus Fox (another Swede), she was going to teach the Confederates – and the British – a lesson.**
BELOW: **In the battle between *Monitor* and *Merrimac* (now renamed *Virginia*) neither ship could really damage the other and when *Monitor* retreated into shallow water, *Virginia* could not follow.** BOTTOM: **This diagram shows the saucer-like profile of *Monitor*. Ericsson also devised a novel turret (not shown here) mounted on a spindle.**

ramming. The USN would have preferred a low-board ironclad with turrets on the Coles principle of a roller bearing, but Ericsson provided a single turret mounted on a central spindle with a bronze skirt resting on a ring of bronze. The turret was 6.1m/20ft in diameter and 2.74m/9ft high, and the roof was made of a grating of railway lines. The turret held two 280mm/11in Dahlgren smoothbore shell guns, and was powered by steam. The steam mechanism made training the guns jerky and imprecise.

Monitor was unlikely to teach the British Admiralty any lessons but she was well suited for coastal and riverine warfare during the American Civil War.

Built in a few months in the winter of 1861/2 at the Continental Iron Works in Greenpoint, Long Island, *Monitor* left New York after trials on March 6. She experienced heavy weather on her route south, and her exhausted crew reached Hampton Roads two days later. She fought her famous action against the *Merrimac*, the first between two armoured ships, on March 9, 1862. Neither ship could seriously harm the other and a further fight in April, after *Merrimac* had been improved by fitting more armour and now equipped with solid shot, was declined.

Monitor fought in the James River in support of the Army's Peninsular Campaign, before being sent to Washington for improvements that included a telescopic funnel, better ventilation, and davits. However, on December 31, 1862 *Monitor* was returning to operations in the South when she was caught in rough waters off Cape Hatteras and flooded by seawater that drowned her boilers. She foundered and 16 of her crew of 62 were lost.

The wreck of *Monitor* was rediscovered in 1974 and is on display at the Mariners' Museum, Norfolk, Virginia.

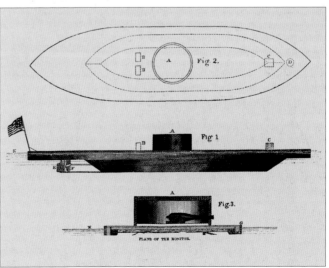

Virginia

After the Federal frigate *Merrimac* was captured alongside and partly burned in Gosport Navy Yard in Norfolk by advancing Confederate forces, she was successfully converted into an ironclad of unusual design. At the same time she was renamed *Virginia*.

Virginia was armed with a mix of guns behind an armoured casemate. This casemate was 51.8m/170ft long sloping inwards and upwards, and covered with layers of plates both horizontally and vertically. She had two significant disadvantages: her engines were not powerful enough for the additional weight of armour so she took a long time to manoeuvre, and she had the draught of a frigate, so that she was unsuited for warfare in estuaries and rivers.

However, on March 8, 1862 she attacked the blockading Federal fleet in Hampton Roads, sank the frigate *Congress* and the sloop *Cumberland*,

and could have turned the tide of the war. The next day when she renewed her attack she found *Monitor* had arrived. Neither ship could harm the other much and *Monitor* escaped into shallower water, where *Virginia* with her deeper draught could not follow.

As Union forces continued to advance, *Virginia* was destroyed by her crew in May 1862.

TOP: The retreating Federal forces burned *Merrimac* to the waterline, so it was a relatively simple matter to convert her to a turtleback ironclad. News of the conversion inspired the North to build *Monitor*.

ABOVE: This turtleback ironclad of unusual design was renamed *Virginia* after conversion. The sloping sides of the armour helped to protect her by letting shot glance off, and she was eventually destroyed by her own crew as the Union forces continued to advance.

Broadside ironclads

The building of broadside ironclads in the late 1850s and 1860s was stimulated by Anglo-French rivalry and the threat of war in northern and southern Europe.

In order to overmatch the French Gloire class, Britain, in addition to building iron-hulled broadside ships, converted a number of 90-gun wooden ships to ironclads in 1860–4, and other navies followed suit. Denmark, which was faced with the inevitability of war with Prussia over Schleswig-Holstein, converted *Dannebrog*, a 72-gun two-deck sailing ship, in 1863. Russia converted two frigates, *Sevastopol* and *Petropavlovsk*, to ironclads, and perhaps the oldest ship to be converted was the Dutch *De Ruyter*, first built as a 74-gun ship in 1831.

Interest in the Gloire class attracted customers to France, where broadside ironclads and central battery ships were built for foreign customers including Germany. The Italian navy, which was created in 1861 from the navies of Naples, Piedmont-Sardinia, Tuscany, the two Sicilies and the Papal States, bought purpose-built ships from yards abroad, including the French-built *Terrible* and *Formidable* and the Regina Maria Pia class, but the two kings, *Re d'Italia* and *Re di Portogallo*, were bought in the USA. As its industry developed, Italy began to design and build her own ships in yards in Genoa and Leghorn. Austria

responded by using her indigenous shipbuilding capacity at Trieste to build the Drache and Kaiser Max classes.

Spain bought one ironclad broadside from France, *Numancia*, and built another, *Tetuan*, at Ferrol, while the iron-hulled *Vitoria* and former wooden screw frigate *Arapiles* were built or converted on the Thames.

Turkey also ordered new-build ironclads from British yards, *Osmanieh, Mahmudieh, Abdul Aziz* and *Orkanieh*. This started the habit of the Royal Navy using foreign ships being built in British yards as a reserve of ships ready to be taken over in time of crisis.

The broadside ironclad was the end of the evolution of the ship of the line rather than a step in the development of the battleship. The new navies of Japan and Germany missed this phase altogether.

BELOW: **It was difficult to mount turrets in ocean-going ships and so broadside ironclads continued to be built for a number of years, including the 1864 French *Surveillante*.** BOTTOM LEFT: **Marking another stage in the evolution of the battleship, while retaining the broadside layout, *Deutschland*'s armament was almost all confined to an armoured central citadel.** BOTTOM: **While looking like a broadside ironclad, the 1865 Italian *Roma* combined several features including a ram and central battery.**

The monitors

Over 50 monitors were ordered during the American Civil War although many were not completed, and most were sold or broken up within ten years. When a new generation of monitors was built, Amphitrite class (1874), Monterey (1889) and Arkansas class (1899), they took the names of Civil War ships of which they were supposed to be "repairs".

In an attempt to make them seagoing, masts and super-structures were added, and the 3,455-tonne/3,400-ton *Miantonomoh* made a trans-Atlantic voyage, mostly under tow, with the Secretary of the Navy, Gustavus Vasa Fox, on board. Despite Fox's ambition that these monitors would teach the British a lesson, *Miantonomoh* had to use Royal Navy resources in Halifax, St John's, Queenstown, Portsmouth and Gibraltar to accomplish her remarkable journey. During a visit to France, Fox called on Napoleon III and his travels took him to Denmark in July 1866. He also visited St Petersburg in August for a month-long visit – although what the autocratic Tsar Alexander II thought of the representative of an upstart republic named after the king of one of his country's bitterest enemies is not known. Fox's aim was to study European naval

ABOVE: ***Cerberus*** **was built in England to the order of the Australian state of Victoria. Her sides were built up and she was ship-rigged for her oceanic voyage of delivery. The remains of** *Cerberus* **can still be seen where she was sunk as a breakwater, though she is probably too far gone ever to be restored, and within a few years she will probably be lost forever.**

technology, though naturally his ship excited much interest. *Miantonomoh* returned via Sweden, Germany, France, Portugal, Spain and Italy and in May 1867 crossed the Atlantic via a more southerly route and one last call, courtesy of the British, for more coal in the Bahamas, a journey of a staggering 28,587km/ 17,767 miles.

Used effectively in the waterways and rivers, the perceived success of the monitors resulted in them being copied by other nations, including Sweden, Norway and the Netherlands. The Swedes built American-style monitors also designed by Ericsson, who gifted guns built by Dahlgren, and the first ship in 1865 was called *John Ericsson*. Though initially armed with two 380mm/15in guns these were replaced in 1881 with 240mm/9.4in guns. *John Ericsson* had two sister ships, *Thordön*

ABOVE: **In addition to her twin 255mm/10in guns *Cerberus* carried a range of lesser guns. Here her crew are demonstrating how those guns would be manned.**
ABOVE RIGHT: **The Swedish monitor *John Ericsson*. Despite his work in the United States, Ericsson retained links with his country of birth and both he and fellow-Swede John Dahlgren represented designs and surplus equipment to the Swedish navy.** RIGHT: **Surprisingly the USN was still operating 19th-century-style monitors in World War I. Some even crossed the Atlantic and others were used as submarine depot ships, for which their low freeboard was especially suitable.**

(1866) and *Tirfing* (1867) and a slighter larger sister ship, *Loke* (1871). All had the low freeboards typical of their type and even in the slightest sea, the upper decks were awash.

Even the Royal Navy built some monitors, the oldest surviving being the *Cerberus*, built at Jarrow on the Tyne in 1867–8 and fitted out at Chatham. At Chatham the Admiralty refused to let her fly the White Ensign or even to provide naval victuals and the civil authorities refused to register her as a merchant ship, while her first Captain died of illness. Finally, an officer was sent from Melbourne to bring her to Victoria, Australia. Since her freeboard was only 0.91m/3ft, temporary bulwarks were fitted and she was rigged with masts and sail, which were useless for making headway but they steadied her when she ran into heavy weather. With bunkers for only 122 tonnes/120 tons of coal, she had to rely on frequent coalings, which gave plenty of opportunity for her crew to desert or mutiny, which they did in Portsmouth and Malta, preferring a spell in prison to the risks of the voyage, and the searing heat between decks. It did not help that another new-fangled ship, *Captain*, had capsized in heavy weather with large loss of life only a few weeks before.

However, *Cerberus* was the first steamship to combine a central superstructure with fore and aft gun turrets, and the first armoured warship built for Australia. In dispensing with sail power she preceded the Royal Navy's *Devastation* by three years, and she was the first steamship to pass through the newly completed Suez Canal. Once *Cerberus* reached Port Philip in 1871 she never left and, apart from an American plan to capture Melbourne prepared during the visit of the Great White Fleet, no one ever challenged the guardian of the hull's four 255mm/10in rifled muzzle-loading Armstrong guns. Her remains – she was scuttled as a breakwater off the Black Rock Yacht Club – are the oldest surviving warship to have served in the Royal Australian Navy.

Although the 20th century would witness a revival of the type, the low-freeboard monitor was a dead-end in battleship development. *Devastation*, with a similar layout but three times the size of *Cerberus*, did however set the pattern for future battleships. Amazingly some USN monitors continued to cross the Atlantic without being swamped and were used as submarine tenders in World War I where their low-freeboard was an advantage.

LEFT: **The French cruiser *Dupuy de Lôme* exhibits an extreme form of the ram. The French navy at the end of the 19th century was well known for its odd, even extreme, designs. Possibly naming this ship after one of the better naval architects was an attempt to legitimize the design.**

The rams

In the American Civil War, several ships were attacked by ramming, causing John Ericsson to design into *Monitor* elaborate features to protect her underwater form from ramming. The French were the first to construct a seagoing ram, the wooden-hulled armoured *Taureau* in 1863, which was built with a turtle deck, a large gun in a barbette and a long-spur ram, however she rarely left harbour.

The French were no more successful with the larger *Cerbere* class in 1865. However, the idea of ramming was boosted by the sinking of the *Re d'Italia* during the Battle of Lissa in 1866. Analysts failed to note that the *Re d'Italia* had already suffered rudder damage and was unable to manoeuvre out of the way.

In 1868, the Royal Navy responded with the ironclad ram *Hotspur*, an iron-hulled ship of 4,064 tonnes/4,000 tons whose ram projected 3.05m/10ft, but the low freeboard gave poor seakeeping qualities and she was only used for coastal defence. The much larger *Rupert* of 5,527 tonnes/5,440 tons was built in 1870 but was not much better, though both ships were modernized and survived into the 20th century.

Then in 1871, the British Admiralty's committee on Designs for Ships of War highlighted what it called the importance of ramming. Consequently, the British built the freakish torpedo ram *Polyphemus* in 1878, and the monstrous 6,096-tonne/6,000-ton turret rams *Conqueror* and *Hero* in 1879 and 1884, armed with 305mm/12in breech-loading guns. Naval officers and architects had just about overcome their nervousness when in 1893 *Camperdown* struck *Victoria*, though *Victoria*'s rapid sinking was due to poor inherent stability. Most pre-Dreadnought battleships were built with rams and Jacky Fisher even chose a design for *Dreadnought* that gave the appearance that she had a ram.

Nevertheless, it was a failed tactic: ramming could be effective only against ships that were unable to manoeuvre, and there was at least as much risk of damage to the ramming vessel as there was to the target in the approach under fire and in any collision. Rams may however have acted as bulbous bows and bestowed some streamlining on the pre-Dreadnoughts, and fear of ramming helped to improve damage control and promote the internal subdivision of ships.

BELOW: **A British battleship in dry dock showing her ram. Note also the open hatches of her forward-firing anti-torpedo-boat guns and booms for her anti-torpedo nets.**

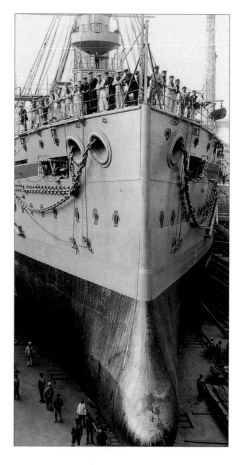

Barbettes

The first ironclad warships mounted guns in broadsides just like their sailing ship predecessors. At first during the battleship revolution ships' sides were protected by iron cladding and then individual guns were protected by shields. At the same time the early monitors and some small warships had turrets with roofs after designs by Coles and Ericsson. Smaller ironclad warships continued to be armed with guns in broadsides, but as the size of gun and the thickness of armour increased they were placed in armoured batteries known as casements.

As gun size increased again warships were generally fitted with fewer guns and these had to be sited on the centreline of low-freeboard ships and placed inside barbettes or fixed iron shields inside which the guns rotated on their mountings. The term barbette came to be applied to the open-topped, armoured enclosure used to protect guns on their turntable together with their crews. The guns fired over the top of their barbettes, but when roofs were added to mountings from the mid-1860s onwards, they became known as turrets again, and the name barbette was applied to the internal substructure which extended below deck. However, when it was introduced the barbette was considered an advance in naval construction as it saved weight when compared to building a larger turret.

For example, the 9,144-tonne/9,000-ton *Devastation* and *Thunderer* of 1869 had muzzle-loading rifled 305mm/12in guns in twin turrets, fore and aft, but *Collingwood* of 1880 was 508 tonnes/500 tons larger and mounted her guns in barbettes. The barbettes in *Collingwood* were pear-shaped, 15.24m/50ft long and 13.72m/45ft wide, with an armoured trunk at the rear of the barbette for the ammunition hoist (compare with *Dreadnought* below), and the general layout proved to be the model for the majority of pre-Dreadnought battleships.

In 1868 the French were the first to build a barbette, to a British design, which penetrated the deck with an armoured trunk resting on the well-protected roller path. This enabled the French to build high-sided ships with their main guns well clear of the water but they proved to be vulnerable to gunfire and the ships of the Hoche class were held to be some of the worst French designs, despite many modifications while building. They were so heavy that most of the armour was underwater but they did have comfortable accommodation and were accordingly known as the grand hotels. The French also introduced splinter shields over the mountings to protect their crews and by the 1890s this was the standard method of mounting heavy guns in battleships.

In Britain the *Royal Sovereign* of 1892 was one of the first designs in which the barbette was extended below deck to afford some protection to the magazine and ammunition hoists. In the *Majestic* of 1895 the barbette revolved with the gun, although the gun still had to return to a fixed angle of elevation and training for loading. The Italian *Re Umberto* of 1893 and British *Caesar* and *Illustrious* of 1895 were the first ships to have guns which could be loaded at any angle.

The design of the barbette required a very large diameter and one of the frequently overlooked but revolutionary aspects of the 1905 *Dreadnought* was her compact turrets with an internal diameter of just 8.23m/27ft.

The earliest ironclads still had wooden mountings with guns on trucks or slides whose recoil was controlled by ropes, but as the guns grew in size so pivoting iron slides and friction and later hydraulic means of restraining the recoil were introduced. The early guns' mountings in their barbettes were trained by hand although steam-powered, hydraulic and eventually electrical systems were later developed. Finally by about 1900 the barbette was no longer a feature of warship design.

LEFT: **The French *Tonnant* (1880) was intended as a coast defence ship to keep the British at bay. Note the barbettes are roofed over to protect the gun's crew from splinters.** ABOVE: **The French persisted in barbette mountings for their guns, as in *Magenta* (1890), though the larger hull enabled their designers to build more seaworthy ships.**

Turret ships

The French are credited with having introduced armoured floating batteries in the Crimea, during the Russian War of 1854–6, in order to attack Russian positions in support of the attack on Kinburn.

It was during the Russian War that British Captain Cowper Coles and the Swede, John Ericsson, made proposals for turret ships. Ericsson, after several years of attempting to interest the Royal Navy in his various inventions, had settled in the USA and there he successfully introduced a design that became known as a monitor. The USA became a prolific builder of monitors, and many other navies took up similar designs. In its simplest form the monitor remained a platform for bombarding the shore, though some of these grew to be quite large. Some subsequent designs such as the coast defence ship had many attributes of the true battleship.

However, real navies needed seagoing vessels capable of standing up to the heaviest ships in any other navy's order of battle. In the late 1850s, Cowper Coles made many proposals for ships fitted with guns mounted in cupolas including an 1859 plan for a ship with ten armoured cupolas. In response, the Royal Navy cautiously tried out an experimental turret in *Trusty* in 1861. The problem was to design a ship capable of crossing oceans, or in the British case the Channel, that could carry sufficient armour and armament to defeat any shallow-water monitor that might be waiting on the other side. Two of Cowper

Coles's designs were the Danish *Rolf Krake* (1863), and the Peruvian *Huascar* (1865), which did indeed cross open waters, but neither could be regarded as successful.

Rolf Krake, also described as an armoured battery ship, entered the Danish navy in 1863. Built by Napier & Sons in Glasgow she was the first Danish ship to be iron-built and carried four 205mm/8in guns in two double turrets mounted on

BELOW: **Showing how alternative designs co-existed, the *Dreadnought* (1875) had her funnels and other top hamper centralized amidships. Here she is cleared for action and her boats are being towed astern.** BOTTOM: **The British *Agamemnon* (1879) had turret mountings and, in an echo of the earlier, failed *Captain* design, these were mounted one deck lower with forecastle and aftercastle and flying bridge to carry the boats, searchlights and so on.**

the centre-line. The turrets rotated on a roller track which also supported their weight (unlike Ericsson's design for the first monitor in which the turret rested and rotated a central spindle). However, the fundamental principle that turrets should be mounted on the centre-line was soon lost as ships grew bigger, and was not rediscovered until the epoch-making *Dreadnought* was built in 1905. *Rolf Krake* took part in the War of Schleswig Holstein in 1854 and although not a decisive influence on the course of the war, she helped to persuade the German emperor that Germany needed to build its own navy.

Huascar was also built in Britain according to a Coles design. She was twice tested in battle, against two unarmoured British cruisers in 1877, and against several Chilean sailing ships and two casemate ships in 1879. *Huascar* was captured by the Chileans and has been maintained as a trophy of war ever since.

The first British turret ship was the *Royal Sovereign*, formerly a three-deck line-of-battle ship, launched in 1849, which was cut down in 1862 and armed with 265mm/10.5in guns in a twin turret and three single turrets. She remained in service for a surprisingly long time as a coast defence ship. The first purpose-built design was the *Prince Albert* in 1866, whose 230mm/9in guns barely qualify her for a mention in this book but which, it is said, remained in commission until 1899 in deference to Queen Victoria's wishes.

The disadvantage with turrets was their weight, the main issue being that as the size of the gun increased, so too did the weight of armour and these large weights could not be carried high in the hull without risk of instability. The result was a number of low-freeboard ships with poor seakeeping qualities.

The problem is clearly demonstrated in the case of the seven battleships of the Royal Sovereign class of 1889–91 and the eighth ship ordered at the same time under the Naval Defence Act, *Hood*. All had similar 340mm/13.5in guns, but in

TOP: **The turret armour-clad *Devastation* at a naval review at Spithead (for the visit of the Shah of Persia) on June 23, 1873, painted by E. Wake Cooke and capturing the power and majesty of the new pre-Dreadnoughts.** ABOVE: **The German *Preussen*, photographed in Malta in 1890, is a turret ship; though even with her sailing rig reduced from the original she still displays many of the characteristics of a former generation of ships.**

the former, they were in barbettes. However, in order to carry the weight of a turret in *Hood*, the guns had to be fitted one deck lower.

The turret was the correct line for development rather than the barbette, but guns in turrets would not become standard until a smaller size of gun was established at 305mm/12in and the effectiveness of armour had also improved. This would allow the turret weight to be reduced, whilst the displacement of the battleship increased significantly.

LEFT: The French navy continued to build coast defence ships in the 1890s, and used many novel designs like the Bouvines class with a high forecastle and the heavy guns mounted aft, one deck lower. BELOW: The French seem temporarily to have lost their eye for good design and to have produced some exceptionally odd ships like the coast defence ship *Hoche*, laid down in 1881 but not completed until 1890.

Coast defence ships

The American Civil War was followed closely in Europe, and particularly in the Royal Navy, where a 121-gun ship of the line, *Royal Sovereign,* was turned into a coast defence battleship. The conversion in 1862 was not as extreme as that of the *Virginia*, because the *Royal Sovereign* was intended to be a seagoing ship, as was shown by her folding bulwarks. Her hull and deck were strengthened but not heavily armoured and she was fitted with a twin and three single 265mm/10.5in guns firing solid shot, later replaced by more effective 230mm/9in muzzle-loaders. Because of Cowper Coles's agitation, the Royal Navy also built the slightly smaller *Prince Albert* from scratch, with four 230mm/9in muzzle-loaders. Soon, however, the Royal Navy abandoned this line of development.

The Brazilian navy built a number of coast defence battleships, but only the low-freeboard, twin-turreted, French-built *Javary* and *Solimoes* had battleship-sized guns. The small Argentine navy possessed two low-freeboard monitors, *La Plata* and *Los Andes* (1874), with a narrow superstructure fore and aft that allowed end-on fire. *Almirante Brown* (1880) was built to an antiquated design with a central battery and single turrets fore and aft mounting eight 205mm/8in guns, which were replaced in 1897/8 with 265mm/10.5in guns.

In Sweden the coast defence ships *Svea, Göta* and *Thule* (1886–93) had 255mm/10in guns in a twin turret and *Thule* had a ram, while *Oden, Thor* and *Niord* (1897–9) had 255mm/10in guns in single turrets. Between 1900 and 1905, the Swedish navy built three more classes armed with 210mm/8.3in guns: *Dristigheten* (1900), four ships of the Äran class (1902–4) and *Oscar II* (1905).

Denmark competed with an unusual design, *Helgoland* (1878), a coast defence battleship with a single 305mm/12in gun and four 260mm/10.2in guns, and *Iver Hvitfeldt* (1886) with two 260mm//10.2in guns. Norway and the Netherlands also built several coast defence ships with guns under 255mm/10in. Austro-Hungary built *Monarch, Wien* and *Budapest* (1893), though these were too small to be effective battleships.

The coast defence ship in all its forms was, however, a byway in the development of the battleship.

BELOW: The German *Siegfried* photographed in 1889 mimicked the French design, but being larger also supported a forecastle mounting. The German Kaiser's navy began a period of rapid expansion, turning itself from a coast defence navy into a high seas fleet which would eventually challenge the Royal Navy.

Royal Sovereign class

Under the Naval Defence Act of 1889, £21 million was provided for the construction of ten battleships, 42 cruisers and other vessels over the next five years. The two-power standard whereby the Royal Navy would be maintained at strength equal to two other foreign powers was also endorsed: the enemies then were France and Russia.

The launch and completion of the seven ships of the Royal Sovereign class in just two years was itself an important message. Designed by Sir Samuel White, they were the most powerful battleships in the world, setting new benchmarks in firepower, armour and speed.

White's design was for an enlarged Admiral class barbette ship. The Royal Navy wanted better seakeeping than previous generations of low-freeboard ships. The armoured belt covered two-thirds of the ship's length and was up to 460mm/18in thick and the gun mountings were pear-shaped with 430mm/17in armour. The areas behind the main and

upper belts of armour were used as coalbunkers for additional protection. To save weight the 340mm/13.5in breech-loading guns remained in barbettes. The freeboard was raised to 5.5m/18ft by building another full-length deck, and the armour extended to cover the barbettes and a heavier secondary armament. On build, they were found to roll heavily but after bilge keels were fitted proved to be good sea-keepers capable of maintaining high speeds.

Such a large class meant that their effectiveness was increased by operating in squadrons. Few ships of this class, however, saw active service. The Royal Sovereigns were deployed in the Channel and Mediterranean Fleets, but after 1902 they served exclusively in home waters. From 1907 onwards, when superseded by the Dreadnoughts, the Royal Sovereigns were placed in reserve and most were scrapped by 1914. Only *Revenge* saw service in World War I, when she was deployed on the Belgian

ABOVE: **A coloured postcard of *Empress of India* (1891) dressed overall. The launch of seven ships of the same class in just two years was intended as a strong message to the world.**

coast to give fire-support to the army in 1914–15. Following this she was renamed *Redoubtable* and made a tender to HMS *Victory* until 1919.

Royal Sovereign class

Class: *Royal Sovereign, Empress of India, Ramillies, Repulse, Resolution, Royal Oak, Revenge.*
Launched 1891–2

Dimensions: Length – 115.8m/380ft
Beam – 22.9m/75ft
Draught – 8.4m/27ft 6in

Displacement: 14,377 tonnes/14,150 tons

Armament: Main – 4 x 340mm/13.5in guns
Secondary – 10 x 150mm/6in, 16 x 6-pdr,
12 x 3-pdr guns and 7 x 455mm/18in torpedoes

Machinery: 2 shafts, 8 boilers, 6,711kW/9,000ihp

Performance: 18 knots

Complement: 712 men

Hood

The debate about the design of the pre-Dreadnought battleship was not quite decided, and, under the Naval Defence Act of 1889, an eighth battleship was built, *Hood*. Although a sister ship to the Royal Sovereign battleships and sharing many features of their internal layout, she retained more of the characteristics of an earlier type, the turret ship.

Hood had similar machinery, armour and guns to the Royal Sovereign class, but instead of barbettes, she was fitted with turrets. The greater weight of the turrets meant that these had to be mounted one deck lower. In consequence *Hood* shipped water in even the slightest seaway and so could not maintain such high speeds as her half-sisters.

The design allowed direct comparison between the old and the new concepts, but was not a success. *Hood* saw service briefly in the Mediterranean but was soon withdrawn, used as a receiving ship and then for trials from 1911–14.

LEFT: *Hood* was the eighth battleship to be built under the Naval Defence Act of 1889. The weight of the turrets required them to be carried lower in the ship, and the value of a high freeboard for ships of an ocean-going navy like the Royal Navy was not as widely accepted as it should have been.

Hood became part of the Royal Navy's growing anti-submarine efforts and was the first ship to be fitted with bulges, intended to absorb the impact of a torpedo hit.

Hood

Class: *Hood.* Launched 1891
Dimensions: Length – 125.12m/410ft 6in
   Beam – 22.86m/75ft
   Draught – 8.38m/27ft 6in
Displacement: 14,377 tonnes/14,150 tons
Armament: Main – 4 x 340mm/13.5in guns
   Secondary – 10 x 150mm/6in, 10 x 6pdr,
   12 x 3pdr guns and 5 x 455mm/18in torpedoes
Machinery: 8 boilers, 2 shafts,
   9,000kW/16,000ihp
Performance: 16.7 knots
Complement: 690 men

Renown

Similar in armament to earlier Royal Sovereigns, *Renown* was 2,032 tonnes/2,000 tons heavier than *Centurion* and because she was beamier drew slightly less water. Her increased size was due to her heavier armour, a trend which every successor ship followed until the battlecruisers were built. The outer edge of the protective armoured deck over the citadel was also sloped to deflect any shells which might penetrate the belt. She was flagship on the North America and West Indies station from 1897–9, and in the Mediterranean from 1899–1902. With her 150mm/6in guns removed, she carried the Duke and Duchess of Connaught and Prince and Princess of Wales on state visits to India. The role of royal (or presidential) yacht was frequently allotted to battleships.

Renown

Class: *Renown.* Launched 1895
Dimensions: Length – 124.34m/408ft
   Beam – 22m/72ft
   Draught – 8.15m/26ft 9in
Displacement: 12,548 tonnes/12,350 tons
Armament: Main – 4 x 255mm/10in guns
   Secondary – 10 x 150mm/6in, 12 x 12pdr,
   12 x 3pdr guns and 5 x 455mm/18in torpedoes
Machinery: 8 boilers, 2 shafts.
   6,711kW/9,000ihp
Performance: 17.5 knots
Complement: 674 men

RIGHT: *Renown* was a handsome, comfortable ship much in demand by admirals as a flagship or as a royal yacht. She saw service in the Atlantic and Indian Oceans, the West Indies and Mediterranean.

Centurion and *Barfleur*

Centurion and *Barfleur* were the smallest of the British pre-Dreadnoughts and officially rated as second-class battleships. Their size enabled them to enter the major Chinese rivers. Although they could not stand up to other, larger Russian and Japanese ships, they could run down any armoured cruiser and as such, they might be regarded as the first battlecruisers.

A revolving armoured hood covered circular barbettes, marking an intermediate stage in the development of the turret. Both ships could reach 17 knots, and slightly higher speeds with forced draught. Both ships were reconstructed in 1901–4 when the 120mm/4.7in guns were replaced with the more usual 150mm/6in ordnance.

Both *Centurion*, which saw service on the China station between 1894 and 1905, and *Barfleur*, which served in the Mediterranean from 1895–8 and then on the China station until 1902, were recalled to home waters after Fisher's redeployment of the British fleet.

Centurion class

Class: *Centurion, Barfleur*. Launched 1892–4
Dimensions: Length – 109.73m/360ft
    Beam – 21.3m/70ft
    Draught – 7.8m/25ft 6in
Displacement: 10,668 tonnes/10,500 tons
Armament: Main – 4 x 255mm/10in guns
    Secondary – 10 x 120mm/4.7in, 8 x 6pdr,
    12 x 3pdr guns and 7 x 455mm/18in torpedoes
Machinery: 8 boilers, 2 shafts,
    6,710kW/9,000ihp
Performance: 18 knots
Complement: 620 men

LEFT AND BELOW: **The two small battleships of the** *Centurion* **class were specialized ships, intended for work overseas and able to enter China's rivers.** *Barfleur* **is seen here in Mediterranean paint scheme in dry dock (left) and at Malta (below). The twin side-by-side funnels were typical of the era.**

Majestic class

The Majestics were the largest single class of battleships ever built. Combining the successful features of the Royal Sovereigns with the improvements in layout adopted in *Renown*, like their predecessors they were good sea-going boats. The 305mm/12in guns became the British standard and proved superior to the previous 340mm/13.5in guns in everything except weight of shell. The extensive armoured belt was 230mm/9in thick and 305mm/12in to 355mm/14in at the bulkheads and barbettes, where, except for a small number of ready-use rounds, the guns had to be trained fore and aft for loading. The bridge, control tower and foremast were combined in the first six ships. By 1908, all carried some oil fuel in addition to coal, and *Caesar* and *Illustrious* had been fitted with new gun-mountings that enabled all-round loading.

All served in the Channel fleet, except *Victorious,* which served on the China station 1898–1900 and *Majestic*, flagship of the Mediterranean fleet 1895–1903. In World War I *Magnificent, Hannibal* and *Mars* were stripped of their guns, which then armed the Lord Clive class of monitors, and were employed as troopships. *Jupiter* escorted the Russian fleet down the English Channel on its way to defeat at the Battle of Tsushima, and after a period as a gunnery training ship was sent to Archangel as an icebreaker in February 1914, and served in the Far East and Middle East.

Illustrious became an ammunition ship. *Prince George*, which had a lucky escape when a torpedo that struck her off Cape Helles in 1915 failed to explode, and was hit by Turkish gunfire during a bombardment off the Dardanelles, survives as a reef off the Netherlands coast, where she foundered on the way to breakers in Germany in 1921. *Majestic* was sunk by a German U-boat. *Caesar* was one of the few pre-Dreadnoughts to see action after World War I, when she supported British operations in the Black Sea against the Bolsheviks.

LEFT: **Besides war fighting, battleships had a diplomatic purpose in peacetime, and this stern view of** *Majestic* **and the admiral's gallery hints at the luxury onboard, at least for one man.** ABOVE: **This Majestic class appears more warlike, painted all over in grey. The class survived World War I and individual ships were broken up in the 1920s.**

Majestic class

Class: *Magnificent, Jupiter, Majestic, Prince George, Victorious, Mars, Hannibal, Caesar, Illustrious.* Launched 1894–6

Dimensions: Length – 128.3m/421ft
Beam – 22.9m/75ft
Draught – 8.2m/27ft

Displacement: 14,445 tonnes/14,890 tons

Armament: Main – 4 x 305mm/12in guns
Secondary – 12 x 150mm/6in, 16 x 12pdr,
12 x 2pdr guns and 5 x 455mm/18in torpedoes

Machinery: 8 boilers, 2 shafts,
8,950kW/12,000ihp

Performance: 17 knots

Complement: 672 men

All (except *Majestic*) were sold for breaking up in 1921–2.

LEFT: British design, after a generation of change, was remarkably consistent during the pre-Dreadnought period. The Canopus class were only smaller versions of their predecessors. They saw service worldwide and also proved useful in World War I. BELOW: The Canopus class were the same length as the Majestics but had their funnels arranged in-line, and with their tall masts made handsome ships and good seagoing vessels.

Canopus class

British battleship construction in this period showed a consistency in design, and the Canopus class were smaller and faster versions of the Majestics, designed for the Far East and intended to counter the growing naval power of Japan. New-style Krupp armour maintained protection while reducing the thickness and saving 2,032 tonnes/2,000 tons in weight. However, 25.4mm/1in and 50.8mm/2in deck armour was fitted when it was rumoured that the French were fitting howitzers in their ships.

The Canopus class had all-round loading, like *Caesar* and *Illustrious*, and the last of the class, *Vengeance*, was fitted with improved mountings that could also be loaded at any elevation. She had improved armour, giving her flat-sided mountings a "modern" appearance. All earlier British pre-Dreadnoughts had had side-by-side funnels but this was now abandoned in favour of a fore and aft arrangement. The Belleville water-tube boilers worked at 21.1kgcm/300psi, compared to the 11kgcm/155psi of cylindrical boilers, and on trials developed 10,100kW/13,500hp giving speeds of over 18 knots.

Typical of her class, *Glory* served on the China Station from 1900 until 1905 when the Anglo-Japanese alliance made her presence unnecessary. Refitted in 1907 with magazine cooling and fire control, she served in the Mediterranean fleet and then the reserve fleet. In 1914, she escorted Canadian troops across the Atlantic and was relegated to the North American and West Indies station as flagship. After briefly being guard-ship in Egypt, *Glory* was sent to Archangel to remain there until 1919 and was sold to breakers in 1920.

Ocean took part in operations in the Persian Gulf in October 1914 and was at the Dardanelles on March 18, 1915 when she was damaged by gunfire and then hit a floating mine. After an orderly abandonment, *Ocean* sank three hours later. In November 1914 *Goliath* took part in the operation against the *Königsberg*, a German commerce-raiding cruiser that had taken refuge far up in the Rufiji River in East Africa. She was hit twice by Turkish gunfire off Cape Helles in April and May 1915, and on May 13, she was torpedoed by the Turkish motor torpedo boat *Muavenet* and sank with the loss of 570 men.

Canopus class

Class: *Albion, Glory, Canopus, Goliath, Ocean, Vengeance.* Launched 1897–9
Dimensions: Length – 128.5m/421ft 6in
  Beam – 22.6m/74ft
  Draught – 8m/26ft 2in
Displacement: 13,360 tonnes/13,150 tons
Armament: Main – 4 x 305mm/12in guns
  Secondary – 12 x 150mm/6in, 10 x 12pdr,
  6 x 3pdr guns and 4 x 455mm/18in torpedoes
Machinery: 20 Belleville boilers, 2 shafts,
  10,100kW/13,500ihp
Performance: 18 knots
Complement: 682 men

LEFT: **British naval architects were certainly able to design good-looking ships to a classic recipe: two double turrets, two funnels and two pole masts.** ABOVE: **The class continued the gradual evolution of the pre-Dreadnoughts.** BELOW: **Their usefulness continued into the Dreadnought era, although** *Formidable* **was sunk by a U-boat in the English Channel in 1915 and** *Irresistible* **by Turkish mines in 1916, and only** *Implacable* **survived World War I.**

Formidable class

The three ships of this class continued the trend in development of the Majestic and Canopus designs, in which the use of lighter Krupp armour was used to give greater protection rather than to reduce size. Similar to Canopus, the armour belt was extended to the stern and bow. The armament was also similar to the earlier ships, but of larger calibre, and, like *Vengeance*, the 305mm/12in guns could be loaded on any bearing and elevation. To achieve this, a deep hoist opened into a working chamber beneath the guns, which also reduced the possibility of fire or blast spreading to the magazines.

They were fitted with inward-turning propellers resulting in improved speed (over 18 knots) and reduced fuel consumption, but at slow speeds they were difficult to manoeuvre.

All served in the Mediterranean from commissioning until 1908, when they were withdrawn to home waters, fitted with fire control and an array of wireless aerials. *Formidable* had been paid-off

into the reserve when World War I broke out, and she was sunk on January 1, 1915, while unescorted on passage in Lyme Bay west of Portland Bill. Struck by torpedoes from the German submarine *U-24,* she sank with heavy loss of life in the cold and darkness, and bad weather.

These pre-Dreadnoughts were not fit to fight in the main theatre of operations, the North Sea, and were relegated to secondary operations such as the landings at Gallipoli, where *Irresistible* was mined and sunk on March 18, 1915. The Turks had covertly laid an extra row of mines where the allies attempted to execute a plan to force their way through to Constantinople. The mines also trapped *Ocean* and the French battleship *Bouvet*: of 16 British and French battleships that took part in the attempt to rush the straits, three were badly damaged and three were sunk. *Ocean* and *Bouvet* sank in minutes, while

Irresistible took several hours to sink and was only saved from drifting on to the shore of Turkey by the strong stream emerging from the Bosporus.

Formidable class

Class: *Formidable, Irresistible, Implacable.*
  Launched 1898–9
Dimensions: Length – 131.6m/431ft 9in
  Beam – 22.86m/75ft
  Draught – 7.9m/25ft 11in
Displacement: 14,733 tonnes/14,500 tons
Armament: Main – 4 x 305mm/12in guns
  Secondary – 12 x 150mm/6in, 16 x 12pdr,
  6 x 3pdr guns and 4 x 455mm/18in torpedoes
Machinery: 20 Belleville boilers, 2 shafts,
  11,190kW/15,000ihp
Performance: 18 knots
Complement: 780 men
Implacable was broken up in 1921.

LEFT: *London* in camouflage and fitted as a minelayer. Her heavy guns were removed and she could carry an outfit of 240 mines. The dazzle patterns were meant to prevent U-boat commanders from achieving a torpedo-firing solution by accurate estimation of speed and course. BELOW: One of the newly completed London class entering Malta very early in the 20th century.

London class

The first three ships of the London class were constructed under the 1898–9 naval estimates and the last two under the 1900–1 estimates. They were largely repeats of the Formidable class with some changes to their armour, which included a longer armoured belt. All had Belleville boilers, except *Queen,* which was fitted with Babcock and Wilcox boilers. The designed displacement was 15,240 tonnes/15,000 tons although there was some variation across the class.

Venerable served in the Mediterranean and then in home waters.

Bulwark was an ill-fated ship. Intended as flagship of the Mediterranean Fleet, delays in her refit meant she joined the Home Fleet instead. In October 1907, she grounded needing repairs. While loading ammunition at Sheerness on November 26, 1914, she was destroyed by a massive internal explosion, with only a dozen survivors from her complement of over 700 officers and men. The cause was widely attributed to the unstable nature of the black powder in use, which destroyed several ships of this epoch.

London was flagship of the Channel Fleet in 1908 and of the Atlantic Fleet in 1910. In 1912, she was used in flying experiments, which included the first take-off from a ship underway, using a 7.3m/24ft ramp built out over a turret and used to launch a biplane. At the outbreak of war she was employed on Channel patrols until sent on the Dardanelles expedition. Transferred to the Adriatic in May 1915, she was based at Taranto until 1917. Her 305mm/12in guns were removed and the after-gun replaced with a 150mm/6in gun when she became a minelayer, carrying 240 mines.

Queen and *Prince of Wales* differed from the rest of the London class by having open 12pdr gun batteries amidships. Like *London,* both ships were engaged on Channel patrols before being sent to support the ANZAC landings at Gallipoli, and were then based in Taranto, partly to check the Austro-Hungarian fleet in the Adriatic. *Queen*'s 305mm/12in guns were removed in Italy and transferred to the Italian Navy in 1918. All were sold for breaking up in 1920.

London class

Class: *London, Bulwark, Venerable, Queen, Prince of Wales.* Launched 1899–1902
Dimensions: Length – 131.6m/431ft 9in
   Beam – 22.86m/75ft in
   Draught – 7.92m/26ft
Displacement: 14,733 tonnes/14,500 tons
Armament: Main – 4 x 305mm/12in guns
   Secondary – 12 x 150mm/6in, 16 x 12pdr,
   6 x 3pdr guns and 4 x 455mm/18in torpedoes
Machinery: 20 boilers, 2 shafts,
   11,190kW/15,000ihp
Performance: 18 knots
Complement: 714 men

LEFT: The battleship *Russell* in the 1900s. She has an extensive suite of radio aerials but no range-finding equipment to enable her to fire her heavy guns accurately at long range. BELOW: Though only a few years old, the Duncan class were made immediately obsolete by the Dreadnought revolution. *Albemarle*, seen here, was used as an icebreaker in World War I. BELOW LEFT: An evocative picture of the Duncans at sea and working as a homogenous squadron.

Duncan class

Four ships were ordered in 1898 in response to a perceived threat from France and Russia, and two more in 1899. Designed before the London class, and intended to catch fast Russian battleships, the Duncan class sacrificed armour for speed. The armour of the belts and around the barbettes was thinner than the Londons, and speed came from four extra boilers and a modified hull form. They were the first British battleships to exceed 19 knots. The Duncans operated in the Mediterranean until 1904–5 and then in home waters, with the exception of *Duncan, Exmouth* and *Russell,* which also served in the Mediterranean from 1908 until 1912.

Albemarle saw service in the Channel and Atlantic Fleets, and was flagship at Gibraltar until she became a gunnery tender in May 1913. At the outbreak of World War I she served on the Northern Patrol, the distant blockade of Germany where in November 1915 she was badly damaged by heavy weather while in the Pentland Firth. After repairs, she served as an icebreaker at Archangel, and after having her guns stripped out she became an accommodation ship at Devonport in 1917.

Cornwallis was the first ship to open fire in the Dardanelles, on February 18, 1915, and she took part in all the operations including the evacuation of troops from the peninsula. She was hit by three torpedoes from German U-boat *U-32* on January 9, 1917 and sank about 100km/60 miles south-east of Malta with the loss of 15 lives.

Exmouth and *Russell* bombarded Zeebrugge in November 1914 and again in May 1915, and both served in the Dardanelles. *Exmouth* returned to Britain and was paid-off in 1917, but *Russell* was mined, reputedly by the German U-boat *U-72*, on April 27, 1916, just off the coast of Malta with the loss of over 100 lives.

Montagu ran aground on Lundy on May 30, 1906, and was wrecked, although her guns were later salvaged.

The surviving ships were sold for scrap in 1920.

Duncan class

Class: *Duncan, Cornwallis, Exmouth, Montagu, Russell, Albemarle.* Launched 1901
Dimensions: Length – 131.7m/432ft
  Beam – 23m/75ft 6in
  Draught – 7.9m/25ft 9in
Displacement: 13,482 tonnes/13,270 tons
Armament: Main – 4 x 305mm/12in guns
  Secondary – 12 x 150mm/6in, 10 x 12pdr,
  6 x 3pdr guns and 4 x 455mm/18in torpedoes
Machinery: 24 Belleville boilers, 2 shafts,
  13,429kW/18,000ihp
Performance: 19 knots
Complement: 720 men

LEFT: **The King Edward VII class or "The Wobbly Eight" were so-called because, although very manoeuvrable ships, the design of their underwater form and balanced rudders caused lateral instability. Completed during and after the Dreadnought revolution, they were workhorses of the fleet.** ABOVE: **When modernized with torpedo bulges and improved fire-control (on tripod masts) they saw action throughout World War I.** BELOW: **Note the funnel bands painted so that one ship could be distinguished from another.**

King Edward VII class

Ordered in three batches between 1901 and 1903, the King Edward VII class marked a departure from the Majestic class derivatives. Their armament including four 235mm/9.2in guns mounted in single turrets on the upper deck and the 150mm/6in casement guns were moved up one deck to a central battery behind 180mm/7in armoured bulkheads. In consequence they were criticized because, not having a uniform secondary armament, it was almost impossible to distinguish between the fall of shot of various guns which prevented good fire control. Completed with fighting tops on pole masts, these were replaced by fire-control platforms on tripod masts.

In the battle of the boilers, the class was fitted with various steam plants. They were also the first British pre-Dreadnoughts to be fitted with balanced rudders, and though this gave them a small turning circle at speed, they had difficulty keeping a steady course and earned the name "The Wobbly Eight".

Most ships served prior to World War I in the Atlantic, Channel and Home Fleets and formed a single unit, the Third Battle Squadron, from May 1912 onwards. In August 1914, the Third Battle Squadron joined the Grand Fleet at Scapa Flow. Towards the end of the war, they were partially reconstructed, given anti-torpedo bulges and a tripod mast with director control platforms, and the 150mm/6in battery was replaced with four 150mm/6in guns placed one deck higher.

King Edward VII served briefly pre-war in the Mediterranean, but after she joined the Third Battle Squadron, was mined off Cape Wrath. Both engine rooms flooded and *King Edward VII* capsized and sank after 12 hours. *Commonwealth* distinguished herself by colliding with the battleship *Albemarle* in 1907 and in the same year by going aground.

The Royal Navy's interest in aviation was highlighted when in May 1912, *Hibernia* was fitted with a 30.5m/100ft-long runway over the forecastle and Commander Sampson made the first ever flight from a British ship, on May 4, 1912. All were culled after the Washington Naval Treaty, along with scores of other battleships in the world's navies, most of them of prewar design.

King Edward VII class

Class: *King Edward VII, Commonwealth, Dominion, Hindustan, New Zealand, Britannia, Hibernia, Africa.* Launched 1903–5
Dimensions: Length – 138.3m/453ft 9in
  Beam – 23.8m/78ft
  Draught – 7.8m/25ft 8in
Displacement: 15,835 tonnes/15,585 tons
Armament: Main – 4 x 305mm/12in and
  4 x 235mm/9.2in guns
  Secondary – 10 x 150mm/6in, 14 x 12pdr,
  14 x 3pdr guns and 4 x 455mm/18in torpedoes
Machinery: 10, 12 or 16 boilers, 2 shafts,
  13,420kW/18,000ihp
Speed: 18.5 knots
Complement: 777 men
  New Zealand was renamed *Zealandia* in 1911.
  King Edward VII was fitted with 10 Babcock and
  Wilcox boilers, *Dominion* and *Commonwealth*
  with 16 Babcock and Wilcox, *New Zealand* with
  12 Niclausse; the others 12 Babcock and Wilcox.

LEFT: The Royal Navy bought the two ships of the Swiftsure class, while under construction, from the Chilean navy in order to end an arms race in South America. *Triumph* (formerly *Libertad*) is seen at anchor at a fleet review.

Swiftsure class

Class: *Swiftsure* (ex *Constitucion*), *Triumph* (ex *Libertad*). Launched 1903
Dimensions: Length – 146.2m/479ft 9in
Beam – 21.6m/71ft
Draught – 7.7m/25ft 4in
Displacement: 11,990 tonnes/11,800 tons
Armament: Main – 4 x 255mm/10in and 14 x 190mm/7.5in guns
Secondary – 14 x 14pdr, 2 x 12pdr guns and 2 x 455mm/18in torpedoes
Machinery: 12 large-tube Yarrow boilers, 2 shafts, 10,490kW/12,500ihp
Speed: 19 knots
Complement: 800 men

Swiftsure class

Chile has long-standing connections with Britain, and it was in Chile's independence struggle that Lord Cochrane repeated and exceeded some of his exploits when he had fought the French and Spanish in the Great War of 1793–1815. Independence did not mean peace and Chile and its neighbours fought a series of wars and civil wars. During a war with Peru, the turret ship *Huascar* was captured in 1879, and so has been preserved. At a battle in 1891, during a revolution in which the Chilean forces supported the forces for change, the government torpedo gunboat *Almirante Lynch* sank the protected cruiser *Blanco Encalada*: this was the first successful use of a self-propelled torpedo against an armoured vessel.

In the 1890s Chile had ordered some ships from France, but when a border dispute threatened war with Argentina, Chile ordered two battleships from Britain: *Constitucion* and *Libertad*, designed by Sir Edward Reed. They were still building when the crisis in South America was settled, and the Royal Navy, which reckoned ships under construction for other governments formed a reserve, bought them both and they were re-named *Swiftsure* and *Triumph*. This also stopped the Russians from acquiring these ships for its war with Japan.

In comparison with other British ships, *Swiftsure* and *Triumph* were lightly armoured and lightly armed, and their beam and draught, limited by the size of Chilean docks, made them relatively long, thin and fast. Despite their powerful secondary armament, they were rated as second-class battleships. If they could not stand up to battleships, they could certainly run down and out-gun any cruiser or merchant ship and so, by 1913, *Swiftsure* became flagship of the East Indies station and *Triumph* had been sent to the China station. *Swiftsure* was scrapped in 1920, but *Triumph* was torpedoed by *U-21* off the Dardanelles on May 25, 1915.

LEFT: These were small battleships by the Royal Navy's contemporary standards and were going to replace *Centurion* and *Barfleur* on the China station, but they were both recalled to the Dardanelles.

Lord Nelson class

The Lord Nelsons were provided under the 1904/5 Estimates, and had a designed displacement of 16,765 tonnes/16,500 tons. The progress towards a heavier armament, first seen in *King Edward VII*, was taken a stage further in this design; all 150mm/6in guns were abandoned in favour of a complete secondary battery of 235mm/9.2in guns all mounted in turrets. This disposed of the unsatisfactory main deck batteries that, despite their limitations, had been repeated in every class since the Royal Sovereigns. The only other gun armament was 12pdr for torpedo boat defence, and these were mounted on a flying deck over an amidships structure reminiscent of Reed's turret ships. Owing to the limited space for shrouds, a tripod mainmast was adopted. The vessels were slightly heavier than the King Edward VIIs but docking restrictions required that their length be limited, so beam and draught were increased, and a squarer hull form amidships allowed some fining of the lines fore and aft to give a speed of 18 knots. They were good sea-boats and gun-platforms and had exceptional manoeuvrability. On trials, *Lord Nelson* made 18.7 knots with 13,008kW/17,445ihp and *Agamemnon* 18.5 knots with 12,878kW/17,270ihp.

In the long term, they were not successful ships because of the fire control problems with mixed-calibre armament. Their 305mm/12in guns were

new pattern 45-calibre weapons; the guns and mountings originally ordered for them were used in the *Dreadnought* and their completion was delayed while replacement guns were manufactured.

The waterline armour belt extended over the full length of the hull and was 305mm/12in amidships reducing to 230mm/9in and 150mm/6in forward and 100mm/4in aft. The upper belt extended from the stern to the after barbette only, and was 205mm/8in amidships reducing to 150mm/6in and 100mm/4in forward and closed by a 205mm/8in bulkhead at the after end. Between the upper belt

ABOVE: **It was the mixed armament of 305mm/12in and 235mm/9.2in guns, clearly seen here in *Lord Nelson*, photographed in 1917 at Malta, which made these ships pre-Dreadnoughts.** BELOW: ***Agamemnon* bringing up the rear of the British line of battle.**

and upper deck the bases of the 235mm/9.2in mountings were protected by a citadel of uniform 205mm/8in armour extending from forward to aft barbette.

Lord Nelson began her career as flagship of the Fifth Battle Squadron in the Channel Fleet, and in 1915 was sent to the Mediterranean. There she took part in the Dardanelles campaign, in which she hit and was hit by Turkish batteries, but sustained only light damage. She was kept in the eastern Mediterranean to bottle up the German *Goeben* and finally entered the Black Sea in November 1918. *Agamemnon* operated closely with *Lord Nelson*: together they destroyed Kavak Bridge in December 1915 and on October 30, 1918, the Turkish armistice was signed onboard *Agamemnon*, before both ships passed through the Dardanelles.

Lord Nelson class

Class: *Lord Nelson, Agamemnon.* Launched 1906
Dimensions: Length – 135.2m/443ft 6in
    Beam – 24.2m/79ft 6in
    Draught – 7.9m/26ft
Displacement: 16,348 tonnes/16,090 tons
Armament: Main – 4 x 305mm/12in and
    10 x 235mm/9.2in guns
    Secondary – 24 x 12pdr, 2 x 3pdr guns
    and 5 x 455mm/18in torpedoes
Machinery: 15 boilers, 2 shafts,
    12,490kW/16,750ihp
Speed: 18 knots
Complement: 800 men

LEFT: **Spain was wrongly blamed for the loss of USS *Maine* in 1898. Twentieth-century scientific investigation suggested an innocent explanation but the USA was looking for an excuse for war.**

Maine

Class: *Maine.* Launched 1889
Dimensions: Length – 97.23m/319ft
   Beam – 17.37m/57ft
   Draught – 6.55m/21ft 6in
Displacement: 6,789 tonnes/6,682 tons
Armament: Main – 4 x 255mm/10in and
   6 x 150mm/6in guns
   Secondary – 7 x 6pdr, 8 x 1pdr guns and
   4 x 355mm/14in torpedoes
Machinery: 4 boilers, 2 shafts, 6710kW/9,000ihp
Speed: 17 knots
Complement: 374 men

Maine

Authorized in 1886, *Maine* rated as a second-class battleship, forming part of the USN's North Atlantic Squadron when she was sent to Havana, Cuba, to protect American property and life during a revolutionary struggle against Spain.

On February 15, 1898, shortly before 22.00, an explosion tore *Maine* apart, shattering the forward part of the ship, sinking her and killing 260 officers and men. Although an official report concluded that Spain (then the colonial power in Cuba) could not definitely be blamed for the disaster, the USA was stirred into frenzy and two months later "Remember the *Maine*" became the war cry that started the Spanish-American War. *Maine* was raised and towed out to be sunk in the Gulf of Mexico in 1912. Her mainmast is in Arlington National Cemetery and her mizzenmast at the US Naval Academy, Annapolis.

Several ships of this era blew up suddenly, this usually being blamed on unstable ammunition, but in 1976 Admiral Hyman Rickover conducted a new investigation and decided that the cause was spontaneous combustion in *Maine*'s coalbunkers.

Texas

Part of the American flying squadron that blockaded Cienfuegos, Cuba, in May 1898, *Texas* later reconnoitred Guantanamo Bay. On June 16, she bombarded Cayo del Tore, destroying a fort there from 1,280m/1,400 yards' range in an hour and a quarter.

On May 19, a Spanish squadron under Admiral Pascual Cervera arrived in Santiago harbour on the southern coast of Cuba. While North American troops landed, a USN fleet blockaded the harbour. (These troops included the Rough Riders, a volunteer cavalry regiment led by Theodore Roosevelt who would subsequently do so much to advance the USN.) When the Spanish attempted to break out of Santiago, an unequal fight took place on July 3, 1898, known as the Battle of Santiago, between the Spanish squadron of cruisers and destroyers and the USN flying squadron that included the battleships *Texas, Indiana* and *Oregon*.

The Spanish fleet was annihilated, sealing the fate of the last Spanish colony in the Americas. *Texas* was expended as a target in 1911–12.

LEFT: **These small (6,095 tonnes/6,000 tons) ships suggest that the USN was not yet thinking in oceanic terms, though when war broke out with Spain they proved useful in the Caribbean.**

Texas

Class: *Texas.* Launched 1889
Dimensions: Length – 94.1m/308ft 10in
   Beam – 19.4m/64ft
   Draught – 6.9m/22ft 6in
Displacement: 5,728 tonnes/6,316 tons
Armament: Main – 2 x 305mm/12in and
   6 x 100mm/4in guns
   Secondary – 12 x 6pdr, 6 x 1pdr guns and
   4 x 355mm/14in torpedoes
Machinery: 4 boilers, 2 shafts,
   5,900kW/8,600ihp
Speed: 17 knots
Complement: 392/508 men

Indiana class

Indiana was initially designated "BB1" but she and her sisters were later re-rated as coast battleships. Although larger than previous designs, they were over-armed and had only 3.35m/11ft freeboard. *Indiana* and *Massachusetts* were sunk as targets in the early 1920s while *Oregon* became a museum ship until 1942, an ammunition carrier in 1944, and was finally sold for breaking up in 1956.

During the Spanish-American War *Indiana* was deployed to intercept Cervera's Spanish squadron, which wild invasion rumours alleged was going to steam up the Potomac. *Indiana* did not join in the first phase of the Battle of Santiago, but when the Spanish destroyers *Pluton* and *Furor* emerged from harbour, she overwhelmed them.

Indiana made several training cruises carrying midshipmen of the US Naval Academy, which included a visit to Queenstown, Ireland, when she fired a 21-gun salute for the coronation of King George V. She served during World War I as a gunnery training ship, and afterwards served as a target for aerial bombs, was sunk in 1920 and sold for scrap in 1924. *Massachusetts* also blockaded Cuba,

although she missed the Battle of Santiago. However, she helped force the unarmoured cruiser *Reina Mercedes* ashore on July 6, 1898. Afterwards she served in the USN's North Atlantic Squadron and as a training ship. Scuttled off Pensacola Bar, she was declared Florida state property in 1956.

Oregon was slightly larger than her sisters. On her 22,530km/14,000-mile maiden voyage from San Francisco to Jupiter Point, Florida, to join the fleet assembling for the attack on Cuba, she demonstrated both the capability of the USN to deploy its ships, and the need for the Panama Canal. After the Battle of Santiago, *Oregon* was sent to the USN's Asiatic station. She cooperated with the US army in the Philippine insurrection, and was sent to Taku during the Boxer Rebellion in China. However, on June 28, 1900, she grounded on a rock in the

Straits of Pechili, and was nearly wrecked. In June 1925 she was loaned to the State of Oregon as a floating museum. At Guam in 1948 she broke her moorings during a typhoon and was found some days later 805km/500 miles away. She was finally scrapped in Japan.

Indiana class	🇺🇸

Class: *Indiana, Massachusetts, Oregon.*
Launched 1893
Dimensions: Length – 106.95m/350ft 11in
Beam – 21.1m/69ft 3in
Draught – 7.3m/24ft
Displacement: 10,498 tonnes/10,288 tons
Armament: Main – 4 x 330mm/13in and
8 x 205mm/8in guns
Secondary – 20 x 6pdr, 6 x 1pdr guns and
6 x 455mm/18in torpedoes
Machinery: 6 boilers, 2 shafts, 6,710kW/9,000ihp
Speed: 15 knots
Complement: 473 men

BELOW: **The Indiana class (10,160 tonnes/10,000 tons) was able to deploy within the American hemisphere, from California to Florida, in time to influence the outcome of the war.** RIGHT: **Officially rated as BB-1, the size of *Indiana* is indicated by the sailors standing atop one of the 205mm/8in, side-mounted gun turrets in the 1890s.**

Iowa

The second ship of her name in the USN, *Iowa* served in the Atlantic Fleet. She fired the first shots in the Battle of Santiago on July 3, 1898, and overwhelmed the Spanish cruisers *Infanta Maria Teresa* and *Oquendo* in a one-sided 20-minute fight, setting both ships on fire and driving them ashore. *Iowa* rescued the survivors of these ships and of the cruisers and two other destroyers, including the Spanish commander, Admiral Cervera. The battle, which was the highlight of *Iowa*'s career, was not a true test of her design. After Cuba gained its independence, *Iowa* spent two and a half years in the Pacific, and in 1902 she became flagship of the USN South Atlantic Squadron.

Her subsequent career was typical of many of the USN pre-Dreadnoughts, few of which were seriously tested in battle. She was decommissioned in June 1903, recommissioned on December 23, 1903, and joined the North Atlantic Squadron to participate in the John Paul Jones Commemoration ceremonies in June 1905. *Iowa* was placed in reserve in July 1907, and decommissioned at Philadelphia in July 1908. She was rearmed in 1909 and, in additon to her military or pole foremast, was given a cage or lattice mainmast.

When recommissioned again in May 1910, *Iowa* served as a training ship in the Atlantic Reserve Fleet, making a number of training cruises to northern Europe, and she participated in the naval review at Philadelphia in October 1912. She saw limited service in World War I, first as a receiving ship, then as a training ship, and finally, when the USA had entered the war, as a guard ship in Chesapeake Bay. She was finally decommissioned on March 31, 1919.

TOP: *Iowa* in the white and buff paint scheme, similar to the Royal Navy's, which later gave the name to the "Great White Fleet". ABOVE: After World War I, *Iowa* was stripped of her guns and became a radio-controlled target ship used in bombing experiments. BELOW LEFT: Most large ships of the period carried complements of marines, and here US marines are seen at drill onboard *Iowa*.

Iowa

Class: *Iowa*. Launched 1896
Dimensions: Length – 110.5m/362ft 5in
Beam – 22m/72ft 3in
Draught – 7.3m/24ft
Displacement: 11,593 tonnes/11,410 tons
Armament: Main – 4 x 305mm/12in and
8 x 205mm/8in guns
Secondary – 6 x 100mm/4in, 20 x 6-pdr guns
and 4 x 355mm/14in torpedoes
Machinery: 5 boilers, 2 shafts, 8,900kW/11,000ihp
Speed: 16 knots
Complement: 486/654 men

LEFT: **Besides the Dreadnought revolution, there were other new weapons like the submarine. Here *Kearsarge* and an early USN submarine inspect each other, in about 1898.** BELOW: ***Kearsarge* was retrofitted with lattice or cage masts. The distribution of weight helped to reduce vibration in the spotting tops at the head of the masts and so improved the performance of optical rangefinders.**

Kearsarge class

USN battleships were named after the states of the Union, except *Kearsarge*, which took her name from a steam sloop of the American Civil War that sank the Confederate raider *Alabama* off Cherbourg in 1864.

Kearsarge was flagship of the North Atlantic Station in 1903 and again in 1904. As flagship of the USN European Squadron, the German Kaiser visited her on June 26, 1903 at Kiel and the Prince of Wales on July 13 at Spithead. When the North Atlantic Battleship *Squadron* visited Lisbon, she entertained the King of Portugal on June 11, 1904, and on the Fourth of July in Phaleron, she hosted the King, Prince Andrew and Princess Alice of Greece. During target practice off Cape Cruz, Cuba on April 13, 1906, a powder charge ignited in a 330mm/13in gun killing two officers and eight men; four others were seriously injured.

Kearsarge was one of the Great White Fleet of battleships which President Theodore Roosevelt sent around the world in 1907. *Kearsarge* commenced a modernization programme in the Philadelphia Navy Yard in 1909, but she

had already been made obsolete by the Dreadnought revolution and was not commissioned again until 1915, when she took US marines to Vera Cruz, Mexico.

Kearsarge was used as a training ship for several years and then converted to a 10,160-tonne/10,000-ton crane ship. She retained her name until it was required for an aircraft carrier in 1941, then becoming a crane ship, and finally she was sold for scrap in 1955.

Fitted out in New York, *Kentucky* sailed via Gibraltar and the Suez Canal to become the flagship on the US Asiatic Station from 1901–4, visiting Hong Kong and the principal ports of China and Japan. She landed marines in Cuba in 1906 to protect American interests and property during an insurrection there and in 1907 was one of 16 battleships in the Great White Fleet.

During 1915 and 1916 *Kentucky* patrolled off Vera Cruz, watching American interests during the Mexican Revolution. Post-war she was used as a training ship, and scrapped in 1924 under the Washington Naval Treaty.

ABOVE: ***Kearsarge* leading ships of the USN's European squadron in review past a line of British battleships (not shown) in 1903. She is followed by two cruisers, *Chicago* and *San Francisco*.**

Kearsarge class

Class: *Kearsarge, Kentucky.* Launched 1898
Dimensions: Length – 114.4m/375ft 4in
   Beam – 22m/72ft 3in
   Draught – 7.16m/23ft 6in
Displacement: 11,725 tonnes/11,540 tons
Armament: Main – 4 x 330mm/13in and
   4 x 205mm/8in guns
   Secondary – 14 x 125mm/5in, 20 x 6pdr guns
   and 4 x 455mm/18in torpedoes
Machinery: 5 boilers, 2 shafts, 7,450kW/10,000ihp
Speed: 16 knots
Complement: 553 men

The 205mm/8in turrets were fitted atop the 330mm/13in turrets and trained together as one unit, an arrangement which did work well. Rearmed in 1909–11, both ships were fitted with cage masts fore and aft.

LEFT AND ABOVE: **Like *Kearsarge*, these two pictures show *Wisconsin* as built in the 1900s and *Illinois* (of the same class) after modernization immediately pre-war and in the grey paintwork which the USN adopted after the cruise of the "Great White Fleet".**
BELOW: **A rare picture of the period showing the hull shape of an American pre-Dreadnought – *Illinois* in dry dock in the New Orleans Navy Yard in 1902.**

Illinois class

When *Illinois* was flagship of the USN European Squadron, she ran aground off Christiania (now Oslo), Norway, and had to be docked in the Royal Navy dockyard at Chatham in 1902. Like many ships of her vintage she was used as a training ship in World War I. After the war she was laid up until being sold to the state of New York in 1921 for use by the Naval Militia. Demilitarized under the Washington Naval Treaty, *Illinois* was fitted out as a floating armoury in 1924 and became part of the New York Naval Reserve. She remained in New York until 1941, when she was renamed *Prairie State* so that her name could be given to a projected new battleship. In 1956 *Prairie State* was sold for scrap to the Bethlehem Steel Corporation.

From her commissioning in 1901, *Alabama* took part in fleet exercises and gunnery training in the Gulf of Mexico and the West Indies in the wintertime before returning north for repairs and operations off the New England coast during the summer and autumn. Exceptionally, in 1904, *Alabama*, in company with the battleships *Kearsarge, Maine* and *Iowa,* visited Portugal and the Mediterranean.

Although *Alabama* started out as part of the Great White Fleet, she was delayed for repairs in San Francisco, and did not visit Japan but, accompanied by the new battleship *Maine*, completed her circumnavigation of the globe via Honolulu and Guam, Manila, Singapore, Colombo, Aden and the Suez Canal.

On return to the USA she was placed in reserve, coming out only to be used for training. Eventually *Alabama* was sunk in Chesapeake Bay in bombing tests by planes of the US Army and her hulk sold for scrap in 1924.

Wisconsin was built on the West Coast and served her early years in the Pacific. In 1902 she hosted peace talks between Panama and Colombia which became known as the "The Peace of Wisconsin". From 1903–6 *Wisconsin* formed part of the USN Asiatic Fleet's Northern Squadron, steaming up the Yangtze River as far as Nanking. After her circumnavigation she remained on the East Coast and after an uneventful career was sold for scrap in 1922.

Illinois class

Class: *Illinois, Alabama, Wisconsin.* Launched 1898
Dimensions: Length – 117.6m/386ft
 Beam – 22m/72ft 3in
 Draught – 7.1m/23ft 5in
Displacement: 11,751 tonnes/11,565 tons
Armament: Main – 4 x 330mm/13in and
 14 x 150mm/6in guns
 Secondary – 16 x 6pdr, 6 x 1pdr guns and
 4 x 455mm/18in torpedoes
Machinery: 6 boilers, 2 shafts,7,450kW//10,000ihp
Speed: 15 knots
Complement: 536 men

The dimensions given are for *Illinois*, but there were small differences between all three ships of this class. An unusual feature of the class was their side-by-side funnels. All three ships formed part of the Great White Fleet.

Maine class

The second *Maine* was laid down in Philadelphia a year to the day after the destruction of the first. She was launched in July 1901 and not commissioned until December 29, 1902. Like others of her vintage, she took part in the Great White Fleet, although in company with *Alabama* took a shorter route and arrived back on the Atlantic coast in October 1908 in advance of the rest of the fleet.

Used as a training ship in World War I, *Maine* took part in the review of the fleet at New York on December 26, 1918.

Maine operated with ships of the Atlantic Fleet until May 15, 1920, when she was decommissioned at Philadelphia Navy Yard.

The distinguishing feature of *Missouri*'s career, while serving in the USN Atlantic Fleet in April 1904, was a flashback from the left gun of her after turret that ignited powder charges in their ready stowage. There was no explosion but the subsequent rapid burning suffocated 36 of the gun's crew. Efficient damage-control measures prevented the spread of fire and by June *Missouri* was repaired and ready for service. An investigation into the cause of the fire led to improvements in the design of the turret and magazine, which were incorporated in the British monitor *Raglan*, which had American built turrets, and when *Raglan* suffered a turret explosion she sank without explosion.

All three ships differed in displacement and *Ohio*, built by the Union Iron Works at San Francisco on the west coast, was the smallest. *Ohio* was flagship of the USN's Asiatic Fleet, and at Manila in April 1905 embarked a party which comprised the Secretary of War William Howard Taft and Alice Roosevelt, the daughter of the president of the USA, for a tour of the Far East that included the Philippines, China and Japan.

Missouri and *Ohio* were also part of the Great White Fleet. All three ships were scrapped under the Washington Naval Treaty.

Maine class	
Class: *Maine, Missouri, Ohio.* Launched 1901	
Dimensions: Length – 120.1m/393ft 11in	
Beam – 22m/72ft 3in	
Draught – 7.4m/24ft 4in	
Displacement: 13,052 tonnes/12,846 tons	
Armament: Main – 4 x 305mm/12in and	
16 x 150mm/6in guns	
Secondary – 6 x 75mm/3in, 8 x 8pdrs guns and	
2 x 455mm/18in torpedoes	
Machinery: 12 boilers, 2 shafts,	
11,930kW/16,000ihp	
Speed: 18 knots	
Complement: 561 men	

LEFT: **After her loss in 1898, *Maine* was immediately replaced by a new pre-Dreadnought and sister ship to *Missouri* and *Ohio*.** BELOW LEFT: **A close-up of the forward 305mm/12in gun mounting in *Ohio*.** BELOW: ***Missouri* was modernized pre-war with cage masts, fighting tops and turret-mounted rangefinders.**

LEFT: *Rhode Island* photographed off New York in 1909, clearly showing the superimposed turrets. Also the forward pole mast has been replaced by a lattice with searchlight platforms. ABOVE: *Nebraska*, before acceptance into the USN, making smoke and a bow wave while undergoing speed trials. BELOW: Sailors and marines in *Virginia* with something to cheer. Note the field gun in its component parts on the deck.

Virginia class

The largest single class of USN pre-Dreadnoughts was authorized in 1889 and 1900. They were larger again than their predecessors and, in spite of the unsatisfactory experience in *Kearsarge* and *Kentucky*, the superimposed turret arrangement was repeated. There were more than half a dozen different calibres of guns, with all the problems of ammunition supply and spotting fall of shot. When refitted in 1909–10, the 150mm/6in guns were removed, and the number of 75mm/3in guns reduced. At the same time the pole masts were replaced by cages. On trials, they were the first USN battleships to exceed 19 knots.

Virginia's career in Cuba, The Great White Fleet, in Europe and Mexico was unexceptional. However, coal supplies had been a problem during the fleet's circumnavigation and in 1910, *Virginia* experimented with equipment for coaling at sea. She was in refit at Boston when World War I broke out and her crew were employed boarding interned German merchant ships. *Virginia* made eight trooping voyages, more than any other battleship, from France in 1918 and 1919. She was expended as a target. *Virginia* and *New Jersey* were bombed at anchor by the US Army. The trials were artificial, but gave a significant impetus to the development of aviation in the USN.

Georgia's career was punctuated by an explosion in her after 205mm/8in turret, when black powder ignited, killing ten officers and men and injuring 11, but no permanent or lasting damage to the ship was caused and within a few weeks she was back in service. A veteran of the Great White Fleet, she made five trooping voyages from France. *Georgia* finished her service in the Pacific Fleet.

The remaining three ships of this class had similar careers: they became veterans of the Great White Fleet and were used as troopships post-war. *Nebraska* replaced *Alabama* in the fleet when it arrived at San Francisco in May 1908, and *New Jersey* was expended as a target. *Rhode Island* and her remaining sisters were sold for breaking up in 1923.

Virginia class 🇺🇸

Class: *Virginia, Nebraska, Georgia, New Jersey, Rhode Island*. Launched 1904
Dimensions: Length – 134.5m/441ft 3in
  Beam – 23.2m/76ft
  Draught – 7.2m/23ft 9in
Displacement: 15,188 tonnes/14,948 tons
Armament: Main – 4 x 305mm/12in, 8 x 205mm/8in and 12 x 150mm/6in guns
  Secondary – 12 x 75mm/3in, 12 x 3pdr guns and 4 x 535mm/21in torpedoes
Machinery: 12 Babcock & Wilcox boilers, 2 shafts,18,980kW/19,000ihp
Speed: 19 knots
Complement: 812 men
On commissioning *Virginia* and *Georgia* had 24 Niclausse boilers, later replaced by 24 Babcock & Wilcox.

Connecticut class

Connecticut and Louisiana extended the fashion in the USN pre-Dreadnoughts for multiple calibres of guns, which was mocked by Cuniberti. With so many guns of similar calibre, it was impossible to spot the fall of shot and so to range the guns: in part, the Dreadnought was a reaction to this design trend. Both ships took part in the Great White Fleet's circumnavigation, Connecticut as flagship.

Connecticut was also flagship of the USN Atlantic Fleet between 1907 and 1912. In the pre-war years, she visited the Mediterranean and the Caribbean on various policing and ceremonial duties and in 1913 protected American citizens and interests during disturbances in Mexico and Haiti. Like Louisiana, she was fitted as a troopship, making four voyages in 1919 to bring US soldiers back from France. In the 1920s, Connecticut served on the west coast before being sold for scrap in 1923.

Soon after entering service Louisiana sailed for Havana in response to an appeal by the Cuban president for American help in suppressing an insurrection. The new battleship carried a peace commission led by the US Secretary of War, William H. Taft, who arranged for a provisional government of the island, and Louisiana stood by while this was set up. Next Louisiana became the presidential yacht, taking President Theodore Roosevelt to inspect work on the construction of the Panama Canal and on a brief visit to Cuba.

Louisiana made an extensive visit to Europe in 1910 and 1911 but was soon back in the Caribbean to protect American lives and property during revolutionary disturbances in Mexico in 1913, during tension between the USA and Mexico in 1914 and again in 1915.

During World War I Louisiana was used for gunnery and engineering training and in late 1918 and early 1919 she made four voyages as a troop transport from Brest with returning US soldiers. She was sold for scrap in 1923.

Connecticut class	
Class: Connecticut, Louisiana. Launched 1904	
Dimensions: Length – 139 m/456ft 4in	
Beam – 23.4m/76ft 10in	
Draught – 7.46m/24ft 6in	
Displacement: 16,256 tonnes/16,000 tons	
Armament: Main – 4 x 305mm/12in, 8 x 205mm/8in and 12 x 180mm/7in guns. Secondary – 12 x 3pdr guns and 4 x 535mm/21in torpedoes	
Machinery: 12 boilers, 2 shafts,15,300kW/16,500ihp	
Speed: 18 knots	
Complement: 827 men	

ABOVE: **Connecticut at anchor in the Hudson river on the occasion of the fleet review of 1911. The launch in the foreground is typical of those carried in battleships.** LEFT: **Connecticut steaming at high speed, photographed by Enrique Muller in 1907.** BELOW: **President Roosevelt addresses the ship's company of Connecticut on the quarterdeck on return from their circumnavigation.**

LEFT: **A side-on view of one of the Vermont class. The mixed armament is distinctly pre-Dreadnought, while in Britain a revolution is taking place.**
BELOW: **A detail of the bow decoration of** *New Hampshire* **taken while in dry dock. The picture shows the eagle figurehead, but unfortunately not the shape of the hull.**

Vermont class

American industry was beginning to show its muscle and the Vermont class of ships were repeats of the preceding Connecticut class of ships. Uniformity of build in a successful design was something which only the USN and the Royal Navy could be relied upon to achieve. All six ships were, however, made obsolescent by the Dreadnought revolution. *Vermont* was another of the Great White Fleet, which after her return to the USA joined the Atlantic Fleet. Her service alternated between European cruises and Caribbean deployments until 1914, when she landed a naval brigade (or battalion in USN usage) of 12 officers and 308 seamen and marines at Vera Cruz. The other ships that the USN sent to Mexico included the battleships *Vermont, Arkansas, New Hampshire, South Carolina* and *New Jersey*. There was only one American fatality in the shore fighting which ensued.

Like other pre-Dreadnought battleships *Vermont* was equipped as a troopship in the winter of 1918–19 and made four voyages from France with some 5,000 troops. She was scrapped in 1923.

Apart from the Great White Fleet, *Kansas*'s service was distinguished by making five crossings from Brest as a troopship. In 1920, she was visited by the Prince of Wales at Grassey Bay, Bermuda, and in November attended the inauguration of the new American governor of the German Samoa islands, ceded to the USA after World War I. Her name was struck from the Navy List on August 24, 1923, and she was sold for scrap in the same year.

Another member of the Great White Fleet, *Minnesota* led an unremarkable career until September 29, 1918, when she struck a mine, 32km/20 miles off Fenwick Island Shoal Lightship, which had apparently been laid by the German U-boat *U-117*. She was seriously damaged but suffered no loss of life. Repaired at Philadelphia, she was serviceable again by March 1919, when she brought 3,000 veterans from France. She was sold for scrap in 1924.

On her first deployment, *New Hampshire* carried a Marine Expeditionary Regiment to Colon, Panama, to protect and garrison Panama in 1908, and she attended the fleet review at New York that welcomed back the Great White Fleet. In 1916, *New Hampshire* operated off Santo Domingo, where her captain had a hand in the newly installed government. In 1917 she was part of the convoy escort taking US troops to France, and in 1919 she made four voyages carrying them back again. *New Hampshire* was scrapped in 1923.

Vermont class

Class: *Vermont, Kansas, Minnesota, New Hampshire*. Launched 1905
Dimensions: Length – 139m/456ft 4in
  Beam – 23.4m/76ft 10in
  Draught – 7.6m/24ft 6in
Displacement: 16,256 tonnes/16,000 tons
Armament: Main – 4 x 305mm/12in,
  8 x 205mm/8in and 12 x 180mm/7in guns
  Secondary – 20 x 75mm/3in and
  12 x 3pdrs guns
Machinery: 12 boilers, 2 shafts,
  12,300kW/16,500ihp
Speed: 18 knots
Complement: 880 men
  The four ships of the Vermont class were repeats of the Connecticut class, with only minor differences in the secondary armament and complement.

Mississippi class

Mississippi and *Idaho* were the last of the USN's pre-Dreadnoughts, and were laid down and completed when Fisher's Dreadnought revolution had already made them obsolescent. Like other USN pre-Dreadnoughts, they carried a main battery of heavy, medium and small calibre guns. In a reaction to the rising cost of battleships the US Congress had limited their size, so that *Mississippi* and *Idaho* were actually smaller, slower and shorter-ranged than their predecessors.

Originally, both ships carried a single pole mast forward (known as a military mast) but soon after commissioning they were fitted with a cage or lattice mast aft, and in 1910 the forward pole mast was replaced by a second lattice mast, which balanced the design.

Neither ship saw battle: apart from deployments to the East Coast of North America and to the Caribbean, both made cruises to Europe. However, in June 1912, *Mississippi* landed US marines in Cuba to protect US interests, and carried men and equipment to Pensacola, Florida, to build a naval air station. In April and May 1914, she transported seaplanes and crews to Vera Cruz, Mexico, when an American squadron landed a force of 800 marines and seamen during a period of political unrest. *Mississippi*'s use as a seaplane tender was probably the first overseas deployment of aircraft by the USN. In 1909 *Mississippi* and in 1911 *Idaho* entered the Mississippi River for a tour of central US states with no seaboard. In 1910, both ships visited France and Britain, where they must have looked old-fashioned.

In July 1914, *Mississippi* and *Idaho* were sold to Greece, becoming the only USN battleships ever to be transferred to a foreign power. They were renamed *Lemnos* and *Kilkis* respectively and served in the Greek navy until April 1941 when they were sunk by German dive-bombers at Salamis, thus becoming the first American-built battleships to be lost to air attack.

Mississippi class	
Class: *Mississippi*, *Idaho*. Launched 1905	
Dimensions: Length – 116.4m/382ft	
Beam – 23.5m/77ft	
Draught – 7.5m/24ft 8in	
Displacement: 13,210 tonnes/13,000 tons	
Armament: Main – 4 x 305mm/12in,	
8 x 205mm/8in and 8 x 180mm/7in guns	
Secondary – 12 x 75mm/3in guns and	
2 x 535mm/21in torpedoes	
Machinery: 8 boilers, 2 shafts,	
7,450kW/10,000ihp	
Speed: 17 knots	
Complement: 744 men	

BOTTOM: *Mississippi* at anchor off Philadelphia in 1908 for Founders' Week. The ship's name, ready for illumination, is picked out in lights on the after superstructure. BELOW: Possibly the USN's first carrier air group. A squadron of Curtiss flying boats and floatplanes embarked in *Mississippi* during the Mexican crisis in 1914.

Fuji and Shikishima class

LEFT: *Yashima* and *Hatsuse* were built at the Armstrong Whitworth yard at Elswick. Here is *Hatsuse* at her launch on June 27, 1899. BELOW LEFT: *Fuji* and *Shikishima* were built at the Thames Iron Works on the Thames. Here is *Shikishima* at buoys in Malta, en route to Japan in 1900.

LEFT: *Yashima* and *Hatsuse* were built at the Armstrong Whitworth yard at Elswick. Here is *Hatsuse* at her launch on June 27, 1899. BELOW LEFT: *Fuji* and *Shikishima* were built at the Thames Iron Works on the Thames. Here is *Shikishima* at buoys in Malta, en route to Japan in 1900.

Fuji class

Class: *Fuji, Yashima.* Launched 1896
Dimensions: Length – 125.6m/412ft
  Beam – 22.5m/73ft 9in
  Draught – 8.1m/26ft 6in
Displacement: 12,518 tonnes/12,320 tons
Armament: Main – 4 x 305mm/12in,
  10 x 150mm/6in guns
  Secondary – 20 x 3pdr guns and
  5 x 455mm/18in torpedoes
Machinery: 14 boilers, 2 shafts.
  10,000kW/14,000ihp
Speed: 18 knots
Complement: 637 men

Building a navy was integral to Japan's rapid advance in the second half of the 19th century from feudal state to industrialized society. The first naval construction programme of home-built ships was influenced by the French *jeune école,* which advocated a fleet of cruisers and torpedo boats to counter battleships. However, the Sino-Japanese War of 1894–5 gave Japanese officers an appreciation of their navy's material and strategic necessities, and the Japanese, turning to Britain for battleships, came under the influence of the Royal Navy. Each ship of the 1896 expansion programme showed an improvement over the preceding one, although all six could be operated together.

The Imperial Japanese Navy began to build its strength in response to a perceived threat from the Chinese navy, which had acquired a number of modern German-built ships. The Chinese ships were armoured turret ships but the six ships that Japan bought in Britain were the new generation of pre-Dreadnoughts.

Fuji and *Yashima* were improved Royal Sovereigns, with weight being saved by placing most of the secondary armament behind shields rather than in armoured casemates. *Yashima*'s keel was cut away towards the bow, giving her a smaller turning circle than *Fuji*. The ships were refitted in 1901 when 12pdrs replaced the 3pdrs. Both ships took part in the Russo-Japanese war. *Yashima* was mined off Port Arthur on May 15, 1904, was taken in tow but capsized. *Fuji* fired the last shot at the Battle of Tsushima to sink the *Borodino*. *Fuji* was refitted in 1910 and reclassified as a coast defence ship. Disarmed under the Washington Treaty and used as a school ship, she capsized and was scrapped in 1945.

The two Shikishima class ships were improved British Majestics, and the armament was identical to the Fuji class. Both ships were at the bombardment of Port Arthur on February 9, 1904, and the subsequent blockade, where *Hatsuse* struck a mine on May 15, 1904. She was taken in tow by *Asahi* but struck a second mine whereupon her magazine exploded and she was lost. *Shikishima*, which was at the Battle of the Yellow Sea and the Battle of Tsushima, was classed as a coast defence ship in 1921, became a training ship in 1923 and was scrapped in 1947.

Shikishima class

Class: *Shikishima, Hatsuse.* Launched 1898–9
Dimensions: Length – 133.5m/438ft
  Beam – 23m/75ft 6in
  Draught – 8.4m/27ft 6in
Displacement: 15,088 tonnes/14,850 tons
Armament: Main – 4 x 305mm/12in and
  14 x 150mm/6in guns
  Secondary – 20 x 12pdr, 6/8 x 3pdr
  (6 x 1) guns and 5 x 455mm/18in torpedoes
Machinery: 25 Belleville boilers, 2 shafts.
  10,810kW/14,500ihp
Speed: 18 knots
Complement: 836 men (*Hatsuse* 741)

LEFT: *Asahi* at anchor in Portsmouth in 1900. Built by John Brown on the Clyde, she was one of the last Japanese ships to be built in Britain. BELOW LEFT: *Asahi*'s sister ship *Mikasa* underway. BELOW *Mikasa* still under construction in the Vickers yard at Barrow-in-Furness. The Japanese navy had a strong preference for having their ships built in Britain, and many Japanese naval officers and naval architects also studied in Britain at the end of the 19th century and admired what they found.

Mikasa and *Asahi*

Asahi was similar to the Shikishimas except she had two funnels instead of three. Mined on October 26, 1904, *Asahi* was repaired in time for the Battle of Tsushima. A gunnery training ship at the start of World War I, she was demilitarized after the Washington Naval Treaty, converted to a submarine salvage ship and torpedoed off Indo-China in 1942.

Mikasa was the last of six battleships ordered under the Japanese navy's ten-year programme of expansion. The 305mm/12in guns, which could be operated electrically or hydraulically and loaded at any angle of elevation or training, could fire at the rate of three shells every two minutes.

On February 8, 1904, *Mikasa* was Admiral Togo's flagship for a surprise attack on the Russian Far East Fleet at Port Arthur. When Admiral Vitgeft attempted a breakout to Vladivostok later in the year, he was defeated in the Battle of the Yellow Sea. Vitgeft was killed when the battleship *Tsessarevitch* was hit by a 305mm/12in shell and the Russian fleet took refuge in Port Arthur. *Tsessarevitch* escaped to Tsingtao, where the Germans interned her, and by January 1905, when the Japanese took Port Arthur from the landward, the Russians had lost no less than seven battleships. Admiral Togo was hailed as the new Nelson.

When Admiral Rozhestvensky arrived in the Korea Strait after a 29,000km/18,000-mile journey from the Baltic, Togo's fleet was inferior to the Russian, but the Japanese possessed speed, morale and a tactical scheme. Togo in *Mikasa* out-gunned and outmanoeuvred the Russians, who by the end of the day had suffered six battleships and four others sunk, four captured, and three ships interned. *Mikasa* was hit 32 times but no Japanese ships were lost.

A magazine explosion killed 114 of *Mikasa*'s crew in September 1906, but she was refloated in the same year, and is preserved as a memorial.

Mikasa and *Asahi*

Class: *Asahi, Mikasa.* Launched 1899–1900
Dimensions: Length – 130m/426ft 6in
  Beam – 22.9m/75ft 3in
  Draught – 8.3m/27ft 3in
Displacement: 15,444 tonnes/15,200 tons
Armament: Main – 4 x 305mm/12in and
  14 x 150mm/6in guns
  Secondary – 20 x 12pdr, 6 x 3pdr guns and
  4 x 455mm/18in torpedoes
Machinery: 25 boilers, 2 shafts.
  11,930kW/15,000ihp
Speed: 18 knots
Complement: 836 men
There were minor differences in size between the two ships.

LEFT: **After a number of evolutionary types of warships, the German Brandenburg class is the first recognizable pre-Dreadnought. This is** *Wörth*, **photographed in 1900.** BELOW LEFT: *Brandenburg*. **Lost in the hamper amidships is a third, twin turret, which had to be of lesser calibre than the other main turrets in order to train to port or starboard.**

Brandenburg class

After a number of classes of German-built central battery ironclads and a class of coast defence battleships, the Brandenburgs marked the beginning of a fateful, and fatal, era of German naval expansion. Disparagingly the Royal Navy nicknamed these ships the "whalers". They were unusual in having a midships turret, whose barrels had to be shorter than the fore and aft turrets in order that they could be trained through the centre line to port or starboard. This could have given the Germans a lead in a Dreadnought-type arrangement of all centre-line guns, but the midships mounting, sited aft of the after funnel, caused blast damage and the idea was abandoned. Nevertheless, in a

further manifestation of growing German ambition, ships of this class saw service in China during the Boxer rebellion.

They were modernized in 1902 and 1904 with new boilers and the top-hamper was cut down. One torpedo tube was suppressed and an extra 105mm/4.13in fitted, but their secondary armament was regarded as weak by the standards of the time. They were also the first German warships to be fitted with radio.

In 1910, two ships of this class were sold to Turkey for nine million marks each, *Kurfürst Friedrich Wilhelm* as *Heireddin Barbarossa* and *Weissenburg*, which became the *Turgut Reis*. On August 8, 1915, *Heireddin Barbarossa*

was torpedoed and sunk with the loss of 253 lives by the British submarine *E11*, commanded by Lieutenant Commander Martin Nasmith, in the Dardanelles. *Turgut Reis* became a training ship in 1924 and was broken up 1938.

Brandenburg served overseas in 1900–1 to further German imperial ambitions, but when general war broke out in 1914 she was obsolete, and was relegated to coast defence duties in 1915. She became an accommodation ship at Libau in 1916–18, and was broken up at Danzig in 1920.

Wörth was categorized as a coastal defence ship in 1915 and then used as an accommodation ship at Danzig where she was broken up in 1919.

Brandenburg class

Class: *Brandenburg, Kurfürst Friedrich Wilhelm, Weissenburg, Wörth.* Launched 1891–2
Dimensions: Length – 115.7 m/379ft 7in
    Beam – 19.5m/64ft
    Draught – 7.9m/26ft
Displacement: 10,668 tonnes/10,500 tons
Armament: Main – 6 x 280mm/11in and
    6 x 105mm/4.13in guns
    Secondary – 8 x 90mm/3.46in guns and
    6 x 450mm/17.7in torpedoes
Machinery: 12 boilers, 2-shaft TE,
    7,459kW/10,000ihp
Speed: 16 knots
Complement: 568 men

Kaiser class

LEFT: The Kaiser class were an incremental improvement over the Brandenburgs, but carried a smaller gun which just about qualified them as battleships.

Named after German emperors past and present, these four ships carried a smaller main gun (approximately 240mm/9.4in) but a heavier secondary armament. Some of the 150mm/6in guns were mounted in turrets rather than casemates, and the triple shafts were typical German arrangements. However in other respects the Kaiser class still compared unfavourably with British designs.

Partly in response to the Dreadnought revolution, the Kaisers were reconstructed in 1907–10, with taller funnels, reduced superstructure and some rearrangement of the secondary and tertiary guns. *Kaiser Wilhelm II*, with her complement increased by 63, was fleet flagship until 1906. All ships of this class were disarmed and used as hulks in the war years. *Kaiser Wilhelm der Grosse* became a torpedo training ship, *Kaiser Wilhelm II*

became an HQ ship for the commander-in-chief, and the others became floating prisons. All were broken up in 1920 and 1921. The bow ornament of *Kaiser Freidrich III* is in a museum in Dresden.

Kaiser class

Class *Kaiser Freidrich III, Kaiser Wilhelm II, Kaiser Wilhelm der Grosse, Kaiser Barbarossa,* Launched 1896–1900
Dimensions: Length – 125.3m/411ft
    Beam 20.4m/67ft,
    Draught 8.25m/27ft
Displacement: 11,920 tonnes/11,599 tons
Armament: Main – 4 x 240mm/9.4in, 18 x 150mm/6in guns
    Secondary – 12 x 88mm/3.46in guns and 6 x 450mm/17.7in torpedoes
Machinery: 12 boilers, 3 shafts.
    10,440kW/14,000ihp
Speed: 17 knots
Complement: 651

Wittelsbach class

The Wittelsbach class were improved Kaisers, although the improvements were not great: they carried a similar armament and somewhat extended armour. By World War I they were too slow and vulnerable to stand in the line of battle, and were used for training. By 1916 all ships of this class had been

disarmed, so when Germany signed away the High Sea Fleet in the Armistice of 1918, she was allowed to keep these obsolete ships. *Mecklenburg* became a floating prison, and was scrapped in 1921. Converted towards the end of World War I to depot ships for minesweeping motor launches,

Schwaben and *Wittelsbach* each carried 12 shallow-draught minesweepers, but they too were scrapped in 1921–2. *Zähringen* became a target ship in 1917, and in 1926 was converted so she could be radio-controlled. She was sunk by the British Royal Air Force bombing at Gotenhafen (Gdynia) in 1944.

LEFT: **The Wittelsbachs were slightly larger and improved Kaisers, with the same gun. Unlike the British pre-Dreadnoughts which could be sent to overseas stations, there was nowhere for these ships to go and they were disarmed by the Germans in 1916.**

Wittelsbach class

Class: *Wittelsbach, Wettin, Zähringen, Schwaben, Mecklenburg.* Launched 1900–1
Dimensions: Length – 126.8m/416ft
    Beam – 22.8m/74ft 9in
    Draught – 8m/26ft 4in
Displacement: 12,798 tonnes/12,596 tons
Armament: Main – 4 x 240mm/9.4in and 18 x 150mm/6in guns
    Secondary – 12 x 88mm/3.46in guns and 6 x 450mm/17.7in torpedoes
Machinery: 12 boilers, 3 shafts,
    11,180kW/15,000ihp
Speed: 17 knots
Complement: 683 men

LEFT: *Preussen* underway at speed. The large bow wave seems to be characteristic, indicating perhaps that German naval architects did not quite understand their subject. BELOW: *Hessen* passing through the Kiel Canal, probably in the interwar years. The Braunschweig class were among the small number of ships that the Germans were allowed to keep under the terms of the armistice.

Braunschweig class

The Braunschweigs marked a stepped improvement over the previous two classes of German pre-Dreadnoughts. The forward main gun was mounted on the forecastle instead of one deck above with a battery of lesser guns beneath. The guns were heavier (280mm/11in as opposed to 240mm/9.4in) and the armour was slightly thicker. Although 1,524 tonnes/1,500 tons larger, with extra boilers and three funnels, they produced a speed of 8 knots, which was one knot faster than the Wittelsbachs and Kaisers. However, the 280mm/11in guns were still lighter than the standard British 305mm/12in, and while they were being completed between 1904 and 1906, they were overtaken by the Dreadnought revolution. In the early part of World War I they were stationed in the Baltic, but between 1916 and 1918 they were disarmed.

Preussen and *Lothringen* were converted to depot ships for minesweeping motor boats in 1919 and broken up in 1931. One midships section of the hull of *Preussen* survived as a torpedo target and for explosive trials. Renamed *Vierkant* (meaning "even keel"), she was sunk by bombing in 1944 and not raised and broken up until 1954.

Braunschweig, *Elsass* and *Hessen* were rebuilt as coast defence ships in the 1920s, with much of their original armament, but were sold for breaking up between 1931 and 1935.

Hessen survived as a radio-controlled target ship and was then taken over by the Soviet Union in 1946 and given the name *Tsel*.

Braunschweig class

Class: *Braunschweig, Elsass, Hessen, Preussen, Lothringen.* Launched 1902–4

Dimensions: Length – 127.7m/419ft
Beam – 25.6m/84ft
Draught – 8.1m/26ft 7in

Displacement: 14,394 tonnes/14,167 tons

Armament: Main – 4 x 280mm/11in and 14 x 170mm/6.7in guns
Secondary – 18 x 88mm/3.46in guns, 4 x machine-guns and 6 x 450mm/17.7in torpedoes

Machinery: 14 boilers, 3-shaft TE, 12,677kW/17,000ihp

Speed: 18 knots

Complement: 743 men

LEFT: **Deutschland was the name of the last class of German pre-Dreadnoughts. Here one is seen passing eastbound along the Kiel Canal. Despite their obsolescence they took part in the Battle of Jutland.** BELOW: **A battleship of the Kaiser class firing a broadside to starboard.** BOTTOM: **Paint ship! A task familiar to sailors old and new in every navy. This essential work is not just for smartness but also keeps the hull well-maintained and rust-free.**

Deutschland class

The Deutschlands were the last pre-Dreadnoughts of the Imperial German Navy. They were similar to the Braunschweigs, but had slightly differently shaped funnels and thicker armour. The two twin turrets and the mixed secondary and tertiary armament marked the epitome of the pre-Dreadnoughts. Ordered and laid down amid rumours, and then hard news, of Fisher's Dreadnought revolution, all five ships of the class were completed at great expense while Germany considered its options of how to react to developments in Britain.

Although obsolescent, the Deutschlands took part in the Battle of Jutland in 1916, where concern for their vulnerability and slowness may have influenced Scheer's tactics. The weakness in the protection and magazine arrangements of the secondary armament was reckoned to have caused the loss of *Pommern* when a single torpedo, fired by a British destroyer, hit her and she blew up.

By 1917 all ships of the class had been removed from the line of battle. *Deutschland* was disarmed and broken up in 1920, but the three others survived into World War II. *Schlesien* and *Schleswig-Holstein* were refitted in the 1920s and rebuilt about 1930, when the fore-funnel was trunked into the midships one. Better anti-aircraft (AA) armament was fitted, and in World War II numerous 40mm/1.57in and other light AA guns were added as well.

After World War I, *Schleswig-Holstein* became an accommodation ship and then in 1926 flagship of the Kreigsmarine. Afterwards she became a

training ship for the newly resurgent Reichsmarine, but she was bombed and sunk in 1944.

Schlesien became an accommodation ship at the end of World War I, was refitted in the 1920s, and mined off Swinemunde in 1944.

Deutschland class

Class: *Deutschland, Hannover, Pommern, Schlesien, Schleswig-Holstein.* Launched 1904–6
Dimensions: Length – 127.6m/418ft 8in
   Beam – 22.3m/73ft
   Draught – 8.2m/27ft
Displacement: 14,218 tonnes/13,993 tons
Armament: Main – 4 x 280mm/11in and
   14 x 170mm/6.7in guns
   Secondary – 20 x 88mm/3.46in guns and
   6 x 450mm/17.7in torpedoes
Machinery: 12 boilers, 3 shafts,
   11,930kW/16,000ihp
Speed: 18 knots

LEFT: **French designers produced several high-sided ships with massive superstructures during the 1890s, such as the *Brennus*.**

Brennus

Class: *Brennus*. Launched 1891
Dimensions: Length – 110.3m/361ft 10in
   Beam – 20.4m/66ft 11in
   Draught – 8.3m/27ft 2in
Displacement: 11,370 tonnes/11,190 tons
Armament: Main – 3 x 340mm/13.5in and
   10 x 160mm/6.4in guns
   Secondary – 4 x 9pdr and 14 x 3pdr guns
   4 x 455mm/18in torpedoes
Machinery: 32 Belleville boilers, 2 shafts,
   12,304kW/16,900ihp
Speed: 18 knots
Complement: 673 men

Brennus turret ship

The French built a number of turret ships of which *Brennus* was the last. Her designers tried to cram in too much and her masts and superstructure had to be reduced before she was considered safe. She was heavily armoured with a belt 255mm/10in to 455mm/18in thick, which extended upwards to cover her upper deck and the barbettes. She carried her three, long 340mm/13.4in guns in single and twin barbettes, and,

also unusual for her time, had no ram: this and her high freeboard qualified *Brennus* as the first true ocean-going battleship of the modern age.

In the previous ten years France had built ten mastless turret ships, but the centre-line armoured pivot turrets qualified *Brennus* as the first modern battleship. She was also protected with face-hardened armour made by the Harvey process invented in the USA.

Like many of her predecessors she was overweight and unstable. At just 5 degrees of heel her armoured belt was submerged and hydraulic power to the guns was interrupted, so both the superstructure and the military mainmast had to be reduced.

Charles Martel class

The French built five similar ships, sometimes considered as one class: *Charles Martel, Carnot, Jauréguiberry, Masséna* and *Bouvet. Charles Martel* had a high freeboard forward, a flying bridge between her funnels and was cut down aft. *Carnot* had a reduced superstructure, no flying deck or military mainmast, and her funnels were further apart. *Jauréguiberry* had a shorter hull which brought the guns close to the ends of the

ship, and, in the earlier days of water-tube boilers (needing numerous tight joints), she suffered a boiler explosion. *Masséna* was similar in appearance to *Charles Martel*, and *Bouvet*, generally regarded as the best of these ships, differed in the hull not being cut down and in having two short military masts.

The armament was generally similar: three 305mm/12in guns on the centre-line and two 275mm/10.8in guns

mounted midships on the tumblehome, and six 140mm/5.5in and numerous smaller quick-firing guns that varied throughout the class. These ships also had numerous small compartments, called the *tranche cellulaire*, which could be filled with coal or stores and were intended to limit the effects of damage.

Charles Martel class

Class: *Charles Martel, Carnot, Jauréguiberry,*
   Masséna, Bouvet. Launched 1893–6
Dimensions: Length – 115.5m/378ft 11in
   Beam – 21.6m/71ft
   Draught – 8.4m/27ft 6in
Displacement: 11,881 tonnes/11,693 tons
Armament: Main – 2 x 305mm/12in,
   2 x 275mm/10.8in and 6 x 140mm/5.5in guns
   Secondary – 4 x 9pdr, 12–18 x 3pdr guns and
   2 x 455mm/18in torpedoes
Machinery: 24 Lagrafel d'Allest boilers, 2 shafts,
   10,910kW/14,200 to 12,304kW/16,900ihp
Speed: 18 knots
Complement: 644 men

LEFT: **The five ships of the Charles Martel class were meant to be one class, but as a result of being built in different yards by different designers, individual ships varied.**

Charlemagne class

These were the first French battleships armed with two twin mountings, as was usual in other navies, and the first to have three shafts. Less beamy and lighter in displacement than the Charles Martel class, most observers reckoned they were too small.

It was recognized that early French designs were vulnerable to hull damage, so in the Charlemagne class the belt was extended from 1.5m/5ft below to 45.5cm/18in above the waterline, and in its midships portion it was 355mm/14in thick, tapering to 205mm/8in at the lower edge and 255mm/10in at the extremities. Inboard there was the usual French arrangement of a cofferdam and cellular compartments.

The main 305mm/12in guns were mounted in pivot turrets fore and aft, the 140mm/5.5in guns in a battery at the upper deck level (and two at forecastle deck level) and the tertiary 100mm/4in guns in the superstructure. All the Charlemagne class took part in World War I.

On March 18, 1915, *Gaulois* was engaged and hit by Turkish shore batteries and a single shell hit her port bow below the waterline, tearing off the hull plating. Flooding spread via the ventilation trunking and she had to be beached on Rabbit Island, north of Tenedos. After being refloated she went to Malta for repairs. However, on December 27, 1916, *Gaulois* was on passage from the French base at Corfu to Salonika when the German submarine *UB-47* eluded her escort and torpedoed her: she floated for 25 minutes, sufficient time for most of her crew to be rescued, before settling on an even keel.

Charlemagne was also in the bombardment groups but escaped serious damage, and survived the war to be stricken in 1920.

St Louis served seemingly without distinction or notoriety until she was scrapped in 1933.

TOP: **The French ships looked so big because they were compact. The Charlemagne class were smaller in displacement than their predecessors but more heavily armed.** ABOVE: **Like the British pre-Dreadnoughts, these French ships were relegated to secondary theatres of warfare.** *Gaulois* **was sunk off the Dardanelles, re-floated and sunk again.**

Charlemagne class

Class: *Charlemagne, St Louis, Gaulois.*
Launched 1896
Dimensions: Length – 114m/374ft in
Beam – 20.2m/66ft 5in
Draught – 8.4m/27ft 6in
Displacement: 11,278 tonnes/11,100 tons
Armament: Main – 4 x 305mm/12in,
10 x 140mm/5.5in, and 8 x 100mm/4in guns
Secondary – 20 x 3pdr guns and
2 x 455mm/18in torpedoes
Machinery: 20 Belleville boilers, 3-shafts VTE,
10,810kW/14,500iph
Speed: 18 knots
Complement: 694 men

Iéna class

In general design *Iéna* was an enlarged *Charlemagne* with a complete armoured belt extended above and below the waterline 325mm/12.8in thick amidships and tapering to 230mm/9in at the ends, and there was the usual, French, cellular layer below the armoured deck. The 305mm/12in guns were arranged with the 160mm/6.4in in casemates on the main deck, and the four amidships guns in sponsons over the pronounced tumblehome. Despite being fitted with bilge keels, *Iéna* was known to roll and pitch uncomfortably.

Iéna was one of a list of ships that suffered a spontaneous explosion. The magazine cooling gear had been removed while she was in dry-dock in Toulon, when decomposing nitrocellulose propellant ignited and set light to the after 305mm/12in magazine. The whole after part of the ship was wrecked and the midships section badly damaged, and she was afterwards used as a target.

Suffren, which took four years to complete, differed in that four of her 160mm/6.4in guns were placed in turrets on the upper deck and the rest in casemates. She was hit during the main attack on the Dardanelles on March 18, 1915, when three casemate guns were put out of action and an ammunition fire started. She was reputed to have been saved from explosion because the charges were in metal cases. However, on November 26, 1916, while on her way to refit at Lorient, *Suffren* was torpedoed and sunk by the German submarine *U-52* off the Portuguese coast. There were no survivors.

Henri IV was an experimental ship, not completed until 1903. She had only 1.22m/4ft freeboard over most of her length, except forward where it was built up to normal deck height, and there was the usual cellular layer inboard of the torpedo bulkhead. She had one of the first superfiring turrets, though the blast effects were said to be severe as the muzzle of the 140mm/5.5in gun barrel was too short even to clear the sighting hood of the 275mm/10.8in gun below it. *Henri IV* saw service at Gallipoli, survived World War I and was scrapped in 1921.

LEFT, BELOW LEFT AND BOTTOM: **The three ships seen here,** *Suffren* **(left) and** *Henri IV* **(below left) and** *Iéna* **(bottom), were singletons, built at a time of great change in French design. It was symptomatic that** *Henri IV* **spent over six years from being laid down to completion.**

Iéna class

Class: *Suffren.* Launched 1899
Dimensions: Length – 125.5m/411ft 9in
    Beam – 21.4m/70ft 2in
    Draught – 8.4m/27ft 6in
Displacement: 12,728 tonnes/12,527 tons
Armament: Main – 4 x 305mm/12in, 10 x
    160mm/6.4in and 8 x 100mm/4in guns
    Secondary – 22 x 3pdr guns and
    2 x 455mm/18in torpedoes
Machinery: 24 Niclausse boilers, 3 shafts,
    12,453kW/16,700ihp
Speed: 17.9 knots
Complement: 714 men

Class: *Iéna.* Launched 1898
Dimensions: Length – 122.2m/400ft 9in
Beam – 20.8m/68ft 3in
Draught – 8.4m/27ft 6in
Displacement: 12,050 tonnes/11,860 tons
Armament: Main – 4 x 305mm/12in,
    8 x 160mm/6.4in and 8 x 100mm/4in guns
    Secondary - 20 x 3pdr guns and
    2 x 455mm/18in torpedoes
Machinery: 20 Belleville boilers, 3 shafts,
    12,304kW/16,500ihp
Speed: 18 knots
Complement: 682 men

Class: *Henri IV.* Launched 1899
Dimensions: Length – 108m/354ft 4in
    Beam – 22.2m/72ft 10in
    Draught – 7m/22ft 11in
Displacement: 8,948 tonnes/8,807 tons
Armament: Main – 2 x 275mm/10.8in,
    7 x 140mm/5.5in guns
    Secondary – 12 x 3pdr guns and
    2 x 455mm/18in torpedoes
Machinery: 12 Niclausse boilers, 3 shafts,
    8,575kW/11,500ihp
Speed: 17 knots
Complement: 464 men

LEFT: **At last the French navy was prepared to build big.** *République* **and her sister ship** *Patrie* **were an adequate size, although their design when completed in 1906–8 was obsolescent.**

République class

Class: *République, Patrie.* Launched 1902–3
Dimensions: Length – 133.8m/439ft
 Beam – 24.3m/79ft 7in
 Draught – 8.4m/27ft 7in
Displacement: 14,839 tonnes/14,605 tons
Armament: Main – 4 x 305mm/12in and
 18 x 160mm/6.4in guns
 Secondary – 25 x 3pdr guns and
 2 x 455mm/18in torpedoes
Machinery: 24 Niclausse boilers, 3 shafts,
 13,423kW/18,000ihp
Speed: 19 knots
Complement: 766 men

République class

Previous French designs of pre-Dreadnought battleships had been poor compromises between armament and armour, but in *République* and her sister ships they were at last able to solve their design problem. However, this class took so long to build they were not completed until 1906 and 1908, when Fisher's revolution was well under way.

In appearance, they owed something to the experimental *Henri IV*, with a high forecastle that ran back to the mainmast. Their three funnels, two forward and one well separated aft, and a tall pole mainmast gave them a distinctive appearance. In addition to the armoured belt and decks the cellular construction that the French preferred consisted of a short cofferdam, a passageway and coal bunkers, before reaching a central passageway. The main guns were placed high in the ship and there were six twin-turreted 160mm/6.4in guns at the forecastle deck level. Both vessels saw out World War I in the Mediterranean, when *Patrie's* casemate 160mm/6.4in guns were mounted ashore in Salonica. Both were stricken in the 1920s.

Liberté class

The *Liberté* was very similar to the *République*, the main difference being the secondary armament of ten 190mm/7.6in guns, arranged six in single turrets at forecastle deck level, and two in casemates forward at upper deck and aft at main deck levels.

The armour was similar to the *République*, but following the French practice of farming out construction to different yards all three ships differed slightly in their displacement and draught. The Liberté class also had improved anti-torpedo 9pdr and 3pdr guns, similar to those later fitted in *République*.

Liberté blew up in Toulon harbour in 1911, the cause again being spontaneous ignition of decomposing nitrocellulose propellant, this time in one of the forward 190mm/7.6in magazines. The flooding arrangements were found to be inadequate and the resulting fire and explosion affected all the fore part of the ship. She was a total loss, although the wreck was not raised and scrapped until 1925.

The other three ships stayed in the Mediterranean during World War I and were stricken in the early 1920s.

Liberté class

Class: *Democratie, Justice, Liberté, Verite.*
 Launched 1904–7
Dimensions: Length – 133.8m/439ft in
 Beam – 24.3m/79ft 7in
 Draught – 8.35m/27ft 5in
Displacement: 14,722 tonnes/14,489 tons
Armament: Main – 4 x 305mm/12in and
 10 x 190mm/7.6in guns
 Secondary – 13 x 9pdr, 10 x 3pdr guns and
 2 x 455mm/18in torpedoes
Machinery: 22 Belleville boilers, 3 shafts,
 13,795kW/18,500ihp.
 Justice had 24 Niclausse boilers.
Speed: 19 knots
Complement: 739 men

LEFT: **The French were now also building ships in batches, but still farming out individual units to separate yards.** *Liberté* **is therefore typical of her class but there were minor differences between individual ships.**

Danton class

After the 1904 Anglo-French Entente Cordiale, the French navy agreed to concentrate in the Mediterranean, and the Premier Armée Navale consisted of 21 battleships, including four newly commissioned Dreadnoughts and the six Danton class semi-Dreadnoughts. First, the French fleet escorted troop transports from North Africa and by the end of August 1914, 14 French battleships were based at Malta to forestall a breakout from the Adriatic by the Austro-Hungarian fleet. In September they bombarded Cattaro and Lissa, and two pre-Dreadnoughts joined the British squadron watching the Dardanelles to prevent the battlecruiser *Goeben* from breaking out.

Once Italy entered the war in May 1915, the French fleet moved to bases at Brindisi and Corfu. In the winter of 1915/6 the French evacuated the defeated Serbian army from Albania to Salonika, and in spring 1916 took an active part in the Dardanelles campaign. The pre-Dreadnoughts *Gaulois, Bouvet, Charlemagne* and *Suffren* were badly damaged when hidden Turkish guns came into action during the landings on March 18, 1915, and they ran into a minefield. *Bouvet* was sunk.

In December 1916, French warships forced the pro-German Greek government to support Allied policies, landing sailors in Athens, briefly bombarding the city and seizing Greek warships. Later in the war the French navy concentrated its efforts more on anti-submarine warfare and convoy protection, but in 1918 formed part of the Aegean Sea Squadron deployed to prevent a breakout from the Dardanelles by the Turks.

TOP: **By their date these ships are Dreadnoughts, but they incorporated many pre-Dreadnought features, such as a large calibre secondary armament mounted to port and starboard.** ABOVE: **The Dantons were impressive high-sided ships. *Danton* is seen here with her three portside twin 9-in guns trained out.**

The Danton class ships were the first large turbine-engine ships. Compared to République and Liberté class they were another 3,048 tonnes/3,000 tons bigger, the extra displacement being used for a heavier secondary armament rather than speed. Their large batteries of rapid-fire tertiary guns made them useful in the confined waters of the Mediterranean.

The ships fitted with Belleville boilers made slightly more than 20 knots on trials, while the others were a knot slower. During World War I all ships received additional 75mm/3in anti-aircraft guns, and *Condorcet, Vergniaud* and *Voltaire* had their

Danton class

Class: *Danton, Voltaire, Condorcet, Diderot, Mirabeau, Vergniaud.* Launched 1909–10
Dimensions: Length – 144.9m/475ft 5in
Beam – 25.8m/84ft 8in
Draught – 9.2m/30ft 2in
Displacement: 18,612 tonnes/18,318 tons
Armament: Main – 4 x 305mm/12in,
12 x 240mm/9.4in guns
Secondary – 16 x 75mm/2.95in,
10 x 45mm/1.77in guns and
2 x 455mm/18in torpedoes
Machinery: 26 Belleville boilers, 4 shafts (Parsons turbines), 16,778kW/22,500shp
Speed: 19.2 knots
Complement: 681 men

mainmasts shortened in 1918 so they could carry kite balloons. In 1918, the main guns had their range increased from 13,700m/14,983yd to 18,000m/19,690yd and the class were given a fire control system like other Dreadnoughts. All except *Danton* and *Diderot* were off to Athens in December 1916 when *Mirabeau* fired four rounds over the city as part of a pro-Allied demonstration, one of which landed near the Royal Palace.

Danton was zigzagging south-west of Sicily en route to the Allied blockade lines in the Straits of Otranto when, on March 19, 1917, the German submarine *U-64* torpedoed her. *Danton* was carrying drafts to the fleet greatly in excess of her own crew but fortunately she took some 45 minutes to sink and 296 men were saved. However, 806 men were lost, making this the worst disaster of the war at sea for the French navy.

Voltaire was also off Athens in December 1916 with four of her sisters, and in the Aegean in 1918. On the night of October 10/11, 1918, near Antikythira, she was twice torpedoed by the German *UB-48* but survived with little damage. On November 13, 1918, she was part of the Allied fleet which anchored off Constantinople.

Vergniaud and *Mirabeau* entered the Black Sea to operate off the Crimea against the Red Army. There *Mirabeau* ran aground in a snowstorm on February 13, 1919, and was salvaged in April 1919 only after the forward part of the ship including the main gun had been dismantled. She was used for trials and then stricken in 1921, though she and *Vergniaud* continued to be used for explosives experiments afterwards.

Condorcet, Diderot and *Voltaire* were modernized in the 1920s and fitted with improved underwater protection, but from 1927 onwards they served as training ships, and *Diderot* and *Voltaire* were stricken in the 1930s.

TOP: **This stern view shows how similar in size the main and secondary armaments were.** ABOVE: **The layout of the funnel made for easy recognition of the class.** BELOW: **Their appearance changed little during World War I.**

Condorcet became a depot ship at Toulon, where on November 27, 1942, an attempt to blow her up by loyal French officers was botched and she was taken over by the German navy as a barrack ship. In August 1944, she was bombed by an Allied aircraft and sunk only to be re-floated in September 1944. She was sold and broken up in 1945.

LEFT: **Italian naval architects were not burdened with a huge legacy of previous draughtsmanship. Starting from first principles they produced a balanced design like *Italia*.** BELOW: **A sister ship to *Italia*, *Lepanto* had four instead of six funnels in the same balanced layout. *Italia* was later remodelled into the same funnel configuration. These two ships, which were much admired by Fisher, were for some time the largest and fastest in the world, and might be regarded as the forerunner to the battlecruiser type.**

Italia class

The Italian navy recovered slowly from the disaster of the Battle of Lissa in 1866, but built some fine ships. Italian naval architects were talented and open to new ideas, while the navy concentrated on quality rather than quantity, and so in the pre-Dreadnought era was able to rival the British and French navies in the Mediterranean. The turret ships *Duilio* and *Dandolo* when laid down in 1873 were faster at 15 knots and more heavily armed with 450mm/ 17.7in muzzle-loaders than any other battleship. Although ugly ships, they were admired by Jacky Fisher, then in command of the Royal Navy's largest warship, *Inflexible*.

In the 1870s, the Italian engineer Benedetto Brin designed two ships, *Italia* and *Lepanto*, which in many ways were the forerunners of the battlecruiser. Different sources describe these ships as large, fast battleships or strategic cruisers. The 430mm/17in guns were at the limits of gun technology, and Brin dispensed with side armour, building the hulls of iron and steel and covering the sides with wood and zinc. Although they each took some nine years to complete and were relatively weakly armoured, these two ships were for many years in the 1880s the largest and fastest in the world. Each was also capable of embarking a division of infantry.

Italia as built had six funnels, three forward and three aft, but was rebuilt in 1905–8 to look like *Lepanto* with just four funnels. The guns were sited in pairs amidships around a central control tower and an elegant military mast. They were later fitted with more quick-firing guns and two additional torpedo tubes. The single pole mast was also replaced and two shorter ones were fitted. Neither, however, saw any action.

Lepanto was stricken in 1914 and then *Italia* in 1921, after a career as a floating battery, a cereal carrier and a depot ship.

Italia class

Class: *Italia, Lepanto.* Launched 1880–3
Dimensions: Length – 122m/400ft 3in
  Beam – 22.5m/73ft 11in
  Draught – 8.7m/28ft 8in
Displacement: 13,897 tonnes/13,678 tons
Armament: Main – 4 x 430mm/17in and
  7 x 150mm/5.9in guns
Secondary – 4 x 120mm/4.7in guns and
  4 x 355mm/14in torpedoes
Machinery: 24 boiler, 4 shafts, 8,389kW/11,250ihp
Speed: 18 knots
Complement: 669 men

Ruggiero di Lauria class

On March 8, 1880, one of *Duilio's* huge muzzle-loading guns was double-charged in a drill error and blew up. The accident prejudiced the Italian public against large ships and large guns, which members of the government opposed already on the grounds of cost.

The task of designing a successor ship to the Italia class was given to an engineer called Giuseppe Micheli and for once Italian ingenuity failed. Micheli tried various ideas but could only come up with an improved *Duilio* type. The improvements included a forecastle, which the original design had lacked; placing the breech-loading guns in barbettes and better armour, but the class was already obsolete when they were completed in 1888–91.

Francesco Morisini was used as a target and sunk in 1909; her guns were mounted on an Italian monitor used to provide the army with gunfire support. The other two were stricken in 1911. *Andrea Doria* became a floating battery in World War I and was broken up in 1929, but *Ruggiero di Lauria* survived until 1943 as an oil bunker at La Spezia, and was not broken up until 1946.

BELOW LEFT: **The low freeboard of the Ruggiero de Lauria class harked back to former designs and may have only been suitable for the relatively calm waters of the Adriatic.** BELOW RIGHT: **A rare picture of an Italian warship being built on stocks. Given the lack of tide in the Mediterranean and Adriatic it scarcely seems possible that she will reach the sea.** BOTTOM: **Despite their unusual appearance, the Ruggiero di Lauria class were heavily armed ships carrying 430mm/17in guns.**

Ruggiero di Lauria class

Class: *Ruggiero di Lauria, Francesco Morosini, Andrea Doria.* Launched 1884–5

Dimensions: Length – 100m/328ft 1in
Beam – 19.8m/65ft 1in
Draught – 8.3m/27ft 2in

Displacement: 10,045 tonnes/9,886 tons

Armament: Main – 4 x 430mm/17in and
2 x 150mm/6in guns
Secondary – 4 x 120mm/4.7in guns and
2 x 355mm/14in torpedoes

Machinery: 8 boilers, 2 shafts, 7,898kW/10,591ihp

Speed: 16 knots

Complement: 507 men

LEFT: **This photograph shows the 120mm/4.7in guns run out and trained to starboard as they might be when repelling a torpedo-boat attack.**
ABOVE: **Seen in profile the twin side-by-side funnels merge into one and** *Re Umberto*, **seen here, looks like any other pre-Dreadnought.** BELOW: **Freeboard and its consequent seaworthiness did not impinge much upon Italy's considerations of design, but her architects were open to novel ideas such as single and twin funnels.**

Re Umberto class

Benedetto Brin (1833–98) worked until the age of 40 as a naval engineer. In 1873, the Italian navy minister, Simone Pacoret di Saint Bon, made Brin undersecretary of state, and the two men complemented each other; di Saint Bon had the ideas and Brin accomplished them in his designs for Italian warships. When Brin himself became the navy minister, he developed di Saint Bon's ideas and is credited with creating the first organic scheme for the development of the Italian fleet. He had already designed the turret ships *Duilio* and *Dandolo* and Italy's first battleships, the Italia class, when he temporarily abandoned big ship designs in favour of smaller warships.

The Italian warship-building industry was insignificant when Brin took office, but under his guidance it made rapid progress. During his time, he helped create private shipyards and machine shops, and introduced the indigenous manufacture of armour, steel plates and guns. Brin's appointment as minister for foreign affairs in 1892 was probably an over-promotion, but his previous achievements qualify him as the creator of the Italian navy.

Two ships were ordered in 1883, and when Brin became navy minister for the second time he decided to build a third ship of the same class. The layout showed Brin's hand: a tall central mast, and a symmetrical disposition of the funnels and turrets fore and aft. The forward funnels were, however, a pair that sat abreast of each other. In Brin's design he continued to sacrifice armour for speed and armament, and the armoured belt of the Re Umberto class was only 100mm/4in thick. These ships, like many Italian and French ships of the period, were a long time in building and when they were complete, they rapidly became obsolete. Nevertheless all three ships survived World War I.

Re Umberto was laid up in 1912 but was later used as a depot ship and as a floating battery. When the Italian navy planned to force the Austro-Hungarian port of Pola, she was fitted as an assault ship, stripped of her former armament in favour of 75mm/3in guns and trench mortars. The idea was that she should

rush the harbour followed by a flotilla of small craft, but the war ended before this scheme could be put into effect. *Sicilia* became a repair ship and *Sardegna* a depot ship. All three were stricken in the 1920s.

Re Umberto class

Class: *Re Umberto, Sicilia, Sardegna.* Launched 1888–91
Dimensions: Length – 122m/400ft 3in
Beam – 23.4m/76ft 10in
Draught – 9.3m/30ft 6in
Displacement: 13,892 tonnes/13,673 tons
Armament: Main – 4 x 340mm/13.5in and 16 x 120mm/4.7in guns
Secondary – 16 x 6pdr, 10 x 37mm/1.46in guns and 5 x 450mm/17.7in torpedoes
Machinery: 18 boilers, 2 shafts, 11,180kW/15,000ihp
Speed: 20 knots
Complement: 733 men

Ammiraglio di Saint Bon class

Italian strategists had not fixed on the size or type of ship they wanted, so for their next class of ship they were driven by the government, which wanted ships to be as small and as cheap as possible. So when di Saint Bon died, Brin returned temporarily and he proposed a medium-sized ship with relatively small 255mm/10in guns. The design showed the symmetry of earlier

Italian ships and followed the style that the British had started with *Collingwood* and Brin had copied with *Re Umberto*: two twin guns forward and two aft. The ships took some eight years to complete, but not even Brin could not save the design from its inherent weaknesses: the ships were too slow at 18 knots and small, and their freeboard was only 2.7m/9ft. Overall they were too weak to

ABOVE: **Italian naval architects were beginning to be influenced by overseas developments, but** *Ammiraglio di Saint Bon* **still has the unusual arrangement of a single, central mast.** BELOW LEFT: *Emanuel Filiberto* **at the end of World War I.**

stand in the line of battle and too slow to catch even a cruiser. They saw limited service in World War I and were not broken up until 1920.

Ammiraglio di Saint Bon class		
Class: *Ammiraglio di Saint Bon, Emanuel Filiberto.* Launched 1897		
Dimensions: Length – 105m/344ft 6in		
Beam – 21.1m/69ft 3in		
Draught – 7.7m/25ft 2in		
Displacement: 10,244 tonnes/10,082 tons		
Armament: Main – 4 x 255mm/10in and 8 x 150mm/6in guns		
Secondary – 8 x 55mm/2.24in guns and 4 x 450mm/17.7in torpedoes		
Machinery: 12 boilers, 2 shafts, 10,664kW/14,300ihp		
Speed: 18 knots		
Complement: 557/567 men		

Regina Margherita class

The Italian navy wanted a ship to match the Austro-Hungarian Habsburg class, and so Brin's last effort was the Regina Margherita class. These were intended to be modern, fast and well-armed ships, even at the expense of armoured protection, as in so many Italian designs. With this class the Italians reverted to a larger battleship design although the result was smaller than other contemporary, foreign battleships. Symmetry was carried to an extreme with two funnels amidships, fore and aft, two matching pole masts, and forward and after combined control towers and bridges. Unlike their

immediate predecessors the Ammiraglio di Saint Bon class, which could burn coal or oil, these ships could only use coal. Brin died while the class was under construction and the second ship was named after him.

On September 27, 1915, while in Brindisi harbour, *Benedetto Brin* suffered a fire and exploded killing 450 of her crew including the Italian admiral, an act which was later blamed upon Austrian saboteurs, but was more likely an internal explosion. On December 11, 1916, *Regina Margherita* was sunk off Valona by mines laid by the successful German submarine minelayer *UC-14*.

ABOVE: **The high sides and massive central superstructure on 13,209 tonnes/13,000 tons displacement showing perhaps some French design influence on** *Regina Margherita*. BELOW: **The ship's company lined up for their photograph.** BELOW LEFT: **A stern view of this fine ship in 1910. In profile they looked like full-grown battleships.**

Regina Margherita class

Class: *Regina Margherita, Benedetto Brin.* Launched 1901

Dimensions: Length – 130m/426ft 6in
Beam – 23.8m/78ft 2in
Draught – 8.8m/28ft 11in

Displacement: 13,427 tonnes/13,215 tons

Armament: Main – 4 x 305mm/12in and
4 x 205mm/8in guns
Secondary – 20 x 75mm/3in guns and
4 x 450mm/17.7in torpedoes

Machinery: 28 boilers, 2 shafts.
16,249kW/21,790ihp

Speed: 20 knots

Complement: 812 men

Regina Elena class

Vittorio Cuniberti succeeded Brin as the leading Italian ship designer and he was tasked with planning a ship with 12 205mm/8in guns, moderate armour and a speed of 22 knots. Cuniberti produced a design with two single 305mm/12in guns in addition to the required 12 205mm/8in guns.

Cuniberti was also first to produce a design for an all-big-gun battleship. However, such a ship was too ambitious for the Italian navy even given its record of innovation. Instead Cuniberti was given permission to publish an article abroad, and in 1903 *Jane's Fighting Ships* printed "An Ideal Battleship for the British Fleet", in which Cuniberti proposed a warship of 17,273 tonnes/ 17,000 tons armed with 12 305mm/12in

guns in single and double turrets, with 305mm/12in armour (which would certainly have been unusual for the Italian navy) and high speed of 24 knots. An article by Cuniberti three years earlier in *Marine Rundschau* entitled "*Ein neuer Schlachtschifftypus*" had gone unnoticed. However, his *Jane's* article was read in London just when the British Admiralty, where Jacky Fisher was First Sea Lord, was considering the lessons learned from the Battle of Tsushima and the design of its next generation of battleships. It is therefore clear that Cuniberti's ideas contributed to the design for Dreadnought.

Meanwhile in Italy, Cuniberti's design for a battleship that was faster than any British or French ship and stronger than

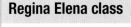

Regina Elena class

Class: *Regina Elena, Vittorio Emanuele, Roma, Napoli.* Launched 1904–7

Dimensions: Length – 132.6m/435ft
Beam – 22.4m/73ft 6in
Draught – 7.9m/25ft 11in

Displacement: 12,751 tonnes/12,550 tons

Armament: Main – 2 x 305mm/12in and
12 x 205mm/8in guns
Secondary – 16 x 75mm/3in guns and
2 x 450mm/17.7in torpedoes

Machinery: 28 boilers, 2 shafts.
14,392kW/19,300ihp

Speed: 22 knots

Complement: 742 men

---

any armoured cruiser became the successful Regina Elena class. Two ships were authorized in 1901 and two more the following year. They were elegant ships with fine lines and scalloped fore-ends to provide a forward arc of fire for the 205mm/8in guns which were all mounted in turrets, with a single turret-mounted 305mm/12in gun at each end, and three tall funnels, although these were later cut down with some positive effect on the ship's speed.

LEFT: **The Regina Elena class was armed with two single 305mm/12in guns, mounted one forward and one aft.** BELOW LEFT: *Regina Elena, Roma* and *Napoli* **on manoeuvres off Venice in 1910.** BELOW: *Regina Elena* **at anchor at Messina in December 1908 after the earthquake there.**

Sissoi Veliki

The Russian navy built a number of powerful, and in some cases innovative, ironclad warships after the Russian War 1854–6. The Russians also participated in every stage of ship evolution from the screw line-of-battle ship, broadside and central battery ship, to the turret ship, coast defence monitor, and coast defence turret ship. They first put 300mm/12in guns in the turret ship *Petr Veliki* (1869) and in the circular coast defence ships *Novgorod* and *Vice Admiral Popov* in 1872–4, and this became the standard armament for successive classes of barbette and turret ships from then on.

In 1892 the Russian navy laid down its first battleship of the modern era at the New Admiralty yard in St Petersburg. *Sissoi Veliki* was a small ship for her armament, presumably intended for operations in the Baltic and to be the largest warship of any navy bordering on the Baltic coast, when the Swedes were still seen as the Russian navy's traditional enemies. However she had a high freeboard, was ocean-going and twice deployed from the Baltic to the Far East.

Sissoi Veliki suffered a serious accident in 1897 when one of her main guns fired before the breech was closed, but she was repaired in time to be part of the allied naval forces off China in 1900 during the Boxer Rebellion. The international fleet consisted of American, Austrian, British, French, German, Italian, Japanese and Russian ships under the command of the British admiral, Sir Edward Seymour. Seymour had landed sailors and marines to defend the embassies in Peking and these had become cut off. As part of the relief operations, the allied fleet bombarded the Taku forts at the entrance to the Peiho River and a squadron of ships forced their way upstream.

Sissoi Veliki's armoured belt was 405mm/16in to 305mm/12in thick and the turret armour 305mm/12in, which were to prove their worth at the Battle of Tsushima on May 27, 1905. She was one of six battleships lost there – the greatest number in any single battle of the steam age. The Russian pre-Dreadnoughts *Sevastapol, Kniaz Suvarov, Osliabia, Borodino, Imperator Alexander III* and

ABOVE: **A picture from the British Admiralty files dated 1910 of** *Sissoi Veliki.* **Despite the small size of these ships, Russian designers managed to fit them with two double turrets.** *Sissoi Veliki* **also made two voyages to the Far East, though on the second occasion to defeat at the Battle of Tsushima.**

Navarin were sunk by Japanese guns and torpedoes. *Sissoi Veliki* was hit by about 12 large-calibre shells, suffered serious bow damage near the waterline and was torpedoed in the stern, but did not sink until her crew scuttled her.

Sissoi Veliki

Class: *Sissoi Veliki.* Launched 1894
Dimensions: Length – 107.2m/351ft 10in
Beam – 20.7m/68ft in
Draught – 7.8m/25ft 6in
Displacement: 10,567 tonnes/10,400 tons
Armament: Main – 4 x 305mm/12in and
6 x 150mm/6in guns
Secondary – 12 x 3pdr, 18 x 1pdr guns and
6 x 455mm/18in torpedoes
Machinery: 12 Belleville boilers, 2 shafts,
6,400kW/8,500ihp
Speed: 16 knots
Complement: 586 men

Admiral Ushakov class

The Admiral Ushakov class were built as part of a Baltic naval arms race, and in particular to counter the Swedish coast defence ships of the Svea and Oden classes. Mounting four 255mm/ 10in guns on a displacement of under 5,080 tonnes/5,000 tons (and 15 per cent overweight compared to their design) they were hardly suitable for a voyage to the Pacific in 1904–5, although some sources say that these ships were good sea-keepers.

The three ships differed slightly: *Admiral Seniavin* was the heaviest ship and drew more water, while *Admiral General Graf Apraksin* had only one gun fitted in the after turret. The armour on all three ships was only 150mm/6in to 230mm/9in thick.

The gun was unsuccessful: designed for the Russian army and navy, both to be fitted in ships and mounted in coastal batteries, the naval version was too lightly constructed, suffered from weak barrels and thus had poor ballistic qualities. The land version had better ballistic qualities but it had primitive

mountings which restricted its rate of fire. Nevertheless four guns were mounted in the Black Sea battleship *Rostislav* in 1898. The Russian army had a battery of these guns at Port Arthur by 1904, and they became the main coast defence guns of the Russian navy until World War I.

At the Battle of Tsushima in 1905 *Admiral Ushakov* fought bravely. She was hit twice below the waterline and once above by Japanese heavy shells, and was left behind by the Russian fleet. The next day, May 28, out of ammunition and surrounded by Japanese armoured cruisers, *Admiral Ushakov* was scuttled by her own crew.

Admiral Seniavin was badly damaged on May 27 and surrendered to the Japanese the next day. Renamed

BELOW: **The proportions of *General Admiral Graf Apraksin* make her look like a lake steamer. She was not designed for the oceanic voyage to the Battle at Tsushima in 1905.** RIGHT: ***Admiral Seniavin* at speed. The clouds of smoke reveal the logistic and strategic weakness of these coal-burners.**

Admiral Ushakov class

Class: *Admiral Ushakov, Admiral Seniavin, General Admiral Graf Apraksin.* Launched 1893–6
Dimensions: Length – 87.3m/286ft 6in
Beam – 15.85m/52ft
Draught – 5.9m/19ft 6in
Displacement: 5,051 tonnes/4,971 tons
Armament: Main – 4 x 255mm/10in and
4 x 120mm/4.7in guns
Secondary – 6 x 3pdr, 10 x 1pdr guns and
4 x 380mm/15in torpedoes
Machinery: 8 boilers, 2 shafts, 4,288kW/5,750ihp
Speed: 16 knots
Complement: 404 men

Mishima, she remained in service with the Imperial Japanese Navy until 1928. *General Admiral Graf Apraksin* also surrendered, and served as the *Okinoshima* until being scrapped in 1926.

Petropavlovsk class

Named after important Russian victories on land, the Petropavlovsk class were flush-decked ships with an appreciable tumblehome. Like earlier Russian battleships they were overweight, in this case by about 10 per cent compared to their design. However, they followed what had now become a standard pattern with twin 305mm/12in turrets, one forward, one aft. Eight of the 150mm/6in guns were mounted in turrets and four in a central battery, port and starboard. Like earlier Russian ships they were seemingly well armoured with belts tapering from 305mm/12in to 205mm/8in thick.

All three ships formed part of the Russian First Pacific Squadron based at Port Arthur and were there at the outbreak of the Russo-Japanese War. *Petropavlovsk* struck a mine and blew up on April 13, 1904, with heavy loss of life including the Commander-in-Chief of the Russian Pacific Fleet, Admiral Makarov.

The other ships of the class proved to be much more resilient. At the Battle of the Yellow Sea on August 10, 1904, *Poltava* survived being hit by over a dozen rounds of 305mm/12in and 205mm/8in shells. She was hit again at the siege of Port Arthur with howitzer shells fired by the Japanese army, caught fire and sank. She was raised by the Japanese and commissioned as the *Tango*. In 1916 she was sold back to the Russians and this time named *Tchesma* (the name *Poltava* having already been taken for a Russian Dreadnought-type) and sent to the White Sea. *Sevastopol* was also mined on June 23, 1904, and again on August 23, 1904, but survived both incidents. She sustained several hits during the Battle of the Yellow Sea, and at the siege of Port Arthur, after being hit five times by 280mm/11in shells, sallied from the harbour. Her captain, Essen, took her to a new anchorage outside the harbour but close inshore and there, behind boom defences, she survived nightly attack for seven nights in December 1904 by Japanese torpedo boats. Three torpedoes exploded in her nets without causing much damage to *Sevastopol*, but a fourth torpedo hit her stern. On January 2, 1905, Essen had *Sevastopol* towed into deep water where he scuttled her.

The Russian ships in the Far East were generally courageously fought, and proved themselves capable of sustaining much damage. The Russian fleet owed its defeats, through the Russo-Japanese War, more to the lack of logistic support than to a want of bravery, until by 1905 morale had also begun to collapse.

BELOW: ***Petropavlovsk*** **and her two sisters formed the Russian First Pacific Squadron and were in the Far East when the Russo-Japanese war broke out. Despite their limitations they fought bravely but were inevitably overwhelmed by the Japanese.**

Petropavlovsk class

Class: *Petropavlovsk, Poltava, Sevastopol.* Launched 1894–5

Dimensions: Length – 112.5m/369ft
Beam – 21.3m/70ft
Draught – 7.8m/25ft 6in

Displacement: 11,536 tonnes/11,354 tons

Armament: Main – 4 x 305mm/12in and 12 x 150mm/6in guns
Secondary – 12 x 3pdr, 28 x 1pdr guns, 6 x 455mm/18in torpedoes and 60 mines

Machinery: 12 boilers, 2 shafts, 8,389kW/11,250ihp

Speed: 16.5 knots

Complement: 632 men

Rostislav

The battleship *Rostislav*, laid down in 1894, is notable for being the first oil-fired battleship in the world, although she was also capable of burning coal. Originally intended to be a copy of the *Sissoi Veliki*, she was supplied with rather unsatisfactory 255mm/10in guns and the Nicolaiev yard on the Black Sea made other changes. Constructed to the same length as *Sissoi Veliki* she emerged with two turrets in the contemporary layout, but with an extra two 205mm/8in guns in the central battery. She also displaced about 1,524 tonnes/1,500 tons less than *Sissoi Veliki*. Although slow and weak, she saw plenty of action in World War I.

Learning the lessons of the Battle of Tsushima, the Russian Black Sea battleship squadron was formed into a single firing-unit of 305mm/12in-gunned ships, from which *Rostislav* was excluded. The fall of her 255mm/10in rounds were so different from the larger shells of the other battleships, and potentially confusing to the fire controller, that she was actually forbidden from firing tactically on the same target.

However, as early as November 1914 *Rostislav* was used to bombard Turkish shore facilities at Zonguldak, and she was present at the first action of World War I when battleships engaged each other. As the Russian Black Sea fleet was returning to Sevastopol on November 18, it was intercepted by the German-manned and Turkish-flagged *Goeben* and *Breslau*. While *Goeben* duelled with the battleship *Evstafi* and her sisters, *Rostislav* engaged the *Breslau* and drove her to the disengaged side of *Goeben*.

Rostislav returned several times in 1915 to bombard facilities and prohibit sea traffic on the south coast of Turkey, and in 1916 she was employed supporting the Russian troops in the Caucasus. On September 2, 1916, while at anchor in the Romanian port of Constanta, she was hit by a bomb dropped from a German seaplane.

At the end of the war *Rostislav* was captured alongside by advancing armies under German command, but retaken by British and French forces supporting the Whites during the Russian revolution.

ABOVE: **In theory the Black Sea in World War I should have been dominated by the German battlecruiser *Goeben*, but the Russian Black Sea Fleet of pre-Dreadnoughts were well handled and were able to operate widely throughout the theatre.**

Her internal machinery had been wrecked, so in November 1920 *Rostislav* was grounded off Kerch as a fixed battery. *Rostislav* survived until 1930 when she was broken up, being the last surviving battleship of the Imperial Russian Navy.

Rostislav

Class: *Rostislav*. Launched 1896
Dimensions: Length – 107.2m/351ft 10in
 Beam – 20.73m/68ft
 Draught - 6.7m/22ft
Displacement: 9,022 tonnes/8,880 tons
Armament: Main – 4 x 255mm/10in and
 8 x 150mm/6in guns
 Secondary – 20 x 3pdr guns and
 6 x 455mm/18in torpedoes
Machinery: 12 boilers, 2 shafts.
 6,488kW/8,700ihp
Speed: 16 knots
Complement: 650 men

Peresviet class

The Peresviet class with their three funnels, length and extended forecastle deck, and French-style tumblehome, French-type turrets, weak armament and miserable speed were thoroughly unsatisfactory. Besides two twin 255mm/10in turrets they had five 150mm/6in guns in casemates port and starboard and a bow chaser. The *Peresviet* and *Osliabia* were built by the New Admiralty yard in St Petersburg and *Pobieda* was built by the Baltic Works in St Petersburg and incorporated some minor changes. The main belt of armour, Russian-made "Harvey-ized" in the first units, and steel alloy in *Pobieda,* was 95m/312ft long and 2.44m/8ft deep.

Peresviet was seriously damaged at the Battle of the Yellow Sea. The Japanese captured a hill overlooking Port Arthur and used it to spot the fall of shot of the advancing army's 280mm/11in howitzers. *Peresviet* was hit by at least 23 rounds and was scuttled on December 7, 1904.

The Japanese raised her and named her *Sagami*. In 1916 Russia needed warships to guard her White Sea ports against the Germans and *Sagami* was repurchased and given back her old name. However, she ran aground off Vladivostok on May 26, 1916, and stuck fast for two months. Then on January 4, 1917, *Peresviet* struck a mine laid by the German minelayer *U-73* and sank 16km/10 miles from Port Said, this time for good. Few ships can claim to have been sunk twice.

Osliabia was in the Baltic when the Russo-Japanese war broke out, and was sent to the Far East as part of the Russian Second Pacific Squadron. She was sunk by gunfire at the Battle of Tsushima. During the Russo-Japanese War *Pobieda* struck a mine on April 13, 1904, but the force of the explosion was

BELOW: ***Pobieda* was mined in 1904 and heavily shelled at Port Arthur. However, she was raised and served on as the Japanese *Suwo* until 1922.**

largely absorbed by a coal bunker and she was repaired in time to be present at the Battle of the Yellow Sea in August 1904. She was finally sunk on December 7, 1904, at Port Arthur. Despite 21 280mm/11in howitzer hits, the Japanese were able to raise her and bring her into service as the *Suwo*. She was finally scrapped in 1922.

Peresviet class

Class: *Peresviet, Osliabia, Pobieda.* Launched 1898–1900

Dimensions: Length – 132.3m/434ft
Beam – 21.8m/71ft 6in
Draught – 7.9m/26ft

Displacement: 12,887 tonnes/12,683 tons

Armament: Main – 4 x 255mm/10in and
11 x 150mm/6in guns
Secondary – 20 x 11pdr, 20 x 3pdr,
8 x 1pdr guns and 5 x 380mm/15in torpedoes

Machinery: 32 Belleville boilers, 3 shafts.
11,186kW/15,000ihp

Speed: 18 knots

Complement: 752 men

LEFT: The battleship *Potemkin*, also known under other names, was made famous by Sergei Eisenstein's classic black and white film of the 1905 mutiny onboard which presaged the Russian Revolution. Although she may have flown as many as five different national flags, it is as *Potemkin* that she will always be known.

Potemkin

The pre-Dreadnought *Kniaz Potemkin Tavricheski* is universally known as the battleship *Potemkin* and for the mutiny which took place aboard on June 25, 1905. Following "Bloody Sunday", when Cossacks had savagely suppressed a protest march on the Winter Palace in St Petersburg on January 22, 1905, the Black Sea port of Odessa remained calm until strikes were called that spring. Socialists had been agitating in the fleet since 1903, but *Potemkin* was regarded as one of the most loyal of ships. However, a mutiny was planned during gunnery exercises, the eventual cause being a refusal to eat maggot-infested meat. *Potemkin*'s captain assured his men that the meat was edible while his second-in-command threatened to shoot 12 sailors chosen at random. There were shouts, small arms were seized and within a few minutes seven officers had been killed and their bodies thrown over the side.

A People's Committee took the ship to Odessa, where the mutineers threatened to bombard the city. However, after several hundred pro-mutiny demonstrators were massacred by Cossacks near the Richelieu Steps,

Potemkin's guns remained silent because the mutineers did not know who to fire on. That night rioting broke out and some 6,000 people were killed by soldiers and looters.

When the barbette ships *Georgi Pobiedonsets* and *Dvenadtsat Apostolov*, and the turret ship *Tri Sviatitelia* approached Odessa, *Potemkin* ordered them to "Surrender or we fire" and the Russian admiral retired to join his commander-in-chief at Tendra Island. When the squadron returned, reinforced by the battleship *Rostislav* and the barbette ship *Sinop*, *Potemkin* steamed out again and this time the barbette ship *Georgi Pobiedonsets* surrendered to mutineers onboard and returned to Odessa with the *Potemkin*.

Over the summer the mutiny subsided and *Potemkin* took refuge in nearby Constanta, Romania, where she was scuttled in shallow water and the crew stole away. By July 11, *Potemkin* had been pumped out and towed back into Russian waters. The mutiny that foreshadowed the Russian Revolution by 12 years was over. In October the Tsar exorcised *Potemkin*'s black history by renaming her *Pantelimon*, and she saw

service in World War I until in April 1917 the Provisional Government renamed her *Potemkin* and, a month later, *Boretz zu Svobodu*. She changed hands several times as independence-seeking Ukrainians, the German army, and counter-revolutionaries occupied Sevastopol. While the British temporarily held Sevastopol, men from the cruiser *Calypso* disabled her engines on April 25, 1919, and in November 1920 the Red Army finally seized control.

Potemkin, immortalized in Sergei Eisenstein's classic silent film *Battleship Potemkin*, was broken up in 1922.

Potemkin

Class: *Kniaz Potemkin Tavricheski*. Launched 1900
Dimensions: Length – 115.4m/378ft 6in
  Beam – 22.25m/73ft
  Draught – 8.2m/27ft
Displacement: 12,784 tonnes/12,582 tons
Armament: Main – 4 x 305mm/12in and
  16 x 150mm/6in guns
  Secondary – 14 x 11pdr guns and
  5 x 380mm/15in torpedoes
Machinery: 22 Belleville boilers, 2 shafts,
  7,904kW/10,600ihp
Speed: 16.5 knots
Complement: 750 men

LEFT: *Retvisan*, another Russian ship which was fought bravely and survived the Russo-Japanese War until sunk by the besieging artillery.

Retvisan

These two similar ships were ordered from foreign yards as the Imperial Russian Navy built up its three fleets, in the Baltic, the Black Sea and the Pacific. *Retvisan* was a three-funnelled, flush-deck ship, while the *Tsessarevitch,* though similar in length and displacement, had two funnels and her pronounced tumblehome gave away her French origins. They had similar main armament, but *Retvisan*'s 150mm/6in guns were mounted four in casemates and eight in a main deck battery. *Tsessarevitch* had her 150mm/6in guns in turrets and she was slightly more heavily armoured. Undoubtedly they were the best Russian battleships to date, and they were sent to join the Russian fleet based at Port Arthur. There they were joined by the battleships *Petropavlovsk, Poltava, Sevastopol, Pobieda* and *Peresviet* as well as many cruisers, gunboats and auxiliaries.

Retvisan

Class: *Retvisan*. Launched 1900
Dimensions: Length – 117.9m/386ft 8in
 Beam – 22.2m/72ft 8in
 Draught – 7.9m/26ft
Displacement: 13,107 tonnes/12,900 tons
Armament: Main – 4 x 305mm/12in and
 12 x 150mm/6in guns
 Secondary – 20 x 11pdr, 24 x 11pdr, 24 x 2pdr,
 8 x 1pdr guns 6 x 380mm/15in torpedoes
 and 45 mines
Machinery: 24 Niclausse boilers, 2 shafts,
 12,677kW/17,000ihp
Speed: 18 knots
Complement: 738 men

Tsessarevitch

LEFT: *Tsessarevitch*, onboard which the Russian Admiral Vitgeft lost his life when a Japanese shell struck the bridge during the Battle of the Yellow Sea in August 1904.

Tsessarevitch

Class: *Tsessarevitch*. Launched 1901
Dimensions: Length – 118.5m/388ft 9in
 Beam – 23.2m/76ft 1in
 Draught – 7.9m/26ft
Displacement: 13,122 tonnes/12,915 tons
Armament: Main – 4 x 305mm/12in,
 12 x 150mm/6in guns
 Secondary – 20 x 11pdr, 20 x 3pdr guns,
 4 x 380mm/15in torpedoes and 45 mines
Machinery: 20 Belleville boilers, 2 shafts,
 12,304kW/16,500ihp
Speed: 18.5 knots
Complement: 782 men

Japan broke diplomatic relations with Russia on February 6, 1904, and two Russian ships were sunk at sea on February 8, although war was not declared when on February 8 and 9, Japanese destroyers attempted to "Copenhagen" the Russian ships in Port Arthur, which was un-expecting and gaily lit. Of 20 torpedoes fired, two reached *Retvisan* and *Tsessarevitch*, which ran aground, though both were soon raised and repaired. Despite its disorder the *Tsessarevitch* steamed out the next day to thwart a major Japanese attack.

Later, when the fleets met on August 10, 1904, in the Battle of the Yellow Sea, both sides concentrated fire on the head of the other's line, the battleships *Mikasa* and *Tsessarevitch* respectively. A dozen 305mm/12in rounds crashed into *Tsessarevitch*, killing Rear Admiral Vitgeft and hitting the control tower, causing *Tsessarevitch* to veer out of control. She was later interned in Kiao Chau, a German concession on the Chinese coast.

Retvisan was also hit nearly a score of times but managed to return to Port Arthur where she was besieged with the rest of the Russian fleet and sunk by howitzers of the Japanese army on December 6, 1904. She was raised and repaired by the Japanese navy and commissioned as the *Hizen*, the only American-built battleship in the steam age to be captured by an enemy or to have flown two flags. She was sunk as a target in 1924.

In World War I, *Tsessarevitch* served in the Baltic and was engaged by the German Dreadnought *Kronprinz* on October 17, 1917, but escaped with only two hits. She was scrapped in 1922.

Borodino class

The five battleships of the Borodino class took the *Tsessarevitch* as their model. However, post-battle analysis of the Russo-Japanese war revealed some serious flaws in the French design. The class had a very pronounced tumblehome, with the hull sides curved sharply inward from the waterline, and they proved to be extraordinarily manoeuvrable, but under certain conditions of flooding the centre of gravity of these ships could change rapidly. This created instability and a large overturning momentum, just as the French battleship, *Bouvet,* demonstrated when she capsized after striking a mine off the Dardanelles in March 1915.

Previous Russian warships, whatever their defects, stood up well to battle damage, and the Borodinos, though their armoured belt was thinner and narrower than in the *Tsessarevitch* prototype, also sustained a great deal of damage before four of them succumbed at the Battle of Tsushima.

Borodino, Imperator Alexander III, Orel and *Kniaz Suvarov* were all at the Battle of Tsushima and in theory these modern ships should have acquitted themselves

well, but material weaknesses and perhaps human exhaustion made these an ill-fated group of ships. The Russians fought their ships hard, but as *Kniaz Suvarov* led the line she became the first target for the Japanese gunners. When her steering gear was damaged, she was forced out of line, and repeatedly hit by shellfire, torpedoed and sank.

Imperator Alexander III took the lead but was soon enveloped in flames and began to list heavily from a hit in the bows. This caused flooding and she later capsized. *Borodino*'s end was even quicker and more dramatic: she suffered a magazine explosion and blew up.

Orel's superstructure was badly damaged and although she survived the day, she surrendered the following day. Once repaired, *Orel* served the Japanese as *Iwami* until being scrapped in 1922.

Only the last ship of the class, *Slava*, was not ready and so did not sail for the Far East. In World War I she fought the German Dreadnought *König* off Moon Sound in the Gulf of Riga on October 17, 1917, when she flooded so much that she grounded and was scuttled by torpedo. The wreck was broken up in 1935.

ABOVE: **The Borodino class was a successful development of *Tsessarevitch* and their presence gave some homogeneity to the Russian line at the Battle of Tsushima. Only *Slava* was not ready in time to steam to the Far East, but she gave a good account of herself in the Baltic in World War I. At Tsushima *Borodino*, seen here, blew up after a shell hit a magazine. *Slava*, a sister ship, had more success against a German Dreadnought in World War I, but ran aground and was sunk by her own side.**

Borodino class

Class: *Borodino, Imperator Alexander III, Orel, Kniaz Suvarov, Slava.* Launched 1901–3

Dimensions: Length – 121m/397ft
Beam – 23.2m/76ft 2in
Draught – 8m/26ft 2in

Displacement: 13,733 tonnes/13,516 tons

Armament: Main – 4 x 305mm/12in and
12 x 150mm/6in guns
Secondary – 20 x 11pdr, 20 x 3pdr guns and
4 x 380mm/15in torpedoes

Machinery: 20 Belleville boilers, 2 shafts,
12,155kW/16,300ihp

Speed: 18 knots

Complement: 835 men

LEFT: **The Russians learned valuable lessons from the Battle of Tsushima and when they next faced battle *Evstafi* and *Ioann Zlatoust* acquitted themselves well.**

Evstafi class

Evstafi class

Class: *Evstafi, Ioann Zlatoust.* Launched 1906
Dimensions: Length – 118m/387ft 3in
　　Beam – 22.6m/74ft
　　Draught – 8.2m/27ft
Displacement: 13,046 tonnes/12,840 tons
Armament: Main – 4 x 305mm/12in,
　　4 x 205mm/8in and 12 x 150mm/6in guns
　　Secondary – 14 x 11pdr and 6 x 3pdr guns and
　　3 x 455mm/18in torpedoes
Machinery: 22 Belleville boilers, 2 shafts,
　　8,054kW/10,800ihp
Speed: 16.5 knots
Complement: 879 men

Generally similar to *Potemkin* and laid down in 1898, these two ships spent some time on the slips while the Russians considered the lessons of the Russo-Japanese War. As a result their armour was improved, especially to the upper deck which was increased to 205mm/8in. The trend towards larger guns was followed and the Evstafis were fitted with 205mm/8in guns. Later in World War I they were also fitted with additional anti-aircraft guns.

The Russian navy as a whole learned other lessons from the Russo-Japanese War, and the Russians developed a system whereby the centre ship of a squadron of three would control the fire of all ships. Equipment and procedures for transmitting the range and correction data between ships were devised and the range-tables for all major guns were revised. New shells with more reliable and predictable trajectories were designed and gun mountings improved,

including smoke-extraction fans to keep the turrets clear. With these gunnery improvements and more thorough training, *Evstafi* and *Ioann Zlatoust* formed the core of a squadron which acquitted itself well when it came up against the more recent *Goeben*.

Imperator Pavel class

LEFT: **The last pre-Dreadnoughts of the Russian navy seen at anchor together in the Baltic.**

Imperator Pavel class

Class: *Imperator Pavel, Andrei Peroswanni.*
　　Launched 1906–7
Dimensions: Length – 140.2m/460ft
　　Beam – 24.4m/80ft
　　Draught – 8.2m/27ft
Displacement: 17,679 tonnes/17,400 tons
Armament: Main – 4 x 305mm/12in,
　　14 x 205mm/8in and 12 x 120mm/4.7in guns
　　Secondary – 4 x 3pdr guns and
　　3 x 455mm/18in torpedoes
Machinery: 22 Belleville boilers, 2 shafts,
　　13,423kW/18,000ihp
Speed: 17.5 knots
Complement: 933men

These were the last pre-Dreadnoughts to be built for the Imperial Russian navy and showed all the lessons of the Russo-Japanese war. A large number of 205mm/8in secondary guns were mounted in turrets and casemates, and the hulls were completely armoured – even to the removal of scuttles and

deadlights. Originally fitted with slender US-style cage or lattice masts, these were cut down to funnel height and replaced with pole masts. They took little part in the Baltic fighting in World War I.

Imperator Pavel, renamed *Respublika* in 1917, was scrapped in 1923. *Andrei Peroswanni* was torpedoed in Kronstadt

harbour on August 18, 1919, long after the war in the rest of Europe was over, during an attack by British coastal motorboats. She was scrapped in 1925.

LEFT: **Austro-Hungarian naval architects had some help from their German-speaking cousins, but generally their designs were their own. The Habsburg class were small, well-proportioned vessels.**

Habsburg class

Habsburg class

Class: *Habsburg, Arpad, Babenburg.*
Launched 1900–2
Dimensions: Length – 114.55m/375ft 10in
Beam – 19.8m/65ft
Draught – 7.5m/24ft 6in
Displacement: 8,364 tonnes/8,232 tons
Armament: Main – 3 x 240mm/9.4in and
12 x 150mm/6in guns
Secondary – 10 x 12pdr guns and 2 torpedoes
Machinery: 16 boilers, 2 shafts.
14,307kW/16,000ihp
Speed: 19.85 knots
Complement: 638 men

Austro-Hungarian provinces in the northern and eastern Adriatic Sea gave the otherwise landlocked empire access to the sea. From the mid-1800s a significant navy was developed, modelled on British lines, and the first ship was a steam frigate ordered from England at the end of the Russian War 1854–6. The first torpedoes were designed and built in Austria, and the Austro-Hungarian navy distinguished itself in fighting the Danes in the North Sea in support of their allies the

Prussians in 1866. The empire, however, had a continental outlook and the navy was starved of funds. Nevertheless, the Austro-Hungarians, although often building only single ships, took part in the development of the battleship from broadside ironclad to centre-battery ship and coast defence ships, sometimes mounting quite large guns.

The three units of the Habsburg class are listed here because, though their guns were less than 255mm/10in, they were heavily armoured, seagoing and

had a significant impact upon the regional balance of power. Although modified before the war, when the superstructure of *Habsburg* was reduced by one deck, they were obsolete by 1914, when Austro-Hungary fought Italy. Although used on isolated operations, as when *Babenburg* shelled the Italian port of Ancona in 1915, by the end of the war their crews had been drafted into the submarine and air services. All three were ceded to Britain in 1920 and scrapped in Italy in 1921.

Erzherzog Karl class

LEFT: **The Erzherzog Karl class was a successful design for a small pre-Dreadnought. Like other ships then building on the slips, they were made obsolescent by the launch of *Dreadnought*. In World War I they were used for bombardment.**

At the end of the war all three ships were seized at Pola by the newly independent state of Yugoslavia, but *Erzherzog Karl* and *Erzherzog Friedrich* were ceded to France and *Erzherzog Ferdinand Max* to Britain, but all were broken up in 1920/1.

Erzherzog Karl class

Class: *Erzherzog Karl, Erzherzog Friedrich,
Erzherzog Ferdinand Max.* Launched 1903–5
Dimensions: Length – 126.2m/414ft 2in
Beam – 21.8m/71 ft 5in
Draught – 7.5m/24ft 7in
Displacement: 10,640 tonnes/10,472 tons
Armament: Main – 4 x 240mm/9.45in and
12 x 190mm/7.48in guns
Secondary – 12 x 70mm/2.76in and
4 x 47mm/1.85in guns
Machinery: 2 shafts, 13,423kW/18,000ihp
Speed: 20.5 knots
Complement: 700 men

These were the three largest and last pre-Dreadnoughts of the Austro-Hungarian navy. Like previous designs, they were compact ships, limited by the size of the dockyard facilities at Trieste, though compared to their Italian rivals they were better armoured. They also displayed some advances, and for the first time the secondary guns in their casemates were electrically operated.

Launched in 1903–5, however, the class was rendered obsolete while the ships were being completed by the launch in Portsmouth of *Dreadnought*.

During World War I they were limited to the role of shore bombardment, including a raid on May 24, 1915, on the city and ancient ferry port of Ancona. In early 1918 they were used in helping to suppress a mutiny at Cattaro.

World War I

There were very few fleet engagements after the Battle of Trafalgar in 1805, the most studied being the Battle of Tsushima in 1905 between the Japanese and Russians. The annihilation of the Russian fleet altered the balance of power in Europe, which coincided with the resurgence of the USN and the rise of the German navy. Germany had imperial ambitions and though its fleet was only intended for a limited purpose, German naval armament was perceived as a threat by Britain, then the greatest naval power in the world. A deadly arms race started across the North Sea which became a symptom, if not the cause, of World War I. In the event the German warships outside the North Sea were quickly rounded up, and though the Germans adopted tactics intended to defeat the Royal Navy by attrition, they never succeeded. Der Tag, the day when the two fleets would meet in decisive battle, was a disappointment to both sides although the Germans won materially, tactically, and in terms of propaganda. The Germans realized too late that submarine warfare was the only way that they could have won the war at sea.

LEFT: **The British built warships for navies throughout the world, although in war they frequently took them over for their own use. The Chilean *Almirante*, seen here, served in World War I as the British HMS *Canada*.**

Dreadnought

The change from the mixed calibres of previous designs to the all-big-gun armament, which Cuniberti had advocated and which Fisher adopted, was a direct result of increasing gun ranges and the need for a single calibre whose fall of shot could be distinguished by spotters.

British naval architects were already considering an all-big-gun design when Cuniberti's article was printed in English, and when Admiral Sir Jacky Fisher became First Sea Lord in October 1904 he tasked a committee to look at various arrangements of turrets. The USN had similar proposals under review and their analysis of the Battle of Tsushima would also convince the Japanese. Spotters needed to see the fall of shot in order to calculate range, but the gun range was increasing so much that the splashes of large- and medium-calibre guns could not be told apart. The obvious solution was to fit guns all of the same calibre.

Naval officers were also impressed by the economy of carrying only one outfit of ammunition and spares. However, the greatest improvement in *Dreadnought* was a result of the bold decision to fit four turbine-driven shafts. This was only four years after the Royal Navy had sent its first turbines to sea fitted in destroyers. The decision-making process was marked by Fisher's energy. The Committee on Design met on January 3, 1905, and by the end of February had made its

TOP: **HMS *Dreadnought*, which gave her name to the type she founded. In the background is Nelson's *Victory* and coming up the harbour are three submarines which were also part of Fisher's revolution.** ABOVE: ***Dreadnought*, again with *Victory* in the background, consciously linking the new great ship to the concept of the Royal Navy's supremacy at sea.**

recommendations. *Dreadnought* was laid down on Trafalgar Day, October 21, 1905, launched on February 10, 1906, and completed in December of the same year. This was something of a record even for the super-efficient Royal Dockyard of Portsmouth, although it was a little longer than the 12 months that Fisher claimed. Nevertheless, Fisher had energized everybody and everything and deserves much of the credit for her quick build.

LEFT: **With the commissioning of *St Vincent* in 1910 there were seven Dreadnoughts in the First Division of the Home Fleet. A. B. Cull's picture shows the first time that such a powerful squadron put to sea.**
BELOW: **A familiar picture of *Dreadnought* just after her launch, which nevertheless is unique because it shows her underwater form. Fisher had decided among his other revolutionary ideas to do away with the ram, although the designers managed to retain a bulbous shape which helped streamline the ship.**

Her naval architects deserve some credit, too. The decision to fit turbines instead of reciprocating engines saved space and about 1,016 tonnes/1,000 tons of weight and when this was combined with the hull form it allowed *Dreadnought* unprecedented speed, in excess of 20 knots. This had been rigorously tested in the model ship tanks at Haslar. Her sea trials were highly successful. The high forecastle kept *Dreadnought* dry, the wide beam to accommodate turrets on each side of the superstructure kept down the roll and the turbines reduced vibration. Consequently foreign navies immediately wanted to copy her. Nevertheless, the first German Dreadnoughts, the Westfalens, were not ready until 1909, and the first Japanese Dreadnoughts, *Satsuma* and *Aki,* and the first Americans, the South Carolina and Delaware classes, in 1910.

The designers made two mistakes, probably forced upon them by naval officers, among them the gunnery expert and future Commander-in-Chief of the Grand Fleet, John Jellicoe. The two wing turrets had limited arcs of fire; it would have been better to place an extra turret on the centre line and accept the increased weight penalty. As it was, fully loaded she was 3,556 tonnes/3,500 tons more than her designed displacement and *Dreadnought* sat so low that her armoured belt was under water and useless. Also, to provide a convenient support for a derrick to hoist her boats, the foremast with its gun-direction platform was placed aft of the fore funnel. This meant that if smoke or heat haze did not obscure the gun director then the acrid exhaust gases would choke the crew. These defects could not be rectified, although later she was armed with more light guns, her topmasts were cut down and she received a larger gun-direction platform and searchlight control positions.

Dreadnought saw the start of World War I as flagship of the Fourth Battle Squadron, until superseded by the more modern *Benbow*. On March 18, 1915, in the Pentland Firth, she became the first and only battleship to sink a submarine, the German *U-29*. In May 1916 she became flagship of the Third Battle Squadron of the Edward VII class ships at Sheerness, guarding the Thames, and so missed the Battle of Jutland, and on June 14, off Dunnet Head, *Dreadnought* attempted but failed to ram a second submarine. She returned to the Grand Fleet in 1918, was placed in reserve in 1919 and scrapped in 1922. *Dreadnought* was a singleton; she named not a class but a type of ship.

Dreadnought

Class: *Dreadnought.* Launched 1906
Dimensions: Length – 160.6m/527ft
  Beam – 25m/82ft
  Draught – 9.5m/31ft
Displacement: 18,400 tonnes/18,110 tons
Armament: Main – 10 x 305mm/12in guns
  Secondary – 24 x 12pdr guns and
  5 x 455mm/18in torpedoes
Machinery: 18 Babcock and Wilcox boilers,
  4 shafts, 17,375kW/23,300shp
Speed: 21 knots
Complement: 695 men

Bellerophon class

This class was very similar to the *Dreadnought* and the ships were also built very rapidly. Internally the propulsion machinery was the same, but they were also fitted with an inner longitudinal bulkhead designed to localize damage from a torpedo hit, known as a torpedo bulkhead. The tripod foremast was placed over the bridge superstructure and thus clear of funnel gases, but a second tripod mainmast was added with a "fighting top" which was exposed to the fumes of both funnels. While these two masts gave the Bellerophons a more balanced look than *Dreadnought*, the fire control position on the mainmast proved useless and was removed along with the topmasts during the war.

The secondary armament was also improved from 12-pounders (75mm/3in) to 100mm/4in guns. Initially some guns were sited on the main turrets' roofs, but these were later placed in casemates in the superstructure. Other changes during World War I included the removal of torpedo nets and the after torpedo tube, more extensive radio aerials, searchlight platforms, additional anti-aircraft guns,

and funnel caps. By 1918 all three ships had ramps on the A and Y turrets and could fly off either a Sopwith Pup fighter biplane or a Sopwith Strutter reconnaissance aeroplane.

Bellerophon joined the Home Fleet in 1909 and the Fourth Battle Squadron of the Grand Fleet in August 1914, and fought at the Battle of Jutland. Her career was remarkable for two collisions, one with *Inflexible* at Portland in 1911 and one with a merchantman in 1914. She was placed in reserve at the war's end and broken up in 1921.

Superb was flagship of the Fourth Battle Squadron at Jutland. In November 1918 she led the Allied Fleet through the Dardanelles, was paid off in 1919, briefly

TOP: ***Bellerophon*** **underway. The design fault of placing the foremast behind the funnel has been corrected.** ***Bellerophon***'**s jack, not normally flown at sea, appears to indicate she is dressed for some occasion.** ABOVE: ***Superb*** **in the Hamoaze at Plymouth.** BELOW: ***Temeraire*** **in Plymouth Sound.**

a target and broken up in 1921. *Temeraire* followed a similar career, but was used as a seagoing training ship until being scrapped in 1921–2. The war service of these ships proved the soundness of the basic Dreadnought design.

Bellerophon class

Class: *Bellerophon, Superb, Temeraire.*
   Launched 1907
Dimensions: Length – 160.3m/526ft
   Beam – 25.2m/82ft 6in
   Draught – 8.3m/27ft 3in
Displacement: 19,100 tonnes/18,800 tons
Armament: Main – 10 x 305mm/12in guns
   Secondary – 16 x 100mm/4in guns and
   3 x 455mm/18in torpedoes
Machinery: 18 boilers, 4 shafts,
   17,151kW/23,000shp
Speed: 21 knots
Complement: 733 men

St Vincent class

The third class of ships of the basic Dreadnought design followed a trend of gradual improvement and increase in size. Horsepower was increased to offset the rise in displacement and the hull form began to be refined, so the St Vincents were slightly slimmer and longer. As in the Bellerophons the after fire-control position proved useless and was later removed.

A new 305mm/12in gun was introduced with a longer barrel, although this did not prove effective as the higher muzzle velocity shortened the barrel life and reduced accuracy at longer ranges. Pre-war modifications included lowering the topmasts and moving the secondary armament from the main gun roofs. Wartime modifications were similar to the Bellerophons with the addition of funnel caps, searchlight towers and aircraft ramps.

St Vincent was commissioned into the Home Fleet as flagship in 1910, fought at the Battle of Jutland as part of the First Battle Squadron, and was broken up.

The future King George VI served as a Lieutenant on *Collingwood* at Jutland. Later this class moved from the First to the Fourth Battle Squadron. *Collingwood* was sold for scrap in 1922. *Vanguard* followed her sisters into the Home and Grand Fleets and Jutland, and between them these ships fired over 250 305mm/ 12in rounds at the German High Sea Fleet, and received no hits. On July 9, 1917, *Vanguard* suffered a violent explosion and sank with appalling speed, killing 804 men. This was later attributed to faulty ammunition.

In this period a number of ships blew up when not in action. Although sometimes attributed to sabotage or other covert enemy action, the cause was invariably the spontaneous combustion of ammunition.

BELOW: ***Vanguard* (with other Dreadnoughts beyond her) approaching Portsmouth.** RIGHT: ***Vanguard* followed by another St Vincent class. The artist A. B. Cull has captured the winter weather when these ships operated in the North Sea.**

St Vincent class

Class: *St Vincent, Collingwood, Vanguard.* Launched 1908–9
Dimensions: Length – 163.4m/536ft
  Beam – 25.7m/84ft 2in
  Draught – 7.9m/25ft 11in
Displacement: 19,875 tonnes/19,560 tons
Armament: Main – 10 x 305mm/12in guns
  Secondary – 20 x 100mm/4in guns and
  3 x 455mm/18in torpedoes
Machinery: 18 boilers, 4 shafts,
  18,270kW/24,500shp
Speed: 21 knots
Complement: 718 men

Invincible, Indomitable and *Inflexible*

One of Fisher's more debatable ideas concerned the armoured cruiser. Fisher wanted a cruiser that was larger and faster than any other cruiser, which could protect trade by hunting down and destroying every other smaller cruiser and could also act either as a heavy scout in pursuit of an enemy or as support of the van of the battlefleet. In official words: "To engage the enemy battlecruisers in a fleet action, or, if none are present, by using their speed to cross the bow of the enemy and engage the van of his battlefleet".

The result was the battlecrusier (so named in 1913) of which the Invincibles were the first. They were long ships so that they could accommodate the number of boilers needed to give them their high speed, and like *Dreadnought* they mounted a uniform large-calibre armament. However, when compared to the battleships they were lightly armoured although externally they looked very similar. Like *Dreadnought* they had twin rudders and four turbine-driven shafts which made them very effective. They were however vulnerable not just against battleships but also against ships of their own type firing large-calibre guns. In the case of the Invincibles the wing turrets, P and Q, had very limited-beam firing arcs. Later in the war *Indomitable* was fitted with flying-off ramps over these turrets.

At the Battle of Jutland the Fifth Battle Squadron had been loaned to the Battlecruiser Fleet and the Invincibles, who formed the Third Battlecruiser Squadron, had been lent to the Grand Fleet. Inevitably Jellicoe placed the three battlecruisers in the line of battle, where they suffered accordingly. Although *Invincible* and *Indomitable* disabled the *Wiesbaden* and *Pillau* and hit *Lützow*, when *Invincible* came under sustained fire from the German battleships *Derfflinger, Lützow* and *König*, a shell hit Q turret causing a huge explosion that blew her in half. There were only six survivors from a crew of over 1,000.

Previously *Invincible* had taken part in the first naval engagement of the war, the Battle of Heligoland Bight on August 28, 1914. In November 1914 she had been ordered to sail from Devonport still with dockyard labourers onboard to hunt for Admiral Graf von Spee's squadron in the South Atlantic. On December 8, 1914, she had fought at the Battle of the Falkland Islands, when *Invincible, Inflexible* and their consorts sank the German *Scharnhorst* and *Gneisenau*, the light cruisers *Leipzig* and *Nürnberg*, and two colliers. During the battle *Invincible* was hit 22 times by smaller-calibre shells, but without fatalities.

As a new ship *Inflexible* visited New York in 1909. At the outbreak of World War I she was flagship of the British Mediterranean Fleet and with *Indomitable*, in August 1914, was involved in the unsuccessful hunt for the German battlecruisers *Goeben* and *Breslau*. She joined *Invincible* in the hunt for *Graf Spee* and the Battle of the Falkland Islands. In February and March 1915 she wore out her guns' barrels during bombardments in the Dardanelles, where she was flagship of the British Dardanelles Squadron. On March 18, 1915, *Inflexible* was hit nine times by Turkish batteries and ran on to a mine, needing to be beached for temporary repairs before

going to Malta for full repairs. At the Battle of Jutland she fired 88 305mm/12in rounds and received no damage herself. On August 19, 1916, *Inflexible* was attacked unsuccessfully by the German submarine *U-65*, and on January 31, 1918, she collided with a British submarine in the ironically named Battle of May Island. She was sold for scrap in 1921.

On commissioning *Indomitable* carried the Prince of Wales on a visit to Canada. At the outbreak of World War I she took part in the chase of the *Goeben* and *Breslau*, and in November 1914 participated in a preliminary bombardment of the Dardanelles forts that may have alerted the Turks to future British and allied intentions. She joined the Second Battlecruiser Squadron and fought at the Battle of Dogger Bank on January 25, 1915. There she fired on *Blücher*, closing the range to 5,490m/6,000yd, and received no damage herself. Afterwards *Indomitable* towed *Lion* back to Rosyth. At the Battle of Jutland *Indomitable* fired 175 305mm/12in rounds, hitting *Derrflinger* (three times), *Seydlitz* (once) and the pre-Dreadnought *Pommern*. She was sold for scrap in 1921.

OPPOSITE AND ABOVE: *Invincible* and her sisters were conceived as fast armoured cruisers, but inevitably in the case of ships with an armament of 305mm/12in guns fleet commanders wanted to place them in the line of battle and they were restyled battlecruisers. The lack of fire control equipment clearly indicates that the heavy guns had outranged the means of laying them accurately – especially in the frequent mists and fogs of the North Sea.

BELOW: The fine photograph of a previous *Inflexible*, taken from the ramparts of the fortress of Malta, shows how far warship design had evolved since the masted turret ship *Inflexible* of 1874–1903.

Invincible, Indomitable and *Inflexible*

Class: *Invincible, Indomitable, Inflexible.*
  Launched 1907
Dimensions: Length – 172.8m/567ft
  Beam – 23.9m/78ft 6in
  Draught – 8m/26ft 2in
Displacement: 17,652 tonnes/17,373 tons
Armament: Main – 8 x 305mm/12in guns
  Secondary – 16 x 100mm/4in guns and
  5 x 455mm/18in torpedoes
Machinery: 31 boilers, 4 shafts,
  30,574kW/41,000shp
Speed: 26 knots
Complement: 784 men

LEFT: *Neptune* at anchor and working her boats. She is wearing the flag of the Commander-in-Chief, Home Fleet. ABOVE: *Neptune* at anchor in the fleet anchorage of Scapa Flow during World War I. Note that the after tripod mast and flying bridges have been removed. BELOW LEFT: A period picture postcard showing *Hercules* dressed overall while underway. The Royal Navy was fond of reusing the famous names of its ships, and chose the classic names of earlier wooden-walled battleships, like *Hercules*, to remind the world that Britainnia ruled the waves.

Neptune, Colossus and *Hercules*

When the American and the Argentine navies built Dreadnoughts which would fire 10 and 12 guns on the broadside, the British staggered their midships turrets, on a longer hull, so that both midships turrets could be fired across the deck. To leave the boats clear and open the firing arcs, a flying bridge was introduced linking the islands of the superstructure.

The roof-mounted 100mm/4in guns were suppressed and placed in the superstructure behind armoured shields. Pre-war a searchlight platform was added, the after control position was removed, the fore funnel heightened and a clinker cowl fitted.

Neptune was the fastest British battleship to date, making nearly 23 knots on trials. She fought at Jutland, where she suffered no damage, and was broken up in 1919. *Colossus* and *Hercules*, the last two 305mm/12in-gunned battleships of the period, were half-sisters to *Neptune*.

Realizing that in battle the wreckage from the flying bridges would fall on P and Q turrets, this was reduced in size, and in 1917 removed completely. The after control position was never fitted but, in a retrograde step, the forward mast and control position were placed abaft the fore funnel. In *Colossus* the 100mm/4in guns in the superstructure were protected by dropping ports; *Hercules* had shields. Pre-war the fore funnel was raised and later the torpedo nets were removed.

Colossus was hit at Jutland by two shells, the only Grand Fleet battleship at Jutland to be damaged. In 1919–20 she was painted in Victorian black, white and buff livery and served as a training ship at Devonport for cadets. She was broken up in 1928. *Hercules* also fought at Jutland. In November 1918 she carried the Allied Naval Commission to Kiel, and was sold for breaking up in 1921.

Neptune

Class: *Neptune.*
Launched 1909
Dimensions: Length – 166.42m/546ft
Beam – 25.9m/85ft
Draught – 8.7m/28ft 6in
Displacement: 19,996 tonnes/19,680 tons
Armament: Main – 10 x 305mm/12in guns
Secondary – 16 x 100mm/4in guns and
3 x 455mm/18in torpedoes
Machinery: 18 Yarrow boilers, 4 shafts,
18,643kW/25,000shp
Speed: 21 knots
Complement: 759 men

Colossus and *Hercules*

Class: *Colossus, Hercules.*
Launched 1910
Dimensions: Length – 166.4m/546ft
Beam – 25.9m/85ft
Draught – 8.8m/28ft 9in
Displacement: 20,550 tonnes/20,225 tons
Armament: Main – 10 x 305mm/12in guns
Secondary – 16 x 100mm/4in guns and 3 x
535m/21in torpedoes
Machinery: 18 boilers, 4 shafts,
18,643kW/25,000shp
Speed: 21 knots
Complement: 755 men

Indefatigable class

As successions of Dreadnought-type battleships and battlecruisers were built year on year, their design improved. However this class has been criticized because *Indefatigable* was a near replica of *Invincible,* which had been laid down three years before. *Australia* and *New Zealand* were laid down at the same time as the Lion class battlecruisers, which incorporated all the lessons learned so far, were bigger by 8,128 tonnes/8,000 tons, more heavily armed (340mm/13.5in guns) and better armoured (230mm/9in on the belt), matching the increases in equivalent ships being built in Germany. There is no direct evidence why this should be so, other than speculation that it was done on grounds of dockyard capacity, speed, cost (£1.7 million – *Australia* and *New Zealand* were paid for by their namesake countries) or to produce a second homogeneous division of battleships.

The class were some 6m/20ft longer than *Invincible,* which allowed greater staggering and better arcs of fire to the

midships turrets, P and Q. The fore funnel was increased in height to help clear smoke from the bridge and the after control position was initially fitted but soon dismantled. Various light guns were added during the war, and after Jutland, *Australia* and *New Zealand* were given an additional 25mm/1in of armour between P and Q turrets. They also received searchlights, range clocks, and, in 1918, flying-off platforms over the midships turrets. These two ships already differed from *Indefatigable* in their internal arrangement of armour and their bridge layouts, and had 745.7kW/1,000shp more power.

Indefatigable served in the British Mediterranean Fleet and took part in the unsuccessful chase of *Goeben* and *Breslau.* In November 1914 she bombarded Cape Helles in the Dardanelles, before joining the Second Battlecruiser Squadron. At the Battle of Jutland *Indefatigable* was hit by *Von der Tann.* Two rounds entered the after (X) magazine, causing an explosion,

ABOVE: *Indefatigable* was one of three similar battlecruisers. Fast but lightly armoured, she was hit by *Von der Tann* at the Battle of Jutland and blew up. The fundamental weakness of these ships was their lack of armour, but some ships had laid great emphasis on rapid rate of fire (rather than accuracy).

and as *Indefatigable* veered out of line a second salvo hit her forward and she blew up.

Indefatigable class

Class: *Indefatigable, Australia, New Zealand.*
  Launched 1909–11
Dimensions: Length – 179.8m/590ft
  Beam – 24.4m/80ft
  Draught – 7.9m/26ft
Displacement: 18,800 tonnes/18,500 tons
Armament: Main – 8 x 305mm/12in guns
  Secondary – 16 x 100mm/4in guns and
  3 x 455mm/18in torpedoes
Machinery: 32 boilers, 4 shafts,
  32,811kW/44,000shp
Speed: 25 knots
Complement: 800 men

Australia

At the start of World War I the Admiralty in London and the government in Canberra struggled over *Australia*'s deployment. The Australian government wanted *Australia* as a deterrent and defence against a raid by the German East Asiatic Squadron, yet was anxious to strike its own blow in the war. Therefore after mustering the Australian fleet in Sydney, *Australia* escorted Australian and New Zealand troops for the capture of the German colonies of Samoa and New Guinea.

In September 1914 *Australia* steamed east to Fiji. Japan had declared war on Germany and *Australia* was sent to join Japanese ships off California which were intended to prevent the Germans using the Panama Canal. When the news came of the Battle of the Falklands, *Australia* was sent to join the British Grand Fleet at Scapa Flow; as she was too long for the Panama Canal she made passage via Cape Horn in late December 1914.

In the South Atlantic she sank the German merchantman *Eleonore Woermann*, thus ending enemy coaling arrangements. She was made flagship of the Second Battlecruiser Squadron, although following a collision with her sister ship *New Zealand* she missed the Battle of Jutland. Between January 1915 and November 1919 *Australia* steamed some 91,565km/56,908 miles, mostly on the Northern Patrol, the distant blockade of Germany. She became the first aircraft-carrying ship of the Australian navy, using a platform built over the guns from which Sopwith fighters were launched as scouts and to attack Zeppelins.

After her return to Australia in May 1919, she once more became flagship of the Royal Australian Navy and played a leading role in the visit of the Prince of Wales in another battlecruiser, the British *Renown*. However, *Australia* consumed too much of the navy's budget and manpower, and by 1920 she was

ABOVE: *Australia*, paid for and manned by Australians, played an active part in World War I and became a source of pride for the new nation.
BELOW: Following the Washington naval treaty, *Australia* was de-equipped and scuttled in April 1924 off Sydney.

downgraded to a drill ship at Flinders Naval Depot with a secondary role as a fixed defensive battery. In November 1921 she was paid off into reserve.

Australia was included in the tonnage allowed the British Empire under the terms of the Washington Treaty. There were efforts to have her preserved as a monument, but she was stripped, and in April 1924 towed to sea, where the pride of the Australian navy was scuttled, amid much public lament – the battlecruiser *Australia* had been a symbol of the country's burgeoning nationhood.

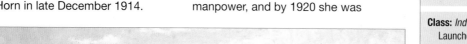

Australia	

Class: *Indefatigable, Australia, New Zealand.* Launched 1909–11
Dimensions: Length – 179.8m/590ft
Beam – 24.4m/80ft
Draught – 7.9m/26ft
Displacement: 18,800 tonnes/18,500 tons
Armament: Main – 8 x 305mm/12in guns
Secondary – 16 x 100mm/4in guns and 3 x 455mm/18in torpedoes
Machinery: 32 boilers, 4 shafts, 32,811kW/44,000shp
Speed: 25 knots
Complement: 800 men

New Zealand

In 1909 the Prime Minister of New Zealand decided to set an example to the other British Dominions by offering to fund a "first class battleship" for the Royal Navy. In the event New Zealand paid for an Indefatigable class battlecruiser and a sister ship to *Australia*, which was rather cheaper than the super-Dreadnoughts which were being introduced.

The British Admiralty sent *New Zealand* on a tour of the Dominions in 1913 to show them what could be done, before sending her to join the First Battlecruiser Squadron of the Grand Fleet. There she took part in the Battles of Heligoland Bight and Dogger Bank, and when Beatty's own flagship *Lion* was damaged at Dogger Bank, he transferred his flag to *New Zealand*.

In April 1916 *New Zealand* and *Australia* collided in fog in the North Sea. *New Zealand* was repaired just in time to rejoin the fleet before the Battle of Jutland, but *Australia* missed the great battle. As if to make up for this *New Zealand* fired more rounds at Jutland than any other ship in the battle – a total of 420 305mm/12in shells. In turn she was hit just once by a shell which landed on X turret without major damage or casualties.

In November 1917 *New Zealand* also fought in the Second Battle of Heligoland Bight. Unlike *Australia*, who was manned largely by Australians, there were mostly British and very few New Zealanders in the battlecruiser *New Zealand*. Nevertheless her captain had been presented with a Maori battledress and it was thought to be unlucky if he did not wear this when going into battle.

In 1919–20 Admiral Jellicoe was sent on a world tour to assess the Empire's needs for defence – the British Admiralty still hankered after an Empire navy and Jellicoe was supposed to report what contributions the Dominions could make. He chose *New Zealand* as his flagship and she was specially modified to provide him with suitable office and living accommodation. It has been reckoned that nearly one-third of the population of her home country saw the battlecruiser *New Zealand* while she was in New Zealanad waters. *New Zealand* was scrapped in 1923.

ABOVE: *New Zealand* became Jellicoe's flagship for his 1919 mission to advise on the naval requirements of the British Empire. The photograph shows his specially built quarters on the port side forward of the funnels. ABOVE RIGHT: *New Zealand* bows-on showing the fine lines of this class of ship. LEFT: Visitors' day on *New Zealand*. Although only a handful of the ship's company were in fact New Zealanders, the population of New Zealand took a proprietary interest in the affairs of their ship, and her captain was expected to wear Maori costume when going into action.

New Zealand

Class: Indefatigable, Australia, New Zealand. Launched 1909–11

Dimensions: Length – 179.8m/590ft
Beam – 24.4m/80ft
Draught – 7.9m/26ft

Displacement: 18,800 tonnes/18,500 tons

Armament: Main – 8 x 305mm/12in guns
Secondary – 16 x 100mm/4in guns and
3 x 455mm/18in torpedoes

Machinery: 32 boilers, 4 shafts,
32,811kW/44,000shp

Speed: 25 knots

Complement: 800 men

LEFT: **Port bow photograph of one of the Orion class. For some extraordinary reason the foremast has been put back behind the funnel where the gunnery control optics, and their operators, will be affected by the smoke and haze.** BELOW: **A starboard profile of this class of ship, showing the hot fumes which must have made climbing the foremast a noxious experience. Producing four Dreadnoughts a year was about the industrial capacity of Great Britain.**

Orion class

The 305mm/12in, 50-calibre gun had proved inaccurate and caused too much barrel wear, so the 340mm/13.5in gun, not seen since the 1890s, was reintroduced in the Orion class. The lower muzzle velocity and larger shell was successful in reducing instability in flight and increased accuracy, and, with increased elevation of firing, the 340mm/13.5in gun could hit a target at 21,950m/24,000yd. The shell when it arrived was also considerably heavier (635kg/1,400lb) than the 305mm/12in version (567kg/1,250lb).

The Orions incorporated many minor improvements. The awkward arrangement of placing guns midships to fire athwartships was abandoned and all were mounted on the centre line. The forward turrets, A and B, and the after ones, X and Y, were super-firing. On the other hand, blast through the sighting hoods of the lower turrets prevented these guns being fired ahead. Side armour was extended up to the main deck, overcoming the problem that at full load the armoured belt tended to be submerged and therefore useless. The mainmast was reduced to a small pole

mast. Bilge keels were fitted to reduce roll.

Once more the foremast and its control position were placed aft of the fore funnel, and the only reason for this can be a continued emphasis on seamanship (the need for a derrick to hoist boats) over gunnery. However, the interference this caused with optics and the hazard to health was much reduced because the funnel served fewer boilers.

When *Thunderer* was fitted with the Scott director aiming system in 1912 and took part in a competitive shoot against *Orion* she scored many more hits.

During World War I the topmasts were reduced and torpedo nets removed, the fire-control platform extended, plating over magazines increased and flying-off platforms fitted over B turret. *Thunderer* had an additional runway over X turret.

Monarch rammed *Conqueror* in December 1914, damaging her bows, and *Revenge* collided with *Orion* causing similar damage. These four ships formed the Second Battle Squadron at the Battle

of Jutland, where they fired 198 rounds but neither caused nor sustained any damage. Discarded after the Washington Treaty, *Thunderer* survived until 1926 as a cadet training ship, then, like her sisters in 1922, was broken up.

Orion class

Class: *Orion, Conqueror, Monarch, Thunderer.*
Launched 1910–11
Dimensions: Length – 177.1m/581ft
Beam – 27m/88ft 6in
Draught – 7.3m/24ft 1in
Displacement: 22,560 tonnes/22,200 tons
Armament: Main – 10 x 340mm/13.5in guns
Secondary – 16 x 100mm/4in guns and
3 x 535mm/21in torpedoes
Machinery: 18 boilers, 4 shafts,
20,134kW/27,000shp
Speed: 21 knots
Complement: 752 men

Lion class

The Lion class battlecruisers were 6 knots faster than the Orion class battleships. To achieve this they had 42 rather than 18 boilers, and were 36.6m/120ft longer. To reduce weight the maximum thickness of armour was reduced from 305mm/12in to 230mm/9in and the super-firing after turret was removed. Nevertheless, the displacement increased by over 4,064 tonnes/4,000 tons to 22,556 tonnes/22,200 tons.

They were handsome ships, known in the fleet as the "Cats", and were the subject of much favourable comment inspired by the Admiralty, which encouraged rumours exaggerating their speed and armoured strength.

When launched *Lion* had the foremast placed between the closely spaced first and second funnels, but the heat was so intense that the crew in the gun-direction platform were stranded. The direction platform was re-sited forward of the fore funnel on a pole mast and this was reinforced by struts, turning it into a tripod.

Lion was Admiral Beatty's flagship in the Battle Cruiser Force. She took part in the Battles of Heligoland Bight, Dogger Bank and Jutland. At Dogger Bank she fired nearly 250 rounds but made only four hits; one on *Blücher*, one on *Derfflinger* and two on *Seydlitz*. In turn she was hit by 16 280mm/11in and

305mm/12in rounds and had to be towed back by *Indefatigable*. She was also damaged at Jutland, and saved from explosion by the heroism of one man who ordered the flooding of a magazine. Q turret was temporarily removed in late 1916. She made numerous other sorties, but was scrapped in 1924.

Princess Royal fought at the Battle of Heligoland Bight before escorting the first Canadian troops across the Atlantic in September 1914, and guarding the North America and West Indies station during the hunt for Admiral Graf von Spee's squadron. She was also in action at Dogger Bank. At Jutland she was hit by *Derfflinger*, *Markgraf* and *Posen*, but although suffering damage, casualties and on fire, she remained in action. *Princess Royal* was part of the covering force during the Second Battle of Heligoland Bight on November 17, 1917. She was sold for scrap in 1922.

Lion class

Class: *Lion, Princess Royal.* Launched 1910–11
Dimensions: Length – 213.4m/700ft
Beam – 27m/88ft 6in
Draught – 8.4m/27ft 8in
Displacement: 26,690 tonnes/26,270 tons
Armament: Main – 8 x 340mm/13.5in guns
Secondary – 16 x 100mm/4in guns and 2 x 535mm/21in torpedoes
Machinery: 42 boilers, 4 shafts, 52,199kW/70,000shp
Speed: 27 knots
Complement: 997 men

ABOVE: *Lion*, flagship of Admiral Sir David Beatty's First Battlecruiser Squadron, leads *Princess Royal* to sea and into action on May 31, 1916. LEFT: *Lion* being towed into Armstrong's yard at Newcastle upon Tyne for repairs after the Battle of Jutland. BELOW: The Lion class were graceful ships well equipped with radio, which Beatty did not seem to want to use at Jutland and so lost control of the Fifth Battle Squadron that was allocated to him.

Queen Mary and *Tiger*

Superficially similar to the Lion class, *Queen Mary* incorporated several minor improvements. An additional 3,729kW/5,000shp gave her half a knot extra speed, the armoured belt was modified, and the larger main armament shell gave even greater stability in flight and accuracy, though for a period she could shoot at greater ranges than the guns could be sighted. Wartime modifications included a larger bridge and gun-direction platform with director control in 1915, reduced topmasts, and additional legs for the foremast.

Queen Mary was at the Battle of Heligoland Bight but missed the fighting at Dogger Bank. At Jutland she was another ship of the Battle Cruiser Force which came under fire from the German *Derfflinger*. She had fired about 150 rounds at *Seydlitz* when she was hit on Q turret and shortly afterwards between A and B turrets. The forward magazines exploded and the fore part of the ship disappeared and as she settled, listing to port, a further enormous explosion occurred, barely half an hour after the battle had started.

BELOW: *Queen Mary* and *Tiger* were at first glance the same as the Lion class, but they were half a knot faster and bigger-gunned. BOTTOM: *Tiger* with *Renown* beyond her, steaming at full speed into a heavy swell in the North Sea (1917 or 1918). Together, *Lion*, *Tiger*, *Princess Royal* and *Queen Mary* were known as the Cats.

The Tiger class were half-sisters to *Lion* and *Princess Royal*, together known as the Cats. Externally the difference was the rearrangement of the turrets, Q turret now being placed aft of three equally spaced funnels. For the first time in a British battlecruiser, the secondary armament consisted of 150mm/6in guns. Internally, improved boilers gave *Tiger* 63,385kW/85,000shp, but the speed increase this enabled was disappointing while the fuel consumption increased alarmingly. Protection (230mm/9in maximum armour) was just as poor as in other battlecruisers.

At the Battle of Dogger Bank, *Tiger* exchanged fire with German opponents, and was hit by six large-calibre hits. At Jutland, she was hit 15 times without her ammunition exploding, thus seemingly proving that in ships where the rules of handling ammunition were followed there was less risk of disaster.

Queen Mary

Class: *Queen Mary*. Launched 1912
Dimensions: Length – 214.4m/703ft 6in
    Beam – 27.1m/89ft
    Draught – 8.5m/28ft
Displacement: 27,200 tonnes/26,770 tons
Armament: Main – 8 x 340mm/13.5in guns
    Secondary – 16 x 100mm/4in guns and
    2 x 535mm/21in torpedoes
Machinery: 42 boilers, 4 shafts,
    55,928kW/75,000shp
Speed: 27.5 knots
Complement: 997 men

Tiger

Class: *Tiger*. Launched 1913
Dimensions: Length – 214.6m/704ft
    Beam – 27.6m/90ft 6in
    Draught – 8.7m/28ft 6in
Displacement: 28,885 tonnes/28,430 tons
Armament: Main – 8 x 340mm/13.5in guns
    Secondary – 12 x 150mm/6in guns and
    4 x 535mm/21in torpedoes
Machinery: 39 boilers, 4 shafts,
    63,385kW/85,000shp
Speed: 29 knots
Complement: 1,121 men

LEFT: **The four ships of this class formed the newest squadrons of Dreadnought, until *Audacious* was sunk by a mine off Northern Ireland in October 1914.** BELOW: ***King George V* lying under a huge crane at Portsmouth and being fitted out after launch. The crane is being used to begin to assemble *King George V*'s 355mm/14in guns.**

King George V class

This class was similar to the Orions, but with the foremast placed forward of the funnels and modified during World War I, including the fitting of flying-off ramps in 1918. Almost the last of the Dreadnoughts to be built before the outbreak of war, the King George V class was the epitome of the type.

King George V served the war in the Grand Fleet and became a post-war gunnery training ship. She was finally scrapped in 1926 (under the terms of the Washington Treaty) when *Nelson* and *Rodney* were completed.

Ajax served the war in the Grand Fleet and operated in the Black Sea against Russian revolutionaries in 1919. She was scrapped in 1926. *Centurion* also served the war in the Grand Fleet and after operations in the Black Sea was converted to a radio-controlled target ship. She was used as a decoy in World War II and then sunk as a block ship off Normandy in France on June 9, 1944.

In October 1914 the converted German liner *Berlin* laid a minefield off Malin Head on the north coast of Ireland, where the British Grand Fleet was using Loch Swilly as a base whilst the anti-submarine defences of Scapa Flow were being improved. On the morning of October 27, 1914, as she steamed out

on exercises with the other super-Dreadnoughts *Centurion*, *Ajax*, *King George V*, *Orion*, *Monarch* and *Thunderer*, the *Audacious* struck a mine on her port side amidships, quickly developed a list and lost power. Most of her crew were taken onboard the White Star liner *Olympic*. *Audacious* slowly settled by the stern and, at nightfall, after the rest of her crew had been rescued, she capsized, there was an explosion, and she sank.

No lives were lost, and the sinking was blamed on the weakness of the longitudinal bulkheads which were buckled in the initial explosion and had allowed floodwater to spread, though it seems that the damage control procedures in the ship could not have been very proficient.

Ludicrously, since the incident had been witnessed by American passengers onboard *Olympic*, the Commander-in-Chief of the Grand Fleet, Jellicoe, persuaded the British Admiralty to try to keep the sinking a secret. While everyone but the British acknowledged the loss, the British kept *Audacious* in the Navy List and reticence on the subject damaged British credibility. *Audacious* was the first loss of a major warship in World War I.

King George V class

Class: *King George V, Centurion, Audacious, Ajax.*
Launched 1911–12
Dimensions: Length – 182.1m/597ft 6in
Beam – 27.1m/89ft
Draught – 8.7m/28ft 8in
Displacement: 23,370 tonnes/23,000 tons
Armament: Main – 10 x 340mm/13.5 guns.
Secondary – 16 x 100mm/4in guns and 2 x 535mm/21in torpedoes
Machinery: 18 boilers, 4 shafts, 23,117kW/31,000shp
Speed: 21 knots
Complement: 782 men
Former name of *King George V* was *Royal George*

Iron Duke class

Similar in many respects to the King George V class, the Iron Dukes were 7.7m/25ft longer and 0.3m/1ft wider in the beam. However they were 2,032 tonnes/2,000 tons heavier, mainly because of the increase in the secondary armament from 100mm/4in to 150mm/6in to meet the greater ranges at which torpedo-boats could fire their improved weapons. A large direction platform was fitted on build, and these were also the first battleships to be fitted with anti-aircraft guns – two 12pdr on the after superstructure of *Iron Duke* in 1914. The stern torpedo tubes which had been a feature of design until now were suppressed.

The secondary armament casemates were, however, a problem: the hinged plates that closed off the revolving turrets were vulnerable in any kind of seaway and once washed away or damaged allowed seawater to flood on to the mess decks. The problem was solved by fitting dwarf bulkheads and rubber seals, but the design fault was that the guns were mounted too low in the hull. After Jutland searchlights and increased armour were fitted.

Iron Duke was flagship of the Home Fleet under Admiral Callaghan, and then of the Grand Fleet, under both Jellicoe and Beatty. In 1919–26 she was part of the British Mediterranean Fleet, and bombarded Red Army positions in the Black Sea in support of the White Russians during operations there in 1919–20. While the others of her class were scrapped under the terms of the Washington Treaty, *Iron Duke* was retained in a demilitarized state as a training and depot ship. Demilitarization included removal of B and Y turrets, and

BELOW: *Iron Duke* in 1914 as flagship of the Grand Fleet under Admiral Sir John Jellicoe. *Iron Duke* served on into World War II when she was an accommodation ship at Scapa Flow.

a substantial part of her armour, and limiting her speed, through the removal of boilers, to 18 knots. *Iron Duke* spent World War I at Scapa Flow, with the rest of her armament removed, was damaged by bombs in 1939 and finally sold for scrap in 1946. *Benbow* served her time in the Grand Fleet, joined the British Mediterranean Fleet between 1919 and 1926 and, like others of her class, provided gunfire support for White Russians in the Black Sea in 1919–20, and was sold for scrap in 1931. *Emperor of India*, whose former name was *Delhi*, spent World War I in the Grand Fleet (but missed Jutland because she was in refit), and was in the Mediterranean between 1919 and 1926. She was sunk as a gunnery target in 1931.

Between them the Iron Dukes fired 292 rounds of 340mm/ 13.5in ammunition during Jutland, of which *Marlborough* fired 162. She was torpedoed amidships and a hole 21m x 6m/70ft x 20ft was blown in her side, abreast the boiler rooms, where she was only protected by coal bunkers. Unlike *Audacious* she was able to keep station at 17 knots and did not cease firing until her guns were prevented from bearing by her list. She made her way to the Humber, and after three months' repairs on the Tyne she rejoined the Grand Fleet. *Marlborough* served with the rest of her class in the Mediterranean until 1926, then the Atlantic Fleet until 1929, and was scrapped in 1932.

TOP: *Iron Duke* enters Portsmouth. On the left is *Queen Elizabeth* and on the right is *Victory*. All three ships are flying the St George cross signifying an Admiral in command. ABOVE LEFT: *Emperor of India*, showing how with a following wind the bridge and in particular the gunnery direction platform could be enveloped in smoke and funnel gases. ABOVE: An over-flight of biplanes portends the coming struggle between the surface ship and the aircraft.

Iron Duke class

Class: *Iron Duke, Marlborough, Emperor of India, Benbow.* Launched 1912–13
Dimensions: Length – 189.8m/622ft 9in
Beam – 27.4m/90ft
Draught – 8.8m/29ft
Displacement: 25,400 tonnes/25,000 tons
Armament: Main – 10 x 340mm/13.5in guns
Secondary – 12 x 150mm/6in guns and
4 x 535mm/21in torpedoes
Machinery: 18 boilers, 4 shafts,
21,625kW/29,000shp
Speed: 21 knots
Complement: 995 men

Queen Elizabeth class

Though armed and armoured as battleships, the Queen Elizabeth class was fast enough to operate with the Battle Cruiser Force, to which, as the Fifth (Fast) Battle Squadron, they were attached during the Battle of Jutland (except *Queen Elizabeth* herself who was in dockyard hands). They were regarded as the finest battleships of their era. Their 380mm/15in guns were one reason for this and another – which her crew appreciated – was that with oil-fired boilers they were cleaner and more spacious than coal-fired ships. The six 380mm/15in guns could deliver a heavier broadside than any five-turret predecessor, and the guns were more accurate and suffered less barrel wear than the 340mm/13.5in. To secure supplies of oil the British government bought shares in Middle Eastern oil companies, thus inadvertently setting the course of foreign policy later in the century.

All five ships were overweight when completed and in practical terms their speed was about 24 knots.

Like other Dreadnoughts they were modified after Jutland and were fitted with range clocks and deflector scales, searchlight towers and additional deck armour. In 1918 all five were fitted with flying-off ramps on B and X turrets.

Although the handling of the Fifth Battle Squadron at Jutland was severely criticized, its participation in the Battle Cruiser Force probably saved Beatty's ships from an even worse mauling. In particular, the Germans were impressed by the accuracy of *Valiant*'s shooting.

Built at Portsmouth, but towed to Fairfield's to be fitted with her engines, as first of class *Queen Elizabeth* had a stern walk and two additional 150mm/6in guns under the quarterdeck, but these were removed in 1915 when they proved wet. Instead single guns with stern arcs were retrofitted port and starboard underneath X turret, as was done in the rest of the class.

TOP: *Queen Elizabeth*, after she had been modernized in the interwar years. The forward tripod had been replaced by a heavy control tower. ABOVE: In peacetime ceremonial duties were part of life on a battleship and here, on *Queen Elizabeth*, seamen and Royal Marines man the side for HM the King, and prepare to salute him in the traditional manner by giving him three cheers.

Queen Elizabeth bombarded forts in the Dardanelles in early 1915, but was recalled to the Grand Fleet although she missed the Battle of Jutland. In 1917, after Beatty had become Commander-in-Chief of the Grand Fleet, he took her for his flagship. Briefly in September 1917 she wore the flag of Admiral Mayo USN. The surrender of the German High Seas

LEFT: **Rough weather when the deck would be out of bounds.** BELOW: **In calm weather the forecastle was a place of work and here** *Queen Elizabeth's* **crew are seen preparing to launch paravanes (used to keep mines clear of striking the hull).**

Fleet was signed onboard *Queen Elizabeth* on November 15, 1918. Refitted and then modernized, she served on into World War II.

Repaired after a collision with *Barham* on December 2, 1915, *Warspite* was ready in time for the Battle of Jutland. She fired over 250 rounds, but was hit herself by some 15 305mm/12in rounds. At a critical moment her steering gear failed and *Warspite* steamed a full circle under the German gunfire but the Grand Fleet came up to drive off the Germans before she could be destroyed, and she limped back to Rosyth. Her repairs were just completed when on August 24 she was damaged in another collision, this time with *Valiant*. *Warspite* was partially modernized in 1924–6 and served in World War II.

The Federated States of Malaya paid for a fifth ship, named *Malaya*. She was ready in time for Jutland where she fired 215 rounds and was hit herself eight times by 305mm/12in rounds. *Malaya* visited Cherbourg for celebrations of the peace in April 1919 and in 1920 visited Germany. In 1921 *Malaya* took Prince Arthur of Connaught to India and on to Malaya. She served in the fleet until 1948.

Valiant served with the Grand Fleet throughout World War I and fired 299 rounds at the Battle of Jutland, receiving only slight splinter damage. She was modernized in 1929–30 and rebuilt in 1937–9.

Barham was named after Lord Barham, First Lord of the Admiralty and architect of the Campaign of Trafalgar in 1803–5. In the fighting at Jutland, *Barham* fired 337 rounds and during the "run to the north" came under heavy fire from the German High Seas Fleet. Midshipman Blackett, who subsequently became one of the greatest scientists of the 20th century and winner of the Nobel Prize for Physics in 1948, described this as "our five minutes' hate". It really lasted much longer and was extraordinarily unpleasant. It is estimated that some 500 305mm/12in bricks were fired at the *Barham* and the

rest of the squadron. "How we survived with so very few hits I have no idea," Blackett said. "Everyone was very relieved that the Grand Fleet had joined up, for it was exceedingly unpleasant alone."

Like her sisters, *Barham* was modernized from 1931–4, emerging with a single smokestack, enhanced protection against long-range plunging gunfire, and additional anti-aircraft guns, as well as a hangar and catapult for two seaplanes.

In World War II, *Barham* was capsized and blew up after she had been torpedoed by a German U-boat in the Mediterranean. The U-boat was returning from a special forces operation in North Africa when it found itself in the path of the British Mediterranean Fleet making a sortie to the west. The U-boat commander was lucky to get in his snapshot and it hit *Barham* with three torpedoes. The loss of *Barham* was recorded on film and makes for poignant viewing, as well as unique footage.

Queen Elizabeth class

Class: *Queen Elizabeth, Warspite, Valiant, Barham, Malaya.* Launched 1913–15
Dimensions: Length – 196.6m/645ft
 Beam – 27.7m/91ft
 Draught – 9.5m/31ft
Displacement: 27,940 tonnes/27,500 tons
Armament: Main – 8 x 380mm/15in guns
 Secondary – 14 x 150mm/6in guns and
 4 x 535mm/21in torpedoes
Machinery: 24 boilers, 4 shafts,
 41,759kW/56,000shp
Speed: 25 knots
Complement: 925 men
A sixth ship, to be named *Agincourt,* was cancelled. All ships of the class were extensively rebuilt between the wars, and their anti-aircraft armament improved.

Royal Sovereign class

Although known as the Royal Sovereigns, the British Admiralty referred to these ships as the Revenge class, and in fact *Ramillies* was the first ship to be laid down. Compared to the Queen Elizabeths their speed was reduced to 21 knots, and the 150mm/6in guns placed further aft to keep them drier. The obvious visual difference was the single, large, centrally placed funnel.

Ramillies was built with 2.1m/7ft-wide bulges faired into the hull to absorb the effect of an exploding torpedo. Filled with wood, tubes, oil and water, the bulges weighed an extra 2,540 tonnes/ 2,500 tons, but did not affect speed or fuel consumption, and were retrofitted in others of the class.

Up to this point all Dreadnoughts had had four shafts and twin rudders, but in this class two in-line rudders were fitted, the smaller, forward rudder intended to reduce vulnerability and make hand-steering, in an emergency, easier. In practice, the ancillary rudder proved ineffective and was removed.

When Fisher returned to office in 1914, he had the designs changed from mixed coal and oil to all oil-fired, with the intention of raising the horsepower and

with this the speed to 23 knots. He also had work on three other ships of this class, *Renown*, *Repulse* and *Resistance*, suspended as he wanted to replace them with battlecruisers.

After Jutland pumping and flooding arrangements were extended to cope better with damage, extra armour was placed over the magazines, and flash-tight doors on ammunition routes improved. Searchlight towers, range clocks and deflection scales were also fitted. By 1918 all ships had flying-off ramps over B and X turrets.

Only *Royal Oak* and *Revenge* fought at Jutland. The *Royal Sovereign* was completed in time, but missed the battle through engine problems. *Ramillies*'s completion was delayed after she had damaged her rudder on launch, and she did not join the Grand Fleet until 1917. *Resolution* was completed too late.

Royal Oak was torpedoed by the German U-boat *U-47* at Scapa Flow in 1939. *Royal Sovereign* was transferred to the Soviet Navy in 1944, and renamed *Archangelsk*, to be returned in 1949 when she was broken up. All others survived World Wars I and II and were sold for breaking up in 1948.

ABOVE: The Royal Sovereign class of ships saw much active service in both World Wars of the 20th century, but were already slow ships when completed. BELOW: *Revenge* on a spring cruise in 1934. The effect of the Atlantic swell, even on a 28,450-tonne/28,000-ton battleship, would have been the same whatever the year, even though architects tried to build their ships for North Atlantic conditions.

Royal Sovereign class

Class: *Ramillies, Resolution, Revenge (ex Renown), Royal Oak, Royal Sovereign.* Launched 1914–16
Dimensions: Length – 190.3m/624ft 3in
   Beam – 27m/88ft 6in
   Draught – 8.7m/28ft 6in
Displacement: 28,450 tonnes/28,000 tons
Armament: Main – 8 x 380mm/15in guns
   Secondary – 4 x 150mm/6in guns and
   4 x 535mm/21in torpedoes
Machinery: 18 boilers, 4 shafts,
   29,830kW/40,000shp
Speed: 21 knots
Complement: 937 men

Erin

The main concern of the Turkish navy in the run-up to World War I was superiority in the Aegean over its former vassal, Greece, and in the Black Sea over its traditional enemy, Russia. To meet these perceived threats, Turkey had ordered several ships in Britain including the new-build super-Dreadnought *Reshadieh*, and *Sultan Osman I* was purchased from Brazil while still in the yard. In addition to two cruisers and four destroyers, none of which were delivered, these ships were paid for in part by public subscription in Turkey. Resentment at their requisition in August 1914 by the Royal Navy, after the crews had arrived to steam them home, helped to bring Turkey into the war on the side

of Germany. As a result the Turkish navy was commanded by a German admiral on the side of the central powers.

Reshadieh (formerly *Reshad V*), renamed *Erin* in the Royal Navy, had the same gun plan as *Orion* and mixed elements of the King George V and Iron Duke class designs, but was slightly shorter and broader. Her extra beam meant that she could not fit into any Royal Navy dry dock and she had to be docked in private yards. She carried a main armament of ten 340mm/13.5in guns in twin turrets in the same layout but her secondary armament consisted of 150mm/6in guns. Her armour was equivalent to her British contemporaries, though she was regarded as rather

Erin	
Class: *Erin*. Launched 1913	
Dimensions: Length – 170.5m/559ft 6in	
Beam – 27.9m/91ft 7in	
Draught – 8.7m/28ft 5in	
Displacement: 23,150 tonnes/22,780 tons	
Armament: Main – 10 x 340mm/13.5in guns	
Secondary – 16 x 150mm/6in guns and	
4 x 535mm/21in torpedoes	
Machinery: 15 boilers, 4 shafts,	
19,761kW/26,500shp	
Speed: 21 knots	
Complement: 1,070 men	
A second ship of the class, *Reshad-i-Hammiss*, was cancelled.	

overcrowded and cramped for accommodation. She was readily recognized by her unusual reverse tripod mast, round funnels, and by Q turret being one deck higher than in her contemporary British designs. *Erin* was given improved fire-control equipment in 1917 and, in 1918, flying-off platforms on B and Q turrets. It is said that Japan's first battlecruiser, *Kongo*, also laid down in 1911 at Vickers, was derived from this design by Sir George Thurston.

Erin spent the war, including the Battle of Jutland, in the Grand Fleet. She was placed in reserve in 1919 and sold to the breakers in 1922, in the era when many ships were culled.

ABOVE: **The Royal Navy's requisitioning of a Turkish battleship which had been partly paid for by public subscription by the Turkish nation, and whose Turkish crew had already been formed, caused much resentment. This helped bring Turkey into the war on the side of Germany.** RIGHT: *Erin* **had a short career. Launched in 1913, she was broken up in 1922. The British Admiralty had a preference for large ships of similar types and equipment-fits:** *Erin* **had too many unique features to make her economic to retain.**

Agincourt

The battleship *Rio de Janeiro* was ordered by the Brazilian Government in November 1910 and she would have been the ultimate expression of the naval arms race between the Argentine, Brazil and Chile. She was to have been the most powerful warship not just in South America, but in the world, and she was for a time certainly the longest. However she was also a long time building as the Brazilians could not agree amongst themselves what armament to give their ships: various designs were considered between eight 405mm/16in and 14 305mm/12in guns, and eventually the latter was chosen, partly on the grounds of standardization of ammunition stock within the Brazilian fleet and partly under the influence of German advisers who were content with their own 305mm/12in guns. In the meantime Brazil's position in the arms race was costing 25 per cent of the national budget, which became untenable when the price of rubber collapsed and with it the Brazilian economy. In December 1913 *Rio de Janeiro* was sold to Turkey and renamed *Sultan Osman I*. Work recommenced and now included some luxury fittings.

The Turkish Government expected delivery of their new super-Dreadnought in July 1914, and her crew had arrived to take her, and *Reshadieh,* home, but as the delivery time neared Armstrong's were approached by the Admiralty to delay the

ABOVE: ***Agincourt*** was also destined for the Turkish navy but forcibly taken over by the Royal Navy. The picture on this page shows her as modified for British service, and opposite shows her with the flying bridges and tripod masts with which she was built.

handover of the ship. Then on July 31, 1914, with war imminent, the First Lord of the Admiralty, Winston Churchill, minuted that "Messrs Armstrong should be informed that in view of the present circumstances the Government cannot permit the ship to be handed over to a Foreign Power or to be commissioned as a public ship of a Foreign Government, or to leave their jurisdiction". Next day a company of Sherwood Foresters with fixed bayonets boarded the *Sultan Osman I* and escorted all the Turkish naval personnel off the ship. Money for the new ship had been raised partly by public subscription in Turkey, and her seizure by Britain strengthened the hand of the pro-German faction in the Turkish government. Two months later Turkey was at war with Britain.

Renamed *Agincourt*, her luxurious fittings gave her the nickname of "The Gin Palace" in the Royal Navy and appropriately her first captain and the core of her first crew came from the Royal Yacht. There were individual cabins for the officers and spacious accommodation for the crew but this

had been achieved by eliminating many watertight bulkheads. Like *Erin*, the armoured protection (maximum thickness 230mm/9in) was not up to Royal Navy standards (305mm/12in). The flying bridges – also known as "Marble Arches" – were no longer a feature of British designs and these, along with the tripod mainmast, were removed. To complete her eccentricity the seven turrets were named after the days of the week, Sunday, Monday, Tuesday, Wednesday, Thursday, Friday and Saturday. So unique was *Agincourt's* appearance that it became common to give stationing orders relative to her.

She was not a success in the Royal Navy: much of her equipment was non-standard and required more frequent visits to the dockyard. The 305mm/12in gun had not been fitted since the Indefatigable battlecruisers, and the single-lever loading arrangements were unusual. Besides concern for control of flooding if torpedoed, it was rumoured that she would break her back or turn turtle if she fired her full broadside.

Nevertheless, at the Battle of Jutland *Agincourt* was one of the first battleships to sight the German High Seas Fleet, and the sight of her 14 guns firing broadsides and enveloping her in a sheet of flame was described as awe-inspiring.

During the war the gunnery direction platform and bridge were enlarged, and searchlight towers around the second funnel were added, together with some extra, light guns.

After the war *Agincourt* was offered for sale to the Brazilian Government, which was not interested; Brazil's challenge to the first navies of the world had ebbed. *Agincourt* was converted to oil-fired boilers and given additional protection, and five turrets (Tuesday to Saturday) were removed so she could be used as a depot ship. However, these plans were dropped and she was scrapped in 1922, along with a great many other ships.

TOP: **As built, originally for the Brazilian government who sold her to the Turks, *Agincourt* had a prominent midships Sampson mast and two tripods.**

ABOVE: **Much of her equipment was, literally, foreign to the Royal Navy but such a powerful ship could not be allowed to go overseas into another navy. Subsequently her career in the Royal Navy was foreshortened.**

Agincourt

Class: *Agincourt.* Launched 1913
Dimensions: Length – 204.7m/671ft 6in
    Beam – 27.1m/89ft
    Draught – 8.2m/27ft
Displacement: 27,940 tonnes/27,500 tons
Armament: Main – 14 x 305mm/12in guns
    Secondary – 20 x 150mm/6in, 10 x 75mm/3in
    guns and 3 x 535mm/21in torpedoes
Machinery: 22 boilers, 4 shafts,
    25,354kW/34,000shp
Speed: 22 knots
Complement: 1,115 men

Canada

There is good evidence that during the period running up to World War I the British Admiralty used ships being built in British yards for foreign navies as a reserve. The Chilean Government had ordered two battleships as their response to the South American arms race, to be named *Almirante Latorre* and *Almirante Cochrane*. Turkish battleships being built in Britain had been seized, but Chile was a friendly country where there were large British business

BELOW: **Unlike Turkey whose ships, which were being completed in Britain, were requisitioned, Chile sold her two incomplete battleships to the Royal Navy.**

interests, and she was an important supplier of nitrates for the ammunition industry. As a result *Almirante Latorre* was purchased, though the hint to the Chilean Government that it should follow Australia, Malaysia and New Zealand in paying for a battleship did not work.

Canada was similar to the British Iron Dukes, but 12.2m/40ft longer and 2–3 knots faster, her funnels were taller and thicker, and she had a pole mainmast. In 1918 she had flying-off ramps on B and X turrets. *Canada* joined the Grand Fleet and fought at Jutland and in 1920 she was returned to Chile. In 1914 *Canada*'s sister ship *Almirante Cochrane* had been built up to the

forecastle deck, and in 1918 she was taken in hand and completed as the aircraft carrier *Eagle*.

Canada

Class: *Canada*. Launched 1913
Dimensions: Length – 201.5m/661ft
  Beam – 28m/92ft
  Draught – 8.8m/29ft
Displacement: 29,060 tonnes/28,600 tons
Armament: Main – 10 x 355mm/14in guns
  Secondary – 16 x 150mm/6in guns and
  4 x 535mm/21in torpedoes
Machinery: 21 boilers, 4 shafts,
  27,591kW/37,000shp
Speed: 23 knots
Complement: 1,167 men

LEFT: **The battlecruiser *Renown* was a familiar site off the coast in 1937.**
ABOVE: ***Renown*'s guns had a range of just over 32km/20 miles. Her rate of fire was about one round per minute and it was claimed that each shell could penetrate up to 1.46m/57in of wrought iron.**
BELOW: **All needs were catered for – large galleys and dining rooms, crowded messes and, on most warships, quiet places such as *Renown*'s chapel, seen here.**

Renown class

The Royal Navy had decided against building more battlecruisers when Fisher returned to office as First Sea Lord. He drew lessons from the Battle of the Falklands and to those who said that World War I would be over within a year, he promised to build his new ships quickly enough to participate. Using the material assembled for two Royal Sovereign class ships, Fisher ordered instead two fast battleships. They were 61m/200ft longer and 10,160 tonnes/ 10,000 tons heavier than previous battlecruisers, and armed with 380mm/ 15in guns instead of 305mm/12in, but they suffered from the same basic weakness of the battlecruiser concept in that they were too lightly armoured. However they were fast ships, reaching 30 knots, although not their designed speed of 32 knots.

They were also under-gunned on secondary armament. Under Fisher's influence 100mm/4in guns were selected, which even in triple mountings could not deliver the necessary weight of shells, and needed a disproportionately large crew.

Further, they were not delivered until after the weaknesses of the battlecruisers became tragically evident at the Battle of Jutland. Jellicoe, while still Commander-in-Chief of the Grand Fleet, proposed that both ships should be given increased armour as well as other post-Jutland modifications typical of the British Dreadnought fleet. The architects still could not solve the smoke problem and so the fore funnel was also raised 1.8m/6ft to clear the bridge of funnel gases.

At the end of the war they received more armour again. After World War I both ships were extensively refitted and in the inter-war years they were rebuilt, adding another 6,095 tonnes/6,000 tons.

Neither ship saw much action during World War I, although both led busy lives in the inter-war years and also fought in World War II.

Renown class

Class: *Renown, Repulse.* Launched 1916
Dimensions: Length – 242m/794ft
  Beam – 27.4m/90ft
  Draught – 7.8m/25ft 6in
Displacement: 28,095 tonnes/27,650 tons
Armament: Main – 6 x 380mm/15in guns
  Secondary – 17 x 100mm/4in guns and
  2 x 535mm/21in torpedoes
Machinery: 42 boilers, 4 shafts,
  83,518kW/112,000shp
Speed: 30 knots
Complement: 967 men

Courageous, Glorious and Furious

Fisher's ill-defined plans to "Copenhagen" the German fleet by forcing an entry into the Baltic gave rise to two extremes of his battlecruiser concept. *Courageous* and *Glorious* were thinly armoured, shallow draught, and fast. The hull was so light that on trials *Courageous* suffered buckling between the breakwater and the forward turret and both ships were strengthened. Fisher hoped to fit a 455mm/18in gun but it was not ready in time. Reckoned by some to be "white elephants", they were tried in a number of different roles. They were fitted with additional torpedoes (although there was no recorded incident of a contemporary Dreadnought successfully firing her torpedoes) and *Courageous* was briefly equipped as a minelayer. A significant advance was made in using small-tube boilers for the first time and double-helical turbines. With 18 Yarrow small-tube boilers they could achieve almost the same horsepower as the Renowns with 42 large-tube boilers.

Courageous and *Glorious* took part in an action against German light cruisers in November 1917. Both were converted to aircraft carriers in the 1920s.

BELOW: ***Courageous***, seen here alongside at Devonport, and ***Glorious*** were light battlecruisers in which even armament was sacrificed for speed. Eventually both ships were converted to aircraft carriers.

Furious was similar in size to *Courageous* and *Glorious*, even down to her turret rings, but she had, at last, the 455mm/18in gun in single mountings. She was also slightly beamier. However while nearing completion she was converted to an aircraft carrier. Contrary to popular history, the Admiralty was very air-minded, appreciating the value of aircraft both for reconnaissance and as fighters – particularly after the Royal Naval Air Service's success in shooting down airships. Nearly all battleships were converted to carry flying-off ramps, and the decision was taken to platform over the whole of *Furious*'s forecastle, and suppress the forward turret as one large flying-off ramp. There was space for a hangar under the ramp. Derricks were fitted for hoisting seaplanes onboard, but trials showed that an aircraft like the Sopwith Pup could also be landed on the deck.

The conversion was a limited success and in August 1917 *Furious* was taken in hand for a rebuild which would turn her into a through-deck carrier. The Royal Navy is sometimes accused of being too battleship-minded in the inter-war years and criticized for not paying enough attention to naval aviation, but up to April 1, 1918 (when the RAF was formed), it owned one of the largest air forces in the world and the loss of so many men and machines to the RAF was a serious setback.

TOP: **Another view of *Courageous*, this time from the quarter.** ABOVE: ***Furious* also was converted to an aircraft carrier (above left) on board where in the inter-war years the Royal Navy experimented with the first arrester wires (above right). Despite the loss of expertise by the transfer of large numbers of aircraft and airmen to the RAF, the Royal Navy continued to innovate and, despite a lack of modern aircraft, maintained its tactical skill in the use of aircraft. Control of the Fleet Air Arm did not revert to the Royal Navy until just before World War II. Nevertheless, the Fleet Air Arm newly restored to the Admiralty's operational control made rapid progress and distinguished itself well in all theatres of the war, against the German, Italian and Japanese navies.**

Courageous class

Class: *Courageous, Glorious.* Launched 1916
Dimensions: Length – 239.7m/786ft 3in
 Beam – 24.7m/81ft
 Draught – 7.1m/23ft 4in
Displacement: 19,540 tonnes/19,230 tons
Armament: Main – 4 x 380mm/15in guns
 Secondary – 18 x 100mm/4in guns and
 2 x 535mm/21in torpedoes
Machinery: 18 small-tube boilers, 4 shafts,
 67,113kW/90,000shp
Speed: 32 knots
Complement: 828 men

Furious

Class: *Furious.* Launched 1916
Dimensions: Length – 239.7m/786ft 6in
 Beam – 26.8m/88ft
 Draught – 6.4m/21ft
Displacement: 19,826 tonnes/19,513 tons
Armament: Main – 2 x 455mm/18in guns
 Secondary – 11 x 140mm/5.5in guns and
 2 x 535mm/21in torpedoes
Machinery: 18 boilers, 4 shafts,
 67,113kW/90,000shp
Speed: 31 knots
Complement: 880 men

LEFT: *Michigan* at anchor at evening colours. The low light through the lattice masts shows their delicate and elaborate construction. ABOVE: *Michigan* firing a broadside of her 305mm/12in guns during 1912. BELOW: The larger navies were beginning to experiment with replenishment at sea, but operations like this coaling while underway from the bunker ship *Cyclops* to *South Carolina* in 1914 were slow and cumbersome.

South Carolina class

The launch of the British *Dreadnought* with her size, turbine machinery, speed of 21 knots, and main battery of ten 305mm/12in guns shook naval observers everywhere. The USN had already ordered its first all-big-gun ships, but the design was artificially constrained by the US Congress to 16,257 tonnes/ 16,000 tons, and delayed while the USN absorbed the lessons of the Great White Fleet and of the Battle of Tsushima. In the end, *South Carolina* and *Michigan* were similar to earlier US pre-Dreadnoughts, including in the retention of reciprocating engines.

They did, however, have two novel features: lattice masts and super-firing guns. Apparently the original intention had been to install a gun-direction platform amidships on a flying bridge, but this was dropped in favour of the lattice or cage mast. Experiments had shown that this stood up well to shellfire and reduced vibration at the top of the mast and certainly the gun-direction platform could be carried up higher. This did not always work and in 1918 a heavy gale bent *Michigan*'s mast over. Nevertheless, the lattice mast was retro-fitted into many US pre-Dreadnoughts

and became the distinctive recognition mark of future US battleships.

The other novel feature was the super-firing turret. This enabled the full complement of main armament guns to be brought to bear on either beam, giving ships arranged like this a superiority over other Dreadnoughts with guns arranged in echelon or staggered in midships positions. The super-firing gun soon became the norm in every other navy.

South Carolina visited Europe in 1910–11, took part in US interventions in Haiti and Mexico in 1913–14, and spent the rest of World War I on the east coast of the USA. In 1919 she made four round-trips to France, bringing home over 4,000 servicemen, and was scrapped in 1924.

Michigan visited England and France in 1910, and spent the rest of her career in the Atlantic. In spring 1914 she was involved in the Vera Cruz incident when many of her crew served ashore. In World War I she stayed in the western Atlantic, but between January and April 1919 she brought home more than a thousand veterans of the western front. She was scrapped in 1924.

South Carolina class

Class: *South Carolina, Michigan.* Launched 1908
Dimensions: Length – 137.2m/450ft
  Beam – 24.5m/80ft 5in
  Draught – 7.5m/24ft 7in
Displacement: 16,260 tonnes/16,000 tons
Armament: Main – 8 x 305mm/12in guns
  Secondary – 22 x 75mm/3in guns and
  2 x 535mm/21in torpedoes
Machinery: 12 boilers, 2 shafts.
  11,304kW/16,500ihp
Speed: 18.5 knots
Complement: 869 men

Delaware class

The Delaware class, reckoned to be the first true Dreadnoughts in the USN, were 25 per cent larger than the previous class, capable of over 20 knots, and their ten centre-line 305mm/12in guns exceeded anything so far built. The secondary armament consisted of 125mm/5in guns, which became the standard size in the USN.

Absorbing more lessons from the Battle of Tsushima, large but fully enclosed conning towers were intended to reduce the exposure of bridge personnel. *Delaware* was fitted with triple-expansion reciprocating engines, while *North Dakota* was turbine-driven. The reciprocating engine proved more efficient and reliable and – the Americans claimed – *Delaware* was the first ship that could steam for 20 hours at full speed without a breakdown. *North Dakota*'s first turbines proved inefficient and better, geared turbines were installed in 1915 delivering 23,340kW/31,300shp.

LEFT: Quite soon the USN Dreadnoughts like the Delaware class did away with wing turrets and mounted all turrets on the centre line.

Delaware class

Class: *Delaware, North Dakota.* Launched 1909
Dimensions: Length – 155.5m/510ft
  Beam – 26m/85ft 4in
  Draught – 8.3m/27ft 3in
Displacement: 20,707 tonnes/20,380 tons
Armament: Main – 10 x 305mm/12in guns
  Secondary – 15 x 125mm/5in guns and
  2 x 535mm/21in torpedoes
Machinery: 14 boilers, 2 shafts,
  18,640kW/25,000shp
Speed: 21 knots
Complement: 933 men

Delaware served with the British Grand Fleet in the US Sixth Battle Squadron, and was scrapped in 1924. *North Dakota* was reduced to an auxiliary role after World War I and lasted until 1931.

Florida class

LEFT: *Florida*'s after turrets trained out to starboard and ready for action: the men do not appear to be wearing any kind of action clothing and the awning will have to be taken down to prevent blast from the guns from tearing it apart.

Compared to the Delaware class, these ships had an improved 125mm/5in gun with better armour and, once the US Congressional limit had been breached, showed the tendency for US Dreadnoughts to grow in size. Both ships landed seamen and marines during the Vera Cruz crisis in 1914. *Florida* joined the British Grand Fleet at Scapa Flow, and in December 1918 she escorted President Wilson to France and was at New York for the Victory Fleet Review. *Utah* was based in Ireland to cover Allied convoys as they approached Europe. Both ships were modernized in the 1920s when they received bulges, new oil-fired boilers and the funnels were trucked into one. The lattice mainmast was removed and an aircraft catapult fitted over the midships turret. Under the 1930 London Naval Treaty, *Florida* was scrapped and *Utah* was converted to a radio-controlled target ship in 1931. On December 7, 1941, *Utah* was hit by two aerial torpedoes and capsized in the attack on Pearl Harbor, where her wreck can still be seen.

Florida class

Class: *Florida, Utah.* Launched 1909–10
Dimensions: Length – 155.5m/510ft
  Beam – 27m/88ft 3in
  Draught – 8.6m/28ft 3in
Displacement: 22,175 tonnes/21,825 tons
Armament: Main – 10 x 305mm/12in guns
  Secondary – 16 x 125mm/5in guns and
  2 x 535mm/21in torpedoes
Machinery: 12 boilers, 4 shafts,
  20,880kW/28,000shp
Speed: 21 knots
Complement: 1,001 men
Beam increased to 32m/106ft by the addition of anti-torpedo bulges.

LEFT: The outline of USN Dreadnoughts did not change much until some of them were modernized in the 1920s. Here *Wyoming*, taken about 1937, can be compared with ships on the previous page. The most obvious feature is that a pole mast replaces the after cage mast and there is a single funnel.

Wyoming class

Twenty per cent larger again than their predecessors, the Wyomings had two more 305mm/12in guns, and the secondary armament was carried one deck higher. Both ships operated with the British Grand Fleet during World War I and afterwards in the Atlantic and Pacific. After modernization in 1925–7 they emerged with broader beams and thicker deck armour, and their silhouettes changed by single funnels, a pole mainmast and an aircraft catapult.

In 1931 *Wyoming* became a training ship, losing first her armour and six of the main turrets, and, in 1944 when the priority became anti-aircraft training, gaining extra 125mm/5in guns. She was scrapped in 1947.

Arkansas was also used for pre-World War II training, and she supported the occupation of Iceland and escorted convoys in the North Atlantic until refitted in 1942. Emerging with a tripod foremast, she was used for shore bombardment in support of the Normandy landings and off Southern France in 1944. Between February and May 1945, she supported the landings on Iwo Jima and Okinawa. *Arkansas* was expended during atomic bomb tests at Bikini Island in 1946.

Wyoming class

Class: *Wyoming, Arkansas.* Launched 1911
Dimensions: Length – 165.8m/544ft
  Beam – 28.4m/93ft 2in
  Draught – 8.7m/28ft 7in
Displacement: 26,420 tonnes/26,000 tons
Armament: Main – 12 x 305mm/12in guns
  Secondary – 21 x 125mm/5in guns and
  2 x 535mm/21in torpedoes
Machinery: 12 boilers, 4 shafts,
  20,880kW/28,000shp
Speed: 21 knots
Complement: 1,063 men

New York class

LEFT: A second modernization in the 1930s gave these and similar ships two tripod masts and a single funnel. The primary career of both ships was inshore bombardment.

The two New Yorks with their 355mm/14in guns were last in the line of the original US Dreadnoughts. Both ships served with the British Grand Fleet in 1917–18. They were modernized in the 1920s, and became the first USN battleships to have tripod masts. However, oil-fired boilers, a single trunked funnel, additional deck armour and anti-torpedo bulges increased beam and displacement, so that they could no longer make 20 knots. They served throughout World War II, covering convoys in the North Atlantic and supporting the landings in North Africa in November 1942. *Texas* also bombarded targets off Normandy and Southern France in 1944. In the Pacific they supported the Iwo Jima and Okinawa landings in 1945. *New York* was exposed during atomic bomb tests at Bikini Island and in 1948 was sunk as a target off Pearl Harbor. *Texas* is preserved as a memorial at San Jacinto and is the only remaining World War I-era US battleship still in existence.

New York class

Class: *New York, Texas.* Launched 1912
Dimensions: Length – 172.2m/565ft
  Beam – 29.1m/95ft 6in
  Draught – 8.7m/28ft 6in
Displacement: 27,433 tonnes/27,000 tons
Armament: Main – 10 x 355mm/14in guns
  Secondary – 21 x 125mm/5in guns and
  4 x 535mm/21in torpedoes
Machinery: 14 boilers, 2 shafts,
  20,954kW/28,100shp
Speed: 21 knots
Complement: 1,026 men

LEFT: *Oklahoma* passing Alcatraz in the 1930s.
BELOW: Sailors swabbing out the 355mm/14in guns.
The need for this function did not change with the
passing of time. BOTTOM LEFT: *Nevada* operating a
kite balloon off Cuba in World War I. BOTTOM RIGHT:
Nevada at sea with other battleships in the 1920s.

Nevada class

The Nevadas were the first US battleships to carry a super-firing twin turret over a triple turret, thus contracting the heavy broadside into just four mountings. At the time they were also the most heavily armoured USN battleships, with the upper and lower belts merged into one with a maximum thickness of 340mm/13.5in. They were the first to use oil as their primary fuel and the last to have two shafts. *Nevada* had turbines and Yarrow boilers, while *Oklahoma* was the last USN battleship to have reciprocating steam engines (with Babcock and Wilcox boilers) which gave her a range of 12,875km/8,000 miles. They were originally completed with a large battery of anti-torpedo-boat 125mm/5in guns, but these were very exposed to the sea and were suppressed.

The Nevadas were based in Ireland in World War I, covering troop convoys to Europe. They were modernized in 1927–9, when gun elevation was increased, and two distinctive tripod masts were fitted as well as aircraft catapults. Anti-torpedo bulges increased the beam to 32.3m/106ft and additional anti-aircraft guns were added.

Both ships were sunk in the Japanese attack on Pearl Harbor on December 7, 1941. *Nevada* was the only battleship to get underway and became the main objective of the second wave of Japanese aircraft and was stranded. *Nevada* supported the landings at Attu in May 1943, Normandy and Southern France in 1944, and Iwo Jima and Okinawa in 1945, when she was hit by a suicide plane on March 27 and by shore artillery on April 5. Irradiated at Bikini in 1946, she was sunk off Hawaii.

In 1936 *Oklahoma* evacuated during the Spanish Civil War. At Pearl Harbor she was berthed outboard of the battleship *Maryland* and hit by a large number of aerial torpedoes. She rolled over and sank. Her salvage became a matter of pride but with a gaping hole in her side she was beyond repair. The hulk sank while under tow in 1947.

Nevada class

Class: *Nevada, Oklahoma.* Launched 1914
Dimensions: Length – 175.3m/575ft
   Beam – 29m/95ft
   Draught – 8.7m/28ft 6in
Displacement: 27,940 tonnes/27,500 tons
Armament: Main – 10 x 355mm/14in guns
   Secondary – 21 x 125mm/5in guns and
   2 x 535mm/21in torpedoes
Machinery: 12 boilers, 2 shafts,
   20,880kW/26,000shp (*Nevada*)
   19,700kW/24,800shp (*Oklahoma*)
Speed: 20 knots
Complement: 864 men

LEFT: *Pennsylvania* at sea in May 1934, after her first modernization. One of the most significant features was the replacement of the cage masts by tripods, carrying considerably more fire control equipment than these ships used to have.

Pennsylvania class

Class: *Pennsylvania, Arizona.* Launched 1915
Dimensions: Length – 185.3m/608ft
    Beam – 29.6m/97ft
    Draught – 8.8m/29ft
Displacement: 31,900 tonnes/31,400 tons
Armament: Main – 12 x 355mm/14in guns
    Secondary – 22 x 125mm/5in, 4 x 75mm/3in
    guns and 2 x 535mm/21in torpedoes
Machinery: 12 boilers, 4 shafts,
    23,490kW/31,500shp
Speed: 21 knots
Complement: 915 men

Pennsylvania class

The Pennsylvanias were enlarged Nevadas, with four triple turrets. Reconstructed in 1929–31, they received the usual range of improvements. In addition *Pennsylvania*, designated as a flagship, was given a two-tier armoured conning tower. Both were in battleship row when the Japanese attacked Pearl Harbor. *Arizona* blew up and her remains are now an American national memorial.

Pennsylvania was in dry dock and only slightly damaged. Fitted with a large battery of anti-aircraft guns in late 1942, she supported many amphibious operations and was at the Battle of Surigao Strait on October 25, 1944.

On August 12, 1945, *Pennsylvania* was the last major warship to be hit during World War II. A target ship at atomic bomb tests in 1946, *Pennsylvania* was scuttled in 1948.

New Mexico class

LEFT: **An aerial view of *New Mexico* taken in 1919. Compare this photograph of *New Mexico*, more or less as newly completed with distinctive cage masts, and *Pennsylvania* after modernization. All these ships underwent further modernizations after Pearl Harbor in order to combat the threat from the air.**

Mississippi was converted to a gunnery training and weapons development ship in 1946, and in the 1950s to a test ship for the USN's first surface-to-air guided missile, Terrier. She was sold for scrap in 1956. *New Mexico* was hit twice by kamikaze planes, but was present in Tokyo Bay when Japan surrendered on September 2, 1945. She was sold for scrap in October 1947. *Idaho* was also present in Tokyo Bay and she was scrapped in November 1947.

New Mexico class

Class: *New Mexico, Mississippi, Idaho.*
    Launched 1917
Dimensions: Length – 190m/624ft
    Beam – 29.7m/97ft 5in
    Draught – 9.1m/30ft
Displacement: 32,510 tonnes/32,000 tons
Armament: Main – 12 x 355mm/14in guns
    Secondary – 14 x 125mm/5in, 4 x 75mm/3in
    guns and 2 x 535mm/21in torpedoes
Machinery: 9 boilers, 4 shafts,
    23,862kW/32,000shp
Speed: 21 knots
Complement: 1,084 men

The New Mexico class had three triple turrets of an improved design. Some secondary armament was placed in the bow and stern, but had to be removed because they were too wet, and the remaining 125mm/5in guns were in the superstructure. A clipper bow made for better sea-keeping. Initially two ships were intended, but selling two pre-Dreadnoughts to Greece paid for a third. *New Mexico* had a new propulsion system, which had been trialled in the collier *Jupiter*. This used steam turbines to turn electrical generators, which in turn powered the ship's propellers driven by electric motors. All were rebuilt in 1931–4, receiving new superstructures, modern gun directors, new engines, deck armour and anti-torpedo bulges. All three were in the Atlantic in 1941 and so avoided the attack on Pearl Harbor, but were recalled and participated in many landing operations, and *Mississippi* took part in the Battle of Surigao Strait.

Kashima class

Class: *Kashima, Katori.* Launched 1905
Dimensions: Length – 144.3m/473ft 7in
  Beam – 23.8m/78ft 2in
  Draught – 8m/26ft 4in
Displacement: 16,663 tonnes/16,400 tons
Armament: Main – 4 x 305mm/12in and
  4 x 255mm/10in guns
  Secondary – 12 x 50mm/2in guns and
  5 x 455mm/18in torpedoes
Machinery: 20 boilers, 2 shafts,
  11,782kW/15,800shp
Speed: 18.5 knots
Complement: 946 men

Kashima class

These two ships were the last pre-Dreadnoughts built in Britain for the Imperial Japanese Navy, and with one exception represented the last major Japanese warships built anywhere abroad. They were the equivalent of the King Edward VII class. No doubt Japanese officers standing by their ships in Britain would have had plenty of time to study developments in battleship design. The Imperial Japanese Navy had already drawn up plans for an 18,290-tonne/18,000-ton cruiser with 255mm/10in guns, and the lessons of the Russo-Japanese War confirmed to the Japanese their subsequent choice of an all-big-gun ship. *Kashima* and *Katori* saw no action and were broken up in 1924.

Satsuma class

two half-sisters, and *Aki* had three instead of two funnels. Both ships were disarmed under the terms of the Washington Naval Treaty. They were unsuitable for modernization, and expended as targets in 1924.

Satsuma class

Class: *Satsuma, Aki.* Launched 1906–7
Dimensions: Length – 146.9m/482ft
  Beam – 25.5m/83ft 6in
  Draught – 8.4m/27ft 6in
Displacement: 19,683 tonnes/19,372 tons
Armament: Main – 4 x 305mm/12in and
  12 x 255mm/10in guns
  Secondary – 12 x 120mm/4.7in guns and
  5 x 455mm/18in torpedoes
Machinery: 20 boilers, 2 shafts,
  12,901kW/17,300ihp
Speed: 18.25 knots
Complement: 887 men

The Satsuma class is further proof that the idea of an all-big-gun ship arose in several places at about the same time. These ships had been designed before the Battle of Tsushima and were to be armed with 12 305mm/12in guns. However, impoverished by the Russo-Japanese War, the Imperial Japanese Navy could not afford both the 305mm/12in guns it wanted to buy from Britain and the Curtis turbines from the USA. Hence these ships were completed with a mixed armament, all in turrets.

The Japanese learned quickly, and *Aki* benefited from the lessons learned in building *Satsuma*, and the 120mm/4.7in guns were replaced by 150mm/6in guns as the secondary armament. The Japanese did not have the same problems as the USN in making turbines work in their ships and they quickly abandoned the reciprocating steam engine, though a shortage of oil meant that the Japanese used coal-fired boilers for longer than most navies. There were minor differences in size between these

LEFT: *Tsukuba* and *Ikoma* were the first Japanese-built battlecruisers. They were slow and very lightly armoured, and their small size, less than half the tonnage of battlecruisers being built in Europe and America, meant that they served little tactical operational purpose and were very soon obsolete.

Tsukuba class

The Imperial Japanese Navy had a preference for speed and armament over armour, and this included both large battlecruisers and small ones like *Tsukuba* and *Ikoma*. Built as armoured cruisers (when the Royal Navy introduced the term) these were re-rated as battlecruisers and were ordered to replace earlier pre-Dreadnought battleships. Japanese industry, including shipbuilding, was advancing rapidly and

with these and successor ships they demonstrated their ability to build quickly. Nevertheless, despite their rapid construction, by the time these ships were completed in 1907–8 other navies were building yet bigger and faster battlecruisers. *Tsukuba* was a defect-prone ship and suffered an ammunition explosion in 1917. *Ikoma* was re-armed in 1919 as a training ship before being scrapped in 1924.

Tsukuba class

Class: *Tsukuba, Ikoma.* Launched 1905–6
Dimensions: Length – 137.2m/450ft
  Beam – 23m/75ft 5in
  Draught – 7.9m/26ft 1in
Displacement: 13,970 tonnes/13,750 tons
Armament: Main – 4 x 305mm/12in and
  12 x 150mm/6in guns
  Secondary – 12 x 120mm/4.7in guns and
  3 x 455mm/18in torpedoes
Machinery: 20 boilers, 2 shafts,
  15,287kW/20,500ihp
Speed: 20.5 knots
Complement: 879 men

Ibuki class

LEFT: *Ibuki* and *Kurama* were not much better than the Tsukuba class, and were scrapped in the 1920s, when these ships, and their immediate predecessors, had been taken over by the Dreadnought revolution. All of them were too small, apart from any other consideration, to be of further use in the inter-war years.

Ibuki class

Class: *Ibuki, Kurama.* Launched 1907
Dimensions: Length – 147.8m/485ft
  Beam – 23m/75ft 4in
  Draught – 7.9m/26ft 1in
Displacement: 14,870 tonnes/14,636 tons
Armament: Main – 4 x 305mm/12in and
  8 x 205mm/8in guns
  Secondary – 14 x 120mm/4.7in guns and
  3 x 455mm/18in torpedoes
Machinery: 20 boilers, 2 shafts,
  16,778kW/22,500ihp
Speed: 20.5 knots
Complement: 844 men

The Ibuki class was an improved Tsukuba class. *Ibuki* was delayed because the slips at Kure were occupied and she was re-engineered with turbines. Few Japanese ships saw any action in World War I, but *Ibuki* joined the hunt in

the Pacific for the German East Asiatic Squadron. She also escorted convoys of Australian and New Zealand troops across the Indian Ocean in 1914. Warships also operated in support of the Allies in the eastern Meditteranean.

LEFT: *Fuso* in dry dock at Kure. *Fuso* and *Yamashiro* when completed were powerful, elegant ships, but were rebuilt with thick control towers and single funnels in the 1930s. Unlike the Kashima, Satsuma, Tsukuba and Ibuki classes, which were all too small, the 30,480-tonne/30,600-ton *Fuso* and *Yamashiro* incorporated all the lessons of the Dreadnought revolution and were capable of a worthwhile and significant mid-life update which enabled them to see action in World War II.
BELOW: *Yamashiro* at sea in 1934.

Fuso class

The Fuso class was the first of super-Dreadnoughts with guns greater than 305mm/12in. Reckoned by some to be too lightly armoured for their size, the Japanese applied the lesson they had learned from mine and torpedo damage during the Russo-Japanese War and fitted their ships with much greater subdivision of compartments in order to control this damage.

After World War I both ships acquired additional searchlights and improved gun-direction platforms, and *Yamashiro* received a British-style flying-off ramp on B turret. Both ships were extensively modernized in the 1930s. They were lengthened by some 7.6m/25ft, and their beam increased by over 3.7m/12ft with anti-torpedo bulges. New turbines and space-saving boilers nearly doubled their horsepower from 29,828kW/40,000shp to 55,928kW/75,000shp and increased speed by nearly 2 knots, despite the weight of additional deck armour. The change from coal- to oil-fired boilers also increased the ships' range.

Both ships were equipped with aircraft and a catapult, which was mounted on the quarterdeck in *Yamashiro* and initially over Q turret in *Fuso* until removed to the quarterdeck. The secondary and anti-aircraft armament was improved and the elevation of the main guns increased to 43 degrees, giving the 355mm/14in guns a range of 22km/13.5 miles. In the conversion, the fore funnel was done away with entirely, and the elegant tripod mast of the original design was replaced by towering pagodas containing conning positions, light guns, searchlights, rangefinders and gun direction platforms.

Fuso and *Yamashiro* operated together during World War II, either as the covering force to long-range convoys or awaiting the decisive battle which the Japanese thought the Americans might attempt, as the Russians had 40 years before. They were also sunk together.

At the Battle of Surigao Strait on October 25, 1944, *Fuso* and *Yamashiro* encountered a USN fleet which included the six battleships *Mississippi, Maryland, West Virginia, Tennessee, California* and *Pennsylvania*. *Fuso* was sunk by gunfire and *Yamashiro* succumbed to a massed torpedo attack by USN destroyers – although experts are still arguing as to which ship was sunk first and, in the darkness, how.

Fuso class

Class: *Fuso, Yamashiro.* Launched 1914–15
Dimensions: Length – 203m/665ft
  Beam – 28.6m/94ft
  Draught – 8.7m/28ft 6in
Displacement: 30,480 tonnes/30,600 tons
Armament: Main – 12 x 355mm/14in guns
  Secondary – 16 x 150mm/6in,
  4 x 80mm/3.1in guns and 6 x 535mm/21in
  torpedoes
Machinery: 24 boilers, 4 shafts,
  29,828kW/40,000shp
Speed: 22.5 knots
Complement: 1,193 men

Kongo class

The battlecruiser *Kongo* was the very last Japanese capital ship to be built outside Japan. While *Kongo* was designed and built by Vickers, large components were delivered from Britain to Japan for *Kongo*'s three sister ships. *Kongo* was intended as a model ship for Japanese shipyards to emulate, but her evident success, and superiority over the British Lion class which was building at the same time, inspired the changes which led to the Tiger class.

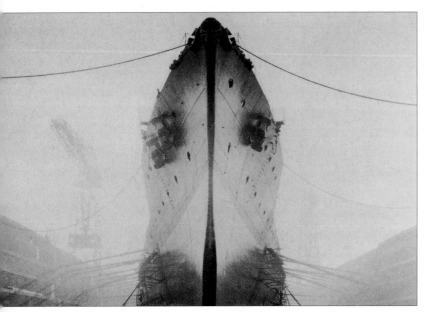

After World War I all four ships were refitted and received pagoda-like control towers, and funnel cowls, and were re-designated as battleships. They were modernized in 1936–7 when the hull was lengthened, and with new machinery they could reach over 30 knots. High speed and heavy guns made the Kongo class useful ships which saw much action in World War II. The Japanese concept was that the Kongos should act as escorts to carrier battle groups. Modifications during World War II to *Kongo* and *Haruna* included the fitting of radar. All ships of the class were sunk in the war.

In December 1941, *Kongo* supported the Japanese invasion of the Malayan Peninsula. She then supported landings in Java, and was part of the force which raided the Indian Ocean. At the Battle of Midway in June 1942, *Kongo* was part of the covering force, and during the Guadalcanal campaign she bombarded Henderson airfield, took part in the Battle of the Santa Cruz Islands and the naval Battle of Guadalcanal. Then in June 1944 she performed her intended function as part of the Japanese carrier escort force at the Battle of the Philippine

TOP: **The battleship *Kongo* from a postcard in the 1920s. Japanese sailors were proud of their ships and wanted postcards to send home. *Kongo* was the last major unit built abroad for the Imperial Japanese Navy, primarily for Japanese constructors to gain experience of the latest British methods. The three other ships of the same class were Japanese-built.** LEFT: **A rare picture of *Kongo* in dry dock at Yokosuka during her reconstruction during the 1930s.**

LEFT: **Four Japanese battleships photographed pre-war: *Nagato*, *Kirishima*, *Ise* and *Hyuga*. The Japanese fleet was powerful but, as the profiles of these ships show, photographed in the 1930s, it relied on a core of World War I ships which had been modernized and some inter-war ships which had not been built in large batches nor followed the same generational and incremental steps from which American and British battleships had benefited.**
BELOW: ***Haruna* was sunk at Edashima in April 1945 by USN carrier aircraft.**

Sea. At the Battle of Leyte Gulf, *Kongo* showed her immense strength, surviving a torpedoing, naval air attacks, and a bombing from high level. However, on November 21, 1944, she was torpedoed by the USN submarine *Sealion*, causing a fire which raged out of control until she blew up and sank. *Kongo* was the only battleship to be sunk by a submarine attack during the war in the Pacific.

Like her sisters, *Kirishima* was modernized in 1927–30, rebuilt in 1935–6, and reclassified as a battleship. She was part of the escort force during the Japanese attack on Pearl Harbor and in spring 1942 part of the fleet that raided the Indian Ocean. Active throughout that year, she received minor damage during a skirmish on November 13. Off Savo Island two nights later she was disabled by the USN battleship *Washington*, during the last ever purely battleship-to-battleship engagement, and was scuttled by her crew.

Haruna was damaged by a mine laid by the German auxiliary cruiser *Wolf* in 1917. In December 1941 she covered the landings in Malaya and in early 1942 she supported the Japanese conquest of the Dutch East Indies. *Haruna* was present at most significant battles throughout 1942: in June she was damaged at the Battle of Midway and in October (with *Kongo*) she devastated Henderson airfield. With the bulk of the Japanese fleet, *Haruna* was held back in Japan for a decisive battle against the US Navy during 1943–4. She was hit by a bomb in June 1944 at the Battle of the Philippine Sea, and also survived the Battle of Leyte Gulf. Damaged by near-misses in October 1944, *Haruna* was finally sunk at Kure by carrier aircraft on July 28, 1945.

Hiei was the only one of her class to be demilitarized under the terms of the Washington Naval Treaty. However, in the 1930s she received the same modernization as her sisters and returned to the Japanese order of battle. She was present at the attack on Pearl Harbor, the invasion of the Dutch East Indies, and the Japanese sortie into the Indian Ocean. During

the campaign off Guadalcanal she showed great resilience, like *Kirishima*, surviving more than 100 hits from the USN cruisers *Portland* and *San Francisco*, and torpedoes from the destroyers *Cushing* and *O'Bannon*. She was finally hit and sunk by high-level bombing on November 13, 1942.

Kongo class

Class: *Kongo, Hiei, Haruna, Kirishima.*
Launched 1912–13
Dimensions: Length – 215m/704ft
Beam– 28m/92ft
Draught – 8.5m/27ft 7in
Displacement: 27,940 tonnes/27,500 tons
Armament: Main – 8 x 355mm/14in guns
Secondary – 16 x 150mm/6in,
8 x 80mm/3.1in guns and
8 x 535mm/21in torpedoes
Machinery: 36 boilers, 4 shafts,
47,725kW/64,000shp
Speed: 27.5 knots
Complement: 1,221 men

Ise class

These were improved versions of the Fuso class, being slightly longer and larger. The midships P turret was moved and raised into a super-firing position over Q turret, thus making better use of the between decks and enabling an improved machinery room space.

They were modernized in two stages. In 1926–8 the two tripod masts were replaced by a pole mainmast and a pagoda foremast, the fore funnel received a cowl, and a catapult was mounted on X turret (this was removed to the quarterdeck in 1933). Total conversion followed in the 1930s, when they were lengthened, the armour increased, bulges fitted, boilers upgraded, fore funnel suppressed, main gun elevation improved and they received additional light guns.

After the Battle of Midway, both ships were modified into semi-aircraft carriers. The after turrets were suppressed and a short flight deck installed, with two

TOP: *Ise* was launched in 1916 and with her sisters modernized in the 1920s. ABOVE: *Hyuga* sitting on the bottom at Kure after an air attack in 1945. RIGHT: A close-up of B turret. The forward turret is submerged.

powerful catapults, however neither ship seems to have carried aircraft and the concept was never proved.

Hyuga was at the Battle of Midway, and converted to a semi-carrier in 1942–3. However, she saw action as a battleship during the battle for Leyte Gulf. She received some damage and was sent to Kure for repairs, where she was bombed again in March and July 1945. She settled on the bottom on July 24, where she was broken up in 1946.

Ise followed an almost identical career, and was sunk on July 27, 1945.

Ise class ●

Class: *Ise, Hyuga.* Launched 1916–17
Dimensions: Length – 206m/675ft
    Beam – 28.6m/94ft
    Draught – 8.9m/29ft 1in
Displacement: 31,762 tonnes/31,260 tons
Armament: Main – 12 x 355mm/14in guns
    Secondary – 20 x 140mm/5.5in,
    4 x 80mm/3.1in guns and
    6 x 535mm/21in torpedoes
Machinery: 24 boilers, 4 shafts,
    33,557kW/45,000shp
Speed: 22.5 knots
Complement: 1,360 men

Nassau class

A battleship considerably more powerful than the archetypal pre-Dreadnought was being contemplated by the German navy when the news of Fisher's *Dreadnought* spread abroad. The consequence was a three-year delay while the Germans worked out exactly what Fisher had achieved. The resulting design was the first German Dreadnought, with 12 large-calibre guns in a hexagonal layout of twin turrets. This was not ideal as only a maximum of four turrets could be brought to bear on any one target, but the Germans rationalized that the two turrets on the disengaged side formed a reserve. These ships were easily identified by the two prominent gooseneck cranes carried amidships. The Nassau class rolled dangerously even on a smooth sea and bilge keels had to be fitted.

The class operated as a unit and in April 1916 were part of the covering force during the German bombardment of Scarborough and Yarmouth. At the Battle of Jutland, *Nassau* was hit twice and soon repaired, *Westfalen* and *Rheinland* were both hit once and slightly damaged, and *Posen* was undamaged.

In August and again in October 1916 attempted sorties into the North Sea were frustrated, but in April 1918 *Nassau* progressed as far as the latitude of Stavanger, Norway, before turning back without achieving very much. *Westfalen* was torpedoed by the British submarine *E-23* in August 1916 but repaired.

In 1918 *Westfalen* was sent into the Baltic to assist the Finns in their uprising against the Russians and the ensuing civil war. *Rheinland* accompanied *Westfalen* to the Baltic, but ran aground in April 1918 off the Åland islands. She was salvaged (involving the removal of 6,503 tonnes/6,400 tons of coal, armour, ammunition and guns) three months later and was towed to Kiel where she became a barracks ship.

Posen first entered the Baltic and then accompanied *Nassau* north to Norway. All ships of the class were deleted from the German navy in November 1919. *Nassau* was allocated to Japan, and *Westfalen* and *Posen* were allocated to Britain. All ships of the class were scrapped in 1920–4 under the terms of the Armistice, leaving Germany with only some very obsolete battleships.

Nassau class

Class: *Nassau, Westfalen, Rheinland, Posen.*
Launched 1908

Dimensions: Length – 137.7m/451ft 9in
Beam – 26.9m/88ft 5in
Draught – 8.1m/26ft 6in

Displacement: 18,870 tonnes/18,570 tons

Armament: Main – 12 x 280mm/11in guns
Secondary – 12 x 150mm/6in,
16 x 88mm/3.46in guns and
6 x 455mm/18in torpedoes

Machinery: 12 boilers, 3 shafts,
16,405kW/22,000ihp

Speed: 19.5 knots

Complement: 1,008 men

BELOW: **A starboard bow view of the** *panzerkreuzer* *Westfalen.* BOTTOM: **The four ships of the Nassau class,** *Nassau, Westfalen, Rheinland* **and** *Posen,* **alongside, possibly in pre-war Hamburg.**

ABOVE LEFT: **The German battle fleet at sea.** *Oldenburg* **is nearest to the camera.** ABOVE: **Post-war** *Ostfriesland* **was sunk during aerial bombing trials by the USAAF.** LEFT: **The bombing trials were somewhat artificial as the targets were both stationary and not firing back at the bombers. Nevertheless, although it took several attempts by the bombers to get photographic evidence like this, the pictures had a powerful influence on decision-makers in the USA.**

Helgoland class

While retaining the inefficient hexagon layout of the main armament, the Helgolands were a considerable improvement over their predecessors. Compared with the Dreadnoughts building in Britain, they were like most German ships of this period, lighter and beamier. They also had better internal subdivision and greater pumping power, and the German ammunition was safer when hit because it was inclined to burn rather than explode. The Germans retained reciprocating steam engines for longer than the Royal Navy, but this class introduced the 305mm/12in gun to the German navy.

The class acted as a unit, and was part of the covering force for the bombardment of Scarborough and Yarmouth in April 1916, and fought at Jutland in May. *Helgoland* and *Oldenburg* received one hit each and were quickly repaired. *Ostfriesland* hit a mine but was repaired by the end of July. All ships took part in the Battle of Dogger Bank, but were inactive for most of the remainder of the war. After Germany's defeat in World War I, *Helgoland, Ostfriesland, Thüringen* and *Oldenburg* were handed over to Britain, USA, France and Japan respectively.

Interned at Scapa Flow, *Ostfriesland* was not scuttled with the rest of the German High Seas Fleet because she had been moved to Rosyth, prior to being taken over by the USN. She was steamed to New York where she was decommissioned and dry-docked so that USN naval architects could examine her design. She was then expended as a target in July 1921 while at anchor. *Ostfriesland* survived many bomb hits and near-misses. She would probably have avoided any damage if she had been underway and, even if hit, been saved if damage control measures had been taken. Carefully edited film of her eventual sinking was used to help promote the use of air power. In 1920 *Thüringen* survived an attempted scuttling off Cherbourg by her German crew. In 1920s she was used as a target, then was sold for scrap. A large portion of the hull still remains off the beach at Gavres and continued to be used for target practice until the 1990s.

Helgoland class

Class: *Helgoland, Ostfriesland, Thüringen, Oldenburg.* Launched 1909–10
Dimensions: Length – 167.2m/548ft 7in
Beam – 28.5m/93ft 6in
Draught – 8.2m/26ft 11in
Displacement: 22,800 tonnes/22,440 tons
Armament: Main – 12 x 305mm/12in guns
Secondary – 14 x 150mm/6in,
14 x 88mm/3.46in guns and
6 x 510mm/20in torpedoes
Machinery: 15 boilers, 3 shafts,
20,880kW/28,000ihp
Speed: 20 knots
Complement: 1,113 men

LEFT: *Prinzregent Luitpold* immediately pre-war showing off the range and elevation of her 305mm/12in guns.

Kaiser class

Kaiser class	
Class: *Kaiser, Friedrich der Grosse, Kaiserin, König Albert, Prinzregent Luitpold.* Launched 1911–12.	
Dimensions: Length – 172m/564ft	
Beam – 29m/95ft 3in	
Draught – 8.3m/27ft 3in	
Displacement: 25,095 tonnes/24,700 tons	
Armament: Main – 10 x 305m/12in guns	
Secondary – 14 x 150mm/6in guns and 5 x 510mm/20in torpedoes	
Machinery: 18 boilers, 3 shafts, 18,640kW/25,000hp	
Speed: 21 knots	
Complement: 1,088 men	

Kaiser class

The Kaisers were the first German battleships to be fitted with turbines and with an oil-burning capability. Like other German ships they had three (rather than the British arrangement of four) propellers. It was intended to provide *Prinzregent Luitpold* with a diesel to drive her central shaft but this was not fitted and the space was left empty. The use of turbines made it easier to mount the midships guns *en echelon*, and with one after turret mounted in a super-firing position the Kaisers – despite having one less turret compared with their predecessors – could still bring one more turret (all five) to bear on either beam.

Kaiser took part in most of the German naval operations of World War I in the North Sea: the bombardments of the English east cost, the First and Second Battles of Heligoland Bight, the Battle of Dogger Bank and the Battle of Jutland, where she was hit twice. In 1917 she also operated in the Baltic. All four sister ships followed similar careers. In addition, *Friedrich der Grosse* was flagship of the German High Seas fleet until March 1917.

König class

LEFT: The *linienschiff König* from a pre-war postcard. The class was new at the time of Jutland, where they saw much fighting, and they also fought in the Baltic.

These ships followed the pattern of operations for the High Sea Fleet and were in the thick of the fighting at Jutland, firing between them some 700 rounds of 305mm/12in munitions. They received hits as follows: *König*, ten; *Grosser Kurfürst,* eight; *Markgraf,* five. *Kronprinz* escaped undamaged. *König* went on to destroy the Russian battleship *Slava* on October 17, 1917, in the Baltic. Commander Noel Laurence in the British submarine *J-1* has the distinction of being the only submariner to hit two battleships in one go, when he fired a salvo of torpedoes at *Kronprinz* and *Grosser Kurfürst* on November 5, 1916, but in neither case was the damage fatal. *Kronprinz* was renamed *Kronprinz Wilhelm* in 1918.

Grosser Kurfürst holds something of a record for accidents: she collided with *König* in December 1914, ran aground in 1917, collided with *Kronprinz* also in 1917, hit a mine in the same year, damaged herself entering Wilhelmshaven in 1918, and ran aground off Heligoland on May 30, 1918.

All ships of both the Kaiser and König classes were interned at Scapa Flow and scuttled on June 21, 1921. They were then broken up from the 1930s onwards.

König class	
Class: *König, Grosser Kurfürst, Markgraf, Kronprinz (Wilhelm).* Launched 1913	
Dimensions: Length – 177m/580ft	
Beam – 29m/96ft	
Draught – 8.4m/27ft 6in	
Displacement: 25,910 tonnes/25,000 tons	
Armament: Main – 10 x 305mm/12in guns	
Secondary – 14 x 150mm/6in guns and 5 x 510mm/20in torpedoes	
Machinery: 18 boilers, 3 shafts, 25,350kW/34,000hp	
Speed: 21.5 knots	
Complement: 1,100 men	

Bayern class

LEFT: *Baden* seen here pre-war as fleet flagship. Neither ship was available in time for *Der Tag* (the Battle of Jutland) and they were the last Dreadnought battleships to be completed for the German Kaiser's navy. Others were planned and even laid down, but all were cancelled. ABOVE: *Bayern* had a relatively short life. She was laid down in 1914, launched in 1915 and scuttled in 1919. BELOW LEFT: *Bayern*, showing the German three-shaft arrangement, being towed to the breakers in 1935. BELOW: *Bayern* was mined in the Gulf of Riga in 1917.

This class introduced the 380mm/15in gun to the German navy as well as double-ended super-firing turrets, which meant that with just four twin turrets, all guns could fire over wide arcs on the beam. The German navy considered fitting triple turrets, but after studying the Austro-Hungarian battleships of the Viribus Unitis class, they decided against it on the grounds of weight, ammunition supply, rate of fire, torque and loss of fighting capability should one turret be hit. Instead the Germans opted for the larger-calibre gun. The two outer shafts were turbine-driven, and the centre line shaft was diesel-driven.

Bayern and *Baden* missed the Battle of Jutland but *Bayern* supported German landings in the Gulf of Riga in October 1917 against Russian-held positions. Ten German battleships were opposed by two Russian pre-Dreadnoughts, cruisers and three small British C-class submarines. Off Moon (Muhu) in the northern entrance to the gulf *Bayern* and *Grosser Kurfürst* hit mines on October 12, and *Bayern* suffered serious flooding through her forward underwater torpedo flat.

However, on October 17, the battleships *König* and *Kronprinz* damaged the Russian pre-Dreadnought *Slava* so badly that she had to be scuttled, and hit *Grazdanin* (formerly *Tsessarevitch*) which retired to the east and north. The badly flooded *Bayern* did not reach Kiel until October 31. She was scuttled at Scapa Flow and broken up in 1934–5. *Baden* took over from *Friedrich der Grosse* as flagship of the German High Fleet. She saw no action and was scuttled at Scapa Flow but beached by the British before she could sink, and eventually expended as a target during battleship practice in 1921.

Two slightly larger ships, *Sachsen* and *Württemberg*, were laid down in 1913 and 1914 but not completed and broken up on the slips in 1921.

Another class of fast battleship, this time with 420mm/16.5in guns, was designed but work on these ships was never started.

Bayern class

Class: *Bayern, Baden.*
Launched 1913-15
Dimensions: Length – 179.8m/589ft 10in
Beam – 30m/98ft 5in
Draught – 8.4m/27ft 8in
Displacement: 28,525 tonnes/28,074 tons
Armament: Main – 8 x 380mm/15in guns
Secondary – 16 x 150mm/6in,
8 x 88mm/3.46in guns and
5 x 600mm/23.6in torpedoes
Machinery: 14 boilers, 3 shafts.
35,794kW/48,000shp
Speed: 21 knots
Complement: 1,187 men

Von der Tann

Starting in 1908 the Hamburg shipyard of Blohm and Voss built a series of successful battlecruisers, the first ship in response to the British Invincible class being *Von der Tann*.

This first German battlecruiser was bigger all-round than the *Invincible*, and more heavily armoured. Anti-roll tanks were originally fitted but these proved ineffective and bilge keels were installed instead and the additional space was used for extra fuel. *Von der Tann* was also the first German capital ship to have turbines. Although the speed was about the same, her endurance was greater. The secondary armament (150mm/6in) was heavier than the *Invincible*'s (100mm/4in), and the German 280mm/11in main gun was almost as good as the British 305mm/12in, while the British ammunition was inferior. Although the midships turrets were placed *en echelon*, they were far enough inboard to have a good arc of fire on the opposite beam, and in most situations the broadside consisted of eight guns as compared to *Invincible*'s six. German ships generally had more thorough damage control arrangements, and so *Von der Tann* was a much better design and a superior warship to the Invincibles.

Von der Tann was present at most of the major naval engagements of World War I, starting with the Battle of Heligoland Bight in August 1914. She bombarded the English towns of Yarmouth on November 3, 1914, Scarborough on December 16, 1914, and Lowestoft on April 24, 1915.

At Jutland *Von der Tann* engaged *Indefatigable,* where one salvo caused an explosion in X magazine and another hit *Indefatigable*'s forecastle, whereupon she blew up, after only a quarter of an hour of the first phase of the battle. By comparison *Von der Tann* was also hit but withstood the damage. Two 380mm/15in and two 340mm/13.5in rounds put two turrets out of action and damaged two others, and she was without her main armament for one hour and fifteen minutes, but she was fully repaired by August 1916.

Her other sorties were less successful and late in 1916 and again in 1917 she required repairs to her turbines. She was scuttled with the rest of the German High Seas Fleet, but raised in 1903 and broken up at Rosyth in 1931–4.

BELOW: *Von der Tann* **photographed in 1910 before she was handed over to the German navy. She was reckoned to be a considerably better fighting ship than any British battlecruiser, primarily because she could withstand more damage.** RIGHT: *Von der Tann* **under tow to the breakers. Some of the work was contracted abroad and these tugs, in the mid 1930s, are flying the Nazi swastika.**

Von der Tann

Class: *Von der Tann.* Launched 1909
Dimensions: Length – 171.7m/563ft 4in
  Beam – 26.6m/87ft 3in
  Draught – 8.1m/26ft 6in
Displacement: 19,370 tonnes/19,064 tons
Armament: Main – 8 x 280mm/11in guns
  Secondary – 10 x 150mm/6in,
  16 x 88mm/3.46in guns and
  4 x 455mm/18in torpedoes
Machinery: 18 boilers, 4 shafts.
  32,513kw/43,600shp
Speed: 24.75 knots
Complement: 923 men

Moltke and *Goeben*

Moltke and *Goeben* were further improvements over *Von der Tann*, being slightly larger, with a streamlined hull form and, as with *Von der Tann*, bilge keels replaced the anti-rolling tanks. The main improvement and external difference was an additional super-firing after turret, bringing the broadside up to a possible ten 280mm/11in guns.

Moltke was present at most surface actions in World War I, took part in the bombardment of the English east coast and was torpedoed twice. She was hit forward by a torpedo fired by Lieutenant Commander Noel Lawrence of *E-1* (who would later torpedo *Kronprinz* and *Grosser Kürfurst* while in command of the submarine *J-1*) on August 19, 1915, in the Gulf of Riga but the damage was slight. On April 25, 1918, during a sortie by the German High Seas Fleet, *Moltke* lost a propeller, damaged the water inlet of one of her condensers and an engine room was flooded. She was under tow by *Oldenburg* when she was torpedoed by *E-42*; nevertheless she reached Germany and was repaired. Scuttled at

Scapa Flow, *Moltke* was raised in 1927 and broken up in 1927–9.

Goeben was flagship of the German Mediterranean division and was visiting Trieste when World War I broke out. Under the command of Admiral Souchon she made a feint against French troop convoys assembling in North Africa and then made a dash for the Bosphorus, chased unsuccessfully by the British *Indomitable* and *Indefatigable*. Once she arrived at Constantinople she was sold to Turkey, to replace capital ships which the British had confiscated, and played a major role in turning the balance of power in the region. The renamed *Yavuz* saw active service in the Black Sea, including some of the few engagements between pre-Dreadnoughts and Dreadnoughts, and she sank the British monitors *Raglan* and *M-28* on January 20, 1918, but ran into a minefield. She survived until 1974.

TOP: **The battlecruiser *Moltke*, photographed pre-war.** ABOVE: ***Moltke* being towed under the Forth Bridge on her way to the breakers at Rosyth.**

Moltke class

Class: *Moltke, Goeben.* Launched 1910
Dimensions: Length – 186.5m/611ft 11in
  Beam – 29.5m/96ft 10in
  Draught – 9m/29ft 5in
Displacement: 22,979 tonnes/22,616 tons
Armament: Main – 10 x 280mm/11in guns
  Secondary – 12 x 150mm/6in,
  12 x 88mm/3.46in guns and
  4 x 510mm/20in torpedoes
Machinery: 24 boilers, 4 shafts,
  38,776kW/52,000shp
Speed: 25.5 knots
Complement: 1,053 men

LEFT: **The damaged *Seydlitz*, down by the bows, after the Battle of Jutland. Despite the damage she was able to return to Germany for repair, before eventually being scuttled at Scarpa Flow and raised for scrap in 1928.**

Seydlitz

Class: *Seydlitz.* Launched 1912
Dimensions: Length – 200.5m/657ft 11in
　　Beam – 28.5m/93ft 6in
　　Draught – 8.2m/26ft 11in
Displacement: 24,989 tonnes/24,594 tons
Armament: Main – 10 x 280mm/11in guns
　　Secondary – 12 x 150mm/6in,
　　12 x 88mm/3.46in guns and
　　4 x 510mm/20in torpedoes
Machinery: 27 boilers, 4 shafts,
　　46,979kW/63,000shp
Speed: 26.5 knots
Complement: 1,068 men

Seydlitz

Blohm and Voss continued their incremental changes to their battlecruisers. *Seydlitz* was larger again than the Moltke class and had a raised forecastle and the forward turret was one deck higher. Anti-rolling tanks still featured, but were not used. Like her predecessors *Seydlitz* had tandem rudders, but the forward rudder was ineffective and all these ships had excessively large turning circles. The British obtained the plans for *Seydlitz*

although they were not influenced by them. At the Battle of Dogger Bank *Seydlitz* received two or three 340mm/13.5in hits from *Lion* that caused a rapid fire that burned out both after turrets. During the raid on Lowestoft she struck a mine and shipped nearly 1,524 tonnes/1,500 tons of sea water.

At Jutland, *Seydlitz* fired on *Queen Mary* and helped to sink her. She also received a score of large-calibre hits herself and was torpedoed twice by the

destroyer *Petard* (or maybe *Turbulent*). Both after turrets were again burned out, and she shipped 5,385 tonnes/5,300 tons of water, increasing her draught to 14m/46ft. However, like other German designs which had good subdivision, *Seydlitz* proved capable of sustaining much damage. She reached Germany and was repaired at Wilhelmshaven. She was interned, scuttled at Scapa Flow and then raised for scrap in November 1928.

Derfflinger class

LEFT: ***Lützow*, one of the three Derfflinger class, was sunk at the Battle of Jutland in 1916. This proved to be the exception and other ships, such as *Seydlitz* above, proved to be very resistant to British firepower in battle.**

Flush-decked and with a pronounced sheer which became characteristic of later German warships, the Derfflingers had two super-firing turrets at each end. At the Battle of Dogger Bank *Derfflinger* was hit by three 340mm/13.5in shells, causing superficial damage. At Jutland she fired on *Queen Mary* and *Invincible,* which both blew up, but *Derfflinger* was hit by a score of heavy rounds, including ten 340mm/13.5in shells from *Revenge.* Both after turrets were put out of action,

fires started and she was flooded, but she was repaired by October 1916. She was interned, scuttled and raised at Scapa Flow in 1934 and her remains were finally scrapped in 1948.

At Jutland *Lützow* is credited with sinking *Invincible*, and probably the cruiser *Defence*, but took at least 24 heavy shells and was badly damaged. Her crew was rescued by a German torpedo boat who then torpedoed *Lützow*, which sank in two minutes.

Hindenburg was completed too late for Jutland, saw little action and was scuttled at Scapa Flow. She was broken up in 1931–2.

Derfflinger class

Class: *Derfflinger, Lützow, Hindenburg.*
　　Launched 1913–15
Dimensions: Length – 210.4m/690ft 3in
　　Beam – 29m/95ft 2in
　　Draught – 8.3m/27ft 3in
Displacement: 26,600 tonnes/26,180 tons
Armament: Main – 8 x 305mm/12in guns
　　Secondary – 12 x 150mm/6in,
　　4 x 88mm/3.46in guns and
　　4 torpedoes of various sizes
Machinery: 18 boilers, 4 shafts,
　　46,979kW/63,000shp
Speed: 26.5 knots
Complement: 1,112 men
Hindenburg's displacement was 26,938 tonnes/
　　26,513 tons. *Hindenburg* was 2.44m/8ft longer.
　　The secondary armament and size of torpedoes
　　varied across the class.

Courbet class

The French navy was late in entering the Dreadnought race, and then built these four low-profile racy-looking ships, though following French procurement methods each was built at a different yard. Armed with twelve 305mm/12in guns, the forward and after guns were in super-firing turrets but the two wing turrets could only fire on their respective beams. Unlike the Dreadnought prototype, they also carried a substantial battery of medium-calibre guns. The thickness of the armour was generally less in these ships than in equivalent American and British battleships, but a minimum of 180mm/7in armour was carried well below the waterline. Originally they also carried a small outfit of mines: however, though some battleships were used as minelayers, it was not a happy combination of functions. The medium-calibre armament was suppressed in the 1920s and 1930s when these ships were also fitted with new boilers and the funnel arrangements were altered. In 1918 *Courbet* carried an observation balloon, and in 1920 *Paris* experimented with an aircraft ramp over B turret.

Jean Bart was completed in time to carry the French President on a pre-war state visit to St Petersburg in July 1914. In accordance with joint British and French naval plans, all four ships were employed in the Mediterranean during World War I, and on August 16, 1914, were involved in a battle off the Albanian coast in which the Austro-Hungarian cruiser *Zenta*

BELOW: **In 1940 some of the French fleet escaped to England. This close-up of** *Courbet* **shows British sailors cheering for the camera. After** *Courbet* **reverted to the Free French navy, she was grounded as an anti-aircraft battery off Ouistreham during the Normandy landings.**

LEFT: **Although they were a long time building and obsolescent when complete, the Courbet class (except for** *France* **which was wrecked in 1922) lasted until World War II.** BELOW: **The funnel arrangements and tall thin pole of military masts were reminiscent of some Italian designs of battleships. The layout lacks control equipment and rangefinders high over the ship, which nearly every other navy found essential for operations. These ships were not risked in the North Sea against the German High Sea Fleet.**

was sunk. *Jean Bart* was heavily damaged by the Austro-Hungarian submarine *U-12* in the Strait of Otranto in December 1914 and repaired at Malta. These modern ships were not risked during the Dardanelles campaign, but in 1919 *Jean Bart* took part in operations in the Black Sea against the Bolsheviks. *France* ran aground in Quiberon Bay in 1922 and was wrecked. *Jean Bart* (renamed *Ocean* in 1937) was scuttled in Toulon, used by the Germans as a target, and sunk by the Allies in 1944. *Paris* and *Courbet* saw action against the advancing German army in 1940, and were interned in Britain after the fall of France. *Paris* was offered to the Free Polish navy as a depot ship and finally scrapped in Brest in 1956. *Courbet* was a hulk, powered by an old railway locomotive lashed to her deck, when she was scuttled as a block ship off Ouistreham on the eastern edge of the Normandy landings where she was repeatedly attacked by German manned-torpedoes.

The French navy's operations in World War I were to convoy troops from North Africa to metropolitan France, then to counter the Italian and Austro-Hungarian fleets in the Mediterranean.

Courbet class

Class: *Courbet, Jean Bart, France, Paris.*
   Launched 1911–12
Dimensions: Length – 158.5m/520ft
   Beam – 27.89m/91ft 6in
   Draught – 8.99m/29ft 6in
Displacement: 22,545 tonnes/22,189 tons
Armament: Main – 12 x 305mm/12in guns
   Secondary – 22 x 135mm/5.4in guns and
   4 x 455mm/18in torpedoes
Machinery: 24 boilers, 4 shafts, power
   20,880kW/28,000shp
Speed: 20 knots
Complement: 1,085 men

When Italy joined the allies the French were released to support the allied landings at Gallipoli, while the Italians guarded the Austro-Hungarians. The Royal Navy was responsible for closing the Channel and North Sea to the Germans.

Bretagne class

These ships were developments of the Courbet class, but as French resources were increasingly directed towards her army, their completion was delayed and they saw little action during World War I.

The heavy guns were 340mm/13.5in, but instead of wing turrets they carried a centre-line midships turret which could fire on either beam. Unlike the Courbet class they were regularly modernized in the 1920s and 30s, during which they were converted to oil-burning, and the torpedo tubes and minelaying capability were suppressed. The after funnel was also raised. After trials in these ships with balloons and ramps in the 1930s, Lorraine's funnel was also moved aft and the midships turret removed so she could carry up to four aircraft.

All three ships operated with the British Mediterranean Fleet in early 1940. However, after the fall of France, the British demanded that the French navy should agree to measures of internment or disarmament to stop them falling into German hands, and when the French admiral at Mers-el-Kebir could not agree, Provence, Bretagne and other warships

were shelled on July 3, 1940, by the British battleships Hood, Barham and Resolution. Bretagne blew up with large loss of life. Provence was sunk and then salvaged by the French, and taken to Toulon where she was scuttled in 1942 by patriotic Frenchmen. She was then raised by the Germans so that her guns could be installed in coastal batteries, and finally broken up in 1949.

In July 1940 Lorraine was in the British naval base of Alexandria, where she agreed to internment, and subsequently joined the Free French navy at Dakar in 1943. She took part in the Allied landings in southern France in 1944, bombarding French soil, and in 1945 in the reduction of a remaining German stronghold, near the mouth of the Gironde. She was scrapped in 1954.

The Vasilefs Konstantinos (also Re Constantino) was built in France for the Greek navy in 1914. She was very similar in design to the Provence class, and with the outbreak of war she was taken over by the French navy and given the name Savoie but never completed.

TOP: **French shipbuilding programmes were often leisurely and the Bretagne class took four years to complete, 1912–16.** ABOVE: **One of the class at a speed trial in 1914. The class saw little action in the war. Two ships suffered under the guns of the British, and a third ship was used to bombard southern France and ports along the French Atlantic coast.**

Bretagne class

Class: Bretagne, Provence, Lorraine. Launched 1913
Dimensions: Length – 164.9m/541ft
Beam – 26.9m/88ft 3in
Draught – 8.9m/29ft 2in
Displacement: 23,600 tonnes/23,230 tons
Armament: Main – 10 x 340mm/13.5in guns
Secondary – 22 x 135mm/5.4in guns and
4 x 455mm/18in torpedoes
Machinery: 24 boilers, 4 shafts,
21,625kW/29,000shp
Speed: 20 knots
Complement: 1,124 men

Normandie class

In the midst of growing tension in Europe, France announced an ambitious programme in 1912 to achieve a strength of 28 battleships by 1922. It was envisaged that this would be reached by building battleships, and battlecruisers or fast battleships, in divisional numbers, of two and even three units per year. However, with the outbreak of World War I, France placed her priority for resources on her army and the Royal Navy was left to guard the northern flank of the allied armies on the Channel and North Sea coast. With this nearly all work on designing or building capital ships in France slowed to a stop.

Construction of five ships of the Normandie class began in 1913 and 1914. The French had also designed a quadruple 340mm/13.5in turret, which was planned for this class, and adoption of which would have enabled French designers to reduce the length and weight of the armoured citadel. This class would therefore have had three turrets, one each forward, midships and aft. Work continued as far as to allow the hulls to be launched, but thereafter they were robbed of their equipment, the boilers were taken for smaller warships and the guns for the army. Some of these guns were captured by the German army and turned against their builders. The hulls of *Normandie, Languedoc, Flandre* and *Gascogne* languished uncompleted for many years until the Washington Naval Treaty sealed their fate and they were deleted in 1922 from the French order of battle and scrapped. Work on *Vendée* recommenced in 1918 and after some experiments she was completed as the aircraft carrier *Béarn* in 1927.

Normandie class

Class: *Normandie, Vendée, Flandre, Gascogne, Languedoc.* Not launched

Dimensions: Length – 194.5m/638ft 2in
Beam – 29m/95ft 2in
Draught – 8.65m/28ft 5in

Displacement: 29,465 tonnes/29,000 tons

Armament: Main – 16 x 340mm/13.5in guns
Secondary – 24 x 135mm/5.4in guns and
6 x 455mm/18in torpedoes

Machinery: 21 or 28 boilers, 4 shafts,
23,862kW/32,000shp

Speed: 23 knots

Complement: 1,200 men

BELOW: **None of the Normandie class was completed, but one hull was taken to convert to France's first aircraft carrier, *Béarn*. She was too small and slow to be successful, although after conversion in World War II by the Americans she finished her career as a submarine tender, finally broken up in 1967.**

LEFT: **As a design,** *Dante Alighieri* **was clearly in the line of succession of Cuniberti's elegant proposals for the all-big-gun ship, and one which was copied by the Russian navy. This aerial photograph gives a very good idea of Cuniberti's concept: a relatively clear upper deck without large numbers of secondary or tertiary guns, and the main guns able to bear over wide angles of fire.** BELOW: **Firing a broadside from the midships two turrets.**

Dante Alighieri

The Italian warship designer Vittorio Cuniberti had already designed a number of ships for the Italian navy when he had published an article in *Jane's Fighting Ships* on what he thought would be the ideal battleship for the Royal Navy. This ship had 12 305mm/12in guns in single and double turrets and secondary armament was to consist of 75mm/3in guns. Cuniberti also placed emphasis on speed, sacrificing armour if need be, and proposed a ship which has a displacement of 17,273 tonnes/17,000 tons.

However, Admiral Fisher took up Cuniberti's all-big-gun idea in Britain, while Cuniberti and the Italian navy were still building distinctly pre-Dreadnought ships like the Vittorio Emanuele class. These were small battleships (13,209 tonnes/13,000 tons) with two single 305mm/12in guns in fore and aft mountings and a range of medium- and small-calibre guns. These ships were laid down in 1901–5 and although completed they took some six years each to build while the Italians absorbed intelligence about *Dreadnought*.

The Italian Government joined the Dreadnought race by authorizing the *Dante Alighieri* in 1907, although she was not laid down until 1909. The Cuniberti-designed ship had 12 305mm/12in guns, all on the centre line, one forward and one aft, and two amidships. A novel feature of the design was that the guns were for the first time in any navy placed in triple mountings. This arrangement enabled the boiler rooms to be widely separated and the engine room to be placed in the centre of the ship. *Dante Alighieri* also had two in-line rudders and four shafts. When completed she was capable of 24 knots and reckoned to be the fastest battleship in the world, although critics suggested that the armour was too light.

Dante Alighieri's only noteworthy action in World War I was the bombardment of Durazzo in the Adriatic during the army's struggle with the Austro-Hungarians. She was modified in 1923 and given a tripod foremast, taller

fore funnels and an aircraft ramp on C turret, but was scrapped in 1928.

The type was copied by the Russians in both their Gangut and Imperatrica Marija classes.

Dante Alighieri

Class: *Dante Alighieri*. Launched 1910.
Dimensions: Length – 158m/518ft 5in
 Beam – 26.6m/87ft 3in
 Draught – 8.8m/28ft 10in
Displacement: 19,835 tonnes/19,522 tons
Armament: Main – 12 x 305mm/12in guns
 Secondary – 20 x 120mm/4.7in,
 13 x 75mm/3in guns and
 3 x 455mm/18in torpedoes
Machinery: 23 boilers, 4 shafts,
 26,360kW/35,350shp
Speed: 24 knots
Complement: 950 men

Conte di Cavour class

These three ships were the epitome of Cuniberti's ideas. They carried a main armament of 305mm/12in guns and 18 120mm/4.7in guns in casements around the superstructure as defence against torpedo boats. The arrangement of the heavy guns was novel. The Italians adopted the principle of super-firing guns and placed a twin turret above a triple turret forward and aft, and also a triple turret amidships on the centre line, giving the unusual number of 13 main armament guns. This was only one gun less than the then most heavily armed ship in the world, the Brazilian 14-gun *Rio de Janeiro* (later the British *Agincourt*), but in two fewer turrets.

Critics again thought that these ships were too lightly armoured, and that, in the tradition of Italian warship building, too much had been sacrificed for speed. This was tacitly acknowledged in the inter-war years when heavier armour and the Pugliese system was fitted, but by then the output of the machinery had also been increased from 22,371kW/ 30,000hp to 67,113kW/90,000hp.

Conte di Cavour and *Giulio Cesare* were modified in the 1920s after the Washington Naval Treaty. The foremast was moved to a better position, before the fore funnel (a mistake the British had made in *Dreadnought* by placing the mast where it would be wreathed in funnel smoke) and both ships were fitted with catapults for aircraft. In one more demonstration of innovation in Italian design, the catapult was placed on the forecastle and the aircraft stored on the roof of the A turret.

Leonardo da Vinci sank as a consequence of an internal magazine explosion in 1916 at Taranto harbour, and although she was raised, was scrapped in 1921. This explosion was blamed on saboteurs, but it is more likely that it was one more in a series resulting from unstable ammunition. Neither *Conte di Cavour* nor *Giulio Cesare* saw any action in World War I, and they were so

TOP: **The silhouette was transformed when the Conte di Cavour class was modernized in the 1930s.**
ABOVE: *Guilio Cesare*, **followed by** *Conte di Cavour*, **off Naples for the Italian fleet review of 1938.** BELOW LEFT: **A rare picture of** *Conte di Cavour* **flying off her aircraft from the forecastle-mounted catapult.**

largely rebuilt, starting in 1933, and their appearance changed, that they also appear under separate entries in *Battleships of World War II*.

Conte di Cavour class

Class: *Conte di Cavour, Giulio Cesare, Leonardo da Vinci.* Launched 1911

Dimensions: Length – 168.9m/554ft 1in
Beam – 28m/91ft 10in
Draught – 9.3m/30ft 6in

Displacement: 23,360 tonnes/22,992 tons

Armament: Main – 13 x 305mm/12in guns
Secondary – 18 x 120mm/4.7in,
13 x 75mm/3in guns and
3 x 455mm/18in torpedoes

Machinery: 20 boilers, 4 shafts,
23,324kW/31,278shp

Speed: 22.2 knots

Complement: 1,197 men

Caio Duilio class

Similar in layout to the Conte di Cavour class with their two tall funnels and tripod mast mounted before each, these two ships had the trademark 13 heavy guns mounted in five turrets, and retained the medium guns in casements, but increased the calibre from 120mm/4.7in to 150mm/6in. This increased the displacement by 2,032 tonnes/2,000 tons without any serious adverse affects upon the speed of about 21 knots. Other Italian features included two in-line rudders. Neither ship saw action during World War I.

From 1926 onwards they carried an aircraft launched from a rail over the forecastle, and the familiar arrangement of rangefinders in Italian ships whereby they were mounted vertically one over the other revolving around the forward conning tower. *Caio Duilio* was damaged by an internal explosion in 1925, and with the *Andrea Doria* was rebuilt in the years 1937–40.

In 1914 Italy also ordered four larger battleships (29,465 tonnes/29,000 tons) *Francesco Morosini, Francesco Caracciolo, Cristoforo Colombo* and *Marcantonio Colonna* but work on these ships came to a halt during World War I. They were intended to be fast battleships, similar to but faster than the British Queen Elizabeth class, and a direct response to the Austro-Hungarian Ersatz Monarch class which were building in Triestino. The 380mm/15in guns intended for these ships were used in several monitors.

Under the Washington Naval Treaty Italy was allowed 71,120 tonnes/70,000 tons and plans were drawn up for three 23,370-tonne/23,000-ton 380mm/15in-gun battleships in 1928. This was partly in response to news of the French Dunkerque class, but eventually a larger design was chosen which became the Vittorio Veneto class.

TOP: *Caio Duilio* as she appeared in World War I, showing the classic lines of a Dreadnought battleship and her similarity to the contemporary British designs. ABOVE: Photographed in about 1912, the guns have been installed but the builders have not yet left or removed their mess.

Caio Duilio class

Class: *Caio Duilio, Andrea Doria.* Launched 1913
Dimensions: Length – 165.8m/544ft 1in
   Beam – 28m/91ft 10in
   Draught – 9.4m/30ft 10in
Displacement: 23,324 tonnes/22,956 tons
Armament: Main – 13 x 305mm/12in guns
   Secondary – 16 x 150mm/6in, 19 x 75mm/3in
   guns and 3 x 455mm/18in torpedoes
Machinery: 20 boilers, 4 shafts.
   22,371kW/30,000shp
Speed: 21 knots
Complement: 1,198 men

Gangut class

This class was a compromise. Whilst the Tsar wanted these ships, his Duma did not and the naval staff favoured a design by Cuniberti but a technical committee preferred a Blohm and Voss design. The German design was opposed on principle and John Brown and Co. from Britain was brought in to re-work the drawings. The resulting ship was a Baltic-Dreadnought, close to Cuniberti's original ideas. British (Yarrow) boilers instead of French (Belleville) boilers gave a speed of 24.5 knots on trials, at the expense of some armour and although the armour was thinner it was spread over the full hull. Ice-breaking bows were also fitted.

All four ships formed part of the Russian First Battleship Brigade based in the Baltic, where they conducted a series of minor operations until they came under Bolshevik control during the Russian Revolution, and were demobilized at Kronstadt in 1918.

Petropavlovsk engaged Royal Navy destroyers in May 1919, during British intervention in the Russian civil war, and on August 17 she was sunk by torpedoes from British coastal motor boats which raided Kronstadt harbour. She was raised and modernized

between 1926–8 and participated in the 1937 fleet review at Spithead as *Marat*. In 1939 *Marat* bombarded Finnish positions, and in 1941 was hit by German long-range artillery and aerial bombs while alongside at Kronstadt, where she settled on the bottom. Partially repaired in January 1944, she was used as a fixed battery to fire on German army positions south of Kronstadt. She was renamed *Petropavlovsk* in 1943, and broken up in about 1953.

Poltava caught fire in 1922, sank and was plundered for spares for her sisters. Repairs were commenced on her under the name of *Frunze* in 1926–8 but she was hulked again in the 1930s. Her remains were sunk at Leningrad in 1941 and she was broken up in the 1950s.

Sevastopol operated with *Gangut* during World War I, and was modernized in 1928 as *Parizhkaya Kommuna*. While on passage to the Black Sea she was forced into Brest for repairs in 1929. She was modernized again in 1936–9 and during World War II bombarded the seaward flank of the advancing German army. She reverted to her old name in 1942, and was broken up in the late 1950s.

ABOVE: *Gangut* at anchor. A comparison with the aerial picture of *Dante Alighieri* shows how similar these ships are to the original Italian design. Considering their length and variety of service, these were successful and long-lived ships which withstood a great deal of damage.

Gangut was refitted in 1926–8 and 1931–4, and renamed *Oktyabrskaya Revolyutsiya*. In World War II she duelled with Finnish and then German positions, and on September 23, 1941, was hit by several bombs. Repaired at the Baltic Shipyard, she was ready to bombard the flank of the retreating German army in 1944. She was finally broken up in 1959.

Gangut class

Class: *Gangut, Petropavlovsk, Poltava, Sevastopol.* Launched 1911
Dimensions: Length – 180m/590ft 6in
Beam – 26.6m/87ft 3in
Draught – 8.4m/27ft 6in
Displacement: 23,735 tonnes/23,360 tons
Armament: Main – 12 x 305mm/12in guns
Secondary – 16 x 120mm/4.7in guns and
4 x 455mm/18in torpedoes
Machinery: 25 boilers, 4 shafts.
31,319kW/42,000shp
Speed: 23 knots
Complement: 1,126 men

Imperatritsa Mariya class

Similar to the Ganguts but adapted for operations in the Black Sea, the Russian naval staff wanted bigger guns to counteract the battleships ordered in Britain for Turkey. However, to avoid delay in acquiring 355mm/14in guns, 305mm/12in main armament was accepted. John Brown and Co. advised in their construction as with the Ganguts. A heavier armoured belt was provided, but the problem of blast from the main guns affecting the secondary armament in its casemates was not resolved. There were minor differences between these ships when completed, and a bewildering series of name changes.

Imperatritsa Mariya bombarded the Turkish and Bulgarian coasts in 1915 and 1916 and on July 22, 1916, fought the ex-German Turkish-flagged light cruiser Breslau. On October 20, 1916, she suffered an internal explosion, whilst alongside in Sevastopol. Sabotage was suspected, but the most likely cause was a spontaneous explosion of unstable ammunition. The wreck was raised in 1918 and broken up in 1922.

Imperator Alexander III was not completed until after the Russian Revolution in February 1917, when she was renamed Volya. In April 1918, for a few months, she flew the flag of the independent state of Ukraine, but on October 1, 1918, she was seized by the Germans and renamed (perhaps mistakenly) Volya. In 1919 she sailed briefly under the British flag, and during the war between the Red and White Russians she fought on the side of the Whites under the name of General Alekseev. She was steamed to Bizerta, where the French government offered to give her up to the newly installed Soviet rulers of Russia, but she was sold for scrapping in 1924 and finally broken up in 1936.

Imperatritsa Ekaterina Velikaya (ex Ekaterina II) also undertook bombardment operations, and she fought the ex-German battlecruiser Goeben on January 7–8, 1916, and the light cruiser Breslau on April 4–5, 1916. In April 29, 1917, she was renamed Svobodnaya Rossiya and under this name she again fought Breslau on June 24–5, 1917. Under the terms of the armistice she should have been handed over to the Germans but escaped from Sevastopol to Novorossijsk where she was sunk by torpedoes from the destroyer Kerch on June 18, 1918.

Imperatritsa Mariya class

Class: *Imperatritsa Mariya, Imperator Alexander III, Ekaterina II*. Launched 1913–14

Dimensions: Length – 167.8m/550ft 6in
Beam – 27.3m/89ft 6in
Draught – 8.4m/27ft 6in

Displacement: 22,960 tonnes/22,600 tons

Armament: Main – 12 x 305mm/12in guns
Secondary – 20 x 130mm/5.1in guns and
4 x 455mm/18in torpedoes

Machinery: 20 boilers, 4 shafts.
19,761kW/26,500shp

Speed: 21 knots

Complement: 1,220 men

Imperator Alexander III renamed *Volya* and *Ekaterina II* renamed *Imperatritsa Ekaterina Velikaya*. *Ekaterina II* was slightly longer and larger than her sisters.

ABOVE: *Imperator Alexander III*, seen here from a distance, entered service after the February 1917 revolution in Russia, when she was renamed *Volya*. *Volya* later flew the flag of independent Ukraine and later still under White Russian authority she was known as *General Alexieff*. LEFT: *Volya* also spent some time under German and then British control as revolution raged around the Black Sea. The clean lines and minimum of superstructure, with the emphasis on keeping free the big guns' arcs of fire, show the influence of Italian design. Under German control she was briefly known as *Volga*.

LEFT: **Although the Bolsheviks renamed *Imperator Nikolai I* in 1917 and called her *Demokratiy*, she was never finished.**

Imperator Nikolai I

Intended as a fourth ship of the Imperatritsa Mariya class, *Imperator Nikolai I* was a larger ship all round, which enabled her designers to give her increased armour. She was built on the Black Sea and intended to counter the acquisition by Turkey of the *Rio de Janeiro* (which became the British *Agincourt*) from the Brazilian navy. Although 355mm/14in and even

400mm/16in guns were contemplated for this ship, the guns never became available. In any case, *Imperator Nikolai I* was not completed: she fell into German hands in 1918 and into the Allies' hands in 1919. Although the Germans started to break her, construction was later recommenced until the Allies decided to demolish her to prevent her being commissioned by the Reds.

Imperator Nikolai I

Class: *Imperator Nikolai I.* Launched 1916
Dimensions: Length – 188m/616ft 9in
    Beam – 28.9m/94ft 9in
    Draught – 9m/29ft 6in
Displacement: 27,740 tonnes/27,300 tons
Armament: Main – 12 x 305mm/12in guns
    Secondary – 20 x 130mm/5.1in guns and
    4 x 455mm/18in torpedoes
Machinery: 20 boilers, 4 shafts.
    19,243kW/27,300shp
Speed: 21 knots
Complement: 1,252 men

Borodino class

The Russian battleships and battlecruisers all had a similar silhouette, except that in the Borodino class the forward triple turret was carried one deck higher on an extended forecastle. The forward secondary guns in their casemates were still wet, and suffered from blast effects by continuing

to be placed beneath the main turrets. As World War I developed the Russians had difficulty in sourcing equipment for the Borodino class, especially the turbines. None were completed. Consideration was given to converting the most advanced ship, *Izmail*, to an aircraft carrier but all were broken up.

Borodino class

Class: *Borodino, Izmail, Kinburn, Navarin.*
    Launched 1915–16
Dimensions: Length – 221.9m/728ft
    Beam – 30.5m/100ft
    Draught – 10.2m/33ft 6in
Displacement: 33,020 tonnes/32,500 tons
Armament: Main – 12 x 355mm/14in guns
    Secondary – 24 x 130mm/5.1in guns and
    6 x 535mm/21in torpedoes
Machinery: 25 boilers, 4 shafts,
    50,708kW/68,000shp
Speed: 26.5 knots
Complement: 1,250 men

LEFT: **Like other nations, the Russians named ships after famous victories on land. Borodino, sunk in 1905 was to have been replaced by one of four ships built at St Petersburg, but they were overwhelmed by the Russian revolution and never completed. Except in the Black Sea, the Russian navy never recovered from its defeat at the Battle of Tsushima.**

Radetzky class

These ships, the last of the Austro-Hungarian pre-Dreadnoughts, were designed by Siegfried Popper. Popper wanted to build an all-big-gun ship but could not fit the necessary gun layout into a ship of less than 16,257 tonnes/ 16,000 tons to which he was constrained by the size of the available docks.

Although small and seemingly over-armed for their displacement, the Radetzkys were well suited to warfare in the Adriatic, even if their active service was against shore targets rather than against other warships. Some speed was given up for increased armour, which was similar to British Dreadnoughts, while they were not much slower than their Italian equivalents. Popper emphasized underwater protection, and when underwater explosive experiments failed to inform him, he devised a satisfactory mathematical model for his design of an armoured double bottom.

Erzherzog Franz Ferdinand was named after the Austrian crown prince whose assassination at Sarajevo marked the start of World War I.

Radetzky was at the British Coronation Review in 1911 and all three ships of the class made training cruises in the eastern Mediterranean in 1912. In 1913 they formed part of an international squadron which demonstrated in the Ionian against the Balkan War.

In the spring of 1914 *Zrinyi* made a training cruise with the two new Dreadnoughts, *Viribus Unitis* and *Tegetthoff*, in the eastern Mediterranean and visited Malta.

In the opening moves of World War I, the Radetzkys covered the German Admiral Souchon's escape from the Adriatic, and bombarded Montenegro and Ancona and other coastal targets, but after the summer of 1915 they took little active part in the war.

Austro-Hungary wanted to give her fleet to the Yugoslavs in order to keep it out of Italian hands but *Erzherzog Franz Ferdinand* was interned at Venice. However Yugoslav officers steamed *Radetzky* and *Zrinyi* from Pola. On sighting a superior Italian force, the two battleships hoisted American flags and

ABOVE: **Not many pictures of the Austro-Hungarian fleet have survived: this is *Radetzky* photographed in 1911. Her only action was the bombardment of Ancona in Italy. She fell, briefly, into Yugoslav hands at the end of the war, but was allocated to the USA and scrapped in Italy.**

sailed south down the Adriatic coast to Split, where a flotilla of USN submarine chasers accepted their surrender. However, all three ships were eventually ceded to Italy and scrapped in 1920–6.

Radetzky class

Class: *Erzherzog Franz Ferdinand, Radetzky, Zrinyi.* Launched 1908–10
Dimensions: Length – 137.44m/450ft 11in
   Beam – 24.59m/80ft 8in
   Draught – 8.15m/26ft 9in
Displacement: 14,740 tonnes/14,508 tons
Armament: Main – 4 x 305mm/12in guns
   Secondary – 8 x 240mm/9.4in,
   20 x 100mm/4in guns and
   3 x 455mm/18in torpedoes
Machinery: 12 Yarrow boilers, 2 shafts.
   14,765kW/19,800ihp
Speed: 20.5 knots
Complement: 876 men

Tegetthoff class

The Tegetthoff class was the Austro-Hungarian response to news of the building of the Italian Dreadnought, *Dante Alighieri*. Although German experts had been consulted, the design was all-Austrian and the decision to fit triple turrets was influenced more by the desire to match the Italians. When financial authority for these ships was slow in forthcoming, the Austrian Commander-in-Chief, Admiral Montecuccoli, took out a personal loan for these ships, some months before parliament approved their construction.

The ships were compact, yet strongly armed and armoured. Their main weaknesses were the lack of reserve displacement and poor underwater protection, which led to the loss of two ships of the class.

In June 1918, Admiral Horthy planned a major raid on the Otranto barrage, in coordination with the Austro-Hungarian army. His battleships left Pola in two poorly protected groups: *Viribus Unitis* and *Prinz Eugen* on June 8, and *Szent Istvan* and *Tegetthoff* the next evening. *Szent Istvan*'s engines gave her trouble, reducing speed and making excessive smoke, and she was intercepted in the early hours of the morning by two Italian torpedo-boats on an unrelated mission

off the island of Premuda. *Szent Istvan* was hit with two torpedoes and the bulkhead between the boiler rooms collapsed. She quickly flooded and within three hours she had capsized. The sinking was filmed from *Tegetthoff*, making it one of the rare sequences of a battleship being sunk. The planned bombardment was aborted and the Austro-Hungarian navy returned to harbour for the last time.

On October 6, 1918, the Austrian emperor gave the Austro-Hungarian navy to the National Council of Slovenians, Croats and Serbs, and the fleet allegedly hoisted the Croatian flag. That night, while the end of the war was celebrated ashore and afloat, two Italian divers placed mines under the brightly lit *Viribus Unitis*, which blew up at dawn. Four days later Italian troops entered Pola and captured *Tegetthoff* and *Prinz Eugen*.

ABOVE: **One of the Tegetthoff class at speed. She was named after one of the few Austro-Hungarian naval leaders.** LEFT: *Szent Istvan* **was sunk by Italian torpedo-boats in 1918 and settled slowly, giving sufficient time for her loss to be filmed from her sister ship,** *Tegetthoff,* **and for some unique and poignant footage to be captured.**

Prinz Eugen was ceded to France and expended in underwater explosive tests as a bomb target and finally sunk by the guns of the French battleships *Jean Bart, Paris* and *France. Tegetthoff* was ceded to Italy and broken up in 1924–5.

In 1914–16 the Austro-Hungarian navy laid down four improved Tegetthoff ships, but these were never launched.

Tegetthoff class	

Class: *Viribus Unitis, Tegetthoff, Prinz Eugen, Szent Istvan*. Launched 1911–14
Dimensions: Length – 151m/495ft 5in
  Beam – 27.3m/89ft 8in
  Draught – 8.9m/29ft
Displacement: 20,334 tonnes/20,013 tons
Armament: Main – 12 x 305mm/12in guns
  Secondary – 12 x 150mm/6in,
  18 x 65mm/2.6in guns and
  4 x 535mm/21in torpedoes
Machinery: 12 boilers, 4 shafts
  (*Szent Istvan* 2 shafts). 20,134kW/27,000shp
Speed: 20.5 knots
Complement: 1,087 men

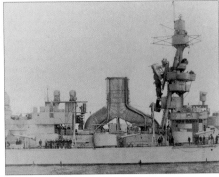

LEFT: *Drottningen Victoria* **is seen here during her sea trials in 1921. The photograph shows her as newly completed, but all three ships were modernized before World War II.** ABOVE: **Perhaps the most unusual flying accident occurred in 1939 when an aircraft crashed into the foremast of** *Gustav V.* BELOW: **An unusual photograph of a torpedo firing trial in 1893. Many battleships carried torpedoes in underwater tubes which were never photographed.**

Sverige class

By the beginning of the 20th century Sweden possessed a large fleet although some of the hulls were elderly. Even the *John Ericsson*, which was almost 50 years old, having been upgraded three times, was still available. Between 1900 and 1905 the Swedish navy decided to build three classes of coast defence ships, Dristigheten, Oscar II and five ships of the Åran class.

However, Sweden's traditional enemy was Russia and larger ships were needed to increase the enemy's risk by forcing her to commit her own battleships in the event of an invasion. After considering a range of designs the so-called F-boat was decided upon in 1911, only for a change of government in 1912 to cancel the order on economic grounds. A remarkable battleship-club was started that rapidly raised more than enough money to build the first ship of a new class, and the government had little option but to thank the people and begin construction of *Sverige*.

The second and third ships of this class, *Drottningen Victoria* and *Gustaf V*, although ordered during World War I, were not completed until 1921 and 1922. The design of the later ships also changed slightly, they were larger and had two shafts instead of four and icebreaking stems instead of rams. After successive modernization all three ships differed from each other, all were given heavy tripod masts, but in *Gustaf V* the two funnels were combined into one, while *Sverige* was given an S-shaped fore funnel, and *Drottningen Victoria* retained her upright funnels. There were different arrangements of gun directors, and at each modernization the anti-aircraft weaponry was improved. Coal-fired boilers were also replaced by oil.

Swedish battleships successfully helped to safeguard their neutrality in two world wars, and the fate of other navies meant that for many years in the 20th century the Swedish navy was master of the Baltic, but by 1957 the Swedish battleships had been decommissioned. All that remains of Sweden's battleship ambitions are various guns which were set up in fixed defensive batteries.

Sverige class

Class: *Sverige, Drottningen Victoria, Gustaf V.*
Launched 1915–18
Dimensions: Length – 120.9m/396ft 8in
Beam – 18.6m/61ft
Draught– 6.2m/20ft 4in
Displacement: 7,240 tonnes/7,125 tons
(*Sverige* 6,935 tonnes/6,825 tons)
Armament: Main – 4 x 280mm/11in guns
Secondary – 8 x 150mm/6in, 6 x 75mm/3in guns
and 2 x 535mm/21in torpedoes
Machinery: 12 boilers, 2 shafts,
17,830kW/23,910shp
Speed: 22.5 knots
Complement: 427 men

De Zeven Provincien

While armed and armoured like a small battleship, *De Zeven Provincien* was in fact the last of the long line of Dutch coast defence ships. *De Zeven Provincien* saw little action in World War I, in which the Netherlands were neutral, and in 1912 was sent to the Dutch East Indies, the vast archipelago which later became Indonesia.

When a mutiny broke out onboard in 1933, *De Zeven Provincien* was bombed by a Dutch seaplane which hit her forecastle, killing 23 men. In 1935–6 she was used as a training ship, and in 1937 she was substantially modified and re-commissioned under the name *Soerabaia*. *De Zeven Provincien* was badly damaged in a Japanese air attack on February 18, 1942, and scuttled a few days later.

Meanwhile, a Dutch Royal Commission in 1912–13 recommended the building of a new fleet for the Royal Netherlands Navy to defend the Netherlands, protect her colonies and police the East Indies. The fleet would have included nine battleships of about 20,320 tonnes/20,000 tons and capable of 21 knots, armed with 340mm/13.5in guns. The number of ships was determined by the perceived need to maintain a squadron in the Far East, a squadron in home waters, and a reserve. It was a long-term, rolling programme which envisaged the earlier ships being replaced by more modern ships over a 30-year period.

The Dutch got as far as asking German and British firms for proposals when World War I broke out and these plans were abandoned. The leading design was by Germaniawerft and provided for a ship of 21,000 tonnes/20,668 tons, 21 knots, and armed with eight 340mm/13.5in, 16 150mm/6in and 12 75mm/3in guns.

De Zeven Provincien class

Class: *De Zeven Provincien.* Launched 1909
Dimensions: Length – 101.5m/333ft
   Beam – 17.1m/56ft
   Draught – 6.2m/20ft 3in
Displacement: 6,635 tonnes/6,530 tons
Armament: Main – 2 x 280mm/11in and
   4 x 150mm/6in guns
   Secondary – 10 x 75mm/3in guns
Machinery: 8 boilers, 2 shafts,
   5,966kW/8,000ihp
Speed: 16 knots
Complement: 452 men

ABOVE: **The Dutch contemplated building a proper battleship, but only managed a coast defence ship, which they armed with 280mm/11in guns. She survived from 1910 to 1942.** LEFT: **One of the smallest post-Dreadnoughts to appear in these pages, *De Zeven Provincien* saw much of her service in the Dutch East Indies, where she was scuttled to prevent her falling into Japanese hands. *De Zeven Provincien* lies in the line of development between the pocket battleship and the monitor.**

España class

These three small battleships were built in Spain to British plans and largely under the supervision of British architects. The intention of their ingenious design was to incorporate the Dreadnought principles of an all-big-gun warship into the size of a pre-Dreadnought battleship. This was typical of a long tradition that British designers could be so adventurous with designs for foreign navies while at home the Admiralty was much more cautious about innovation. At less than 16,257 tonnes/16,000 tons they were the smallest and slowest Dreadnoughts and the variant was not copied elsewhere.

Their eight 305mm/12in guns were mounted in one turret forward and aft and two midships turrets mounted *en echelon*. The secondary armament was mounted in casemates. Distinctive recognition features were the boats mounted on the roofs of the midships turrets, the single upright funnel almost in the centre of the ship, and two tall tripod masts.

España ran aground off Morocco in 1923 and her large-calibre guns were salvaged but the wreck was broken up in the heavy surf which pounds that coast almost continually throughout the year.

Jaime I was not completed before the outbreak of World War I, when Britain was unable to supply further material. In 1923–5 she took part in what was known as the Riff revolt and was hit from a shore battery. In the Spanish Civil War she fought on the side of the Republicans, and bombarded Ceuta and Algeciras, but she was bombed in Malaga in 1936 and further damaged by an internal explosion in 1937. She was finally scrapped in 1939.

Alfonso XIII, which took the name *España* in 1931, declared for the Nationalists in the Spanish Civil War and bombarded Bilbao in April 1937, but soon afterwards hit a mine and was sunk – though at the time the Nazis claimed one of their aircraft had been involved.

Three more ships of a class named *Reina Eugenia* were supposed to be laid down during World War I, but plans were abandoned in favour of more affordable cruisers and destroyers. During World War II Franco approved a plan to build four modern battleships but financial weakness prevented this being taken up.

TOP: **A handsome picture of one of the España class (probably the renamed *Alfonso XIII* which was renamed *España* after the name ship had been wrecked) which shows a passing resemblance to Italian and Russian designs and faithfulness to Cuniberti's concepts.** ABOVE: ***España* declared for the nationalist government and was sunk by a mine off Santander. At the time the Germans thought that Basque government aircraft were responsible for the loss.**

España class

Class: *España, Jaime I, Alfonso XIII.*
  Launched 1912–14
Dimensions: Length – 132.58m/435ft
  Beam – 24m/78ft 9in
  Draught – 7.77m/25ft 6in
Displacement: 15,700 tonnes/15,453 tons
Armament: Main – 8 x 305mm/12in guns
  Secondary – 20 x 100mm/4in guns
Machinery: 12 boilers, 4 shafts.
  11,558kW/15,500shp
Speed: 19.5 knots
Complement: 854 men

Kilkis and Lemnos

Kilkis and Lemnos were both 13,209-tonne/13,000-ton battleships, originally built as two of the Mississippi class pre-Dreadnoughts completed in 1908 for the USN. Their place might properly be regarded as belonging to an earlier period, but they had careers that spanned both World Wars of the 20th century. The Greeks and Turks fought at sea in the Balkan Wars 1912–13, which saw the first use of aviation in modern warfare and the first use of submarine torpedo attack.

The Hellenic navy consisted of ships bought in from several navies, and two battleships were ordered, one from Germany and the other from France, but neither ship was finished. The American 355mm/14in guns intended for a German-built ship named Salamis were purchased for the British Abercrombie class monitors, and the unfinished Salamis was not scrapped until 1932. An unnamed French-built battleship of 23,369 tonnes/23,000 tons was to have been similar to the Provence class.

However, Greece did purchase two pre-Dreadnoughts from the USA in 1914, while Turkey hoped to acquire modern battleships from Britain. Kilkis, the name ship of the class, was taken over at Newport News, Virginia, in July and served in the Royal Hellenic Navy until 1932 when she became a training ship. Lemnos was in the Mediterranean on a training cruise with USN midshipmen when she was handed over.

The Lemnos was originally the Idaho and she was amongst the Greek naval ships temporarily seized by France in 1916 during a constitutional crisis in Greece. Lemnos was active in Turkish waters during the chaotic period following the end of World War I, but went out of active service during the 1930s and was retained as a hulk. Kilkis and her sister ship Lemnos became two of the longest-surviving pre-Dreadnoughts until they were both sunk at Salamis by German dive-bombers on April 23, 1941, during the German invasion of Greece. The wrecks were salvaged for scrap in the 1950s.

LEFT: **Kilkis** and **Lemnos** retained the lattice masts which the USN had fitted before World War I. Apart from two Argentinian battleships built to order in the USA, they were the only USN battleships to pass out of American service and to fly a foreign flag.
ABOVE: Both ships were sunk by German aircraft while at anchor at Salamis in 1941. The picture was taken from a German bomber as it dived on *Kilkis* at anchor. The ships had not been modernized and were no match for modern air power.

Kilkis class

Class: Kilkis (ex *Idaho*), Lemnos (ex *Mississippi*). Launched 1905
Dimensions: Length – 116.4m/382ft
Beam – 23.5m/77ft
Draught – 7.5m/24ft 8in
Displacement: 13,210 tonnes/13,000 tons
Armament: Main – 4 x 305mm/12in,
8 x 205mm/8in and 8 x 180mm/7in guns
Secondary – 12 x 75mm/3in guns and
2 x 535mm/21in torpedoes
Machinery: 8 boilers, 2 shafts,
7,457kW//10,000ihp
Speed: 17 knots
Complement: 744 men

Yavuz Sultan Selim

The Turks had two old German pre-Dreadnought battleships, *Kurfürst Friedrich Wilhelm* and *Weissenburg,* which had been modernized and renamed as *Heireddin Barbarossa* and *Turgut Reis* and saw active service in World War I. *Heireddin Barbarossa* was sunk by the British submarine *E-11* in the Sea of Marmara on August 8, 1915. *Turgut Reis* survived as a hulk until she was broken up in 1956–7.

The Turks made several attempts to improve their battleship strength by purchasing ships in Britain. However, *Resadiye* was confiscated by the Royal Navy and commissioned as *Erin*, and two other ships of this class, *Mahmud Resad V* and *Fatik* were cancelled. *Sultan Osman I* (ex *Rio de Janeiro*) was also taken over as *Agincourt*.

Consequently, when the German battlecruiser *Goeben* and the cruiser *Breslau* escaped from the British Mediterranean Fleet, arriving off Istanbul on August 10, 1914, it was natural that the Turks were interested in acquiring these ships. *Goeben* transferred to the Turkish flag six days later, while retaining most of her German crew and thereafter led perhaps the busiest and longest life of any ship of the period.

Goeben was twice bested by the Russian Black Sea pre-Dreadnought squadron. On November 18, 1914, and again in May 1915, she exchanged fire with *Evstafi*, which hit *Goeben*, whereupon the German-Turkish ship again had to use her speed to avoid being outgunned by the Russian squadron.

On January 20, 1918, this time in the Dardanelles, *Goeben* sank the British monitors *Lord Raglan* and *M-28* but as the German-Turkish ships shaped a course for Lemnos island, *Breslau* hit a mine, and while *Goeben* attempted a tow *Goeben* hit three mines herself, while *Breslau* hit several more and sank rapidly. *Goeben* then ran aground on Nagara Point, where she was attacked by British seaplanes from *Ark Royal,* but the bombs used were too small to be effective. The British submarine *E-14* was diverted from her patrol in the Otranto Straits but by the time she arrived, *Goeben* had been towed off by *Turgut Reiss.*

Yavuz survived under the Turkish flag until 1973–6 when she was broken up shortly before her diamond jubilee – one of the longest surviving ships of her era.

LEFT: **The German battlecruiser *Goeben* was sold to the Turks in 1914 and is here seen under a prominent Turkish flag, although the German crew remained onboard to man her. She was not finally handed over to the Turkish authorities until November 1918.**
BELOW: **Under her new owners – whatever the nationality of the crew – *Yavuz Sultan Selim* took part in many actions in the Black Sea. In 1918, during a brief sortie from the Black Sea, she sank the British monitor *Raglan.***

Yavuz Sultan Selim

Class: *Yavuz* (as *Goeben*). Launched 1910
Dimensions: Length – 186.5m/611ft 11in
Beam – 29.5m/96ft 10in
Draught – 9m/29ft 5in
Displacement: 22,979 tonnes/22,616 tons
Armament: Main – 10 x 280mm/11in guns
Secondary – 12 x 150mm/6in,
12 x 88mm/3.46in guns and
4 x 510mm/20in torpedoes
Machinery: 24 boilers, 4 shafts,
38,776kW/52,000shp
Speed: 25.5 knots
Complement: 1,053 men

Rivadavia class

In the 1870s the Argentine navy consisted of a few cruisers, and although *La Plata* (1874), *Los Andes* (1874), *Libertad* (1890), and *Independencia* (1891) were classed as coast defence battleships they were small and poorly armed. Only *Patagonia* (1885), a protected cruiser built in Italy, had a single gun of 255mm/10in size and she was reconstructed in 1909 as a survey ship. However, when Argentina's quarrel with Chile over boundaries in Patagonia and territorial limits in the Beagle Channel was settled (for the time being) by British arbitration in 1902, the British thoughtfully wrote into the treaty clauses concerning the limitation of naval arms. The Royal Navy bought two pre-Dreadnought battleships from Chile which were under construction in Britain and Argentina sold two cruisers to Japan which were building in Italy.

In 1904 the Brazilian Government decided upon a programme of naval expansion, and Argentina asked foreign companies to tender plans for new battleships. Fore River won the competition and the ships became the only Dreadnoughts built in the United States for a foreign navy. Although the Argentine decision was based on technical and financial grounds, there was another, unintended consequence of choosing American yards. Unlike orders placed by foreign nations in European yards where the ships being built were taken over by the warring powers, American neutrality during the early years of World War I allowed a timely delivery of both Dreadnoughts. As a result Argentina got her warships, whereas Brazil and Chile did not.

They were a combination of ideas from capital ship design, with battleship and battlecruiser features, good protection, significant armament and relatively high speed. The superimposed turret arrangement was American, and the wing turrets showed British design influence. The secondary 150mm/6in battery was attributed to German influence as were the triple shafts, but engine-room and boiler-room layout was similar to the Italian Dante Alighieri class. The forward cage mast was entirely American.

ABOVE: *Rivadavia* and *Moreno* were possibly the only major warships to be built in the USA for export. Their design incorporated features from American, British, German and Italian naval architecture. This picture shows the profile after modernization.

Both ships underwent modernization in the 1920s. In 1937 *Moreno* attended the Coronation Review at Spithead while *Rivadavia* tactfully visited Brest, and later both ships visited Wilhelmshaven. Neither ship fired her guns in anger during World War II, and in 1956 they were stricken from the navy list.

Rivadavia class

Class: *Rivadavia, Moreno.* Launched 1911
Dimensions: Length – 181.3m/594ft 9in
  Beam – 30m/98ft 4in
  Draught – 8.4m/27ft 8in
Displacement: 28,388 tonnes/27,940 tons
Armament: Main – 12 x 305mm/12in guns
  Secondary – 12 x 150mm/6in, 16 x 100mm/4in
  guns and 2 x 535mm/21in torpedoes
Machinery: 18 boilers, 3 shafts,
  29,455kW/39,500shp
Speed: 22.5 knots
Complement: 1,130 men

Minas Gerais class

Minas Gerais and *Sao Paulo* were the most powerful warships in the world when completed. They were built amid rumours that they were destined for another power, or for the Royal Navy, and had two super-firing turrets fore and aft and two wing turrets. The Brazilian Government ordered them even before the first Dreadnought was commissioned. The only outdated thing about these ships was that they were powered by reciprocating engines and not turbines. As a direct consequence the USA started to court Brazil as a pan-American ally, but a downturn in the economy and a mutiny halted the Brazilian Dreadnought programme. Therefore, when Brazil declared war on the Central Powers in 1917 and promised to send her battleships to join the Grand Fleet at Scapa Flow, both ships were in need of refit. *Sao Paulo* was sent to New York in June 1918 to be modernized, and though her refit outlasted the war, *Minas Gerais* was also sent north and completed her refit in 1923.

Minas Gerais was modernized in 1934–7, but *Sao Paulo* was judged to be in too poor a condition to justify the cost. Neither ship saw action in World War II. *Sao Paulo*, en route to Britain for breaking, broke her tow in the North Atlantic in 1951 and was never seen again. *Minas Gerais* was towed to Italy to be broken up in 1954.

In 1910 Brazil ordered a yet more powerful warship, which would have been the largest in the world. However a mutiny in the navy had undermined public support for buying Dreadnoughts, and eventually *Rio de Janeiro* was sold to Turkey as *Sultan Osman I*, and was about to be steamed away from Britain when the Royal Navy confiscated her under the name of *Agincourt*. In 1921 Great Britain offered to sell *Agincourt* back to Brazil but after consideration the idea was rejected.

The Brazilians contemplated a fourth Dreadnought, to be known as *Riachuelo*, and four designs were considered for a battleship of 32,005 tonnes/31,500 tons to 36,580 tonnes/36,000 tons with main batteries of 355mm/14in, 380mm/15in or 405mm/16in guns. Construction was never started and the idea was dropped on the outbreak of World War I.

TOP: *Sao Paulo* **as built and photographed at Rio de Janeiro in 1918.** ABOVE: *Minas Gerais*, **date unknown, but showing features of World War I, the range clock, and World War II, what appear to be radar domes.** BELOW LEFT: *Minas Gerais* **in 1909. The structure apparently extending to port and starboard are in fact spans of the bridge over the River Tyne in England, where this was photographed.**

Minas Gerais class

Class: *Minas Gerais, Sao Paulo.* Launched 1908–9
Dimensions: Length – 165.5m/543ft
  Beam – 25.3m/83ft
  Draught – 7.6m/25ft
Displacement: 20,378 tonnes/19,281 tons
Armament: Main – 12 x 305mm/12in guns
  Secondary – 22 x 120mm/4.7in and
  8 x 3pdr guns
Machinery: 18 boilers, 2 shafts,
  17,524kW/23,500shp
Speed: 21 knots
Complement: 900 men

Almirante Latorre class

As part of the South American naval arms race, Chile ordered two Dreadnoughts to counter the ships that the Argentine had built in face of the perceived threat from Brazil. The first ship was named *Valparaíso*, then *Libertad*, and thirdly *Almirante Latorre*. Work on *Almirante Latorre* started in 1911, but ironically work could not start on *Almirante Cochrane* until the Brazilian *Rio de Janeiro* had left the slip. The design was similar to the British Iron Duke class but with 355mm/14in guns in lieu of 340mm/13.5in, however neither ship was delivered to the Chileans.

At the outbreak of World War I the Royal Navy purchased *Almirante Latorre* from its ally and renamed her *Canada*, and for a while considered purchasing *Almirante Cochrane* to be renamed *India*. Being less advanced, work was halted on *Almirante Cochrane* until 1917, when she was taken in hand to be finished as

the aircraft carrier *Eagle*. *Almirante Latorre* (*Canada*) was modified at the end of the war and flying-off ramps were fitted over B and X turrets.

Chile finally took over *Canada* and gave her back her original name. The Chilean navy also wanted their second Dreadnought and asked for *Eagle* to be reconverted, but they were offered instead the battlecruiser *Inflexible*. This was refused and the Chileans settled for just one capital ship and several minor war vessels.

Almirante Latorre was modernized in Devonport in 1929–31 and converted to oil-fired boilers. Anti-torpedo bulges were fitted which raised her beam to 31.4m/103ft, and she was given new gunnery control systems. An Italian-designed catapult was fitted on the quarterdeck. She remained in service until 1958 when she was towed to Japan to be broken up.

TOP: *Almirante Latorre* in 1913. Soon after this photograph she was purchased by the Royal Navy and renamed *Canada*. ABOVE: *Almirante Cochrane* at the time of her launch. In 1917 the uncompleted hull was purchased and finished by the British as the aircraft carrier *Eagle*.

Almirante Latorre class

Class: *Almirante Latorre* (as *Canada*), *Almirante Cochrane*. Launched 1913
Dimensions: Length – 201.47m/661ft
  Beam – 28.04m/92ft
  Draught – 8.84m/29ft
Displacement: 29,060 tonnes/28,600 tons
Armament: Main – 10 x 355mm/14in guns
  Secondary – 16 x 150mm/6in guns and
  4 x 535mm/21in torpedoes
Machinery: 21 boilers, 4 shafts,
  27,591kW/37,000shp
Speed: 23 knots
Complement: 1,167 men

World War II

The battleship, which had benefited from every kind of advance in technology in the 19th century, was threatened in the next century by two new weapons: the submarine and the aeroplane. The oldest and most powerful navy in the world, the Royal Navy realized this and at the start of World War I had not only the largest fleet of battleships but also the largest fleet of modern submarines. The Royal Navy was also the first to experiment with taking aircraft to sea and by 1918 the Royal Naval Air Service was one of the largest air forces in the world. Even as these new weapons increased in numbers and effectiveness, the battleship held sway up to the beginning of World War II. Throughout the war there were sporadic clashes between British and Italian, British and German, and American and Japanese capital ships. However tactics and operations involving aircraft evolved so rapidly that by 1942 the aircraft carrier rather than the battleship was regarded as the new capital ship of the fleet. By the end of World War II such battleships as remained were not being replaced, though a few lingered on in active service with the USN.

LEFT: **Japanese battleships in line ahead in the 1940s – still the optimum formation for bringing the maximum number of guns to bear upon an enemy, whatever technical changes had taken place over the previous century.**

Hood

When commissioned in 1920 *Hood* was the largest warship in the world, and between the wars she became an icon not just for the Royal Navy, but for the British Empire. *Hood* was generally regarded, in respect of the combination of fighting power, speed and protection, to be the most powerful ship in the world. She was also thought to be one of the most beautiful. During a ten-month world cruise in 1923–4 *Hood*, with the battlecruiser *Repulse* and their escorts, visited the British dominions and crossed the Pacific to the USA and Canada, reminding the world that the Royal Navy was still the most impressive in the world.

Hood was ordered in response to the wartime German 28-knot Mackensen class battlecruisers, none of which were commissioned. Her design was modified in light of the lessons learned from the loss of battlecruisers *Queen Mary*, *Indefatigable* and *Invincible* at the Battle of Jutland, and extra armour was added. Although usually referred to as a battlecruiser, *Hood* was really a fast battleship and an improved version of the Queen Elizabeths, with the same main armament of eight 380mm/15in guns, a sloped armoured belt and improved torpedo protection. Nevertheless, magazine protection remained one of her weak spots and her deck armour was only 75mm/3in thick. Small-tube boilers and a longer hull-form gave *Hood* a speed of 31–2 knots, 7 knots faster than the Queen Elizabeths. However, the extra weight made her sit lower in the water than designed and she had a

ABOVE: *Hood* was made famous by her inter-war world cruise when she was admired for her handsome looks. She was sunk by the German battleship *Bismarck* after a few minutes' fight.

tendency to dig in, fore and aft, in any seaway and at speed. Four ships of the same class were originally ordered, but work on *Hood*'s three sisters, who were to be named *Rodney*, *Howe* and *Anson*, was halted in 1917.

Hood was modernized twice, once in 1929 and again in 1939. There were proposals to remove or reduce the 610-tonne/600-ton conning tower and make further improvements to her deck armour, but World War II came too soon to allow this.

Hood, marked with red, white and blue stripes to indicate her neutrality, was part of the international force which intervened in the Spanish Civil War. On St George's Day, 1937, *Hood* covered a convoy of three British merchant ships as they delivered food to the besieged population of Bilbao and evacuated refugees, training her guns on the Spanish Nationalist cruiser *Almirante Cervera* as she did so.

At the outbreak of World War II *Hood* was with the Home Fleet at Scapa Flow, taking part in the chase of *Scharnhorst* and *Gneisenau*, and escorting convoys in the North Atlantic. In June 1940 she was attached to Force H, the British force established at Gibraltar after the collapse of France and their commitment to defend the western Mediterranean. On July 3,

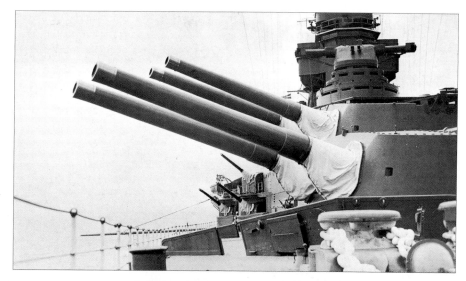

RIGHT: *Hood*'s main 380mm/15in guns and secondary armament trained out to starboard. BELOW: **Two sailors demonstrating loading drill on a 100mm/4in anti-aircraft gun.** BELOW RIGHT: **Nearly all battleships of the period had underwater torpedo tubes. Although much vaunted they were little used.** BOTTOM RIGHT: *Hood*'s **crew of nearly 1,500 men required mass-catering on her mess deck.**

1940, Force H opened fire on the French fleet at Mers-el-Kebir where the battleship *Bretagne* was blown up and *Provence* and *Dunkerque* were badly damaged.

In May 1941 *Hood* and the new *Prince of Wales* formed Vice Admiral Holland's Battle Cruiser Force sent to intercept the even newer German battleship *Bismarck* and the heavy cruiser *Prinz Eugen* as they made their breakout into the Atlantic. The Germans were found by the patrolling cruisers *Norfolk* and *Suffolk* and shadowed on radar. Reports by wireless enabled Holland to bring his ships into action on the morning of May 24 in the Denmark Strait, between Iceland and Greenland. Both sides opened fire shortly before 06.00 hours but as Holland closed the range *Bismarck*'s fifth salvo hit *Hood* amidships, starting a fire in her 100mm/4in ammunition. The fire spread to the main magazine, causing a catastrophic explosion which tore through the ship, breaking her hull in several places. Only three of her 1,418 ship's company survived.

The news shocked the British and the Prime Minister Winston Churchill ordered that "*Bismarck* must be sunk at all costs". The German ship had been damaged in the brief exchange of shot with *Hood* and *Prince of Wales*; two days later she was crippled by aircraft from the carrier *Ark Royal*, wrecked by the battleships *King George V* and *Rodney* on the morning of May 27, and finally despatched by torpedoes. Revenge was complete and commerce raiding by German surface warships was brought to an end.

Hood

Class: *Hood.* Launched 1918
Dimensions: Length – 262m/860ft
  Beam – 32m/105ft
  Draught – 8.7m/28ft 6in
Displacement: 43,355 tonnes/42,670 tons
Armament: Main – 8 x 380mm/15in guns
  Secondary – 12 x 140mm/5.5in, 4 x 100mm/4in
  guns and 6 x 535mm/21in torpedoes
Machinery: 24 boilers, 4 shafts.
  107,381kW/144,000shp
Speed: 31 knots
Complement: 1,477 men

Queen Elizabeth – modernized

The Queen Elizabeth class was reconstructed between the wars, emerging from the modernization with a single funnel, improved deck armour, additional anti-aircraft guns, and a hangar and catapult for two seaplanes.

In 1941 *Queen Elizabeth* joined the British Mediterranean Fleet at Alexandria where on December 19, 1941, she and *Valiant* were attacked by Italian frogmen. Both ships settled on an even keel and the extent of the damage was kept secret. *Queen Elizabeth* was repaired at Norfolk, Virginia, and *Valiant* at Durban in 1943, and later both ships bombarded Japanese positions in the Dutch East Indies. *Queen Elizabeth* was scrapped in Scotland in July 1945.

Valiant was modernized in 1929–30 and again in 1937–9, and in World War II served in every theatre of war: she took part in the Norway campaign in Spring 1940; she exchanged fire with the French battleship *Richelieu* at Dakar in September 1940 during an operation to put De Gaulle in power there; she fought at the Battles of Cape Matapan in March and Crete in May 1941; and provided covering fire during the Allied landings on Sicily in July and at Salerno in September 1943. In August 1944, *Valiant* was in dry dock at Trincomalee in Ceylon (now Sri Lanka) when the dock collapsed. She was never fully repaired and was sold for scrap in 1948.

At the Second Battle of Narvik in April 1940 *Warspite* led a flotilla of destroyers into the fjord where eight German destroyers and a U-boat were sunk. At the Battle of Calabria in July 1940, a single shot from *Warspite* hit the Italian battleship *Giulio Cesare* at nearly 24km/15 miles range and the Italian fleet retreated, however *Warspite* was too slow to catch up. At the Battle of Matapan in March 1941, *Warspite* sank two heavy cruisers. In the battle for Crete she was bombed and was sent to Puget Sound for repairs. In 1942 she was flagship of Force A in the Indian Ocean which brushed with Admiral Nagumo's Japanese fleet. She was hit by a German glider bomb during the Allied landings at Salerno in 1943, putting X turret out of action. Nevertheless, she bombarded the coast during the Normandy landings and again at Walcheren in 1944. *Warspite* was sold for scrap in early 1947, but broke her tow and ran aground in Mounts Bay, Cornwall, where she was eventually broken up.

On December 28, 1939, *Barham* was torpedoed by *U-30*, but repaired in Liverpool. She joined the Mediterranean Fleet and at the Battle of Matapan, she sank the Italian cruiser *Zara* and the destroyer *Alfieri* on the night of March 28, 1941. In May of that year, *Barham* was again severely damaged off Crete and repaired at Durban. Finally her luck ran out and on November 25, 1941, she was torpedoed by *U-331*. The German submarine was returning from having landed a small patrol to blow up a railway bridge on the Egyptian coast and her meeting with the *Barham* was by chance, her commanding officer doing well to get in a snap attack. *Barham* was hit by three torpedoes and within five minutes had rolled over to port,

LEFT: **An aerial view of one of the Queen Elizabeth class at anchor in Weymouth Bay: the number of small craft alongside and the work on deck hint at the logistic effort which each battleship needed, even in peacetime.** BELOW: **A multiple pom-pom or "Chicago piano" was retrofitted to many battleships for anti-aircraft defence. Note that the seamen wear knives on lanyards as their ancestors did in the age of sail.**

Queen Elizabeth class

Class: *Queen Elizabeth, Warspite, Valiant, Barham, Malaya.* Launched 1913–15

Dimensions: Length – 197m/645ft 9in
Beam – 27.6m/90ft 6in
Draught – 8.8m/28ft 9in

Displacement: 27,940 tonnes/27,500 tons

Armament: Main – 8 x 380mm/15in guns
in four twin turrets
Secondary – 16 x 150mm/6in, 2 x 75mm/3in
and 4 x 3pdr guns

Machinery: 24 boilers, 4 shafts.
55,928kW/75,000shp

Speed: 25 knots

Complement: 925 men

All ships of the class were extensively rebuilt
between the wars, and anti-aircraft
armament improved.

one or more of her magazines blew up and she sank with the loss of more than two-thirds of her crew. Cunningham acknowledged that the sinking of *Barham* was a most daring and brilliant performance on the part of the U-boat. He described the sinking:

> I saw the Barham, *immediately astern of us, stopped and listing heavily over to port. The poor ship rolled nearly over on to her beam ends, and we saw men massing on her upturned side. A minute or two later there came the deep rumble of a terrific explosion as one of her main magazines blew up. The ship became completely hidden in a great cloud of yellowish-black smoke, which went on wreathing and eddying high into the sky. When it cleared away the* Barham *had disappeared. There was nothing but a bubbling, oily-looking patch on the calm surface of the sea, dotted with wreckage and the heads of swimmers. It was ghastly to look at, a horrible and awe-inspiring spectacle when one realized what it meant.*

TOP: **The end of *Barham*, torpedoed off Sollum on November 25, 1941.** ABOVE LEFT: **A gun crew at a drill while at anchor in Alexandria, 1940. The French battleship in the background would later be demilitarized.** ABOVE: **Even a 30,481-tonne/ 30,000-ton battleship could be moved by the waves. If the length matched the frequency of a wave, even a large ship could be moved like this.**

Malaya alone did not receive the second major refit like her sisters. She was at the Battle of Calabria, and then employed on escort duties in the North Atlantic. In March 1941, while escorting convoy SL67, *Malaya*'s aircraft spotted *Scharnhorst* and *Gneisenau* off the Cape Verde Islands, which turned away. Later she was torpedoed off the coast of West Africa by *U-106* and steamed to the USA for repairs. She ended her life moored in a Scottish loch as a stationary target for the RAF and was scrapped in 1948. *Malaya*'s ship's bell hangs in the East India Club, London.

Royal Sovereign class

Also known as the Revenge class, these ships were progressively modernized during their lives. *Revenge* and *Royal Oak* were the only ships of this class at the Battle of Jutland. They were envisaged as smaller versions of the Queen Elizabeths, designed to use coal or oil to fire the boilers. During and immediately after World War I the class received anti-torpedo bulges which increased their beam to 31m/102ft, director fire-control for the secondary armament, and flying-off ramps over B and X turrets. In the inter-war years various 150mm/6in guns were removed and replaced by 100mm/4in high-angle anti-aircraft guns. By 1939 the torpedo tubes and aircraft platforms were removed and anti-aircraft armament increased by two and later three octuple 2pdr mountings. Also the deck armour over the magazines was increased to 100mm/4in thickness. *Resistance*, *Renown* and *Repulse* were cancelled in 1914, but the steel which had been assembled for the latter two was used for two new battlecruisers of the same names. As a class they were too slow to be effective in World War II.

Ramillies and *Revenge* were deployed to Izmir during the brief Turko-Greek war after World War I. In 1939 *Ramillies* escorted troop convoys in the Channel and in 1940 in the Indian Ocean. On August 18, 1940, she bombarded Bardia, and in November fought at the Battle of Cape Spartivento while transferring from Alexandria to Gibraltar. She was escorting convoy HX106 when she was sighted by *Scharnhorst* and *Gneisenau* on February 8, 1941, and they turned away.

In May 1941 she took part in the hunt for *Bismarck*. By May 1942 she was back in the Indian Ocean where she bombarded Diego Suarez, but on May 20 she was torpedoed by a Japanese midget submarine. Repaired at Durban and at

TOP: *Royal Sovereign* **entering Malta in April 1935. Malta was the kingpin of British strategy in the central Mediterranean where the British had had interests since the 1600s.** ABOVE: **Three pictures on these two pages show the different camouflage schemes in use. These were intended not to disguise the ships but to fool the enemy's optical rangefinders. Here** *Resolution* **is in wartime camouflage in May 1942.**

Devonport, *Ramillies* bombarded German positions during D-Day and the Allied landings in southern France. She was sold for scrapping in 1948.

Revenge carried British bullion reserves to Canada in 1939 and escorted Canadian troopships back to England. In September 1940 *Revenge* bombarded Cherbourg to interrupt German preparations for Operation Sealion, the invasion of Britain. *Revenge* sailed from Halifax, Nova Scotia, to participate in the hunt for *Bismarck*. After a year in the Indian Ocean, *Revenge* returned home to be taken out of service and was sold for scrap in 1948.

Resolution also took bullion to Canada. During the Norway Campaign on May 18, 1940, she was hit by a large bomb which penetrated three decks, but was soon repaired. As part of Force H she bombarded the French fleet at Mers-el-Kebir on July 3, 1940. She took part in operations against the Vichy French at Dakar when she was torpedoed by the French submarine *Bévéziers*. When repairs at Portsmouth became impossible because of German air raids she was sent to Philadelphia. *Resolution* then escorted troop convoys in the

Royal Sovereign class

Class: *Ramillies, Resolution, Revenge (ex-Renown), Royal Oak, Royal Sovereign.*
Launched 1914–16

Dimensions: Length – 190m/624ft
Beam – 27m/88ft 6in
Draught – 8.7m/28ft 6in

Displacement: 28,450 tonnes/28,000 tons

Armament: Main – 8 x 380mm/15in guns
Secondary – 14 x 150mm/6in guns and
4 x 535mm/21in torpedoes

Machinery: 18 boilers, 4 shafts.
29,828kW/40,000shp

Speed: 21 knots

Complement: 908–997 men

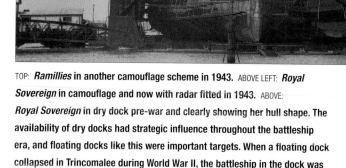

Indian Ocean, but by early 1944 had become a training ship and was scrapped, also in 1948.

Royal Sovereign was in the Home Fleet during 1939 and on Atlantic convoy duty in 1940–1. She was part of the British Mediterranean Fleet at the Battle of Punto Stilo on July 18, 1940, when Cunningham, with the battleships *Warspite, Malaya, Royal Sovereign*, and the carrier *Eagle*, met the two Italian battleships *Giulio Cesare* and *Conte di Cavour*. *Warspite* hit *Giulio Cesare* at long range, but Cunningham was hampered by the slow speed of *Malaya* and *Royal Sovereign*, though he pursued the Italians to within 80km/50 miles of the coast of Calabria. *Royal Sovereign* spent 1942–3 refitting in the USA after just one month in the Indian Ocean and then returned home. On May 30, 1944, *Royal Sovereign* was loaned to the Soviet navy and renamed *Arkhangelsk*. She was returned in 1949 and subsequently scrapped.

Royal Oak was sunk at Scapa Flow on October 14, 1939, by the German submarine *U-47*, when 833 men were killed, the wreck subsequently being preserved as a war grave. Recently, divers have worked on the wreck to prevent leaking oil tanks causing pollution.

One 380mm/15in gun from *Resolution* and another from *Ramillies* are displayed outside the Imperial War Museum in London.

Battle of Cape Spartivento

Operation Collar aimed to pass a fast convoy eastward through the Mediterranean, which Admiral Somerville with Force H from Gibraltar would cover with the battlecruiser *Renown* and the carrier *Ark Royal*. Meanwhile aircraft carriers of the British Mediterranean Fleet would raid targets as far apart as Tripoli

TOP: *Ramillies* in another camouflage scheme in 1943. ABOVE LEFT: *Royal Sovereign* in camouflage and now with radar fitted in 1943. ABOVE: *Royal Sovereign* in dry dock pre-war and clearly showing her hull shape. The availability of dry docks had strategic influence throughout the battleship era, and floating docks like this were important targets. When a floating dock collapsed in Trincomalee during World War II, the battleship in the dock was severely damaged.

and Rhodes, and pass the battleship *Ramillies* through the Mediterranean from east to west. Despite their setback at Taranto earlier in November 1940, the Italian navy was still a significant force, and when *Ramillies* was about to join Force H off the coast of southern Sardinia, Somerville encountered a superior Italian fleet including the battleships *Vittorio Veneto* and *Giulio Cesare* and several cruisers.

The Battle of Cape Spartivento, or Tuelada as it is known to the Italians, started with Somerville chasing towards the Italians, but he was hampered by the slow speed of *Ramillies*, and though shots were exchanged at long range, the British could not overhaul the faster enemy. Air strikes also failed to slow the Italians down. The battle ended when Somerville felt obliged to turn back from the Italian coast to protect the convoy. Curiously the British Admiralty ordered a board of enquiry for not continuing the pursuit of the Italians, but Somerville was exonerated.

LEFT: *Nelson* in the Thames for the Silver Jubilee in 1977. Ships of the fleet were anchored at various ports in the Thames to show themselves off to their public. The odd layout of these ships gave them a peculiar profile from wherever they were viewed.
ABOVE: *Nelson* and *Rodney* at sea together, bristling with guns.

Nelson and *Rodney*

The Royal Navy had various proposals for fast battleships or battlecruisers at the end of World War I, and *Nelson* and *Rodney* were lineal descendants of remarkable ships planned under the designation "G3". These plans were cancelled following the Washington Naval Treaty, but revived as heavy battleships incorporating the lessons learned in the war. However, the restriction on displacement to 35,560 tonnes/35,000 tons standard (a measure now defined for the first time by treaty) was in part responsible for their unusual layout of guns, which was intended to reduce the length of the armoured belt. The planned 119,312kW/160,000shp giving 30 knots was also reduced and they had only a quarter of that horsepower and the low speed of barely 23 knots.

The design aimed to produce the heaviest armament and best protection possible for the least displacement. They were amongst the best armoured of all British battleships with an internal belt of armour 305–355mm/12–14in thick, inclined at 15 degrees to the vertical and extending from A turret to the after 150mm/6in guns. The armoured deck was 165mm/6.5in over the magazines and 95mm/3.75in thick over the machinery, not including the 25mm/1in plating underneath.

The internal bulges were designed to withstand a 340kg/750lb warhead, and comprised an empty outer chamber, a water-filled chamber, a 38mm/1.5in torpedo bulkhead inboard and another compartment to limit flooding if the torpedo

bulkhead was strained. *Nelson*'s armour was further increased in 1937–8. Triple drum boilers enabled the actual number of boilers to be reduced to eight.

The three triple turrets were all forward of the superstructure, with B turret at a higher level than A and C. The 150mm/6in guns on either beam repeated this arrangement. In World War II a large number of smaller-calibre guns were added, especially the octuple 2pdr known as a "Chicago piano" and single 20mm/0.79in guns. Initially the 405mm/16in guns suffered some mechanical problems which compared badly to the tried and tested British 380mm/15in gun, and the power-operated 150mm/6in and 120mm/4.7in guns were slow. The performance of all these guns had improved by the outbreak of World War II.

Some other navies copied features of *Nelson* and *Rodney*. On rebuild the USN's *Idaho*, *Mississippi* and *New Mexico* were given tower masts, the French *Dunkerque* and *Strasbourg* were given Nelson-like gun layouts, and the Japanese and Russian navies also toyed with similar designs.

In October 1939 when Germany tried to repeat a World War I tactic by sailing the battlecruiser *Gneisenau* and other ships to draw the Home Fleet within U-boat range, *Nelson* and *Rodney* with *Hood*, *Repulse*, *Royal Oak* and the carrier *Furious* searched but made no contact with the enemy. When the armed merchant cruiser *Rawalpindi* was sunk on November 23

ABOVE LEFT: The triple 405mm/16in guns of *Nelson* and her ship's company preparing for inspection. ABOVE RIGHT: *Nelson*'s main armament at maximum elevation. LEFT: *Rodney*, an Admiral class battleship of 1884, showing how far battleship design had come in 50 years. BELOW: *Rodney* ammunitioning with 405mm/16in shells, a slow, cumbersome, manpower-intensive task and the techniques were little improved since the days of sail.

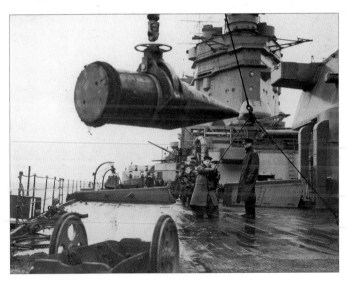

by *Scharnhorst* and *Gneisenau*, *Nelson* was one of the ships which prevented their breakout into the Atlantic, but returning to base she was damaged by a mine laid by *U-31* off Loch Ewe. Once repaired, *Nelson* joined Force H and was part of the escort for most of the important Malta-bound convoys in 1941 and 1942, although on September 27, 1941, during Operation Halberd, she was damaged by an Italian aircraft torpedo. *Nelson* was repaired well in time for Operation Torch, the Allied landing in North Africa in November 1942 and in July 1943. Together with *Rodney*, *Warspite* and *Valiant*, she was part of a fleet of over 2,500 American and British warships assembled for the invasion of Sicily.

One of the bombarding ships during the Normandy landings, *Nelson* was damaged by a mine on June 18, 1944. Repaired in Philadelphia, she briefly saw action in the Far East before becoming a training ship. She was used as a target ship in 1948 and scrapped in 1949.

Rodney had a similar wartime career to *Nelson*, except she took part in the Norway Campaign in 1940, where she was hit by a large bomb which penetrated three decks but did not explode. Her most famous action was the sinking of *Bismarck*. On May 27, 1941, *King George V* and *Rodney* caught up with the crippled German battleship and opening fire at about 08.45 reduced *Bismarck* to a wreck in an hour and a half, thus revenging the loss of *Hood*.

Nelson and *Rodney*

Class: *Nelson*, *Rodney*. Launched 1925
Dimensions: Length – 216m/710ft
  Beam – 32m/106ft
  Draught – 10m/33ft 6in
Displacement: 33,848 tonnes/33,313 tons
Armament: Main – 9 x 405mm/16in guns
  Secondary – 12 x 150mm/6in, 6 x 120mm/4.7in
  guns and 2 x 620mm/24.5in torpedoes
Machinery: 8 boilers, 2 shafts.
  33,557kW/45,000shp
Speed: 23 knots
Complement: 1,314 men
Rodney was larger at 33,370 tons and both ships at deep load were well over 40,000 tons

King George V class

The King George V class were designed just as the inter-war naval treaties expired, and the Royal Navy needed modern fast ships to match the German *Bismarck* and *Tirpitz*. The critical path for construction lay through the manufacture of guns, which the British had been trying to limit to 355mm/14in as they thought this the optimum size to fit into a treaty-sized 35,560-tonne/35,000-ton hull. The arrangement of two quadruple turrets, fore and aft, and a double turret in B position was a trade-off between armament and armour.

The secondary armament consisted of a new 130mm/5.25in dual-purpose gun mounted in eight twin power-operated turrets, and the other, lighter close-range anti-aircraft weaponry was upgraded during the war by fitting eight-barrelled pom-poms and 20mm/0.79in guns. Some ships were fitted with a rocket, which fired a trailing wire and an explosive

BELOW: **King George VI visiting the battleship named after his father "in northern waters" during World War II. A comparison (see opposite) with a similar view of an earlier ship of the same name shows how far warship construction and equipment had advanced in 20 years.**

charge, but this proved more dangerous to the firer than to any enemy aircraft. Armoured protection was better than in the Nelsons, including the anti-torpedo bulges being divided into a sandwich, the middle layer being used for fuel or water. They had four shafts each driven by an independent set of machinery, and space-saving Admiralty pattern three-drum boilers. Speed to catch the enemy was important, and the class was designed to reach 27.5 knots, 6 knots faster than *Nelson* and *Rodney*.

As a class they were commissioned in the war, decommissioned in the late 1940s and scrapped in 1957–8, a life of about 16 years. *King George V* was completed in October 1940 and in March 1941 covered a commando raid on the Lofoten islands. She then covered convoys in the North Atlantic and Arctic and, on May 27, 1941, while flagship of the British Home Fleet, she brought *Bismarck* to bay. Churchill had ordered that *Bismarck* must be sunk at all costs and suggested that this might mean towing *King George V* home, but the order was as unnecessary as it was unusual. She gave gunfire support during the landings on Sicily and at Salerno in 1943,

King George V class

Class: *King George V, Prince of Wales, Duke of York, Anson, Howe.* Launched 1939–40

Dimensions: Length – 227m/745ft
Beam – 31m/103ft
Draught – 8.9m/29ft

Displacement: 37,316 tonnes/36,727 tons

Armament: Main – 10 x 355mm/14in guns
Secondary – 16 x 130mm/5.25in and
32 x 2pdr guns

Machinery: 8 boilers, 4 shafts.
82,027kW/110,000shp

Speed: 28 knots

Complement: 1,422 men

ABOVE FAR LEFT: **An aerial view of one of the class underway.** ABOVE LEFT: **King George VI is seen here inspecting his father's namesake.** LEFT: **By comparison the World War I battleship called** *King George V* **(scrapped in the 1920s) had torpedo nets, very little fire control equipment when first built, and a stern gallery which was a design feature left over from the days of sail. Radar, of course, was not available until World War II.**

and in December brought Churchill home from the Tehran Conference. *King George V* was refitted before joining the British Pacific Fleet in October 1944, and was in Tokyo Bay at the Japanese surrender on September 2, 1945.

Duke of York was ready for service in November 1941, was employed on Arctic convoys, and covered the landings in North Africa in October 1942. In December 1943 she was covering convoy JW55B when the German battlecruiser *Scharnhorst* sortied from her lair in the Norwegian fjords. On December 26, in appalling weather, *Duke of York*'s radar-controlled guns scored several hits on *Scharnhorst,* enabling the escorting cruisers to torpedo the German battlecruiser. *Duke of York* was flagship of the British Pacific Fleet at the Japanese surrender.

Howe covered Arctic convoys until May 1943, but in July she transferred to the Mediterranean for the invasion of Sicily. In 1944 she became flagship of the British Pacific Fleet during the Okinawa campaign, in the new role for the battleship of bombardment and providing an anti-aircraft umbrella for the fleet. In June 1945 she was sent into dock at Durban and so missed the Japanese surrender. *Anson* covered Arctic convoys until June 1944, when she was sent to Plymouth for refit. In

April 1945 *Anson* and the *Duke of York* sailed for the Far East and on August 30, 1945, *Anson* helped liberate Hong Kong two days before the formal Japanese surrender at Tokyo. *Anson* never fired her 355mm/14in guns in anger.

When *Bismarck* escaped from the Norwegian fjords into the Atlantic she was intercepted, on May 24, 1941, in the Denmark Strait by *Hood* and *Prince of Wales*. *Hood* blew up after a brief engagement. *Bismarck* shifted her fire on to *Prince of Wales* and damaged her, but not before *Prince of Wales* had hit *Bismarck,* causing damage and fuel leaks which led eventually to the German ship's demise.

In August 1941, *Prince of Wales* took Churchill across the Atlantic to meet President Roosevelt in Newfoundland, where together they drafted the first Atlantic Charter. Later that year *Prince of Wales* together with *Repulse* formed Force Z at Singapore, which sailed to stop Japanese troops landing on the Malay coast. On December 10, 1941, Force Z was overwhelmed by Japanese bombers and torpedo aircraft: they were the last two American or British capital ships in the Pacific. Following Pearl Harbor, air power, which the British Fleet Air Arm had done so much to develop in the Mediterranean, had truly come of age.

Lion class and *Vanguard*

This four-ship class of battleships was an enlarged version of the King George V class and was contemplated pre-war with two ships, *Lion* and *Temeraire*, being laid down in 1939. Under the London Naval Treaty these ships would have had 405mm/16in guns on a 45,720-tonne/45,000-ton displacement. Similar in layout and silhouette the Lion class would have had a transom stern, an armoured conning tower and a pole mainmast. The turbines and boilers were arranged as in *King George V*, but the 405mm/16in gun would have been a development over *Nelson's* guns, with a shell 15 per cent heavier. Construction was suspended on the outbreak of World War II and cancelled in 1943–4. The Royal Navy realized very early that the era of the battleship was drawing to a close.

Vanguard was the last battleship to be built for the Royal Navy. Built on Clydebank, she was launched on November 30, 1944, but did not serve in the war. She was the biggest British battleship with a deep load displacement of 51,820 tonnes/51,000 tons. Her guns were reputedly those of *Glorious* and *Courageous* and had been in storage since the 1920s when it was decided to convert the ships to aircraft carriers.

The heavy anti-aircraft armament was what might be expected for war in the Pacific, but soon after the end of World War II many of the single 40mm/1.57in guns were removed. In 1947, when *Vanguard* took part in a royal tour to South Africa by King George VI, the anti-aircraft mounting above B turret was replaced by a reviewing platform.

Vanguard was refitted at Devonport in 1947–8, and then used as a training ship at Portsmouth where she became something of a fixture. She was sold for scrapping in 1960, and thousands of people gathered to wave farewell to this icon of British sea power on August 6. As *Vanguard* was being towed out through the narrow entrance to Portsmouth harbour, she broke free of her tugs and threatened to crash into a public house on the Portsmouth side and cut through the Custom House jetty. However she ran aground. She was towed off later that day, and finally scrapped at Faslane just a few miles from Clydebank where she was built. This was the end of an era. For reasons of cost, manpower, technical advance and operations, the world's greatest navy gave up the construction of battleships forever.

ABOVE: *Vanguard*, the last battleship of a long line in the Royal Navy – although outwardly different, she was similar to the King George V class. TOP LEFT: A handsome picture of *Vanguard* from the air. TOP RIGHT: *Vanguard* from the stern, a view which the architect seems to have neglected, but the transom stern was intended to increase her length and, with a pronounced sheer to the bow, to give her better seagoing qualities. RIGHT: *Vanguard* dressed overall and beautifully framed.

Vanguard

Class: *Vanguard*. Launched 1944

Dimensions: Length – 248m/814ft 4in
Beam – 33m/108ft
Draught – 9.4m/30ft 9in

Displacement: 45,215 tonnes/44,500 tons

Armament: Main – 8 x 380mm/15in guns
Secondary – 16 x 130mm/5.25in and
73 x 40mm/1.57in guns

Machinery: 8 boilers, 4 shafts.
96,941kW/130,000shp

Speed: 30 knots

Complement: 1,893 men

Colorado class

Four ships were ordered in 1916 and were completed in the 1920s, apart from *Washington*, which was never finished, and represented the first 405mm/16in battleships of the USN. Apart from the size of the guns, the design and layout of the Colorado class were an evolution of the Tennessee class, and like all USN battleships were characterized by lattice masts. *Maryland* was the first American battleship to be fitted with a catapult. Later these ships carried three catapults, two on the quarterdeck and one on X turret.

Modernization for all three ships was approved in 1939, but rising tension worldwide delayed this until 1941. Modernization had started at Puget Sound on *Colorado*, when *Maryland* and *West Virginia* were sunk at Pearl Harbor, but both were raised and also went to Puget Sound for their delayed modernizations. They emerged in 1942 with additional armour and anti-torpedo bulges. Further refits during the war progressively improved the radars, gunnery directors and anti-aircraft armament.

Colorado returned after her refit to Pearl Harbor in August 1942. From December 1942 to September 1943 she was deployed in the New Hebrides and the Fiji islands as part of a blocking force against further Japanese expansion. In November 1943 she provided gunfire support for the American landings on Tarawa, and was then sent back to the USA for a further upgrade. During early 1944 *Colorado* covered landing operations at Kwajalein, Eniwetok, Saipan, Guam and Tinian. At Tinian on July 24, shore batteries found her range and she

ABOVE: *Colorado* passes under the Golden Gate bridge into San Francisco in 1945. This iconic scene was repeated many times over – and continues to be so – but for many ships at the end of World War II it was also a last scene as the USN was run down and ships placed in reserve during the post-war period.

was hit 22 times. Repaired on the West Coast, *Colorado* arrived in Leyte Gulf where on November 27 she was hit by two kamikazes. Many of the ship's crew were killed or wounded and the attack caused extensive damage. Nevertheless, a few days later she bombarded Mindoro in December before going to Manus Island for temporary repairs. Off Luzon in January 1945, *Colorado* bombarded Japanese positions in Lingayen Gulf where she was hit once more. In April and May 1945 *Colorado* covered the invasion of Okinawa and in August and September was in Tokyo Bay. At the end of the war, in a repeat of the use of USN battleships after World War I, *Colorado* made "magic carpet" voyages, bringing over 6,000 troops home. She was placed in reserve in 1947 and sold for scrapping in 1959.

At Pearl Harbor *Maryland* was berthed inboard of *Oklahoma* and thus was protected from the fury of the attack. Although hit by bombs she was able to steam to Puget Sound after temporary repairs. The pattern of employment for all this class of ships was dictated by their age and lack of speed, and since they were too slow to operate with the aircraft carriers, *Maryland*, though repaired at Puget Sound in two months, missed the main actions of the Battle of Midway. Later

TOP LEFT: **A Colorado class battleship, with storeships alongside, is preparing for her next action. This picture is reminiscent of many others: battleships with their huge crews were hungry beasts with a constant demand for stores.** ABOVE: *Maryland* **firing point-blank during the bombardment of Tarawa.** LEFT: *Colorado* **firing her 405mm/16in guns to starboard, sometime in the 1940s. Note how the technique of lattice mast construction has been retained.** BELOW: **Skills like signalling with flags survived even the age of the battleship. One sailor is sending semaphore and another is reading a message: in ideal conditions this method could be used at the extremes of visibility.**

Maryland joined *Colorado* in protecting the routes to Australia through the Fiji islands and the New Hebrides. Her main role during the extensive amphibious campaigning in the Pacific was to provide gunfire support, as she did at Tarawa in the Gilberts, at Kwajalein Atoll in the Marshalls and at Saipan.

On June 22, 1944, while at anchor off Saipan, a Japanese aircraft missed *Pennsylvania* but torpedoed *Maryland*, opening a gaping hole in her side. Nevertheless she was repaired at Pearl Harbor within two months and was ready to cover beach clearance operations in the Palau islands.

On October 25,1944, *Maryland* took part in the Battle of Surigao, part of the larger Battle of Leyte Gulf, when the Japanese battleships *Fuso* and *Yamashiro* tried to force the straits. The Japanese were detected by a layered defence of torpedo boats, destroyers, cruisers and battleships, and the remnants of the Japanese force were then annihilated by naval aircraft.

In November *Maryland* was hit by a kamikaze plane which crashed between A and B turrets. Again repaired at Pearl Harbor, *Maryland* was back for the Okinawa campaign, where on April 7, a kamikaze plane hit her, this time on X turret causing heavy casualties, especially amongst the exposed 20mm/0.79in gunners. *Maryland* was sent back to Puget Sound for permanent repairs and was there on VJ-Day. On the "magic carpet" run she brought back more than 8,000 troops. Placed in reserve in 1947, *Maryland* was scrapped in 1959.

Colorado class (continued)

ABOVE: **A dramatic picture of *Maryland* in the thick of action in November 1944. The action was not at night, but the brightness of the explosion on *Maryland*'s forecastle has resulted in the film being under-exposed. Nevertheless, the melodramatic mood of the picture is accurate.**

At Pearl Harbor on December 7, 1941, *West Virginia* lay in battleship row, berthed outboard of *Tennessee*, where in the first waves of attack she was hit by seven 455mm/18in aircraft torpedoes in her port side and two bombs. The bombs caused fires and the detonation of ammunition, wrecking two of *West Virginia*'s aircraft and setting light to their aviation fuel. The torpedoes badly damaged the port side but prompt damage control prevented her capsizing. *West Virginia*'s captain was killed by shrapnel from a bomb landing on *Tennessee*. *West Virginia* settled on an even keel and fires drove her crew off the ship: others were trapped below decks and suffered a lingering death. The fires were only subdued after 24 hours and she was refloated six months later to be rebuilt at Puget Sound over the next two years.

Like her sisters, the lattice masts were removed, a new superstructure was fitted and a very large number of 40mm/1.57in and 20mm/0.79in anti-aircraft guns fitted. The 125mm/5in guns in casemates were also replaced by dual-purpose 125mm/5in guns in turrets. The two funnels were trunked into one, giving *West Virginia* a very different silhouette to other ships of the class.

At the Battle of Surigao *West Virginia* led *Maryland*, *Mississippi*, *Tennessee*, *California* and *Pennsylvania* in a line that, for the last time in history, crossed the T of the enemy's line, and sank the Japanese battleship *Fuso*. Other operations included covering the landings in Lingayen Bay and the invasions of Iwo Jima and Okinawa, finishing in Tokyo Bay on August 31, 1945. After this *West Virginia* played host to thousands of visitors for Navy Day on October 27 in San Diego,

and was part of the "magic carpet" bringing home thousands of US servicemen. The "Wee Vee" was decommissioned in the late 1940s and sold for scrapping in 1959.

The Battle of Leyte Gulf

This action arose from a Japanese attempt to interrupt American troop-landings there. A Northern Decoy Force with four carriers (but not many aircraft) and two partially converted battleship-carriers steamed south from Japan. A Centre Strike Force including five battleships closed Leyte Gulf from the north-west through San Bernadino Strait, while a Southern Strike Force including two battleships closed from the south-west through the Surigao Straits in a pincer.

On October 24, in the Battle of Sibuyan Sea, the Centre Strike Force was attacked by aircraft of the US Third Fleet, and the giant battleship *Musashi* was sunk. Next the Northern Decoy Force succeeded in luring the Third Fleet north leaving the San Bernadino Strait open, with only escort carriers and old battleships of the US Seventh Fleet to protect the landings.

Overnight on October 24/25, the Southern Strike Force of the battleships *Fuso* and *Yamashiro* entered the Surigao Strait where they suffered successive attacks from smaller ships, during which *Yamashiro* was lost. When *Fuso* met six US battleships formed into line she too was sunk.

LEFT: *West Virginia* on fire and aground after being torpedoed in battleship row, Pearl Harbor, 1941. BELOW: After the Japanese attack, *West Virginia* was raised and repaired and she is seen here in dry dock, June 1942. The recovery and repair of ships after the Japanese attack on Pearl Harbor became a matter of pride for the USN, even after it was realized that aircraft carriers were needed more than battleships.

ABOVE: The incomplete battleship *Washington* in 1922. She was destined to be sunk in experiments during 1924. The name was used in a new ship of a subsequent class.

Early on October 25, the remains of the Centre Strike Force with four battleships steamed through the San Bernardino Strait to attack the escort carriers and accompanying destroyers of the Seventh Fleet. Japanese surface ships and kamikaze aircraft sank or destroyed two escort carriers and several smaller ships, but just when the Centre Strike Force should have smashed the amphibious shipping, the Japanese turned away.

Meanwhile at the Battle of Cape Enga, aircraft of the US Third Fleet sank all the main units of the Northern Decoy Force, *Chitose*, *Chiyoda*, *Zuiho* and *Zuikaku*. Centre Strike Force, having failed in its objective, escaped from the returning US Third Fleet.

Colorado class

Class: *Maryland, Colorado, Washington, West Virginia*. Launched 1920–1
Dimensions: Length – 190m/624ft
   Beam – 29.7m/97ft 5in
   Draught – 9.2m/30ft 2in
Displacement: 33,123 tonnes/32,600 tons
Armament: Main – 8 x 405mm/16in guns
   Secondary – 12 x 125mm/5in, 8 x 75mm/3in
   guns and 2 x 535mm/21in torpedoes
Machinery: 8 boilers, 4 shafts.
   19,985kW/26,800shp
Speed: 21 knots
Complement: 1,083 men

North Carolina class

The name North Carolina was taken from a ship ordered in 1917, laid down in 1920, but cancelled under the terms of the Washington Naval Treaty.

In the new North Carolina the armament was increased from 355mm/14in to 405mm/16in during their design, but too late to alter other features of the class. However, for the first time in a USN ship the guns were arranged two forward and one aft, with secondary armament in turrets. There were no scuttles in the hull and habitability suffered accordingly. Their hulls had to be strengthened after both ships experienced severe vibrations on trials and during World War II both were refitted, when they received enclosed bridges, improved radars, and a very large number of anti-aircraft guns. Post-war there were proposals to convert North Carolina and Washington into satellite launch ships, helicopter ships, or fast-replenishment ships but these came to nothing.

North Carolina was the first of her class to be built after the expiry of the Washington Naval Treaty in 1936. She was regarded as the first of the modern battleships, receiving so much publicity that she was nicknamed "Showboat".

When the Pearl Harbor attack took place North Carolina was undergoing trials off the East Coast of America. She entered the Pacific in June 1942 and covered the landings at Guadalcanal and Tulagi in August 1942. The USN had developed the concept of battle groups consisting of carriers and battleships, in which long-range strike capability was provided by the carrier's aircraft and the purpose of the battleship was as an anti-aircraft battery. In this role, North Carolina was on the screen of the aircraft carrier Enterprise during the Battle of the Solomons, August 23–25. During this

ABOVE: **North Carolina photographed in 1941. The USN battleships of this class were the first to be built after the expiry of the Washington Treaty. This picture shows North Carolina as she was designed and built, but very soon afterwards she was taken in hand again and fitted with a massive anti-aircraft armament, radars and improved fire-control systems.**

engagement North Carolina claimed to have shot down between seven and fourteen Japanese aircraft in one eight-minute action. On September 6, 1942, North Carolina was torpedoed by a Japanese submarine but she was repaired at Pearl Harbor and ready for action in November.

From then on North Carolina's actions read like a roll call of the American island-hopping advance through the Pacific: Tarawa, Makin, Kwajalein, Majuro, Truk, Marianas, Palau, Yap, Ulithi, Woleai, Ponape, Satawan, New Guinea, Wake, Saipan and the Battle of the Philippine Sea.

In 1945 during preparations for the landings on Okinawa, North Carolina played the battleship's dual role of providing heavy bombardment and an anti-aircraft umbrella. On April 6 while under attack by kamikaze aircraft she was hit by friendly fire and needed repairs at Pearl Harbor before joining a carrier battle group for the attack on the Japanese home islands. In the final days of the assault she bombarded factories near Tokyo, and she landed seamen and marines ashore for "preliminary occupation duty".

North Carolina provided the "magic carpet" for troops on passage between Okinawa and the US East Coast, made one training cruise for midshipmen and was then deactivated. In 1961 she was given to the people of North Carolina, where she is now a museum ship at Wilmington.

LEFT: *North Carolina*'s launch in June 1940. ABOVE: *Washington*, equipped with all her wartime additions. BELOW LEFT: *North Carolina* on her maiden voyage, but apparently not yet fully fitted, showing off the elevation of her guns.

North Carolina class

Class: *North Carolina, Washington.* Launched 1940
Dimensions: Length – 222m/728ft 9in
    Beam – 33m/108ft 4in
    Draught – 10m/33ft
Displacement: 38,086 tonnes/37,484 tons
Armament: Main – 9 x 405mm/16in guns
    Secondary – 20 x 125mm/5in, 16 x 28mm/1.1in
    and 12 x 13mm/0.5in guns
Machinery: 8 boilers, 4 shafts.
    90,230kW/121,000shp
Speed: 28 knots
Complement: 1,880 men

A battleship named *Washington* was ordered in 1916 but cancelled in 1921 when the hull was already built, and she was sunk as a target in 1924. In the early part of 1942 the new battleship *Washington* was deployed in the North Atlantic and Arctic with the British Home Fleet. On May 1, *King George V* rammed the British destroyer *Punjabi,* cutting her in two, and *Washington* passed between the sinking halves while *Punjabi's* depth charges exploded beneath her. *Washington* escaped with only a minor leak and whip damage to her fire-control radars.

In August 1942 *Washington* entered the Pacific, and on the night of November 14–15 took part in a battle off Savo Island. The Japanese were trying to reprovision their positions at Guadalcanal when *Washington* and *South Dakota* met the Japanese battleship *Kirishima* in a night action. *Kirishima* concentrated her fire on *South Dakota* who was forced to retire, but was badly damaged by *Washington's* accurate radar-controlled gunnery and had to be scuttled the next

morning. This was the only battleship-to-battleship action that took place during World War II.

Washington was involved in another collision in February 1943 when she rammed *Indiana*, crumpling her bows. A temporary bow was fitted at Pearl Harbor and she was sent to Puget Sound for permanent repair. From then on *Washington* formed part of various carrier battle groups and took part in the Battle of the Philippine Sea in June 1944 when together with six other battleships, four heavy cruisers, and 14 destroyers she formed the screen.

Like other battleships, *Washington's* anti-aircraft armament was steadily improved throughout the war until by the end she sported 15 x quadruple 40mm/1.57in, 1 x quadruple 20mm/0.79in, 8 x twin 20mm/0.79in, and 63 x single 20mm/0.79in guns. *Washington's* last refit carried her through VJ-Day and she made only one brief sortie into the Pacific before being sent to Europe to bring troops home. She was decommissioned in 1947, and scrapped in 1961.

South Dakota class

This class generally resembled the North Carolinas but were shorter and more heavily armoured as they were designed to provide protection against 405mm/16in shells, but on the same displacement as the earlier ships, and with the same speed and armament. Two ships were planned and two more added to the programme at the outbreak of World War II in Europe. Underwater, the outboard propeller shafts were encased in fins and the inboard shafts were placed entirely between the fins. Overall the design was rather cramped, causing problems of habitability between decks and operationally for the placing of anti-aircraft guns around the superstructure. All four ships were ready for service in 1942.

During the war the 28mm/1.1in and 13mm/0.5in anti-aircraft guns were replaced with larger numbers of 40mm/1.57in and 20mm/0.79in weapons. In addition, the radar suite was upgraded and the bridges were enclosed. Like other battleships post-war plans were made for conversion to missile ships, satellite launch ships, helicopter assault ships, and fast replenishment ships, but none of these ideas came to fruition.

South Dakota was fitted as a force flagship and her conning tower was one level higher than other ships of the class, compensating for the extra weight by having two fewer 125mm/5in guns and an extra pair of quadruple 28mm/1.1in guns. She made an inauspicious start on September 6, 1942, when she struck an uncharted pinnacle in Lahai Passage and suffered extensive damage to her hull needing several weeks of repairs at Pearl Harbor.

In October 1942 South Dakota was part of a battle group centred on the carriers Enterprise and Hornet which met a much larger Japanese carrier force preparing for a major assault on Henderson Field. In what became known as the

TOP: **South Dakota** taken on August 9, 1943. In this picture **South Dakota**'s anti-aircraft armament has been greatly increased over her original design. ABOVE: **South Dakota** in line astern somewhere in the Pacific in 1945. There was no other formation in which the number of guns bearing on a target could be maximized.

Battle of Santa Cruz, Hornet was sunk and Enterprise was temporarily put out of action while the Japanese carrier Shokaku was damaged. While protecting Enterprise during the third wave of air attacks, South Dakota was hit on her A turret by a 227kg/500lb bomb, but she was also credited with having shot down 26 Japanese planes.

On October 30, South Dakota and the destroyer Mahan were in collision and South Dakota's bows crumpled, requiring a repair at Noumea. However, by November 13, 1942, she was able to join the battleship Washington and four destroyers for a night sweep off Guadalcanal, while a Japanese flotilla consisting of the battleship Kirishima, several cruisers and destroyers were approaching to bombard Henderson Field.

In the moonlight of November 14/15, the enemy were sighted from South Dakota at a range of 16,550m/18,100yds. Washington opened fire shortly before South Dakota and the salvoes from both ships straddled the Japanese. South Dakota then fired on another target until it disappeared from her radar screen. As South Dakota's after main turret fired on a third target, it demolished her own planes, whilst her 125mm/5in

TOP LEFT: **Colours on the last evening as** *South Dakota* **is decommissioned (the guns under the dome are already "mothballed").** ABOVE: *South Dakota* **manoeuvring while under air attack from a Japanese Kamikaze aircraft.** FAR LEFT: **The guns of** *Indiana* **on commissioning day, April 30, 1942.** LEFT: **One of the South Dakota class firing her broadside at a shore target. Despite all the investment in battleships, this and anti-aircraft defence was, at the end of their era, their principal role.**

guns engaged targets close inshore, thought to be enemy destroyers. *South Dakota* was then illuminated by searchlight at about 5,485m/6,000yds from ships as they cleared Savo Island, and she came under fire from several warships including the battleship *Kirishima*, taking considerable damage. A fire started in the foremast, she lost power temporarily, her radios failed, her radars and radar plot were demolished, and, as she turned away from the onslaught, she lost track of her consort. *Washington* continued the engagement, damaging *Kirishima* so badly that the Japanese scuttled her next morning. The Americans lost three destroyers, the Japanese cruisers *Takao* and *Atago* were hit and, besides *Kirishima*, the destroyer *Ayanami* was also scuttled.

South Dakota was again repaired at Noumea and she was sent to New York for refit in December 1942. For a few months she operated in the North Atlantic as convoy escort before returning to the Pacific in September 1943, where the actions she was involved in were the familiar roll-call of the American advance across the Pacific. On June 19, 1944, the first day of the Battle of the Philippine Sea, the battleship escorts were

placed so as to be able to continue supporting the army and marines on Saipan while being prepared to intercept a Japanese surface force which was known to be approaching from the west. *South Dakota* was hit during a heavy air raid by a 227kg/500lb bomb which penetrated the main deck, causing minor material damage but over 50 casualties. However, her damage control was sufficient to keep her in action until she was sent to Puget Sound for repair in July.

In May 1945, while loading ammunition from a stores ship, an explosion caused a fire and her magazines were flooded to prevent further damage. Then on July 14, *South Dakota* bombarded the Kamaishi Steel Works on Honshu, the first time that the home islands of Japan had been attacked by ships since the Royal Navy had bombarded Shimonseki and Kagoshima in the 19th century.

South Dakota was in Tokyo Bay for the formal Japanese surrender, leaving there on September 20, 1945, to be refitted in Philadelphia in 1946. In 1962, after 15 years in reserve, she was sold for scrapping. A wave of nostalgia meant that other ships of her vintage were preserved as museum ships.

South Dakota class (continued)

Indiana operated in the Pacific throughout World War II. From November 1942 to October 1943 she was part of a fast battle group based around the carriers *Enterprise* and *Saratoga* as the Americans advanced through the Solomons. In November 1943 she was part of the force which re-took the Gilbert Islands, and in January 1944 she bombarded Kwajalein for eight days prior to the landings there. However, on February 1 *Indiana* collided with the battleship *Washington* and needed repairs to her starboard side at Pearl Harbor.

In the Battle of the Philippine Sea, she bombarded Saipan on June 13–14 and on June 19 as four large air raids attacked the American ships, *Indiana* helped the other escorts and the carrier-based fighters shoot down 100 of the enemy in what was called the "Great Marianas Turkey Shoot". In the next months she bombarded targets on Palau and the Philippines, was refitted at Puget Sound, resumed her bombardment role at Iwo Jima and Ulithi, and screened the carriers during raids on Tokyo in February 1945. Between March and June 1945 she supported carrier operations against Japan and Okinawa,

BELOW: **The USN took part in amphibious operations in Europe as well as the Pacific. Here the *Massachusetts* prepares for Operation Torch off the coast of North Africa.**

riding out a terrible typhoon in June. In August she bombarded targets on the Japanese home islands, and on September 5 entered Tokyo Bay. Later she formed part of the Pacific Reserve Fleet until being sold for scrap in 1962. *Indiana*'s mast is erected at the University of Indiana in Bloomington and her anchor is on display at Fort Wayne.

Massachusetts was commissioned in May 1942 and supported the Allied landings in North Africa, Operation Torch, in November 1942. On November 8, off Casablanca, she silenced the guns of French battleship *Jean Bart* and sank two French destroyers. *Massachusetts* was then deployed to the Pacific, first covering the route through the Solomons to Australia, and then in November 1943 escorting the carrier strikes on the Gilbert Islands. In December she shelled Japanese positions on Nauru and in January she bombarded Kwajalein. Other operations followed at Truk, Saipan, Tinian, Guam and again at Truk, and she was at the Battle of Leyte Gulf in October 1944.

Massachusetts experienced the tremendous typhoon in December 1944, with winds estimated at 120 knots, in which three destroyers foundered. In June 1945 she passed through the eye of a typhoon with 100-knot winds. In July and August 1945 she shelled targets on the Japanese mainland, probably

firing in anger the last 405mm/16in shell of World War II on August 9. Since 1965, "Big Mamie", as she is known, has been a museum ship at Fall River, Massachusetts.

Alabama formed part of the British Home Fleet, based in Scapa Flow from May to August 1943, while British battleships were employed in the Mediterranean in support of the Allied landings on Sicily. In June, *Alabama* and her sister ship covered the reinforcement of Spitzbergen. In July, *Alabama* feinted at southern Norway aiming to reinforce German beliefs of a threatened landing there, and perhaps to lure the German battleship *Tirpitz* from her lair in the fjords.

By late 1943 *Alabama* was in the thick of the fighting in the Pacific, including the Battles of the Philippine Sea and Leyte Gulf, and the bombardment of Japan itself. On August 15, 1945, when the Japanese capitulated, *Alabama*'s seamen and marines were among the first American forces to land.

Her war was over when she had retrieved her crew on September 5, in Tokyo Bay, and taken 700 members of the USN's construction battalion home from Okinawa, arriving in San Francisco on October 15, 1945. In 1962 *Alabama* became a museum ship at Mobile, Alabama.

TOP LEFT: **The brand-new *Alabama* in camouflage in December 1942.**
TOP RIGHT: **A stoker puts on a burner of one of *Alabama*'s boilers.** ABOVE FAR LEFT: **A close-up of one of *Alabama*'s 405mm/16in guns.** ABOVE LEFT: **Another view of the business end of *Alabama*.** ABOVE RIGHT: **Old and new technology. Two fire control radars, a direction-finding loop, and signal flags. Flag signals, under the right circumstances, were still a reliable and adequate means of sending orders.**

South Dakota class

Class: *South Dakota, Indiana, Massachusetts, Alabama*. Launched 1941–2
Dimensions: Length – 207m/680ft
Beam – 33m/108ft
Draught – 10.7m/35ft
Displacement: 38,580 tonnes/37,970 tons
Armament: Main – 9 x 405mm/16in guns
Secondary – 20 x 125mm/5in and numerous lighter guns
Machinery: 8 boilers, 4 shafts.
96,941kW/130,000shp
Speed: 27.5 knots
Complement: 1,793 men

LEFT: **Post-war much of the tertiary armament of anti-aircraft guns was removed to produce the clean lines of *Iowa*.** BELOW: **The business of ammunitioning ships did not however end. After a series of disastrous explosions earlier in the century caused by unstable ammunition, it was now normally inert, but was still stowed quickly.**

Iowa class and *Iowa*

The Iowas were the last class of battleships to be completed for the USN and were considered to be the best, certainly the fastest, and with their long forecastles, cowled funnels and relatively low silhouettes, among the most handsome of all their type. They were conceived as stretched versions of the South Dakotas, their length (60m/200ft longer) giving them 5 to 6 knots extra speed (despite an increase of 10,160 tonnes/10,000 tons standard displacement) and making them capable of protecting a force of fast carriers against the swift Japanese Kongo class battlecruisers.

The USN invoked the so-called escalator clause of the London Naval Treaty to exceed the 45,720-tonne/45,000-ton limit, and eventually the full load displacement of these ships was 58,460 tonnes/57,540 tons. Four ships were planned and two more added in January 1941 after the Japanese attack on Pearl Harbor in the previous month.

Although designed to counter Japanese heavy cruisers and battlecruisers, their principal roles were as command ships, in-shore bombardment, and, of course, operating in fast carrier battle groups as air defence ships for which they were fitted with a huge number of anti-aircraft guns (the actual numbers

varied from ship to ship). They underwent the same World War II modifications as other American battleships, including improved electronics, an enlarged and enclosed bridge and yet more anti-aircraft guns.

They were prestigious vessels capable of a number of tasks, but like nearly every other Dreadnought their war complement was much greater than their peacetime complement. *Iowa*, for example, carried 1,000 more men than her given number of 1,921. They were thus expensive ships to maintain in service and though recalled to service in Korea, Vietnam and the Gulf War for their bombardment capability, they were frequently placed in reserve.

When *New Jersey* was recalled for the Vietnam War, where the air threat was minimal, even though all of the 40mm/1.57in and 20mm/0.79in guns were removed, she still needed a complement of over 1,500 to man the main armament and the steam plant. Even when fitted with eight quadruple armoured boxed launchers for Tomahawk cruise missiles and four quadruple canisters for Harpoon surface-to-surface missiles, their very high manpower costs could not be justified. However, in testimony to the powerful iconic status of these

Iowa class

🇺🇸

Class: *Iowa, New Jersey, Missouri, Wisconsin, Illinois, Kentucky.*
Launched 1942–50
Dimensions: Length – 270m/887ft
Beam – 33m/108ft
Draught – 11m/36ft 2in
Displacement: 48,880 tonnes/48,110 tons
Armament: Main – 9 x 405mm/16in guns
Secondary – 20 x 125mm/5in, 80 x
40mm/1.57in and 50 x 20mm/0.79in guns
Machinery: 8 boilers, 4 shafts.
158,088kW/212,000shp
Speed: 33 knots
Complement: 1,921 men

ABOVE: *Iowa* firing her main armament. LEFT: The fire and smoke of a broadside. There was noise too. RIGHT: The blast effect can clearly be seen on the surface of the sea. There was always a risk of self-inflicted damage from blast. These two aerial photographs show, by the flattening of the water around *Iowa*, how far the blast effect reached.

ships, even in the late 1990s some of them were notionally held in reserve, though there was very little probability of them returning to service.

Besides Tomahawk and Harpoon missiles and modern close-in weapons systems, other options included designating them as BBGs or guided-missile battleships but it was realized that the missiles were unlikely to withstand the blast effects of the 405mm/16in guns. They were not modernized for the Korean War, but in the 1980s the electronics were upgraded, the catapults and aircraft were replaced with limited helicopter facilities, and drone launch and recovery systems were fitted. The aircraft crane was suppressed and habitability was improved. They were not, however, refitted as flagships.

As a class they were finally decommissioned in 1990–2. *New Jersey* and *Wisconsin* both still had reserve status in 1996, but *New Jersey* was stricken in 1999 to allow her to become a museum at Camden, New Jersey, and *Wisconsin* is a "museum-in-reserve" at Norfolk, Virginia. *Missouri* is a museum at Pearl Harbor, and *Iowa*, who has been robbed for spares for the other ships, lies at Suisun Bay, California, awaiting preservation.

Iowa was specially fitted as a flagship and her conning tower was one deck higher than her sisters, who nevertheless proved equally capable of the role. She was damaged by grounding on her trials and repaired at Boston. She took President Franklin D. Roosevelt to Casablanca in 1943 on his way to the Tehran Conference, and when she had brought him back she transferred to the Pacific where she operated in support of fast-carrier task forces for the remainder of the war. *Iowa* also bombarded the Japanese home islands in July 1945 and she entered Tokyo Bay with the occupation forces on August 29, 1945.

Iowa was placed in reserve in 1949, re-commissioned in 1951–8, and made one deployment in the Korean War when she bombarded North Korean positions. She was modernized and commissioned again in 1984, but in 1989 her B turret was damaged by an internal explosion, and the centre gun was never restored. Despite being used for spares, she was reinstated on the register of naval vessels in 1999, but after years lying at Philadelphia she was towed to California to be a museum. Besides the Mikasa in Japan, and some shipwrecks, all the preserved battleships of the modern era are in the USA.

New Jersey

The second *New Jersey*, and the first of three similar ships built in the same yard, was launched at the Philadelphia Naval Shipyard on the anniversary of the Japanese attack on Pearl Harbor. She transited the Panama Canal in January 1944 to join the US Fifth Fleet which was in the Ellis Islands, preparing for the assault on the Marshall Islands. Her first employment was screening a carrier task force as they flew strikes against Kwajalein and Eniwetok. On January 31, the Fifth Fleet landed troops on two atolls, the undefended Majuro and the bitterly defended Kwajalein. The stubborn Japanese defence continued well into the month, while US forces assaulted another atoll, Eniwetok, on January 17. When the Japanese threatened to mount relief operations by forces based at Truk 1,127km/700 miles away, *New Jersey*, now flagship of the Fifth Fleet, led a raid which successfully disrupted their operations.

In June *New Jersey* supported the American invasion of the Marianas. The Japanese fleet was ordered to annihilate the American invasion force, which led to the Battle of the Philippine Sea, also known as the "Marianas Turkey Shoot" because the Japanese lost so many of their aircraft. *New Jersey*'s role was in providing anti-aircraft close support to the

ABOVE: **USN battleships survived post-war and ships such as *New Jersey*, seen here with a modern suite of electronics, was used to bombard shore targets during the Vietnam War. Here *New Jersey*, photographed in March 1960, is seen firing on targets near Tuyho in central South Vietnam.**

carriers. The loss of some 400 aircraft, three carriers and many trained pilots was a disaster for the Japanese. Following this *New Jersey* became flagship of the Third Fleet as fast carrier task forces struck at targets throughout the theatre of war. In September the targets were in the Visayas and the southern Philippines, then Manila and Cavite, Panay, Negros, Leyte and Cebu. Raids on Okinawa and Formosa (now Taiwan) to debilitate enemy air power began in October in preparation for landings at Leyte.

This invasion brought about the last major sortie of the Imperial Japanese Navy in a three-pronged attack. In the Battle of Leyte, a Northern Decoy Force of carriers, though nearly bereft of aircraft, and two battleships succeeded in drawing away ships which should have been protecting the invasion beaches. This allowed the Japanese Centre and Southern Strike Forces to close Leyte Gulf through the San Bernardino Strait. Both were heavily damaged, but the Centre Strike Force,

RIGHT: *New Jersey* in the Pacific in November 1944. Compare the suite of aerials with those on the opposite page. BELOW: Long Beach Naval Shipyard, California. Overhead view of the aft deck of the battleship *New Jersey* in dry dock while undergoing refitting and reactivation. BELOW RIGHT: The perspective of this photograph emphasizes the long bow of this class of ships even more.

New Jersey

Class: *Iowa, New Jersey, Missouri, Wisconsin, Illinois, Kentucky*. Launched 1942–50
Dimensions: Length – 270m/887ft
Beam – 33m/108ft
Draught – 11m/36ft 2in
Displacement: 48,880 tonnes/48,110 tons
Armament: Main – 9 x 405mm/16in guns
Secondary – 20 x 125mm/5in, 80 x 40mm/1.57in and 50 x 20mm/0.79in guns
Machinery: 8 boilers, 4 shafts.
158,088kW/212,000shp
Speed: 33 knots
Complement: 1,921 men

despite losing the giant battleship *Musashi*, entered the area of amphibious operations. Meanwhile *New Jersey* had gone north and although the Third Fleet sank the decoy force, the landings were at risk. *New Jersey* returned south at full speed, but the Centre Strike Force too had turned back and made its escape. Japan now intensified its suicide attacks and on October 27, in the mêlée which characterized mass kamikaze attacks, *New Jersey* damaged a plane, which crashed into the carrier *Intrepid* while anti-aircraft fire from *Intrepid* sprayed *New Jersey*.

In December 1944 *New Jersey* was part of the Lexington task force which attacked Luzon and then experienced the same typhoon which sank three destroyers.

New Jersey continued her roles at Iwo Jima and Okinawa and off Honshu before a refit at Puget Sound, and from September 17, 1945, to January 28, 1946, she was guardship in Tokyo Bay. Notably, by the end of the war, her anti-aircraft armament consisted of 20 x quadruple 40mm/1.57in, 8 x twin 20mm/0.79in, and 41 x single 20mm/0.79in guns.

Between periods in reserve *New Jersey* saw much post-war action. She twice deployed to Korea, in the familiar role of giving gunfire support ashore, though on several occasions the Koreans reached her with their own shore batteries, and she also operated with Allied warships, notably the British cruiser *Belfast* and the Australian carrier *Sydney* in October 1951.

In the 1960s she was refitted for the Vietnam War, and in operations off the coast of Vietnam *New Jersey* fired some 3,000 405mm/16in shells.

New Jersey was also uniquely engaged in support of US marines in Beirut in February 1984 when she fired nearly 300 rounds into the surrounding hills. Proponents of the battleship argued that they still had a viable role and that with armour more than 305mm/12in thick in many places even an Exocet-type missile would bounce off.

In 1986 *New Jersey*'s deployment in the Pacific was used to support the case for the battleship battle group concept and the battleship modernization programme was validated. Consequently in 1987–8 *New Jersey* visited Korea prior to the Olympic Games, and Australia during the bicentennial there, and exercised in the Indian Ocean and the Gulf. She was decommissioned for the last time in 1991 at Bremerton, which had seen so many battleships during World War II. *New Jersey* opened as a museum ship and memorial in October 2001.

Missouri

Missouri, or the "Mighty Mo", was not ready until the very end of 1944. Her first operations were to escort the carriers of Task Force 58 on strikes on the Japanese islands, and to bombard Iwo Jima. In March 1945 she opened the Okinawa campaign by bombarding the island. During the Battle of the East China Sea, on April 7, Missouri was escorting the carriers of the US Fifth Fleet which sank the giant Japanese battleship Yamato, a cruiser and four destroyers.

In June and again in July Missouri and other ships bombarded Japanese industrial targets on the home islands, and by the end of July the Japanese no longer had control over their own sea and air space. On August 10, the Japanese sued for peace and while negotiations were underway the Commander-in-Chief of the British Pacific Fleet, Admiral Fraser, conferred an honorary knighthood on Admiral Halsey on August 16. On August 21, Missouri landed 200 men for duty with the initial occupation force and she entered Tokyo Bay on August 29, where the surrender took place onboard on September 2, 1945.

In the months immediately after the war, Missouri attended celebrations in New York, carried the remains of the Turkish ambassador to the USA to Istanbul, and balanced this with a

ABOVE RIGHT: **Missouri in action. The area of disturbed water indicates the extent of the blast from the guns. There were similar blast effects on the upper deck of the ship.** BELOW: **Missouri experienced war in the Pacific and was heavily engaged post-World War II as well. She is now preserved as a museum ship.**

visit to Greece. This Mediterranean deployment, lasting until the spring of 1946, was the beginning of a long-term USN commitment to defend the region against Soviet expansion and marked an early stage in the Cold War.

Following this, on September 2, 1947, President Truman celebrated the signing of the Inter-American Conference for the Maintenance of Hemisphere Peace and Security. This extension of the 19th-century Monroe doctrine marked the decline of British naval influence in the region. Truman and his family returned to the USA in Missouri.

On January 17, 1950, Missouri spectacularly ran aground in Hampton Roads, her momentum carrying her three ship-lengths out of the main channel and lifting her some 2m/7ft above the waterline. She was re-floated two weeks later.

The Korean War was business as usual for Missouri. In September 1950 she bombarded shore targets and from

Missouri

Class: *Iowa, New Jersey, Missouri, Wisconsin, Illinois, Kentucky.* Launched 1942–50
Dimensions: Length – 270m/887ft
Beam – 33m/108ft
Draught – 11m/36ft 2in
Displacement: 48,880 tonnes/48,110 tons
Armament: Main – 9 x 405mm/16in guns
Secondary – 20 x 125mm/5in, 80 x
40mm/1.57in and 50 x 20mm/0.79in guns
Machinery: 8 boilers, 4 shafts.
158,088kW/212,000shp
Speed: 33 knots
Complement: 1,921 men

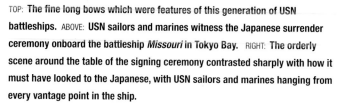

TOP: **The fine long bows which were features of this generation of USN battleships.** ABOVE: **USN sailors and marines witness the Japanese surrender ceremony onboard the battleship *Missouri* in Tokyo Bay.** RIGHT: **The orderly scene around the table of the signing ceremony contrasted sharply with how it must have looked to the Japanese, with USN sailors and marines hanging from every vantage point in the ship.**

then until March 1951 her duties alternated between more bombardments and air defence of carrier task forces. On December 23, 1950, she gave gunfire support to the Hungnam defence perimeter as the last US troops were evacuated.

After two midshipmen's training cruises and a refit which lasted until January 1952, *Missouri* returned to Korea, where her last bombardment was against targets in the Kojo area on March 25, 1953. She was placed in reserve in February 1955, where she remained for nearly 30 years. In 1984–6 she was refitted to help make up the 600-ship USN and in the autumn of 1986 sent on a circumnavigation, following the track of the Great White Fleet. When she emerged from refit her 20 125mm/5in guns had been reduced to 12 and replaced with 32 Tomahawk cruise missiles and 16 Harpoon surface-to-surface missiles. All the 40mm/1.57in and 20mm/0.79in anti-aircraft

guns had been suppressed. In the late 1980s *Missouri* was based in the Pacific, deployed to the Gulf area during an incipient crisis there, and took part in numerous exercises.

After Iraq invaded Kuwait on August 2, 1990, *Missouri* was sent via Hawaii and the Philippines to the Gulf. On January 17, 1991, *Missouri*'s mission was yet again shore bombardment, but this time the weapons used were 28 Tomahawk cruise missiles. In February *Missouri* also used her 405mm/16in guns, the first time they had been fired in anger for nearly 40 years.

At Pearl Harbor on December 7, 1991, *Missouri* took part in a commemoration of the 50th anniversary of the attack there, and she was decommissioned for the last time on March 31, 1992. In 1998 the "Mighty Mo" was given to the USS *Missouri* Memorial Association and opened as a museum ship on January 29, 1999.

LEFT: **A standard aerial three-quarters bow-on shot of *Wisconsin* in the Hampton Roads, showing the battleship in its ultimate state of development. Heavy guns are in place, but a considerable secondary and tertiary armament has been added to give the ship better defence against smaller surface ships and, of course, aircraft.** ABOVE: **Three of the USN's four remaining Dreadnoughts in reserve at Philadelphia Navy Yard during 1967: from left to right, *Wisconsin*, *New Jersey* and *Iowa*. The end of an era, even for the USN, is at hand.**

Wisconsin

The new *Wisconsin* joined the Pacific War in October 1944, screening the fast carriers during operations against the Philippines, Formosa, Lingayen Gulf and French Indo-China. After bombarding Manila on December 18th *Wisconsin* and the fleet were caught by a typhoon when the ships were short of fuel and light in the water; three destroyers were sunk. Her next operation was the occupation of Luzon and anti-aircraft escort for the air strikes on Formosa, Luzon and the islands of Nansei Shoto in January 1945. She also made a sweep of the South China Sea, in the hope that Japanese heavy ships might be met at sea. In February, when Task Force 58 attacked the Japanese home island, under the cover of bad weather *Wisconsin* escorted the main body of ships, and she was at Iwo Jima also in February and Okinawa in March 1945.

When the 66,040-tonne/65,000-ton battleship *Yamato* attacked the American invasion fleet off Okinawa on April 7, she was sunk by carrier planes and *Wisconsin* was not called into action. Meanwhile the US fleet came increasingly under attack from kamikaze aircraft making suicide dives, and on April 12 it was estimated that about 150 enemy aircraft were destroyed in the "divine wind" as *Wisconsin* kept most of the kamikazes away from their targets. In June *Wisconsin* rode out a typhoon, while two carriers, three cruisers and a destroyer

suffered serious weather damage. Operations against Japan resumed on June 8, when the Japanese air effort was already broken. Consequently on July 15 *Wisconsin* was able to close with the coast and bombard steel mills and refineries on Hokkaido, and industrial plant on Honshu, even closer to Tokyo. Battleships of the British Pacific Fleet joined the bombardment.

When *Wisconsin* anchored in Tokyo Bay on September 5, she had already steamed over 160,900km/100,000 miles during her short career. In the immediate post-war period *Wisconsin* provided the "magic carpet" for returning US servicemen, paid visits to South America and cruised with midshipmen embarked to Europe until 1947.

Wisconsin spent two years in reserve until required for the Korean War, where she replaced her sister ship *New Jersey* as flagship of the Seventh Fleet. Operations included screening the carrier attack forces, and as the air threat diminished, frequently joining the "bombline" to provide gunfire support to forces ashore. Targets included artillery positions, bunkers, command posts, harbours, railways, shipyards and trench systems, and on one occasion the illumination with star-shell of an enemy attack. On March 15, 1952, one of *Wisconsin*'s last missions in the Korean War was to destroy a troop train, but she in turn was hit by four 150mm/6in rounds from a shore

Wisconsin 🇺🇸

Class: *Iowa, New Jersey, Missouri, Wisconsin, Illinois, Kentucky.* Launched 1942–50
Dimensions: Length – 270m/887ft
  Beam – 33m/108ft
  Draught – 11m/36ft 2in
Displacement: 48,880 tonnes/48,110 tons
Armament: Main – 9 x 405mm/16in guns
  Secondary – 20 x 125mm/5in, 80 x
  40mm/1.57in and 50 x 20mm/0.79in guns
Machinery: 8 boilers, 4 shafts.
  158,088kW/212,000shp
Speed: 33 knots
Complement: 1,921 men

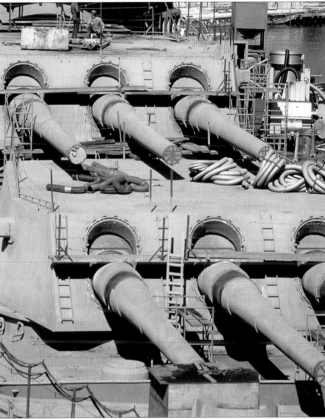

TOP: ***Wisconsin*** **refuelling a destroyer underway in February 1945.** ABOVE: **An informal band concert onboard.** RIGHT: **The beginning of the end of one of the class, whose guns have been cut off but not yet hoisted away for recycling.**

battery. Three seamen were injured but little material damage was done. On April 4 and 5 at Guam, as a test, *Wisconsin* became the first Iowa class battleship to enter a floating dock.

Wisconsin remained in commission throughout the 1950s, alternately employed in training and on exercises, and showing the flag in the Atlantic and Pacific. On May 6, 1956, *Wisconsin* collided with the destroyer *Eaton* in a heavy fog. The long, relatively thin bows of these ships were graceful, but a weakness of the design meant that the collision badly damaged *Wisconsin*. In order to hasten repairs the 109-tonne/ 120-ton, 20.7m/68ft-long bow of the uncompleted *Kentucky* was brought by barge from Newport News to Norfolk, welded in place in a remarkable 16 days, and on June 28 she was ready.

What was thought to be *Wisconsin*'s last deployment in 1956–7 consisted of a midshipmen's training cruise and exercises, visiting Western Europe, the West Indies and the Mediterranean. When *Wisconsin* joined the reserve fleet in 1958, it was the first time since 1895 that the USN had had no battleship in commission. With *Iowa*, she remained at Philadelphia for 26 years until refitted to help make up the Reagan era's 600-ship navy. The 125mm/5in guns were replaced by surface-to-surface missiles and the 40mm/1.57in and 20mm/0.79in guns by 20mm/0.79in radar-controlled,

automatic Phalanx guns. On a typical training cruise she would embark up to 700 midshipmen from colleges across the USA, and visit ports in northern Europe or the Mediterranean and the West Indies. On her penultimate cruise *Wisconsin* sailed from Norfolk on June 19, 1957, transited the Panama Canal, crossed the Equator and visited Chile, whilst on her last cruise she visited the Clyde in Scotland in September and Brest in France. The USN decommissioned *Wisconsin* in 1990, but she was almost immediately required for the 1990–1 Gulf War. With *Missouri*, *Wisconsin* bombarded targets north of Khafji in Saudi Arabia, on Faylaka Island and in Kuwait City.

She was decommissioned for the final time on September 30, 1991, and after languishing in the navy yard *Wisconsin* was berthed in 2000 in downtown Norfolk as a museum ship.

Kentucky and *Illinois*

LEFT: *Kentucky* and *Illinois* were never completed. The bow of *Kentucky* was used to repair *Wisconsin*, and although redesigned several times while building, the hull never progressed much beyond the stage seen here.

Two other ships of the Iowa class were ordered. Originally *Kentucky* and *Illinois* were to have been of the new Montana type but the USN opted for an existing design, the Iowa.

Kentucky was laid down in March 1942 but, when in June the priority for construction became large numbers of landing craft, the double bottom section of the ship was launched and towed away. Work resumed in December 1944 but proceeded slowly and in 1947, when nearly half-finished, work stopped again, restarted briefly in 1948 and stopped again. The hull was re-launched in 1950 to clear the dock for repairs to *Missouri* after her grounding.

Kentucky was redesigned several times in the late 1940s and 1950s, and was designated as BBG-1, a missile-firing ship. However, her bow was cut off in May 1956 to repair *Wisconsin* after her collision. A replacement bow was built but never fitted. She was scrapped in 1959 when her engines and boilers were salvaged and installed in two fast combat-support ships.

The order for *Illinois* was cancelled in 1945, at the end of World War II.

Alaska class

LEFT: Although designated in the USN as CB, indicating a cruiser, these ships carried 305mm/12in guns and were battleships in all but name. They were not, however, regarded as a successful type.

Although armed with 305mm/12-in guns, the Alaska class was more like the heavy cruisers, or "pocket battleships" built without treaty limits, than regular, heavily armoured battleships. They were built to counter the threat of Japanese commerce raiders, a threat that never materialized.

Alaska entered the Pacific theatre in December 1944, when her primary task was to provide an anti-aircraft fire screen for the fast-carrier task forces formed around the fleet carriers *Yorktown*, *Intrepid*, *Independence* and *Langley*. *Alaska*'s secondary role was to direct fighters. *Alaska* destroyed her first kamikaze on March 18, 1945, but also shot down a friendly aircraft. Next day she escorted the heavily damaged carrier *Franklin* out of the fray. On March 27, in her third role, she also bombarded targets on Okinawa. After a busy summer she made a sweep into the East China Sea in July to find that it was empty of enemy ships, and then in August operated against the Japanese mainland.

However, in September, October and November 1945 *Alaska* supported the landing of occupying troops at Inchon in Korea and Tsingtao in China, who took over from Japanese garrisons.

Alaska was expensive in manpower, and by the end of the war there were plenty of cruisers which could perform her roles. She went into reserve in 1946–7 and was never reactivated, being sold for scrap in 1960.

Guam, who operated mainly with *Alaska* in the Pacific, was likewise placed in reserve in 1947 and sold for scrapping in 1961. It was proposed to convert *Hawaii* to a guided-missile ship and then to a command ship, but she was never finished.

Alaska class

Class: *Alaska, Guam, Hawaii*. Launched 1943–5
Dimensions: Length – 246.5m/808ft 6in
  Beam – 27.8m/91ft 1in
  Draught – 9.7m/31ft 10in
Displacement: 30,257 tonnes/29,779 tons
Armament: Main – 9 x 305mm/12in guns
  Secondary – 12 x 125mm/5in, 56 x
  40mm/1.57in and 34 x 20mm/0.79in guns
Machinery: 8 boilers, 4 shafts.
  111,855kW/150,000shp
Speed: 33 knots
Complement: 1,517 men

Montana class

The USN planned five ships of the Montana class: they would have been 282m/925ft long and 37m/121ft in the beam and, freed of treaty limits, the size grew quickly from 45,700 tonnes/ 45,000 tons to over 60,950 tonnes/ 60,000 tons displacement. With 8 boilers generating 128,260kW/172,000shp their designed speed was 28 knots. Originally 455mm/18in guns were considered but the USN settled for 12 405mm/16in guns in four triple turrets. A new large-calibre 125mm/5in gun was planned and they would have had a plethora of 40mm/ 1.57in and 20mm/0.79in guns.

Heavily armoured and bulged, they would not have fitted through the Panama Canal at the time and money was included in the budget to build new locks along the waterway.

Construction work was halted in April 1942, on the grounds of steel shortages, and *Montana*, *Ohio*, *Maine*, *New Hampshire* and *Louisiana* were cancelled on July 21, 1943. The Battle of Midway had shown, as had in different ways the war at sea in the Atlantic and the Mediterranean, that the future need was for aircraft carriers. Consequently the planned Montana class of battleships was cancelled and their place in the USN's construction plans was taken by six carriers of the Midway class.

ABOVE: **The Montana class were cancelled in 1943 when it was realized that the war in the Pacific would be fought principally by aircraft carriers.**
LEFT: **Design progressed as far as this fine model of 1941. The Montana class would obviously have been large ships – although presumably the anti-aircraft armament would have been enhanced before entering the war in the Pacific.**

Nagato and *Mutsu*

Built between 1917 and 1920 the Nagato class were the first all-Japanese-designed warships, the first to be fitted with 405mm/16in guns, and at the time among the fastest battleships in the world. At this stage of international relations the Japanese still had access to British technology and were able to learn the lessons of Jutland: *Nagato* and *Mutsu* were regarded as equivalent to the British Queen Elizabeth class.

Both were modified in 1924 and rebuilt in 1934–5. A characteristic of *Nagato*'s appearance was the six-legged mast festooned with platforms. However, smoke from the fore funnel interfered with the gunnery control positions and in 1921 a tall cowl was added. Later, at the first conversion, the fore funnel was given a distinctive S-shape. Various positions were tried for aircraft ramps and catapults, which aid the dating of photographs.

In 1934 the horizontal armour was reinforced, anti-torpedo bulges were fitted and extended beyond the armoured citadel, the torpedo tubes were removed and there were various additional platforms built around the foremast. New engines and boilers were fitted which allowed there to be one massive central funnel, and the length was increased by extending the stern 8.7m/28.5ft. The heavy guns were given greater elevation (and thus range) and numerous lighter guns were added. Finally an aircraft catapult and crane were added at the weather deck or X turret deck level.

ABOVE: **Designed during World War I but completed in the 1920s, *Nagato* is seen here during her early trials. The massive conning tower is clearly Japanese, but Japanese naval architects had been trained in Britain, and there are still traces of that influence in *Nagato*'s profile, particularly her upright funnels.**

In 1941 *Nagato* was Yamamoto's flagship during the attack on Pearl Harbor. She also took part in the Battles of Midway, the Philippine Sea, and Leyte Gulf.

In May and June 1942 Yamamoto with some 150 ships set out to occupy Midway Island and the western Aleutians, hoping to draw out the US Pacific Fleet to its destruction. As Dutch Harbor in the Aleutians was being invaded by the Japanese, the main carrier battle raged in the south between groups of aircraft carriers. Four Japanese carriers were lost: *Akagi*, *Hiryu*, *Kaga* and *Soryu*, on June 4 and 5, and the American *Yorktown* was badly damaged and sunk by a Japanese submarine on June 7. Yamamoto had spread his forces too widely, and although outnumbered the Americans had been able to concentrate their forces better. The Battle of Midway was the first major victory for the USN in the Pacific. Afterwards the Japanese still had the most ships, including aircraft carriers, but the industrial muscle of the USA would soon change this. So, when *Nagato* and the Japanese fleet retreated from Midway, it marked the high tide of attempts to secure the perimeter of their conquests.

Nagato class

Class: *Nagato, Mutsu.* Launched 1919–20
Dimensions: Length – 216m/708ft
Beam – 29m/95ft
Draught – 9m/30ft
Displacement: 34,340 tonnes/33,800 tons
Armament: Main – 8 x 405mm/16in guns
Secondary – 20 x 140mm/5.5in, 4 x 80mm/3.1in
guns and 8 x 535mm/21in torpedoes
Machinery: 15 oil-burning and 6 mixed-firing
boilers, 4 shafts. 59,656kW/80,000shp
Speed: 26.5 knots
Complement: 1,333 men

Two years later the Battle of the Philippine Sea was also fought at long range and although it involved *Nagato*, as well as four other Japanese battleships, these retreated after disastrous losses of Japanese aircraft.

However, during the Battle of Leyte Gulf, on October 25, 1944, *Nagato* was one of four battleships of the Japanese main Centre Strike Force which passed through the San Bernadino Strait into the amphibious area of operations. There at the Battle of Samar, *Nagato* sank the escort carrier *Gambier Bay* and three destroyers. Kamikaze aircraft also sank the escort carrier *St Lo*, but instead of wreaking havoc among the amphibious shipping, the Centre Strike Force retired through the San Bernadino Strait.

Nagato having been damaged by aircraft bombs off Samar was temporarily repaired, but did not see action again. She was bombed at Yokosuka on July 18, 1945, and badly damaged, and when the Japanese surrendered she was the last surviving battleship afloat. Her end was ignominious: while under tow to Bikini atoll she and her escort broke down and drifted for two days. She had developed a leak and was listing

TOP: *Nagato* or *Mutsu* after her refit of 1924 and before the 1933–4 refit.
ABOVE LEFT: The Japanese fleet leaving Brunei on October 22, 1944, en route to their defeat at the Battle of Leyte: from right to left, *Nagato*, *Musashi*, *Yamato* and cruisers. ABOVE RIGHT: The Japanese *Nagato* seen in the late 1930s preparing for aircraft operations by hoisting a biplane on to a launching ramp on B turret. However, once the war started such aircraft were mostly dispensed with and battleships relied on their carrier escorts for aerial reconnaisance.

and needed three weeks' repairs before she could complete her voyage. However, she survived the first (atmospheric) nuclear test, codename Able, with fairly minor damage, but sank from massive hull damage after the second (underwater), test, codename Baker, on July 25, 1946.

Mutsu was paid for by popular subscription, much of it raised in schools. She survived the cuts imposed on the Japanese Navy by the Washington Treaty, and took part in the attack on Pearl Harbor, the Battle of Midway and the Solomons campaign. However, on June 8, 1943, whilst in Hiroshima Bay, an explosion in the after magazine blew *Mutsu* in two. The cause has never been satisfactorily explained.

Kaga and *Tosa*

After the Russo-Japanese War the Imperial Japanese Navy, with much of its fleet obsolescent notwithstanding its victory at Tsushima, developed the concept of the 8-8 fleet. The Japanese had already thought of the all-big-gun ship when they received news from Portsmouth of Fisher's *Dreadnought* and their 8-8 concept laid emphasis on large, fast battleships. Their idea was that there were ages of ships, the first in the front line, the second operational but aging, and the third in reserve. The concept was that they would have two squadrons of eight ships, each less than eight years old, backed by ships of the other ages. This plan, with variations due to changes of government, finance and international tension, was maintained until the Washington Naval Conference. Meanwhile the Japanese concept had become the 8-8-8 plan, one squadron of ships of each age, and this called for four more battleships and four battlecruisers by 1928. Japan was spending more than one-third of her national budget on naval construction, and it is unlikely that she could have achieved the 8-8-8 plan, but she was resentful at the limits imposed by the Washington Naval Treaty in 1921–2.

The treaty called for the cancellation of *Kaga* and *Tosa*, both laid down in 1920. They were conceived as high-speed battleships with the same speed as the Nagatos but with the main armament increased to ten 405mm/16in guns with an X

ABOVE: **There are no pictures of *Kaga* or *Tosa* as fast battleships, but there are images of hybrid aircraft carriers like *Ise*, seen here in 1943.**

and a Y turret. When cancelled in 1922 under the Washington Naval Treaty, *Tosa* was used for explosives trials and sunk as a target ship in 1925.

Kaga was also cancelled under the treaty, but before she could be broken up, Japan was struck by an earthquake which severely damaged the battlecruiser *Amagi*, scheduled for conversion into an aircraft carrier, and the decision was made to rebuild *Kaga* instead.

The carrier *Kaga* participated in the attack on Pearl Harbor on December 7, 1941, and also in naval operations against Rabaul and Port Darwin in 1942. She was sunk at the Battle of Midway on June 5, 1942.

The Japanese Navy had a tradition of innovation in battleship design, and many proposals were equal to, and sometimes better than, their foreign contemporaries. When *Nagato* was commissioned in the 1920s and *Yamato* in 1941 they were each in their time the world's most powerful battleship. In the 1920s a class of four fast battleships was planned which would have been about 50,000 tonnes/tons and armed with 450mm/18in guns, but these ships were cancelled under the Washington Treaty.

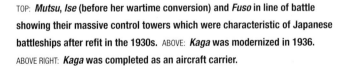

TOP: *Mutsu*, *Ise* (before her wartime conversion) and *Fuso* in line of battle showing their massive control towers which were characteristic of Japanese battleships after refit in the 1930s. ABOVE: *Kaga* was modernized in 1936. ABOVE RIGHT: *Kaga* was completed as an aircraft carrier.

Also a class of large cruisers, like the USN Alaska class, with 150mm/12in or 360mm/14in-guns was envisaged. The Japanese navy had an astonishing ability to redesign and rebuild capitals ships, even given the shortage of raw materials which was the *causus belli* of the attack on Pearl Harbor and the war in the Pacific. During the war resources were shifted from battleships to aircraft carriers, though it was a shortage of experienced pilots as much as any material or technological failure which brought about Japan's defeat.

Kaga class

Class: *Kaga*, *Tosa*. Launched 1921
Dimensions: Length – 231.5m/760ft
    Beam – 30.5m/100ft
    Draught – 10m/33ft 1in
Displacement: 40,540 tonnes/39,900 tons
Armament: Main – 10 x 405mm/16in guns
    Secondary – 20 x 140mm/5.5in,
    4 x 80mm/3.1in guns and
    8 x 610mm/24in torpedoes
Machinery: 12 oil and 4 mixed-fired boilers, 4
    shafts. 67,859kW/91,000shp
Speed: 26.5 knots
Complement: 1,333 men

Yamato class

Japanese war plans were for a pre-emptive strike which would sweep aside the weak opposition of the British, Dutch and French forces (who in the event were preoccupied with the war in Europe), to capture Wake and Guam, and to build and defend a perimeter around a zone of co-prosperity ruled by Japan. The Japanese wanted a quick peace with the USA, but if this was not going to be possible they reckoned that, with the USN exhausted and having suffered attrition during its passage across the Pacific, the Imperial Japanese Navy could meet the USN in a decisive battle close to its home base and annihilate it.

The Japanese navy studied Tsushima and Jutland but not the U-boat campaign of World War I. Little attention was paid to the convoying of Japanese merchant ships or to the attack upon shipping on America's long, vulnerable supply lines, and no plans were made for a long or defensive war. Furthermore, despite the success of carrier aviation at Pearl Harbor, they did not foresee the influence which carrier-borne aircraft would have on the war in the Pacific or have sufficient reserves of aircraft and pilots.

Nevertheless, the plan worked at first, although the attack on Pearl Harbor was counterproductive. Tactically it was a failure because the USN carriers were at sea and escaped

ABOVE: *Yamato,* fitting out at Kure in September 1941, is seen here with her huge 455mm/18in guns in place. Japanese shipbuilding facilities had not progressed as much as their ship design and completion of the Yamato class to this stage was a considerable feat of ingenuity and logistics.

damage. Politically it brought the USA into the war on the side of Britain, and it underestimated the strength of American rage and resolve. Industrially Japan could not match the unprecedented American construction programmes which turned out ships and aircraft and trained men at extraordinary rates. When by the end of 1942 Japanese and American naval losses were about the same (two battleships and four large aircraft carriers), the USN could have been expected to replace their ships whereas the Imperial Japanese Navy, which was already suffering shortages when the war started, could not compete despite desperate efforts.

However, if Japanese plans to consolidate and defend an area of influence in the Far East were to have any chance of success, a navy was needed superior to any rival, and this included the USN. When the Geneva Disarmament Conference broke down, Japan announced its intention to withdraw from the 1922 and 1930 naval treaties when they expired in 1936 and planning started on the giant battleships of the Yamato

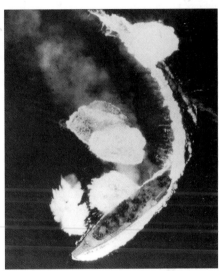

LEFT: *Yamato's* death throes after being attacked by USN aircraft in the East China Sea in April 1945. BELOW LEFT: *Yamato* at speed in December 1941. BELOW: *Yamato* manoeuvring to avoid air attack. By the end of the war USN fliers had been trained in huge numbers, and had the confidence of experience and superior aircraft, so that the Japanese surface fleet was no match for US naval aviation.

class. These ships were built in great secrecy, not excepting a 360-tonne/400-ton camouflage net to cover *Musashi* who at over 31,750 tonnes/35,000 tons was the largest ship to date launched from a slipway. *Yamato* and *Shinano* were built in new or specially enlarged docks, and a purpose-built heavy lift ship was needed to bring the guns and mountings to the shipyard. They were the largest battleships ever built, with the largest guns. Each mounting weighed over 2,270 tonnes/2,500 tons, and their range, at 45 degrees elevation, was 42,940m/ 46,960yd or 23 nautical miles. Their armour was supposed to give protection against 455mm/18in shells or a bomb dropped from 4,575m/15,000ft. The armoured belt was inclined at 20 degrees and below it was an inclined anti-torpedo belt: the weight and thickness of armour was impressive, though trials showed that the connection between the two belts was weak and the bulkheads were insufficiently elastic.

After many tank tests and competitive designs, there was an element of provocation in the final choice: it was reckoned that the largest ship which could pass through the Panama Canal was about 57,000 tonnes/63,000 tons, so if the USN was to

out-build the Imperial Japanese Navy it would have to forgo the advantage of being able to swing its ships between the Atlantic and the Pacific, or widen the canal.

Yamato, the name ship of the class, was built at Kure naval dockyard. Commissioned in December 1941, just over a week after the start of the Pacific war, *Yamato* served as flagship of the Japanese Combined Fleet at the critical battles of 1942, including the Battle of Midway. This battle however was fought between the carrier groups; the battleships of the Japanese main force did not come into action and indeed the opposing fleets never saw each other.

She spent most of 1943 based at Truk and on December 24, 1943, was torpedoed by the American submarine *Skate,* requiring repairs which lasted until April 1944.

Like other Japanese and American battleships of the period, *Yamato's* anti-aircraft battery was hugely increased before she took part in the Battle of the Philippine Sea in June. Again this was a carrier battle, in which Japanese naval air power was annihilated, and the battleships did not come into action and retreated upon Okinawa.

Yamato class (continued)

At the Battle of Leyte Gulf in October 1944 *Yamato* was part of the Japanese Centre Force, four surviving battleships and eight cruisers, which despite losing *Yamato*'s sister ship, *Mushashi*, in the Sibuyan Sea, pressed on into the actual Gulf on October 25. She helped to sink the escort carrier *Gambier Bay* and three destroyers by gunfire. The Centre Force was attacked several times by USN aircraft off the island of Samar, and just when it seemed the invasion forces must be destroyed, the Japanese admiral lost his nerve and retreated back through the San Bernardino Strait.

Yamato received little damage during the Battle of Leyte Gulf, and in Japan in November 1944 was fitted with yet more anti-aircraft guns. She was attacked by USN carrier planes in March 1945, and again slightly damaged. In April she took part in the suicidal Operation Ten-Go, intended to ruin the American invasion of Okinawa. On April 7, 1945, in the Battle of the East China Sea, some 320km/200 miles north of Okinawa, *Yamato* was attacked by a massive force of carrier planes from the USN Fifth Fleet and sunk.

Yamato's remains were located in 1985: she lies split in two at a depth of 305m/1,000ft. Her bows from B turret forward are upright, but the rest is upside down with a large hole close to the after magazines.

Musashi, sister ship of *Yamato*, was built at Nagasaki and commissioned in August 1942. The Japanese still conceived a decisive battle with the main fleet of the USN and in 1943 and 1944 *Musashi* was based at Truk to cover the threat of an American advance. Later she moved to Palau and on March 29, 1944, was torpedoed by the American submarine *Tunny*, needing repairs in Japan. *Musashi*'s anti-aircraft firepower was increased and in June 1944 she took part in the Battle of the Philippine Sea. Her last battle was during the Leyte Gulf campaign. *Musashi* was one of five battleships which formed the Centre Strike Force which, without carrier air support, intended to destroy the American landings on the Pacific coast of Leyte. On October 24, 1944, approaching from the west through the archipelagic Sibuyan Sea, and south of Luzon, *Musashi* and her consorts were attacked by American carrier aircraft. She was hit by 19 torpedoes and 17 bombs and though her armour enabled her to withstand more damage than any other ship might have done, several hours after the last attack she capsized and sank.

BELOW: *Musashi* caught leaving Brunei in October 1944, on what was to be the last major coordinated sortie by the Imperial Japanese Navy. Without aircraft carriers and naval air power to protect her, *Musashi* and her sisters were doomed.

Construction on *Shinano* as a battleship was stopped in 1942, and instead she was completed as an aircraft carrier in late 1944. However, while on trials, she was torpedoed and sunk by the American submarine *Archerfish* on November 29, 1944, as the USN blockade of Japanese waters increased.

Hull number 111 was intended to be a fourth Yamato class but construction on her was suspended in 1941 because of a shortage of skilled labour and materials, and cancelled in 1942; parts were used in three other ships.

Prior to World War II the Imperial Japanese Navy drew up plans for heavy cruisers or battlecruisers which would have been similar to the American Alaska class, and for a class of super-Yamatos, but all these plans were dropped for an emergency construction programme of aircraft carriers.

Yamato class

Class: *Yamato, Musashi, Shinano,* No. 111.
Launched 1940–4
Dimensions: Length – 256m/839ft 9in
Beam – 37m/121ft
Draught – 10.5m/34ft
Displacement: 63,315 tonnes/62,315 tons
Armament: Main – 9 x 455mm/18in guns
Secondary – 12 x 155mm/6.1in,
12 x 125mm/5in and 24 x 25mm/1in guns
Machinery: 12 boilers, 4 shafts.
111,855kW/150,000shp
Speed: 27 knots
Complement: 2,500 men

LEFT: *Musashi* under air attack in the Sibuyan Sea. Cloud off the mountains and blue sky contrast sharply with death from the skies. BELOW: The Emperor Hirohito with officers of the battleship *Musashi* in 1943. Not even an emperor's support could help his navy once the USN had begun to exact its revenge for Pearl Harbor.

LEFT: **The so-called "pocket battleships" proved to be useful commerce raiders and tied up many British resources in the early months of World War II, but by mid-1942 they were either sunk or blockaded.** BELOW LEFT: *Admiral Graf Spee* **on launch. Launches of ships for the new German navy became opportunities for parade and display by the Nazi party.**

Deutschland (*Lützow*) and *Admiral Scheer*

The Treaty of Versailles which ended World War I imposed a displacement restriction on German warships of 10,160 tonnes/10,000 tons. In the 1920s the German navy tried to design an effective capital ship within this limit, varying the armament, armour, length and beam. The possibility of a heavy monitor for coastal defence or a large cruiser were examined and rejected, and eventually the design of a pocket battleship emerged. Weight was saved by using an all-welded construction, and the use of diesel engines gave good range and relatively high speed. The resulting ships were more powerful than any cruiser and faster than any battleship but there was no operational concept which justified these ships: the design was a matter of political and technical compromise. They were, however, well suited for commerce raiding.

Deutschland led an eventful life and survived World War II despite being frequently damaged, including being bombed by Republican aircraft off Ibiza on May 29, 1937, during the Spanish Civil War. *Deutschland* sailed prior to the outbreak of

World War II to a station off Greenland, where she sank two small ships and took another prize, and returned to the Baltic in mid-November, being renamed *Lützow* while still at sea. She took part in the German invasion of Norway, where she was hit by Norwegian coastal batteries on entering Oslo Fjord.

Whilst returning to Germany for repairs she was torpedoed by the British submarine *Spearfish* on April 11, 1940, and severely damaged. Later, while still under repair at Kiel, she was hit by a bomb which failed to explode during a raid by the Royal Air Force.

Then on June 13, 1941, *Lützow* was hit by an air-launched torpedo while en route to Norway, requiring her to return to Kiel for more repairs the next day. She eventually returned to Norway in May 1942, but ran aground and underwent more repairs in Germany. However, in December 1942 *Lützow*, the cruiser *Hipper* and their escorts attacked convoy JW51B off Bear Island and were driven off by a much weaker British squadron. When Hitler learned this he raged for an hour and a half on the theme that capital ships were a waste of men and material, during which time Grand Admiral Raeder "rarely had the opportunity to comment". The subsequent order to draw up plans for decommissioning the German big ships was a turning point in the war for the German navy and Raeder resigned after 14 years in office.

During 1943–5 *Lützow* was used in the Baltic, bombarding the seaward flank of the Soviet army, where on April 16, 1945, *Lützow* was badly damaged during an RAF bombing raid and she settled on the bottom. Her crew fought her as a fixed battery, firing on the advancing Soviet forces, until they blew her up on May 4, 1945. She was salvaged by the Russians and broken up in 1948–9.

Deutschland class

Class: *Deutschland, Admiral Scheer, Admiral Graf Spee.* Launched 1931–4

Dimensions: Length – 186m/610ft 3in
Beam – 21.6m/70ft 10in
Draught – 5.8m/19ft

Displacement: 11,890 tonnes/11,700 tons

Armament: Main – 6 x 280mm/11in guns
Secondary – 8 x 150mm/6in,
6 x 105mm/4.13in, 8 x 37mm/1.46in,
6 x 20mm/0.79in guns and
8 x 535mm/21in torpedoes

Machinery: 8 diesels, 3 shafts.
40,268kW/54,000hp

Speed: 28 knots

Complement: 619–1,150 men

Deutschland was renamed *Lützow* in 1939. Two more ships of the Deutschland class, as well as *Admiral Scheer* and *Admiral Graf Spee* (see over) were started but their material was used to build *Scharnhorst* and *Gneisenau*.

ABOVE LEFT: **Originally launched as *Deutschland*, Hitler later ordered her name to be changed to *Lützow* because he feared the loss of a ship with such a talismanic name.** LEFT: **A detail of *Deutschland* when newly completed, and being admired by onlookers.** BELOW: **Seamen of *Deutschland* receiving training in traditional skills in this photograph dated 1935. Oared craft were retained throughout the 20th century by all navies.**

Like *Deutschland*, *Admiral Scheer* saw service off Spain, and bombarded Almeria on May 31, 1937, in retaliation for the bombing of *Deutschland*. On September 4, 1939, *Admiral Scheer* was bombed in the Schillig Roads; she was also bombed on July 20, 1940, and again escaped damage. In October 1940 *Admiral Scheer* broke out into the North Atlantic where she was attacked by the armed merchant cruiser *Jervis Bay*. *Jervis Bay* was lost together with five ships of convoy HX84, but the remainder of the convoy scattered. *Admiral Scheer* then raided in the Atlantic and Indian Oceans, sinking 16 ships totalling 100,644 million tonnes/99,059 million tons until she returned, undetected, to Kiel on April 1, 1941.

In the summer of 1942 *Admiral Scheer* was part of the threatening fleet of German surface ships that sortied briefly during the debacle of convoy PQ17. She made one more sortie, sinking the Soviet icebreaker *Sibirjakov* on August 26, 1942, and bombarding the Russian coast, before going into a prolonged refit in November 1942. From November 1944 to March 1945 she was employed in coastal operations in the Baltic against the advancing Soviet army. Her luck finally ran out on April 9, 1945, when she was bombed and capsized. She was broken up *in situ*, 1948.

Admiral Graf Spee

Like her sisters, *Admiral Graf Spee* saw limited action off the coast of Spain during the Spanish Civil War. She sailed from Germany on August 21, 1939, to take up her station in the South Atlantic where together with her forays into the Indian Ocean she sank nine ships of 50,893 tonnes/50,089 tons. More than 20 British and French warships in eight groups were formed, each reckoned to be sufficient to despatch any raider of the pocket battleship type, and battleships and cruisers were deployed to act as escorts to ocean-going convoys in the North Atlantic. Thus, one objective of the German raider policy, to scatter and tie down enemy naval forces, was achieved.

The hunting groups were ordered to keep radio silence, which meant the Admiralty in London would not necessarily know about their movements, although they were ordered not to stray very far from concentrations of merchant ships. The Admiralty's orders foresaw that local commanders would need rather more than usual latitude to disregard any order they received, and to use their initiative.

At dawn on December 13, 1939, Force G under Commodore Henry Harwood found the *Admiral Graf Spee* off the River Plate. The battle which followed showed that the Royal Navy had learned a great deal since Jutland. After meeting his

BELOW: ***Admiral Graf Spee*** **attended the British Coronation Fleet Review at Spithead in 1937. Two years later, if** *Admiral Graf Spee* **had been flying her aircraft for dawn reconnaissance off the River Plate in December 1939, she might have avoided the searching British cruisers.** RIGHT: **On launch at Wilhelmshaven on June 30, 1934.**

captains in "Nelson style" onboard his flagship, Harwood gave his orders on the eve of battle in crisp sentences: "My policy with three cruisers in company versus one pocket battleship. Attack at once by day or night. By day act in two divisions ... by night ships will normally remain in company in open order." The three cruisers, the British 205mm/8in-gun cruiser *Exeter*

and the 150mm/6in-gun cruisers *Ajax* and the New Zealand *Achilles* had not operated together before, yet the following morning, no further tactical orders were necessary as the ships split into two divisions to divide the fire of their superior enemy.

Although *Exeter* in particular took terrible punishment from *Graf Spee*'s 280mm/11in guns, she did not blow up, as some of the battlecruisers at Jutland had done: the Royal Navy had clearly re-learned some key lessons about damage control and ammunition handling.

Exeter attacked from the south while the two light cruisers, *Ajax* and *Achilles*, worked around to the north acting as one division. *Admiral Graf Spee* concentrated her heavy armament on *Exeter,* putting her two after turrets out of action and forcing her to retire to the Falklands for repairs, while the two light cruisers dodged in and out of range of *Admiral Graf Spee*'s guns. *Admiral Graf Spee* does not seem to have been well handled and by 08.00, with only superficial damage, she broke off action and headed for the neutral port of Montevideo in Uruguay. She entered Montevideo at midnight with the two light cruisers hard on her heels, and there by diplomatic means she was maintained for several days while other British hunting groups headed for the area. By December 17 the only reinforcement which had arrived was the heavy cruiser *Cumberland* who, whilst refitting at the Falklands, had by a quirk of radio propagation heard the gunnery control signals and correctly interpreted that her presence was needed.

However, Langsdorff, the captain of the *Admiral Graf Spee*, had convinced himself that the entire Royal Navy was waiting for him and, having landed his crew, he scuttled his ship off Montevideo and committed suicide. His funeral was attended by some of the British merchant seamen he had held captive.

TOP: *Admiral Graf Spee* had a relatively low silhouette and consequently her secondary range-finder lacked height.
ABOVE: Photographed at Montevideo where she had taken refuge after the Battle of the River Plate, *Admiral Graf Spee* does not show much sign of damage. LEFT: *Admiral Graf Spee* was scuttled because her captain feared the arrival of British reinforcements to the cruisers who had driven him into port.

Scharnhorst and *Gneisenau*

TOP: **The Germans designed elegant and powerful-looking ships such as** *Scharnhorst*. ABOVE: *Scharnhorst*'s **sister ship** *Gneisenau*.

T he original requirement for these two ships was that they should have the same speed and armament as the Deutschland class pocket battleships, but on a larger displacement – 19,305 tonnes/19,000 tons, allowing for heavier armour. The German navy's view was that if such a vessel was limited to 280mm/11in guns, then they should have a third triple turret, making the displacement 26,415 tonnes/26,000 tons. Hitler rejected this because he still did not want to break the Versailles Treaty and so provoke Britain. However, the Anglo-German Naval Agreement of 1935 allowed for two *panzerschiffe* of 26,415 tonnes/26,000 tons each armed with 280mm/11in guns. The agreement also allowed a maximum calibre of 406mm/16in and Hitler ordered the ships to be built with 380mm/15in guns, but the 280mm/11in triple turrets were available and it would have taken some time to develop a new turret. These new turrets were fitted to *Bismarck* and *Tirpitz* and although it was intended to up-gun *Scharnhorst* and *Gneisenau*, war prevented this. Both ships were refitted with the clipper or Atlantic bow on the eve of World War II, and during the war the close-range armament was increased. Two catapults were fitted, one high over the boat deck and the other on the roof of C turret which was removed pre-war.

Scharnhorst sank the armed merchant cruiser *Rawalpindi* in November 1939 but her planned breakout into the Atlantic was thwarted. On April 9, 1940, during the invasion of Norway she fought a brief battle with the battleship *Renown* but escaped in a snowstorm. On June 8, she sank the carrier *Glorious* and two

destroyers, but the *Acasta* managed a torpedo hit which opened a large hole and flooded her. She was attacked by carrier-borne aircraft but escaped again to Kiel for repairs. In January 1942 *Scharnhorst* succeeded in breaking out into the Atlantic and sank several ships. She was hunted by British battleships but eluded them and reached Brest safely on March 23, 1942, after 60 days at sea and steaming 28,950km/18,000 miles. She was under repair for most of 1943 but in September she bombarded Spitsbergen and in December sallied to attack the Russia-bound convoy JW55B, when on December 26, 1943, she was overwhelmed by the

Scharnhorst class

Class: *Scharnhorst, Gneisenau.* Launched 1936
Dimensions: Length – 235m/770ft 8in
  Beam – 30m/98ft
  Draught – 8m/27ft
Displacement: 35,400 tonnes/34,841 tons
Armament: Main – 9 x 280mm/11in guns
  Secondary – 12 x 150mm/6in,
  14 x 105mm/4.13in, 16 x 37mm/1.46in and
  8 x 20mm/0.79in guns
Machinery: 12 boilers, 3 shafts.
  123,041kW/165,000shp
Speed: 32 knots
Complement: 1,669 men

TOP: *Scharnhorst* **firing her main armament.** TOP RIGHT: **A view of one of the** *schlachtschiff* **(battleship)** *Gneisenau's* **machinery rooms.** ABOVE: **Captain Ciliax, then commanding** *Scharnhorst,* **inspecting his ship's company pre-war. During the war he would make his fame in a German squadron, including leading these two ships, on the Channel Dash.**

battleship *Duke of York* and the cruisers *Belfast, Jamaica* and *Norfolk* and sunk with heavy loss of life.

For much of the war *Gneisenau* operated with *Scharnhorst.* However, on June 20, 1940, she was torpedoed by the submarine *Clyde* and only at the end of the year returned to Kiel for repairs. She broke out into the Atlantic with *Scharnhorst* in January to March 1942, and while in Brest was bombed many times, without serious damage. After being bombed by the RAF in November 1942 *Gneisenau* was taken in hand for the long-anticipated up-gunning. However, work was stopped in early 1943 and her armament used ashore. Three 280mm/11in guns were installed near the Hook of Holland and six in Norway. She was finally scuttled at Gdynia in 1945 and broken up between 1947 and 1951.

Scharnhorst and *Gneisenau* are best known for their Channel Dash or Operation Cerberus. Hitler was convinced that the British were going to invade Norway and personally ordered the Ugly Sisters, as the RAF knew them, home. Taking advantage of foul weather in the English Channel and by a combination of good luck and British failures, the Germans sailed on February 12, 1943, and evaded notice until they were about to enter the Straits of Dover. It was a bad day for the British, relieved only by the incredible bravery of the men of 825 Naval Air Squadron, led by Lieutenant Commander Eugene Esmonde, who was awarded a posthumous VC, for a "forlorn hope" attack in their *Swordfish.*

The dash by German warships up the English Channel was a humiliation for the British. *Scharnhorst* twice hit mines, and *Gneisenau* escaped only to be bombed at Kiel. A serious threat to allied shipping in the Atlantic was over and the German naval commander, Raeder, recognized that he had won a tactical victory but suffered a strategic defeat. The British could now concentrate their efforts against the German surface fleet, whose threat to shipping in the Atlantic had been diminished.

Bismarck

Design work on Germany's first fully-fledged battleships, with armament and armour equivalent to foreign capital ships, began in the early 1930s. Initially this class was supposed to be of 35,560 tonnes/35,000 tons displacement but the design was modified several times, even on the slipway, and after the Anglo-German naval treaty it was recognized that their standard displacement would be nearer 45,200 tonnes/45,000 tons, and eventually their deep load displacement exceeded 50,800 tonnes/50,000 tons.

The actual design was conservative, a development of World War I Baden design, with a main armament of eight 380mm/15in guns in twin turrets, two forward and two aft. Her secondary battery of six twin-turreted 150mm/6in guns were intended for use against destroyers, and her mixed anti-aircraft battery included guns of three different sizes: 105mm/4.1in, 37mm/1.46in and 20mm/0.79in was regarded as inadequate for World War II, given the developments there had been in naval aviation.

Bismarck was, however, very heavily armoured, again along the lines of the Baden class, and her broad beam gave her stability and made her a good, steady gun platform. Her 30-knot speed made for a fast battleship, but the steam plant was fuel-hungry and thus limited range, a defect which the German navy hoped to overcome by fitting diesel engines in all future designs. *Bismarck*'s keel was laid down in July 1936 and even after launch modifications continued, which took two years and included the fitting of a new clipper or Atlantic bow. As a result she was not ready until late in 1940.

ABOVE: *Bismarck* was hit by *Prince of Wales* during their brief battle on May 24, 1941, causing flooding forward which slowed the German ship down. She is seen here from *Prinz Eugen*, shortly before *Bismarck* feinted to the north to allow *Prinz Eugen* to escape. The Royal Navy thought, temporarily, that *Bismarck* was making back towards Norway, but soon resumed the chase to the south. Next, *Bismarck* was attacked from the air.

Germany naval strategy was to avoid set-piece battles with the Royal Navy and to conduct a war on commerce, using surface raiders, both warships and disguised merchant ships, and U-boats. The intention was both to disperse British forces, to force merchant ships into inefficient convoys and then to disrupt the convoy patterns, as well as to destroy shipping. Under this plan battleships and cruisers were to evade the British blockade and break out into the Atlantic, and eventually the Indian and Pacific Oceans. The heavy cruisers *Admiral Hipper* and *Prinz Eugen*, the pocket battleships *Lützow*, *Admiral Graf Spee* and *Admiral Scheer*, the battlecruisers *Scharnhorst* and *Gneisenau*, and, of course, *Bismarck* were faster than most British battleships. This posed a serious threat which was taken very seriously by the Royal Navy and also by the French navy while it was still active in World War II. Germany's strategy was not successful while her navy could be blockaded in the North Sea, but after the fall of France in June 1940, when the German fleet had access to the French Atlantic ports, the strategic balance changed. In December 1940 and early 1941 German surface raiders sank 47 merchant ships, and U-boats sank many more.

Bismarck

Class: *Bismarck, Tirpitz*. Launched 1939
Dimensions: Length – 248m/813ft 8in
    Beam – 36m/118ft 1in
    Draught – 8.5m/28ft 6in
Displacement: 42,370 tonnes/41,700 tons
Armament: Main – 8 x 380mm/5in guns
    Secondary – 12 x 150mm/6in,
    16 x 105mm/4.13in, 16 x 37mm/1.46in and
    12 x 20mm/0.79in guns
Machinery: 12 boilers, 3 shafts.
    102,907kW/138,000shp
Speed: 29 knots
Complement: 2,092–2,608 men

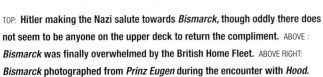

TOP: **Hitler making the Nazi salute towards *Bismarck,* though oddly there does not seem to be anyone on the upper deck to return the compliment.** ABOVE : ***Bismarck* was finally overwhelmed by the British Home Fleet.** ABOVE RIGHT: ***Bismarck* photographed from *Prinz Eugen* during the encounter with *Hood*.**

In May 1941 the German navy sent *Bismarck* and the heavy cruiser *Prinz Eugen* on a raid into the Atlantic. The movement was spotted but in bad weather the Germans got into the Denmark Strait, where they were shadowed by two British cruisers. On May 24, 1941, during a brief battle between the two Germans and the British *Prince of Wales* and *Hood*, *Hood* blew up and *Prince of Wales* was damaged. *Bismarck* however was hit by 355mm/14in shells from *Prince of Wales* which caused her to lose fuel and contaminated several bunkers with salt water. *Prinz Eugen* was detached into the Atlantic while *Bismarck* headed for Brest. Next, presaging the new

relationship between battleship and aircraft which would change naval warfare forever, a strike by nine aircraft from the aircraft carrier *Victorious* hit *Bismarck* with one torpedo, but the damage was slight.

For two days *Bismarck* escaped detection while the hunting British fleet cast to the north, thinking that *Bismarck* might have been returning to Norway. However, she was spotted by the American pilot of a RAF flying boat and in the evening of May 26, and in appalling weather, the aircraft of the carrier *Ark Royal* crippled *Bismarck* by wrecking her steering gear and jamming her rudder. At dawn the next day the battleships *King George V* and *Rodney* opened fire on the German ship at a range of 14,630m/16,000yds, and in an hour and a half *Bismarck* was reduced to a blazing wreck. She was torpedoed and sank some 555km/300 nautical miles west of Ushant. Of her crew of 2,222 men only 110 survived the sinking.

Tirpitz

The sister ship of *Bismarck*, *Tirpitz* was commissioned in February 1941, when she operated in the Baltic on trials and training, and was engaged in support of Operation Barbarossa, the German advance into Russia. However, in January 1942 *Tirpitz* was sent to Norway: Hitler was obsessed that "the fate of the war will be decided in Norway", and throughout the war kept large forces there. Here *Tirpitz* acted like a fleet-in-being and in turn consumed British effort and imagination in plans for her destruction.

One of *Tirpitz*'s few offensive actions was Operation Rösselsprung or "knight's move", a planned attack on convoy traffic in June and July 1942. It was spoilt when three destroyers escorting the German Battle Group I, consisting of *Tirpitz* and the heavy cruiser *Admiral Hipper*, grounded outside Altenfjord. The pocket battleship *Lützow*, belonging with *Admiral Scheer* to Battle Group II, was also stranded and needed repairs in Germany. Both battle groups turned back

BELOW: *Tirpitz* underway for her sea trials in 1941. Her sister ship *Bismarck* had a career which could be measured in months. *Tirpitz*'s career lasted only a handful of years and she saw little action, although her presence as fleet-in-being in a lair in a Norwegian fjord and the threat she represented, in particular to Arctic convoys to Russia, tied up huge resources.

when the Germans suspected an attack by submarines and carrier aircraft. However, when the British Admiralty dispersed the convoy PQ17, 19 of the 36 merchant ships were subsequently lost to German aircraft or U-boats.

At the end of 1942 there was a failed attempt to attack *Tirpitz* at her anchorage by miniature submarines and two-man torpedoes known as chariots, carried into the fjords by a Norwegian fishing boat. The bombing of *Gneisenau* showed that it was unsafe for *Tirpitz* to return to Germany and so she was refitted in the fjords, where in March 1943 she was joined by *Prinz Eugen*, *Scharnhorst* and *Lützow*. On September 8, 1943, *Tirpitz* and *Scharnhorst* bombarded Spitsbergen, which was to be the last time *Tirpitz* fired her main armament in anger.

Back in Kaafjord, the Royal Navy mounted Operation Source in September 1943, an attack using X-craft towed into position by parent submarines. Shortly after 08.00 on September 21, two violent explosions underneath *Tirpitz* forced her upwards several feet. All power was lost and she settled with a list to port. The damage was severe: there were splits in the bottom of the hull, buckling and distortion; a generator room was flooded and electrical generators lifted off their mountings; the propeller shafts were jammed and A and X turrets jumped off their roller paths.

ABOVE: **Hitler inspecting the parade before the launch of** *Tirpitz* **on April 1, 1939. Top left is the hull of** *Tirpitz* **showing the bilge keel which ran each side of the length of the ship.** TOP RIGHT: *Tirpitz* **in her lair with smokescreens put up to obscure her from the air during attack by the Fleet Air Arm.** RIGHT: **Sunk at last after several raids,** *Tirpitz* **turned turtle and was scrapped** *in situ*, **by a Norwegian company. Some portions of her still lie on the bottom of the fjord in her last berth.**

During the winter of 1943–4 the Germans repaired *Tirpitz*, who, despite receiving further shock damage by Soviet bombers in February, was able to begin manoeuvring trials in the following spring. There then began a series of attacks by carrier aircraft of the Royal Navy.

The first of these, Operation Tungsten, comprised the battleships *Duke of York* and *Anson*, the carriers *Victorious*, *Furious*, *Searcher*, *Pursuer* and *Emperor* and a large number of cruisers and destroyers. Fleet Air Arm Barracuda torpedo-bombers, Wildcats and Hellcats struck on April 3, 1944, just as *Tirpitz* was weighing anchor for post-repair trials. The first attack lasted barely a minute and scored six direct hits, and a second attack a few minutes later scored eight direct hits: there were other probable hits and the aircraft descended to strafe *Tirpitz* as well. By 08.00 all the aircraft but three had landed on their carriers.

Similar attacks were cancelled as a result of bad weather, but on July 17, 1944, Operation Mascot scored a near-miss despite improved anti-aircraft defences and *Tirpitz* was only saved from further damage by an effective smokescreen. Nevertheless, *Tirpitz*'s much-delayed sea trials on July 31 and August 1, 1944, were her last.

In August a series of operations all codenamed Goodwood using the carriers *Indefatigable*, *Formidable*, *Furious*, *Nabob* and *Trumpeter* started. Goodwood III on August 24, 1944, was

the heaviest and most determined so far, and even the Germans admired the British skill and dexterity in flying. The effect of all these attacks was to render *Tirpitz* unserviceable from September 1943 onwards.

Finally, on September 15, 1944, 33 Lancaster bombers, which had been pre-positioned in Russia, attacked using 5,445kg/12,000lb bombs nicknamed Tallboys. By now the German anti-aircraft fire included a barge firing next to her 380mm/15in guns, but despite this one bomb hit *Tirpitz* and exploded underneath, flooding the forward part of the ship and shaking much of her machinery off its mountings. *Tirpitz* was towed to shallower water where on November 12 she was again attacked by Lancaster bombers dropping Tallboys. There were two direct hits and several near-misses and an internal explosion, whereupon *Tirpitz* rolled over to port and capsized with heavy loss of life.

Tirpitz was broken up *in situ* between 1949 and 1957 by a Norwegian company.

Tirpitz

Class: *Bismarck, Tirpitz.* Launched 1939
Dimensions: Length – 248m/813ft 8in
   Beam – 36m/118ft 1in
   Draught – 8.5m/28ft 6in
Displacement: 42,370 tonnes/41,700 tons
Armament: Main – 8 x 380mm/15in guns
   Secondary – 12 x 150mm/6in,
   16 x 105mm/4.13in, 16 x 37mm/1.46in and
   12 x 20mm/0.79in guns
Machinery: 12 boilers, 3 shafts.
   102,907kW/138,000shp
Speed: 29 knots
Complement: 2,092–2,608 men

LEFT: **A stern view of** *Dunkerque*, **showing the hangar for her aircraft – then quite an advanced feature of warship design.** ABOVE: **The French battleships** *Strasbourg* **and** *Dunkerque* **at their berth in Mers-el-Kebir in Algeria (then a French colony), where they had taken refuge after the fall of France. While at berth they were attacked by the Royal Navy in July 1940, after the French had refused British proposals to ensure that their fleet would not fall into the possession of the Nazis.**

Dunkerque and *Strasbourg*

These two ships, built as part of France's battleship tonnage allowed by the Washington Naval Treaty, were like the British Nelson class in having all of their main armament forward. France was allowed a total battleship displacement of 177,800 tonnes/175,000 tons under the treaty. Smaller and cheaper ships were sought, but the French navy eventually settled on a design of 26,925 tonnes/26,500 tons, partly in response to the heavy cruisers built in Germany and the new Italian battleships which were known to be in progress. The treaty allowed guns of up to 380mm/15in, but on grounds of economy France chose a new calibre of 330mm/13in.

Other novel features included a large number of medium-calibre and anti-aircraft guns in quadruple mountings and a purpose-built aircraft hangar aft. A prominent feature of these ships was a control tower consisting of three separate structures rotating on a common axis and weighing more than 86 tonnes/85 tons.

In 1939 *Dunkerque* was part of Force I, one of several British and French forces formed to hunt down German raiders in the Atlantic and Indian Oceans. In December she carried French gold to Canada for safekeeping and returned escorting Canadian troop convoys to Britain. After the fall of France, she was badly damaged twice while alongside at Mers-el-Kebir, after senior French officers had refused British proposals to neutralize their fleet to prevent it being used by the Nazis. Consequently the Royal Navy bombarded the port on July 3 and British aircraft attacked on July 6 to stop French warships falling into Nazi hands. After emergency repairs she was taken to Toulon, where on November 27, 1942, she was sabotaged by loyal Frenchmen and stranded in her dry dock for the next three years. She was finally sold for scrap in 1956.

Strasbourg was also involved in the 1939 hunt for the German pocket battleship *Admiral Graf Spee*, which was raiding in the South Atlantic. She suffered a similar fate to *Dunkerque*: although only lightly damaged by British shelling at Mers-el-Kebir, she was scuttled by the French at Toulon on November 27, 1942, and despite attempts at salvage, was sunk again by US aircraft in August 1944 during Allied landings in the south of France. She was sold for scrap in 1955.

Dunkerque class

Class: *Dunkerque, Strasbourg.*
  Launched 1935–6
Dimensions: Length – 214.5m/703ft 9in
  Beam – 31m/102ft
  Draught – 8.7m/28ft 6in
Displacement: 26,925 tonnes/26,500 tons
Armament: Main – 8 x 330mm/13in guns
  Secondary – 16 x 130mm/5.1in,
  8 x 37mm/1.46in and 32 x 13mm/0.52in guns
Machinery: 6 boilers, 4 shafts.
  83,891kW/112,500shp
Speed: 29.5 knots
Complement: 1,431 men

LEFT: *Richelieu* at Dakar in 1941. *Richelieu* exchanged shots with the British *Resolution*, and her sister ship *Jean Bart* exchanged shots with the USN *Massachusetts*.
BELOW: *Richelieu*, having fought the British at Dakar, declared for the Free French, was refitted in New York and fought alongside the British in the Far East.

Richelieu class

After the Anglo-German naval agreement and the abrogation or expiry of the Washington Naval Treaty, France considered herself free to expand her navy. The Richelieu class represented a further development of the Dunkerque class, but was 10,160 tonnes/10,000 tons larger, with 380mm/15in guns, and a speed of 2 to 3 knots faster.

Richelieu and *Jean Bart* escaped from France. *Richelieu* benefited from being completed in New York and gaining from USN experience in the Pacific. *Jean Bart*, which carried very heavy anti-aircraft armament, was damaged during the Allied landings in North Africa and work to complete her did not recommence until 1946. A novel feature of the design included blowers to mix cold fresh air with the hot flue gases and so minimize the effect upon fire-control optics.

Before completion *Richelieu* was moved from Brest to Dakar, where on July 8, 1944, she was damaged by aircraft from the British carrier *Hermes* and again between September 23 and 25 during a duel with the battleship *Resolution*. Once taken over by the Free French navy she sailed for New York where she was finally completed, and in November 1943 began operations with

the British Home Fleet. In 1944 and 1945 she operated with the British East Indies Fleet and then the British Pacific Fleet, visiting Toulon in September 1944 and returning to Cherbourg in March 1946. She was broken up in Italy in 1968.

The incomplete *Jean Bart* escaped from St Nazaire and evaded the advancing Germans in June 1940, eventually reaching Casablanca. There, in November 1942 during Allied landings in North Africa, she exchanged fire with the USN battleship *Massachusetts* and received several gunfire and bomb hits. She was towed to Brest after the war and completed in 1955. *Jean Bart* took part in the Suez campaign in 1956, was decommissioned in the 1960s and scrapped in Japan in 1969.

Clémenceau was only 10 per cent complete when France was overrun by the Germans and she was declared war booty. The hull section was floated out of

dock but never worked on again and was sunk in a US air raid in 1944. *Gascogne* was never started.

A final class of battleships, *Alsace*, *Normandie*, *Flandre* and *Bourgogne* was proposed for 1940 onwards but not actually implemented.

Richelieu class

Class: *Richelieu, Jean Bart, Clémenceau, Gascogne.*
 Launched 1939–40
Dimensions: Length – 247.8m/813ft
 Beam – 33m/108ft 3in
 Draught – 9.65m/31ft 7in
Displacement: 35,560 tonnes/35,000 tons
Armament: Main – 8 x 380mm/15in guns
 Secondary – 9 x 150mm/6in, 12 x 99mm/3.9in,
 8 x 37mm/1.46in and 16 x 13mm/0.52in guns
Machinery: 6 boilers, 4 shafts.
 111,855kW/150,000shp
Speed: 32 knots
Complement: 1,670 men
Jean Bart was fitted with bulges and had a beam of 35.5m/116ft.

Conte di Cavour class

Class: *Conte di Cavour, Giulio Cesare, Leonardo da Vinci.* Launched 1911

Dimensions: Length – 186.1m/610ft 6in
Beam – 28m/91ft 10in
Draught – 9.3m/30ft 6in

Displacement: 24,405 tonnes/23,600 tons

Armament: Main – 10 x 320mm/12.6in guns
Secondary – 12 x 120mm/4.7in guns

Machinery: 8 boilers, 2 turbines.
65,859kW/93,000shp

Speed: 28 knots

Complement: 1,230 men

The specifications given here are for the ships as they were rebuilt in the 1930s.

LEFT: *Conte di Cavour* and *Guilio Cesare* were modernized in the 1930s. The reconstruction amounted to a complete rebuild which totally changed their profile, as well as adding 10.3m/34ft to their length.

Conte di Cavour class (1933)

Starting in 1933 *Conte di Cavour* and *Giulio Cesare* were completely rebuilt. A new bow section added more than 9m/30ft to their length. New oil-fired boilers and turbines driving two shafts, reduced from four, delivered three times more horsepower. This, with the longer hull ratio, produced 6 knots of extra speed. The midships turret was suppressed and the ships were given a completely new superstructure. The 305mm/12in main armament was replaced by 320mm/12.6in guns, and the armoured protection increased. Horizontal armour was increased to 135mm/5.3in and vertical armour around the turrets by an additional 50mm/1.97in. The Pugliese system was installed in which fuel tanks ran the length of the ship, and these contained a large empty cylinder intended as a shock absorber to minimize a hit on or below the waterline.

Conte di Cavour took part in the action off Punto Stilo on July 9, 1940, also known as the Battle of Calabria, when the British battleships *Malaya*, *Barham* and *Royal Sovereign* chased the Italian fleet to within sight of the coast of Calabria. Battles such as this helped to establish the superior morale of the British battlefleet under Cunningham's aggressive command. There followed other largely unsuccessful actions against the British fleet and various Malta convoys. On November 11, 1940, Swordfish torpedo-bombers from the British carrier *Illustrious* attacked the Italian fleet in the harbour of Taranto and *Conte di Cavour* was sunk by a torpedo. Raised and towed to Trieste for repairs, she was sunk again by the Italians to prevent her falling into German hands, only to be raised by the Germans but sunk again by the USAAF in 1945. She was scrapped in 1951.

Giulio Cesare was hit by a 380mm/ 15in-shell from the British *Warspite* during the Battle of Punto Stilo. She took part in the action near Cape Teulada in November 27, 1940, against Force H and the battleships *Renown* and *Ramillies*, and was engaged against British cruisers and destroyers at the First Battle of Sirte on December 17, 1941.

By early 1942 *Giulio Cesare* was reduced to the status of a training and barracks ship. Allocated to the Soviet Union as war reparations, she became the *Novorossijsk*, but was lost in 1955 as a result of striking a mine in the Black Sea.

Leonardo da Vinci was sunk by a magazine explosion in 1916, attributed (probably wrongly) to Austrian saboteurs. Although she was refloated and it was planned to refit the hull, she was scrapped in the 1920s.

Caio Duilio class (1937)

Like their near sisters, the Conte di Cavour class, these ships were completely rebuilt under Mussolini's regime in Italy. The hull was lengthened by inserting a new bow section, and they were given an all-new propulsion plant, driving two shafts. These measures together gave them 6 knots of extra speed, up to 27 knots. The midships turret was removed and they were given new superstructures. The main armament was increased to 320mm/ 12.6in calibre, the secondary armament of 12 135mm/5.3in guns was mounted in four triple turrets, and they also carried numerous lighter anti-aircraft guns. Armour was also increased and they received the Pugliese protection system.

Caio Duilio re-entered service in July 1940 and thereafter was involved in a number of unsuccessful skirmishes against the British Mediterranean Fleet. During the attack on Taranto by aircraft of the Royal Navy's Fleet Air Arm she received one torpedo hit but remained afloat and the following month was at sea on North Africa convoy duties. On December 17, 1941, she fought a brief and unsuccessful action with British cruisers and destroyers in what became known as the First Battle of Sirte. She was surrendered to the Royal Navy on September 9, 1943, when the Italian government signed an armistice with the Allies, and scrapped in 1957.

Andrea Doria was also unsuccessful against the British Mediterranean Fleet, although regularly employed on convoy protection duties to and from North Africa and in attempts to disrupt British convoys to Malta. She escaped damage during the British attack on Taranto harbour on November 11, but did join *Caio Duilio* in the unsuccessful action at the First Battle of Sirte. *Andrea Doria* was surrendered to the Royal Navy at Malta on September 9, 1943, and scrapped in 1957.

Caio Duilio class

Class: *Caio Duilio, Andrea Doria.* Launched 1913
Dimensions: Length – 186.9m/613ft 2in
  Beam – 28m/91ft 10in
  Draught – 9.5m/30ft 10in
Displacement: 21,590 tonnes/23,800 tons
Armament: Main – 10 x 320mm/12.6in guns
  Secondary – 12 x 135mm/5.3in,
Machinery: 8 boilers, 2 turbines.
  59,859kW/87,000shp
Speed: 27 knots
Complement: 1,490 men
The specifications given here are for the ships as they were rebuilt in the 1930s.

ABOVE: **Detail of the port quarter of *Andrea Doria*.** LEFT: **The Caio Duilio class and the Conte di Cavour class were similar ships when first built, with tall funnels, even taller tripod masts and a midships turret, as seen here. Contrast this with the 1930s rebuild opposite, which gave the ships of these two classes a much lower profile. The length was increased too and with more efficient machinery, which nearly tripled the horsepower, the speed was increased in both classes by some 6 knots. Improved armour increased displacement by some 2,032tonnes/2,000 tons.**

Vittorio Veneto class

These handsome battleships were the first to be built by Italy after the Washington Naval Treaty, and were partly a response to the French *Dunkerque* and *Strasbourg*. Clearly the Italians were intent upon breaching the treaty limit of 35,560 tonnes/35,000 tons, and at full load these ships displaced more than 45,720 tonnes/45,000 tons. The guns were 380mm/15in, rather than the 405mm/16in which were permitted by treaty, which was due to the limited capacity of the Italian ordnance industry. However they were long guns capable, in theory, of a range of 42,062m/46,000yds.

With the exception of the 120mm/4.7in guns which were old Armstrong weapons, all the guns were of a new design, and, given the environment in which these ships would operate, the anti-aircraft armament was increased during the war.

The armour which was up to 350mm/13.8in thick was intended to defeat 380mm/15in shells at 16,000m/17,500yds, and there was complex subdivision inside the hull, including the Pugliese system. This consisted of a torpedo bulkhead

ABOVE: **Italian design at its best, *Vittorio Veneto* was built in 1934–40 and scrapped in 1948–51.** BELOW LEFT: **The Vittorio Veneto class were beamy, well-thought-out ships intended for war in the Mediterranean. With its mix of new and modernized battleships and the ability to operate under the cover of aircraft from numerous shore airfields, the Italian navy had the material to dominate the Mediterranean. However, in early encounters Cunningham and his British Mediterranean Fleet established their superior morale.**

which curved inboard and downward to meet the outer bottom. Within this was a compartment containing an empty longitudinal drum which was manufactured under pressure thus absorbing the force of any explosion, however, poor construction technique was blamed for the system not proving as effective in action as was hoped.

As they often showed in battle with the British, this class of ship was capable of high sustained speed. A quarterdeck catapult could launch three reconnaissance planes or, as the war progressed, three fighters. In September 1941 *Littorio* became the first Italian battleship to be fitted with radar.

Vittorio Veneto was the busiest of the Italian battleships. Completed in April 1940, she escaped damage during the attack on Taranto, and was flagship of the Italian fleet during the Battle of Cape Matapan in March 1941. Here she was hit during a torpedo attack by *Formidable*'s aircraft, but was not slowed sufficiently to allow Cunningham in *Warspite* with the British Mediterranean Fleet to catch up. She then underwent repairs until August 1941. Her main employment was as distant cover for Axis Africa-bound convoys and the interdiction of British Malta-bound shipping. On November 8, 1941, the cruisers *Aurora* and *Penelope*, forming the British Force K, sallied from Malta and snapped up a convoy supposedly under the *Vittorio Veneto*'s protection. Then on December 14, 1941, the British submarine *Urge* torpedoed the *Vittorio Veneto* and she required repairs which lasted until early 1942. In June 1943

TOP: *Littorio* (formerly *Italia*) was badly damaged at
Taranto in November 1940 by the British Fleet Air
Arm. ABOVE: *Roma* on her launch in 1940.
LEFT: *Roma* having entered the war against the
British was on her way to surrender at Malta when
she was bombed by her erstwhile allies, the
Germans, and sunk.

she was bombed while at La Spezia. After being surrendered to
the British at Malta in September 1943, she was interned at
Suez and then returned to Italy, being scrapped in 1948.

Littorio, as she is better known, was damaged in Taranto by
three torpedoes delivered by Swordfish aircraft from the British
carrier *Illustrious*. She sank by the bows and remained under
repair at Taranto until August 1941. At the Second Battle of
Sirte on March 22, 1942, she made a determined attempt to
interdict a four-ship convoy protected by British cruisers and
destroyers under the command of Admiral Philip Vian, but
was driven off by superior tactics, including the use of
smokescreens and torpedo attack. She was renamed *Italia* on
July 30, 1943, after the overthrow of Mussolini, and was badly
damaged on September 9, 1941, by German glider bombs but
survived. After internment at Alexandria, she was returned to
Italy in 1947 and scrapped.

Roma was bombed in La Spezia in June 1942 as she was
nearing completion. Repaired, she sailed in September 1943
with the Italian fleet to its surrender under the guns of Malta,
but was struck by a German glider bomb and sank with heavy
losses. *Impero* was never completed and was taken over by

the Germans at the Italian armistice; she was bombed and
sunk in Trieste in 1945, and scrapped in 1950. With the loss of
all its battleships at the end of World War II, Italy's attempt to
join the first rank of navies was brought to an end, despite
leading some of the stages of battleship development and
designing some very graceful ships.

Vittorio Veneto class

Class: *Vittorio Veneto*, *Italia* (ex *Littorio*),
Roma, *Impero*. Launched 1937–40

Dimensions: Length – 224m/735ft
Beam – 32.75m/107ft 5in
Draught – 9.6m/31ft 5in

Displacement: 41,377 tonnes/40,724 tons

Armament: Main – 9 x 380mm/15in guns
Secondary – 12 x 155mm/6.1in,
4 x 120mm/4.7in, 12 x 90mm/3.54in,
20 x 37mm/1.46in and 16 x 20mm/0.79in guns

Machinery: 8 boilers, 4-shaft geared turbines.
96,940kW/130,000shp

Speed: 30 knots

Complement: 1,830–1,950 men

Sovyetskiy Soyuz class

Under the Soviet second five-year plan (1933–7) the old Imperial shipyards at Leningrad and Nikolayev were modernized. In 1938 the *Sovyetskiy Soyuz* was laid down at the Baltic shipyard, known in the Soviet era as the Ordzhonikidze Shipyard (No. 189), and *Sovyetskaya Ukraina* at the Andre Marti Shipyard (No. 198) at Nikolayev on the Black Sea. New yards were also built in the Arctic and the Far East, as well as inland on canals which could be used to take unfinished hulls to the coast for completion. One of the new yards was Shipyard No. 402 at Molotovsk (now Severodvinsk) on the White Sea, where the construction hall was big enough to take two super-battleships of the Sovyetskiy Soyuz class side by side.

After World War I, the Soviet Union was not regarded as a naval power and had not been invited to any of the inter-war naval arms conferences. Stalin apparently studied the strategic writings of the American naval officer, Mahan, who urged

nations (in his case the USA) to obtain a navy for geo-strategic purposes, and wanted a navy for the Soviet Union for reasons of self-esteem as much as for national security. The Soviet Union therefore became a late signatory of the London Naval Treaty and in 1937 signed a bilateral Anglo-Soviet Naval agreement. Stalin ordered his agents to purchase whatever was needed from his capitalist enemies for the Soviet naval programme, and they eventually obtained plans bought from Italy, who had supplied the Imperial Russian Navy, to help work up their own version of a super-Dreadnought. Blueprints were also purchased from the USA, despite objections from the USN, and in 1940 the Soviet navy sought help from Nazi Germany.

The initial Soviet plan was to build a fleet of 16 battleships and 12 heavy cruisers and corresponding numbers of other warships during the next two five-year plans. It is doubtful whether the Soviets ever had the technology to achieve this

LEFT: **Soviet plans to build battleships in the inter-war years came to nothing. However the Soviets did acquire the Italian *Giulio Cesare* as war reparation in 1948. Italian naval officers and men refused to steam *Giulio Cesare* to Russia, and so she had to be manned with a civilian crew.** BELOW: **The British also lent *Royal Sovereign* between 1944 and 1949, seen here flying the Soviet flag.**

Sovyetskiy Soyuz class

Class: *Sovyetskiy Soyuz, Sovyetskaya Ukraina, Sovyetskaya Byelorussiya, Sovyetskaya Rossiya.* Not launched.

Dimensions: Length – 271m/889ft
Beam – 38.7m/127ft
Draught – 10.1m/33ft 2in

Displacement: 60,099 tonnes/59,150 tons

Armament: Main – 9 x 405mm/16in guns
Secondary – 12 x 150mm/6in,
8 x 100mm/4in and 32 x 37mm/1.46in guns

Machinery: boilers, 3 shafts turbo-electric.
172,257kW/231,000shp

Speed: 28 knots

plan or any of its subsequent alterations and it certainly did not have the finance. However four Sovyetskiy Soyuz class battleships were authorized in 1938 and construction of three of them was started. All three were overtaken by war.

The design bore a passing resemblance to the Italian Vittorio Veneto class, with two triple turrets forward, B turret super-firing over A, and an after turret in a tall barbette. They also had a tall tower superstructure forward of two large upright funnels. The Italian Pugliese system of underwater protection was also adopted. None of these ships were completed, and all were broken up in the 1940s.

From May 1944 to February 1949 the Soviet navy was lent the British battleship *Royal Sovereign* under the name of *Arkhangelsk*, pending delivery of an equivalent Italian battleship as part of the Soviet Union's share of war reparations. She was used to escort Arctic convoys, but became something of a target for German U-boats, including an attack by Biber midget submarines, and spent much of the time behind anti-submarine nets. She was returned to Britain in 1949 and broken up.

As for the Sovyetskiy Soyuz class itself, these were by far the largest Russian warships designed, but the German invasion prevented their completion, and the post-war shipyards lacked the capacity and the political direction to continue to build battleships. The name ship of the class, *Sovyetskiy Soyuz*, was well advanced when war broke out, but between 1941 and 1944 most of the armour was removed for use elsewhere in the Soviet war economy. Post-war she was cut into sections and scrapped. Work on the second ship, *Sovyetskaya Ukraina*, was almost 75 per cent complete when the German army occupied Nikolayev on August 16, 1941. When the German army evacuated the city in 1944 they damaged the building slip and the ship, preventing her completion. No progress was made with the other two ships of the class, *Sovyetskaya Byelorussiya* and *Sovyetskaya Rossiya*.

By the end of World War II the Soviet navy still had not recovered from its parlous state after the Battle of Tsushima, and the world had to wait until the Cold War, when it briefly flourished under Admiral Gorshkov.

Glossary

Aft   at or towards the rear or stern

Armourclad   *see* ironclad

Barbette   originally, the open-topped armoured enclosure from which a gun was fired; later, the standing or fixed part of the gun mounting, protecting the hoists and connecting the turret to the magazines

Battle cruiser   ship armed with battleship-sized guns, but in which armour has been dispensed with for speed and manoeuvrability

Beam   the widest part of a ship

Bilge   the lowest part of the hull of a ship, where the side turns into the bottom

Bilge keel   fins or narrow wings at the turn of the bilge, designed to improve stability

Blister   *see* bulge

Block ship   a battleship converted into a floating battery intended to defend habours

Bow   (or bows) the forward end of a ship

Breastwork   raised armoured bulkhead to protect a gun and its moving parts

Bulge   (or blister) a longitudinal space, subdivided and filled with fuel, water or air, to protect against the effects of a torpedo hit

Bulkhead   the internal vertical structures within a ship

Calibre   the internal diameter or bore of a gun, or the ratio of the barrel length to the bore

Capital ship   a generic name given to the largest and most powerful ships in a navy

Casemate   an armoured box or battery in which one or usually more guns were mounted

Chariot   a two-manned torpedo used to attack enemy shipping in harbour

Cofferdam   watertight bulkhead separating and protecting magazines and engine rooms

Copenhagen   reference to the British attack on the Danish capital and fleet in 1807

Dressed overall   a ship dressed *en fête*, flying lines of flags between her masts, when not underway

Dwarf bulkhead   low bulkhead intended to stop the free flood of water

Flotilla   a squadron in the Royal Navy before NATO standardization

Flying deck   a deck suspended between two parts of the superstructure so that the deck below can be kept clear for mounting guns

Forecastle   forward part of a ship

Freeboard   height of the deck above the waterline

Great White Fleet   USN fleet that circumnavigated the globe to demonstrate the coming-of-age of the USA as a sea power

Gunwales   upper edge of the side of a vessel

Heel   lean or tilt of a ship

Ihp   indicated horsepower: the calculated output of a ship's machinery

Ironclad   a ship protected by vertical iron plating

Laid down   reference to when a new ship was first placed on the construction slip

Line ahead   when ships form up in a line

Line-of-battle ship   a ship large enough to be in the line

Metacentre	roll and return to upright slowly
Monitor	low freeboard coast defence vessel
NATO	North Atlantic Treaty Organization
Ordnance	armament and ammunition of a ship
Pole mast	a stick-like mast to carry aerials or flags
Pocket battleship	small German battleship designed in the interwar years to circumvent restrictions on total tonnage and size
Pom pom	the name for a type of 1- or 2-pounder gun derived from the sound of its firing
Port	left side
Quarter	between the beam and the stern
Ram	underwater beak or spur on the bow for striking the enemy
Screw	propellor
Shp	shaft horse power: the actual measured output of a ship's machinery
Starboard	right side
Stern	rear of a ship
Theatre	the area in which a ship or fleet operates or a naval campaign takes place
Tripod mast	a mast having extra legs to carry the weight of direction-finding and gunnery control positions
Tumblehome	inward curve of a ship's side above the waterline
Turret	revolving armoured gun house
USN	United States Navy
Van	the front of a formation of ships

Key to flags

For the specification boxes, the national flag that was current at the time of the ship's use is shown.

 Argentina

 Austro-Hungary

 Brazil

 Britain

 Chile

 France

 Germany

 Germany: World War I

 Germany: World War II

 Greece

 Italy

 Japan

 Netherlands

 Russia

 Spain

 Sweden

 Turkey

 USA

 USSR

Acknowledgements

The publisher would like to thank the following individuals and picture libraries for the use of their pictures in the book. Every effort has been made to acknowledge the pictures properly, however we apologize if there are any unintentional omissions, which will be corrected in future editions.

l=left, r=right, t=top, b=bottom, m=middle, lm= lower middle

Alinari Archives-Florence:
112m (Touring Club Italiano); 112b; 113m (De Pinto Donazione); 113bl; 113br Malandrini Ferruccio); 174t (De Pinto Donazione); 174m; 175t (De Pinto Donazione); 175b (De Pinto Donazione); 176t (De Pinto Donazione); 176m (De Pinto Donazione); 244t (De Pinto Donazione); 245m Instituto Luce); 245b (De Pinto Donazione); 247mr (De Pinto Donazione).

Australian War Memorial:
35mr (H12319); 42 tr (P00433.001); 51ml (P02018.327); 51mr (P02018.345); 51b (P005999.014); 69tl (P00952.003; 134t (300238); 134b (ART09749).

Cody Images: 6t; 6m; 7tr; 7mr; 7bl; 8–9; 10t; 10bl; 11m; 12bl; 12br; 13br; 14t; 14mr; 15tr; 15b; 16t; 16m; 17t; 17ml; 17mr; 25b; 26t; 26bl; 27tr; 27mr; 27br; 28; 29t; 29ml; 29mr; 30b; 31t; 31mr; 31br; 32t; 33tl; 33tr; 34t; 35bl; 37ml; 40t; 4mr; 41tr; 41b; 42tl; 42br; 43tl; 43tr; 43m; 44tl; 44tr; 45; 45mr; 45br; 50t; 53tr; 57tl; 57tr; 62b; 63t; 63mr; 64t; 65t; 65mr; 65br; 68; 69m; 70br; 71bl; 71br; 72mr; 72b; 73t; 73m; 74tl; 74br; 75; 76tl; 82tl; 82bl; 84t; 84b; 85t; 85b; 86t; 88t; 88m; 88mr; 89tl; 89tr; 89mr; 90mr; 91m; 91bl; 91br; 92tl; 92tr; 92mr; 93m; 93bl;

94mr; 96t; 96b; 97t; 98t; 98b; 99t; 99b; 101t; 101m; 101b; 106t; 106m; 107t; 107m; 107b; 108t; 108b; 109ml; 109mr; 109b; 110tr; 111t; 112t; 114t; 115m; 115b; 119t; 120t; 121t; 122t; 122b; 128t; 128m; 128b; 129b; 130; 132tl; 132tr; 132mr; 137mr; 140b; 141ml; 142mr; 143tl; 143tr; 144mr; 145br; 147t; 148t; 149tl; 149tr; 149mr; 152tl; 153t; 153b; 154b; 155t; 158b; 159tl; 159m; 161t; 161m; 162t; 162m; 162mr; 163mr; 163b; 164tl; 164tr; 164m; 165t; 165m; 166tl; 166tr; 166mr; 166b; 167mr; 167b; 168t; 168mr; 169t; 169m; 170–1t; 170br; 171m; 175mr; 177t; 179b; 184t; 184mr; 185mr; 185bl; 186m; 186b; 187t; 188t; 188mr; 193tr; 193ml; 193mr; 1931m; 194bl; 194br; 195tl; 195ml; 195mr; 196t; 196m; 197t; 197ml; 197mr; 198tl; 198tr; 199tl; 199tr; 199ml; 199lm; 201mr; 201b; 204t; 205tl; 205tr; 205ml; 205lm;

206t; 207t; 207mr; 209t; 209ml; 210t; 210m; 210tl; 210tr; 210ml; 212bl; 213br; 214tl; 214tr; 215t; 215ml; 215mr; 217ml; 219mr; 220tl; 220tr; 221t; 221mr; 222t; 223t; 223b; 224t; 225t; 225ml; 225mr; 226; 227t; 227ml; 227mr; 228; 229t; 229ml; 229mr; 230b; 231m; 231b; 232t; 232bl; 233t; 233m; 233b; 234tr; 234b; 235tr; 235mr; 235b; 236t; 236mr; 237tl; 237tr; 237m; 238t; 239t; 239mr; 239lm; 241tl; 241tr; 241mr; 242tl; 242tr; 243tl;

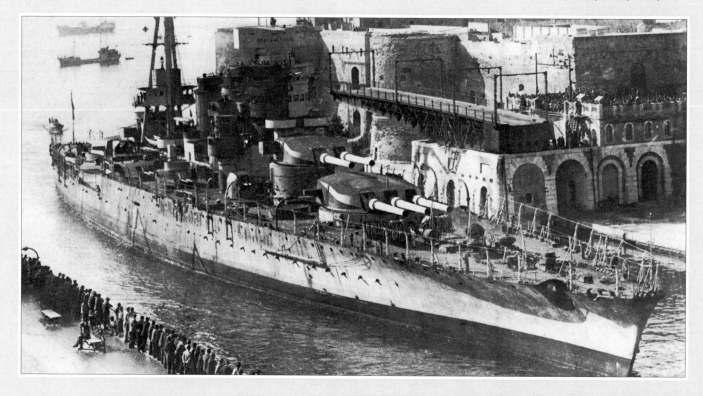

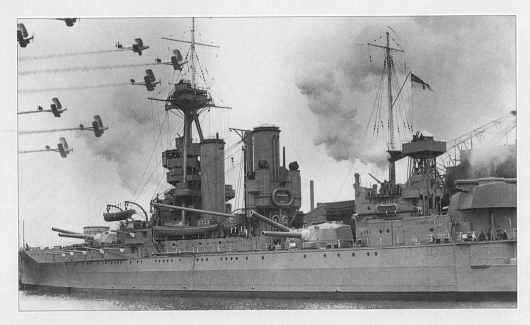

243mr; 246t; 246bl; 247t; 247ml; 248–9; 249tr; 250tr; 250bl; 251; 252tr; 252b; 255tr.

Mary Evans Picture Library: 27ml; 35ml; 60; 158t.

Syd Goodman: 47ml; 47tr; 135ml; 135mr; 135bl; 142t; 144t; 145m; 150b; 151t; 172t; 192t; 200b; 201ml; 202t; 203tl; 203tr; 203mr; 214tl; 214tr; 215tl; 215ml; 215mr; 217ml.

Imperial War Museum Photograph Archive: 11b (Q22212); 13t (Q40607); 20 (Q68264); 21m (MH24467); 23t (Q13942); 23m (Q13941A); 24bl (Q55499); 24br (Q22156); 25tr (Q22155); 30tr (Q38938); 33tr (Q22687); 37t (Q20613); 46m (HU87084); 54br (A8953); 55tl (Q20352); 55lm (A21164); 70t (Q41317); 74tr (Q22284); 100t (Q22357); 102t (Q22258); 102bl (Q41314); 103t (Q22279); 103mr (Q13412); 110tl (Q41298); 110mr (Q41285); 111b (Q19930); 118 (Q22446); 120b (Q41361); 123t (Q70143); 123b (Q70145); 157t (Q22411); 160b (MH6158); 178m (Q20283); 178b (Q20287); 180 (Q22227).

Institute for Maritime History: 182tl; 182tr; 182mr; 183ml; 183b.

Library of Congress: 19tl; 21tr; 38m; 39t.

Maritime Prints and Originals: 32b (Courtesy of Michael French Esq.); 34m (Courtesy of Captain R. A. de S. Cosby LVO RN); 127t (Courtesy of Paul Winter Esq.); 129mr (Courtesy of Captain R. A. de S. Cosby LVO RN); 131t (Courtesy of Commander W. A. E. Hall RN); 141t (Courtesy of Simon Keeble Esq.).

National Archive of Scotland: 97m (UCS 1/116/4).

North Sands Picture Library: 124; 137lm; 139m; 188bl; 189t, 189m; 252bl.

Novosti: 117; 179t.

Curt Ohlsson: 69tr; 182tl; 182tr;182mr.

Royal Naval Museum: 47tr; 47ml; 47mr; 76br; 77m; 77b; 78mr; 78bl; 79t; 79mr; 80tl;

80tr; 80m; 81t; 81mr; 82tr; 83tl; 83tr; 83m; 131m; 133t; 136t; 136mr; 137b; l138m; 138b; 139t; 141mr; 146t; 147mr; 253t.

Erwin Sieche: 15m; 181t; 181b.

Topfoto: 97mr; 157ml.

US _Missouri_ Museum: 218t; 218b; 219tl; 219ml; 253b.

US Naval Historical Center: 1; 2–3; 18tr; 19mr; 36t; 36mr; 37mr; 38t; 39mr; 46tl; 46–7t; 48tl; 48b; 49mr; 49lm; 49br; 50bl; 52t; 53tl; 53mr; 53br; 54t; 55tr; 55ml; 56t; 56m; 57br; 61t; 61mr; 63b; 86bl; 87mr; 87b; 90tl; 91br; 93br; 94t; 100mr; 151ml; 151mr; 152tr; 152mr; 154t; 155tr; 155ml; 155mr; 156tl; 156ml; 160t; 161mr; 190–1; 207ml; 208t; 209tr; 213tr; 213ml; 213mr; 213bl; 216; 217t; 217mr; 219mr; 221ml; 222ml; 240b; 256b.

Walker Archive: 22; 104tr; 104mr; 104bl; 105t; 105b; 172mr.

Index

A

aircraft 31, 43, 44, 46, 48, 49, 51, 237
Argentina
 Rivadavia class 187
Australia 69
 Australia (1911) 33, 134
 Australia 51
 Canberra 50
Austro-Hungary 67
 Battle of Lissa 14–15
 Erzherzog Ferdinand Max 14, 15
 Erzherzog Karl class 123
 Habsburg class 123
 Radetzky class 180
 Tegetthoff class 181

B

barbettes 71
Barents Sea, Battle of the 54–5
Beatty, Vice-Admiral Sir David 32, 33, 34–5, 36
Brazil
 Minas Gerais class 188
 Rio de Janeiro 22
Brin, Benedetti 20
Britain 17, 24–5, 30–1, 38–9
 Acasta 53
 Achates 55
 Agincourt 22, 146–7
 Anglo-German naval race 26–7
 Arethusa 32
 Ark Royal 42, 47, 53
 Audacious (1911) 56
 Barfleur 77
 Barham 42, 43
 Battle of Jutland 7, 25, 29, 33, 34–5

Battle of the Falklands 28–9
Belfast 55
Bellerophon class 128
broadside ironclads 67
Canada 125, 148
Canopus class 79
Captain (1867) 12–13
Centurion 77
Cerberus 56, 68, 69
Clyde 53
Colossus 132
Courageous 150–1
Dorsetshire 47
Dreadnought (1906) 7, 19, 20, 21, 25, 26, 27, 126–7
Duke of York 51, 53, 54, 55, 201
Duncan class 82
Eagle 31
Erebus 31
Erin 22, 145
Excellent 20–1
Formidable 40, 43
Formidable class 80
Furious 31, 150–1
Galatea 34
Glorious 53, 150
Good Hope 28
Hercules 132
Hermes 31, 40, 41
Hood (1889) 56, 73, 76
Hood (1918) 38, 46–7, 52, 192–3
Howe 41
Illustrious 41, 43
Indefatigable 22, 34, 57
Indefatigable class 33, 133
Indian Ocean 40–1
Indomitable (1907) 22, 130–1

Indomitable (1940) 40
Inflexible 24, 28, 29, 130–1
Invincible 28, 29, 32, 35, 57, 130–1
Iron Duke 24
Iron Duke class 140–1
Jamaica 54, 55
Jervis Bay 53
Kent 29
King Edward VII class 83
King George V 41, 47, 51, 53, 200–1
King George V class (1911–12) 139
King George V class (1939–40) 200–1
Lion 33
Lion class (1910) 137
Lion class (1939) 202
London class 81
Lord Clive class 30
Lord Nelson class 25, 85
Lord Warden (1867) 13
M33 56
Majestic class 30, 78
Malaya 42, 43, 53
Monarch (1862) 12
Monmouth 28
Nelson 52, 198–9
Neptune 132
New Zealand 32, 33, 135
Norfolk 46, 55
North Sea actions 1914–15 32–3
Obdurate 54
Obedient 54
Ocean 24, 79
Onslow 54
Orion class 136
Orwell 54
Prince Albert 12, 73, 74
Prince of Wales 46, 47, 50, 57, 201
Princess Royal 33
Queen Elizabeth 41, 43, 194–5
Queen Elizabeth class 142–3, 194–5
Queen Mary 34, 35, 57, 138
Ramillies (1917) 31, 40, 41, 42, 43, 47, 53
Rawalpindi 52
Renown (1895) 76
Renown (1916) 24
Renown (1936) 41, 42, 47, 52–3
Renown class 149
Repulse 47, 50, 52, 57
Resolution 40

Revenge 40
Rodney 47, 52, 198–9
Royal Oak 52, 57
Royal Sovereign (1862) 12, 73, 74
Royal Sovereign (1915) 40, 42
Royal Sovereign class (1891–2) 75
Royal Sovereign class (1914–16) 144, 196–7
St Vincent class 129
Sheffield 46, 47, 54, 55
Suffolk 46
Swiftsure class 84
Terrible 20
Terror 31
Tiger 138
Trusty 12
Valiant 41, 42, 43
Vanguard 202–3
Vernon 24
Victorious 46, 47, 53, 54
Warrior 6, 9, 24, 61, 62–3
Warrior class 62–3
Warspite (1913) 34
Warspite (1934–7) 40, 41, 42, 43, 44
broadside ironclads 14, 67

C

Cape Spartivento, Battle of 197
carriers 31, 40, 41, 42, 43, 45, 47, 51, 53, 150, 223
Childers, Sir Hugh 13
Chile 84, 148
 Almirante Cochrane 31, 148
 Almirante Latorre 125
 Almirante Latorre class 189
Churchill, Winston 24, 25, 30, 35, 200, 201
Clowes, Laird 18
coast defence ships 74
Coles, Cowper Phipps 12–13, 65, 71, 72–3
Cradock, Admiral 28
Crimean War *see* Russian War
Cuniberti, Vittorio 7, 20, 25
Cunningham, Admiral Sir Andrew 42–3

D

Dahlgren, John 11, 65, 68, 69
Denmark 67, 72–3
Dogger Bank, Battle of 33, 34
Dreadnoughts 7, 24–5

E

Ericsson, John 11, 64–5, 69, 70, 71, 72, 73

Esmonde, Lieutenant
Commander Eugene 237
Evans, Rear Admiral "Fighting
Bob" 19

F
Falklands, Battle of the 28–9
Fisher, Admiral of the Fleet Sir
John Arbuthnot 7, 20, 24–5,
27, 28, 70, 126–7, 130, 150
Fox, Gustavus Vasa 11, 65, 68
France 38–9, 43
Brennus 102
Bretagne 42
Bretagne class 172
broadside ironclads 67
Charlemagne class 103
Charles Martel class 102
Courbet class 170–1
Danton class 106–7
Dunkerque 42, 242
Gloire (1856) 6, 10, 60–1
Gloire class 60–1
Iéna class 104
Liberté class 105
Lorraine 42
Normandie class 173
Provence 42
République class 105
Richelieu 41
Richelieu class 243
Strasbourg 42, 242
Fraser, Admiral Sir Bruce 55

G
Germany 22–3, 38, 39, 52–3, 67
Admiral Graf Spee 40, 52, 57,
234–5
Admiral Hipper 53, 54, 55
Admiral Scheer 40, 52, 53,
54, 233
Anglo-German naval race
26–7
Battle of Jutland 7, 25, 29, 33,
34–5
Battle of the Falklands 28–9
Bayern class 166
Bismarck (1940) 46–7, 53,
199, 200, 201, 238–9
Blücher 32, 33
Brandenberg class 98
Braunschweig class 100
Breslau (1914) 22, 23, 186
Derfflinger 32, 33, 37
Derfflinger class 169
Deutschland (*Lützow*) 52, 53,
55, 57, 64, 232–3
Deutschland class 101
Dresden 29
Friedrich Eckoldt 54
Gneisenau 28–9, 46, 52–3,
236–7
Goeben (1914) 22–3,
168, 186

Helgoland class 164
Kaiser class (1896–1900) 99
Kaiser class (1911–12) 165
Köln 32, 54
König class 165
Lützow (*Deutschland*) 52, 53,
54, 55, 57, 232–3
Mainz 32
Moltke 32, 37, 168
Nassau class 163
North Sea actions 1914–15
32–3
Nürnberg 54
Ostfriesland 57
Prinz Eugen 46, 53
Scharnhorst (1914) 28–9, 46,
52–3, 55, 236–7
scuttling of the German fleet
at Scapa Flow 36–7, 38
Seydlitz (1914) 32, 33, 34, 35,
36, 37, 169
Thuringen 57
Tirpitz 46, 53, 54, 57, 240–1
U-331 43
Von der Tann 32, 37, 167
Wittelsbach class 99
Godfrey, Admiral 42
Greece
Kilkis 185
Lemnos 185

H
Harding, Warren 38
Heligoland Bight, Battle of 32, 34
Hipper, Admiral Franz von 32–3,
34, 55
Hitler, Adolf 54, 55

I
Iachino, Admiral 43
India 41
Ingenohl, Admiral Friedrich
von 32
Italy 30, 38–9
Ammiraglio di Saint Bon
class 111
Battle of Lissa 14–15
broadside ironclads 67
Caio Duilio 43
Caio Duilio class (1910) 176
Caio Duilio class (1937) 245
Conte di Cavour 42, 43
Conte di Cavour class (1911)
175, 244
Conte di Cavour class
(1933) 244
Dante Alighieri 174
Giulio Cesare 42
Italia class 108
Palestro (1866) 15
Pola 43
Re d'Italia (1866) 14, 15
Re Umberto class 110
Regina Elena class 113

Regina Margherita class 112
Ruggiero di Lauria class 109
Vittorio Veneto 42, 43
Vittorio Veneto class 246–7

J
Jane's Fighting Ships 20
Japan 38–9, 67
Asahi 97
Atago 48
Battle of Tsushima 16–17, 20,
23, 26, 27
Fuji class 96
Fuso 51
Fuso class 159
Haruna 51
Hiel 48
Hyuga 51
Ibuki class 158
Indian Ocean 40–1
Ise 51
Ise class 162
Kaga 226–7
Kashima class 157
Kirishima 48–9
Kongo 51
Kongo class 160–1
Mikasa 56, 97
Musashi 51
Mutsu 224–5
Nagara 48, 49
Nagato 51, 57, 224–5
Naniwa 16
Pearl Harbor 41, 43, 44–5
Russo-Japanese War 1904–5
16–17
Satsuma class 157
Sendal 48, 49
Shikishima class 96
Takao 48
Tosa 226
Tsukuba class 158
Yamashiro 51

Yamato 51, 57, 218
Yamato class 228–31
Jellicoe, Admiral Sir John
Rushworth 24, 25, 32, 34–5
Jutland, Battle of 7, 25, 29, 33,
34–5

L
Leyte Gulf, Battle of 48, 51, 206–7
Lissa, Battle of 14–15
Lôme, Dupuy de 10, 60, 70
London Conference 1930 and
1935 39
Lütjens, Admiral 46

M
MacArthur, General Douglas 51
Mahan, Alfred 18, 21, 26
Marine Rundschau 20
merchant cruisers, armed 52, 53
Micheli, Giuseppe 20
Milne, Sir Alexander 13
monitors 6, 11, 30–1, 56, 68–9

N
Nagumo, Admiral 40, 41
naval treaties 38–9
Netherlands 67
Buffel 56
De Zeven Provincien 183
Schorpioen 56
New Zealand 32, 33, 135
Nimitz, Admiral Chester W. 50–1
North Cape, Battle of the 55

P
Pearl Harbor 41, 43, 44–5
Persano, Admiral Carlo 14–15
Peru
Huascar 56, 72, 73, 84
Pohl, Admiral Hugo von 34
Poland 39
Piorun 47

pre-Dreadnoughts 7, 16, 33, 59
  barbettes 71
  broadside ironclads 14, 67
  coast defence ships 74
  Majestic class 30, 78
  rams 14–15, 56, 70
  turret ships 11, 12, 56,
    72–3, 102

R
Raeder, Grand Admiral Erich 55
rams 14–15, 56, 70
Reed, Edward 12, 85
Reuter, Admiral Ludwig von 37
Roosevelt, Franklin Delano 45
Roosevelt, Theodore 18–19, 21
  The Naval War of 1812 18
Rozhdestvenski, Admiral 16–17
Russia 39
  Admiral Ushakov class 115
  Almaz 17
  Battle of Tsushima 16–17, 20,
    23, 26, 27
  Borodino class (1901–3) 121
  Borodino class (1915–16) 179
  Evstafi 22, 23
  Evstafi class 122
  Gangut class 177
  Imperator Nikolai I 179
  Imperator Pavel class 122
  Imperatritsa Mariya class 178
  Ioann Zlatoust 22
  Osliabia (1905) 17
  Panteleimon 22
  Peresviet class 118
  Petropavlovsk class 116
  Potemkin 119
  Retvisan 120
  Rotislav 22, 23, 117
  Russian War 1854–6 10,
    11, 72
  Russo-Japanese War 1904–5
    16–17
  Sissoi Veliki 114
  Sovyetskiy Soyuz class 248–9

Tri Sviatitelia 23
Tsessarevitch (1905) 17, 120

S
Scheer, Vice-Admiral Reinhard
  von 34, 37
Scott, Percy 20–1
Seven Weeks War *see* Austro-
  Prussian War
Sherbrooke, Captain Rupert 54
Sims, William 21, 26
Smith, Ensign Leonard B. 46
Somerville, Sir James 40–1, 42
Souchon, Admiral Wilhelm 22–3
Soviet Union *see* Russia
Spain 67, 86, 88
  España (1904) 20
  España class 184
Spee, Admiral von 28–9
Stead, W. T. 24
Stockton, Robert 11
Sturdee, Admiral 28–9
submarines 43. 53
Sweden 68–9
  Sverige class 182

T
Tegetthoff, Admiral Wilhelm von
  14–15
Thomas, C. M. 19
Tirpitz, Admiral Alfred von 26–7
Togo, Admiral Heihachiro
  16–17
Tovey, Admiral Sir John 47
Tsushima, Battle of 7, 16–17, 20,
  23, 26, 27
Turkey 67, 145, 146–7
  Middilli 22
  Resadiye 22
  Sultan Osman I 22
  Sultan Yavuz Selim 22, 23,
    168, 186
turret ships 11, 12, 56, 72–3, 102
Tyrwhitt, Commodore Sir
  Reginald 32

U
United States 11, 31, 38–9
  Alabama (1907) 19
  Alabama 51, 56
  Alaska class 222
  Arizona 44, 45, 57
  California 44
  Colorado 51, 204
  Colorado class 204–7
  Connecticut (1907) 18, 19
  Connecticut class 93
  Delaware class 153
  Enterprise 45
  Florida class 153
  Great White Fleet 18–19, 26
  Idaho 51
  Illinois 222
  Illinois class 90
  Indiana class 87
  Iowa (1896) 88
  Iowa (1942) 51, 56, 215
  Iowa class 214–15
  Kearsarge class 89
  Kentucky 222
  Lexington 31, 45
  Maine (1889) 86
  Maine (1901) 19, 38
  Maine class 91
  Maryland 44, 204–5
  Massachusetts (1893) 56
  Massachusetts 51, 56
  Merrimac 6, 12, 64, 65, 66
  Miantonomoh 11, 68
  Minnesota (1907) 19, 21
  Mississippi 51
  Mississippi class 95
  Missouri 51, 56, 218–19
  Monitor 6, 11, 12, 64–5,
    66, 70
  Montana class 223
  Nebraska 19
  Nevada 44, 45
  Nevada class 155
  New Jersey 51, 56, 216–17
  New Mexico class 9, 156

New York class 154
North Carolina 56
North Carolina class 208–9
Oklahoma 44, 45
Pearl Harbor 41, 43, 44–5
Pennsylvania 9, 44
Pennsylvania class 156
Princeton 11
Prometheus 49
Ranger 31
Saratoga 31, 45
South Carolina class 152
South Dakota 49, 51
South Dakota class 210–13
Tennessee 44, 45
Texas (1889) 86
Texas 56
Utah 44, 45, 57
Vermont class 94
Virginia 66
Virginia class 92
Washington 48, 49, 51, 54
West Virginia 44, 45, 51,
  204, 206
Wisconsin 19, 38, 56, 220–1
Wyoming class 154

V
Vian, Rear-Admiral Sir Philip 47

W
Warrender, Vice-Admiral Sir
  George 32
Washington Naval Treaty 1922
  38–9, 44
White, Sir Samuel 75
Wilhelm II, Kaiser 26–7
World War I 27, 34–5, 38–9, 125
  Battle of Jutland 7, 25, 29, 33,
    34–5
  Battle of the Falklands 28–9
  Black Sea 22–3
  France 106–7, 170–1
  North Sea 1914–15 32–3
World War II 46–7, 48–9,
  50–1, 191
  Atlantic 192–3, 196,
    197, 200
  Battle of the Barents Sea
    54–5
  Battle of the North Cape 55
  Convoy PQ17 54
  German navy 52–3
  Indian Ocean 40–1
  Mediterranean 42–3, 194–5,
    197, 199, 200–1
  Pacific 48–9, 50–1, 204–7,
    210–13, 216–17, 218, 220,
    224–5, 230–1
  Pearl Harbor 41, 43, 44–5

Y
Yalu River, Battle of 16, 17
Yamamoto, Admiral Isoroku 44–5